D0998684

The Presidency of
GEORGE H. W.
BUSH

AMERICAN PRESIDENCY SERIES
Clifford S. Griffin, Donald R. McCoy, and Homer E. Socolofsky, Founding Editors

George Washington, Forrest McDonald
John Adams, Ralph Adams Brown
Thomas Jefferson, Forrest McDonald
James Madison, Robert Allen Rutland
James Monroe, Noble E. Cunningham, Jr.
John Quincy Adams, Mary W. M. Hargreaves
Andrew Jackson, Donald B. Cole
Martin Van Buren, Major L. Wilson
William Henry Harrison & John Tyler, Norma Lois Peterson
James K. Polk, Paul H. Bergeron
Zachary Taylor & Millard Fillmore, Elbert B. Smith
Franklin Pierce, Larry Gara
James Buchanan, Elbert B. Smith
Abraham Lincoln, Phillip Shaw Paludan
Andrew Johnson, Albert Castel
Rutherford B. Hayes, Ari Hoogenboom
James A. Garfield & Chester A. Arthur, Justus D. Doenecke
Grover Cleveland, Richard E. Welch, Jr.
Benjamin Harrison, Homer B. Socolofsky & Allan B. Spetter
William McKinley, Lewis L. Gould
William Howard Taft, Lewis L. Gould
Theodore Roosevelt, Second Edition, Lewis L. Gould
Woodrow Wilson, Kendrick A. Clements
Warren G. Harding, Eugene P. Trani & David L. Wilson
Calvin Coolidge, Robert H. Ferrell
Herbert C. Hoover, Martin L. Fausold
Harry S. Truman, Donald R. McCoy
Dwight D. Eisenhower, Second Edition,
Chester J. Pach, Jr., & Elmo Richardson
John F. Kennedy, Second Edition, James N. Giglio
Lyndon B. Johnson, Vaughn Davis Bornet
Richard Nixon, Melvin Small
Gerald R. Ford, John Robert Greene
James Earl Carter, Jr., Second Edition,
Burton I. Kaufman & Scott Kaufman
George H. W. Bush, Second Edition, Revised and Expanded,
John Robert Greene

The Presidency of

GEORGE H. W.
BUSH

SECOND EDITION, REVISED AND EXPANDED

John Robert Greene

UNIVERSITY PRESS OF KANSAS

Davie County Public Library
Mocksville, North Carolina

© 2015 by the University Press of Kansas
All rights reserved

Published by the University Press of Kansas (Lawrence, Kansas 66045), which
was organized by the Kansas Board of Regents and is operated and funded by
Emporia State University, Fort Hays State University, Kansas State University,
Pittsburg State University, the University of Kansas, and Wichita State University

Library of Congress Cataloging-in-Publication Data
Greene, John Robert, 1955–
The presidency of George H. W. Bush / John Robert Greene. — Revised and expanded
edition.
pages   cm. — (American presidency series)
Previous edition has title The presidency of George Bush.
Includes bibliographical references and index.
ISBN 978-0-7006-2079-1 (cloth : alk. paper) — ISBN 978-0-7006-2080-7 (ebook)
1. United States—Politics and government—1989–1993. 2. Bush, George, 1924–
I. Greene, John Robert, 1955– Presidency of George Bush. II. Title.
E881.G74   2015
973.928092—dc23
2015004158

British Library Cataloguing-in-Publication Data is available.

Printed in the United States of America

10 9 8 7 6 5 4 3 2 1

The paper used in this publication is recycled and contains 30 percent postconsumer
waste. It is acid free and meets the minimum requirements of the American National
Standard for Permanence of Paper for Printed Library Materials Z39.48-1992.

7-15

1826694

University Press of Kansas

For Patty, T. J., Christopher, and Mary Rose
And for my parents, Peg and Jack Greene

CONTENTS

Acknowledgments   ix

Foreword   xiii

1. "One Should Serve His Country"   1

2. "Jugular Politics"   29

3. "The Untouchables"   53

4. Domestic Policies   71

5. Paying for Reaganomics   95

6. "Enlightened Realism" and the End of the Cold War   107

7. Desert Shield   139

8. Desert Storm   163

9. President Bush   179

10. "The Situation Is About as Bad as It Can Be"   193

11. "The President Should Have Fired Us All"   215

12. The "F.L.F.W."   237

Notes   261

Bibliographical Essay   321

Index   347

ACKNOWLEDGMENTS

A noted author once observed that acknowledgment pages in books had grown so lengthy that soon writers would be thanking anyone who had provided them with a paper clip. Perhaps. But writers understand that they succeed only because caring people looked past their often unreasonable demands, fits of impatience, and desire for perfection. I am grateful to everyone who passed on ideas, suggestions, and encouragement—and, in general, put up with me—over the ten years it took to research and write the first edition of this book.

Bright young minds, refusing to accept a shoddy phrase or idea, blow a fresh breeze across the pages of a developing manuscript. I have profited more than I can repay from the ideas of my undergraduate students in history and government at Cazenovia College. Students in my various classes and seminars—particularly those on the Modern American Presidency—have heard pieces of this work. I have utilized with great profit the research essays of Jennifer Cross, Amber Dusenberry, and Debora Hall, and I am also grateful for the research help of Christine Caffrey, Esther Day, Wendy Frias, Kelly Hegedus, Jennifer Hull, and Erin Karasik. Particular thanks are due to Matthew Antonino, who has served as a valued critic, sounding board, and friend for the past four years.

All members of the faculty and staff at Cazenovia College consistently show patience and give their support to any colleague who is undertaking the development of a major project. Every day, I am grateful for their collegiality and encouragement. I am particularly grateful to President Adelaide Van Titus, Dean of the College Michael Fishbein, and Assistant Dean Timothy McLaughlin. I am also grateful for the college's financial assistance, as I could not have completed the research for this book without help from the Cazenovia College Faculty Development Fund.

The George Bush Presidential Library, located on the campus of Texas A&M University in College Station, is the newest addition to the National Archives' Presidential Library System. Many of its treasures, as I have noted in the bibliographical essay, have yet to be opened for scholarly perusal. Nevertheless, its facility is state of the art, and its staff are first-rate, extending themselves to the researcher far beyond the call of duty. I am grateful to Library Director David Alsobrook and to Kate Dillon, Mary Finch, Warren Finch, John Laster, and Debbie Wheeler for their help and good humor. Many other archivists and librarians have helped me. Special thanks are due to Diane Barrie of the Ronald Reagan Presidential Library; Geir Gunderson, David Horrocks, and William McNitt of the Gerald R. Ford Presidential Library; Stanley Kozaczka of the Cazenovia College Library; and Carol Leadenham of the Hoover Institution on War, Revolution, and Peace.

Former president George H. W. Bush was gracious enough to take time out of his busy schedule to be interviewed for this book. I am also grateful to the many other members of his administration, and administration-watchers, who talked with me: James A. Baker III, David Bates, Phillip D. Brady, Douglas A. Brook, Andrew H. Card Jr., Richard B. Cheney, David F. Demarest, Edward Derwinski, Geraldine Ferraro, Barbara Hackman Franklin, C. Boyden Gray, Robert R. Green, Donald P. Gregg, Robert T. Hartmann, Dr. Daniel R. Heimbach, Ronald C. Kaufman, James R. Lilley, Frederic V. Malek, Edward N. Ney, Sean O'Keefe, Michael A. Poling, Rob Portman, Sig Rogich, General Brent Scowcroft, Hugh Sidey, John Sununu, Carol Trimble, Chase Untermeyer, William Webster, and Clayton Yeutter. I also am thankful for the input of those individuals who preferred not to have their names listed here. Without breaking that confidentiality, I have used many of their ideas and insights to corroborate my own thoughts; their anonymity does not diminish the importance of their contribution to this book.

Since 1982, the Hofstra University Cultural Center, in conjunction with the Departments of History and Political Science of that institution, has put on a series of extraordinary conferences dealing with the modern American presidency. Scholars, administration alumni, and often the president himself get together for a series of valuable discussion sessions. The April 1997 conference on the Bush presidency was a real boon to this book. I am grateful to conference coordinators Natalie Datlof and Alexej Ugrinsky and to assistant to the coordinator Athelene A. Collins-Price for their labors.

I am fortunate to be able to publish my work with the University Press of Kansas—an author's house. Special thanks to my friend, director Fred M. Woodward, senior production editor Melinda Wirkus and production editor Rebecca Knight Giusti, marketing director Susan Schott, and copy editor Claire Sutton. All readers of the American Presidency Series owe a debt of gratitude to its general editors—the late Donald McCoy, the late Clifford S. Griffin, and Homer E. Socolofsky. Professor Socolofsky's reading of the manuscript was invaluable, as were the thoughtful comments offered by Professor Robert Divine of the University of Texas.

When a writer talks to a class, the press, or a reviewer, the story of writing tends to become somewhat mythologized, as the project is portrayed in its most positive light. The author's family hears the truth— every day (in fact, they hear more of the truth on those days when a few good pages *don't* seem to get themselves written). It is to my wife and children that my work is always dedicated and to my parents, to whom this particular work is inscribed. But my immediate family hears the same grumbling (as well as stories of literary victories) as I write. I am grateful for their patience and for that of their families: Mark and Carrie Greene, Marsha and Ed Kernan, Bill and Dorothy Messer, Don and Jean Messer, Tom and Sonya Messer, Anne and Bob Reimann, and Doug and Joan Robertson.

I will forget more people than I thank, but among the many others who have given me their support are Cindy and Don Clark and family; Edward Galvin; Mary and Jack Hyla of the Four Seasons Resort in Old Forge (the place I went to *not* write); the staff and faculty of the Jowonio School; Ken, Sherrie, and Julianna Kubiak; and Shirley Anne Warshaw.

When revising and expanding this book to a new edition, I once again received the help of many of these friends; I also incurred additional debts of gratitude.

Once again, the George Bush Presidential Library provided access to the archival material that is at the core of this work. All researchers depend on archivists to be their guide through the thickets of often complicated collections. I had the expert assistance of Rachel Altman, Mary Finch, Warren Finch, Mckenzie Morse, and Rebecca Passmore during my time at College Station, as well as the friendship of many people who befriended me during my many trips to Texas.

My thanks to former secretary of state James A. Baker III, for granting permission both to consult, and to cite and quote from, his papers, donated to the Princeton University, Seeley G. Mudd Manuscript Library, Public Policy Papers. I am grateful to Dan Liedke, University Archivist and Curator of the Public Policy Papers, and Special Collections Assistant Christa Cleeton for helping to make my time at Princeton so profitable.

I particularly want to thank once again the University Press of Kansas. It was Director Emeritus Fred Woodward's idea to take this book into a second edition; I thank him for giving me the chance to apply the new Bush literature and the material opened in the archival record to ideas that were a decade old. To Director Charles Myers, his colleagues Kelly Chrisman Jacques, Karl Janssen, Mike Kehoe, Larisa Martin, and Rebecca Murray, and copy editor Susan Ecklund, I can only say what authors all over the country say about UPK—a comment that, perhaps, only writers would understand: Kansas lets its writers write. I continue to be honored to be associated with this house.

I learned a great deal as a script consultant for *American Experience*: "George H. W. Bush." I thank producer Austin Hoyt for the opportunity. Professor Lewis L. Gould was kind enough to share hints that greatly aided with the recrafting of the manuscript.

At Cazenovia College, I continue to be grateful to the Office of Academic Affairs—particularly Dean Sharon Dettmer, Sarah Diederich, and Anna Marchant—who support my work in every possible way. Students Joseph Celeste and Kasey Sikorsky provided valuable assistance. And once again, to each of my colleagues who has been a part of this effort, my thanks.

Without the patience of my family, each of my books written over the course of my career would have been nothing more than a bullet point on a wish list. *They* made it happen.

Cazenovia, New York
2014

FOREWORD

The aim of the American Presidency Series is to present historians and the general reading public with interesting, scholarly assessments of the various presidential administrations. These interpretive surveys are intended to cover the broad ground between biographies, specialized monographs, and journalistic accounts. As such, each is a comprehensive work that draws on original sources and pertinent secondary literature, yet leaves room for the author's own analysis and interpretation.

Volumes in the series present the data essential to understanding the administration under consideration. Particularly, each book treats the then-current problems facing the United States and its people and how the president and his associates felt about, thought about, and worked to cope with these problems. Attention is given to how the office developed and operated during the president's tenure. Equally important is a consideration of the vital relationships between the president and his staff, the executive officers, Congress, foreign representatives, the judiciary, state officials, the public, political parties, the press, and influential private citizens. The series is also concerned with how this unique American institution—the presidency—was viewed by the presidents, and with what results.

All of this is set, insofar as possible, in the context not only of contemporary politics but also of economics, international relations, law, morals, public administration, religion, and thought. Such a broad approach is necessary because a presidential administration is more than the elected and appointed officers composing it; its work often reflects the major problems, anxieties, and glories of the nation. In short, the authors in this series strive to recount and evaluate the record of each administration and to identify its distinctiveness and relationships to the past, its own time, and the future.

The General Editors

1

"ONE SHOULD SERVE
HIS COUNTRY"

Prescott Bush, an imposing man who could trace his lineage to Henry III of England, was raised in Columbus, Ohio, took his degree at Yale, and served in World War I. His wife, the former Dorothy Walker, was born in Kennebunkport, Maine, and attended private schools in St. Louis and Connecticut. When she met Bush, he was working for the Simmons Hardware Company in St. Louis. They were married in 1921 and moved to New York in 1924, where Bush soon became a partner in the investment firm of Brown Brothers, Harriman. They would have five children. Their second child, George Herbert Walker Bush, was born in Milton, Massachusetts, on 12 June 1924. He was named after his maternal grandfather and also inherited his nickname, "Poppy." Of his father, his second child would later say, "Everything he did was star quality."[1]

When he stepped into the national spotlight, much was made of George Bush's upbringing and background, as he was charged by his political opponents with being out of touch with the masses (Texas governor Ann Richards quipped at the 1988 Democratic Convention: "George can't help it—he was born with a silver foot in his mouth"). But those who dismissed Bush as a coddled member of the upper class did not take into account his rather disciplined upbringing. Both his mother and father were, to be sure, members of the genteel class—well educated, well pedigreed, well mannered, and well connected. They were also wealthy, but not so much so that they could claim membership in the leisure class who lived off their investment income. Prescott Bush did not have the money to engage in conspicuous consumption; even if he had, it would have been quite out of character for this staid New Englander to flaunt his wealth. The world in which the Bush children were raised, then, was one in which comfort was never an issue, but neither were the constant reminders that that comfort could not be taken for granted. Prescott refused to allow his children to loiter their way to adulthood. Rather, he inculcated in them the same values of self-reliance and a mind-set of active service. George Bush's most favorable biographer, Fitzhugh Green, wryly noted that though the Bush family was comfortably insulated from the Great Depression of the 1930s, Prescott "had to work hard to do so. Therefore, it was wrong to leave one's bicycle out in the rain."[2] Prescott Bush used his wealth as a safety net for his children. They were expected to go out, earn their own wealth, and do the same.

Akin to the value of hard work was that of public humility about their accomplishments. Boasting about good fortune, or flaunting their wealth or station, was expressly forbidden in the Bush household. One of his children later remembered with pride that Prescott Bush commuted to New York City from his Greenwich, Connecticut, home by train each day: "He'd *die* now with limos picking them up. He was a straphanger."[3] Doro Bush Koch, George Bush's daughter and one of his future biographers, noted that her father "always heard [his mother's] voice in his head," telling him to keep his ego in check and not to brag about his accomplishments ("How did the *team* do, George?").[4] This did not, however, translate to the preaching of passivity. Both Prescott and Dorothy were athletes of professional caliber, both were intensely competitive, and they expected their children to be likewise. Prescott played on the 1915 Yale baseball team (a first baseman like his son) and was an outstanding golfer (he would serve as a president of the U.S. Golf Association and was often partnered with another outstanding golfer, Dwight Eisenhower).[5] Both Bushes were outstanding tennis players, especially Dorothy (who once reached the finals of the National Girl's Tennis Championship; the Walker's Cup was named after her father), who encouraged her children to excel in the game. Their children were just as competitive, joining and excelling in a variety of sports. Indeed, all games offered an opportunity to smack a sibling: a friend watching a particularly brutal family game of Ping-Pong dryly noted: "I was surprised there was still a ball."[6] Above all, both parents preached the sanctity of family ties. The nickname "Poppy" may have sounded both juvenile and preppy, but it emphasized Bush's direct link to his familial heritage.

Of course, with privilege came privileges. Bush enrolled his sons in the Greenwich Country Day School. They lived at home until they completed the ninth grade, when they went away to prep school at Phillips Academy in Andover, Massachusetts—"Andover." The school's seal, which was designed by Paul Revere, proclaimed the values that Dorothy Bush had already inculcated in her children—"Non Sibi" (not for self) and "Finis Origine Pendet" (the end depends upon the beginning).[7] George was so attached to his elder brother, Prescott Jr., that his parents allowed him to enter Andover one year early, so that the two boys might be together.[8] His time there was far from uneventful. In spring of his junior year, he contracted a serious infection in his right arm. He took the summer off and repeated a year. When he returned to Andover, his classmates were his own age. He became senior class president, president of the Greeks, captain of the baseball and soccer teams, a member of the basketball team, and a participant in many other clubs and groups.[9]

It was also during his senior year, while attending a Christmas dance at the Greenwich Country Club, that George met Barbara Pierce. She was attending Ashley Hall, a girls' finishing school. Her father was the vice president of McCall's Publishing Company, and she could trace her family tree to President Franklin Pierce.[10] Barbara's chief biographer pays tribute to her "caustic tongue"—a trait she shared with her outspoken father.[11] She was sixteen; he was seventeen—Barbara later wrote that George Bush was the first man that she ever kissed.[12] George Bush was smitten. They became "secretly" engaged—a secret that virtually everyone in both families knew.

George Bush learned about the Japanese attack on Pearl Harbor while he was at Andover, walking near the chapel.[13] He later remembered that his reaction "was the same as every other American—'We gotta do something about this one.'"[14] Despite the advice of secretary of war Henry Stimson, who told Bush's graduating class that they should go to college before enlisting, and despite his father's wish for him to go to Yale University, where he had already been accepted, Bush enlisted in the navy on 12 June 1942, his eighteenth birthday.[15] He would later write that at the train station, "that was the first time I saw my father cry."[16] He was assigned to Chapel Hill, North Carolina, to undergo his preflight training. He then went to Minnesota to learn how to fly, and to Corpus Christi, Texas, to learn instrument flying and navigation. On 9

Naval Ensign George H. W. Bush. (Courtesy of the George Bush Presidential Library and Museum)

July 1943, he received his aviator's wings and was promoted to ensign.[17] Just nineteen, Bush was the youngest pilot in the U.S. Navy. For close to a year he traveled across the United States from base to base, practicing his carrier landings and learning to fly Grumman's three-man TBF torpedo bomber, nicknamed the "Avenger." Late in 1943, a rather nonchalant Bush wrote his parents: "True, there is a danger to TB's which you know about, but I don't think we should consider that. Someone has to fly them."[18]

On 15 December 1943, Bush was assigned to the aircraft carrier *San Jacinto*, a "baby flattop" that was part of the navy's Fifth Fleet. He saw plenty of action. During the June 1944 campaign in the Marianas (the greatest aircraft carrier battle in history, it was nicknamed "The Great Marianas Turkey Shoot"), Bush was airborne for more than thirty-two hours; more than half of that time was spent in strikes against Japanese who were dug in on the island of Saipan, where the marines were in the process of landing. During that battle—one week after his twentieth birthday—Bush and his crew were forced to ditch their plane in the ocean immediately after takeoff.[19] Later that summer, Bush flew air cover for the marine landings on the islands of Guam, Iwo Jima, and Chichi Jima.

On 2 September 1944, Bush took off on his fiftieth mission. He and his crew were sent to bomb an enemy radio site at Chichi Jima. Bush remembered that "the minute we pushed over to dive, you could just feel the danger...some way about halfway down the run I was hit."[20] He later described the incident in a letter to his parents: "We got hit....I told the boys in the back to get their parachutes on....The cockpit was full of smoke and I was choking from it....I felt certain that [the crew] had bailed out."[21] Bush made it out of the cockpit, but both his crewmen were killed. When Bush landed in the ocean, he realized that he had not hooked his life raft to his parachute; fortunately, the raft landed only a few yards from him. A half hour later, a submarine patrolling the area, the USS *Finback*, picked him up. Had the *Finback* not been there, the tides would have taken Bush to Chichi Jima, where Americans were well aware of the corroborated stories of the barbaric treatment of American prisoners, which included cannibalism.[22] After his ordeal, Bush returned to his squadron in the Philippines for three further months of combat missions.[23]

Bush was by then eligible for leave. He used it to get married on 6 June 1945 (he reportedly mumbled to his new bride, "Enjoy it. It's the last time I'll ever dance in public").[24] Bush had also earned enough points for a discharge, but instead he opted to return to the Pacific (as he later remembered, "It was different then; 'we gotta go back and do our duty'").[25] However, the atomic bomb was dropped on Japan before he could be shipped back. Bush was discharged on 18 September 1945. He had flown fifty-eight missions, accrued 1,228 hours of flying time, made 126 carrier landings, and earned the Distinguished Flying Cross.[26] Bush later said, "I had faced death, and God had spared me."[27]

After facing death, Bush accepted the invitation to earn the higher education that he had deferred in 1941. When Bush enrolled at Yale in fall 1945, he was part of the blitz on America's college and universities that became known as the "GI Bulge." Many schools had been badly hurt by the drop in enrollment caused when young men left to fight in World War II, so they welcomed returning veterans, the vast majority of whom had their way paid by the GI Bill, with open arms: Bush's class of some 8,000 freshmen was the largest entering class in Yale's history.[28] Colleges also made the effort to help veterans catch up for lost time with innovative—and abbreviated—programs. Bush enrolled in an accelerated program that allowed him to earn his BA in economics in only two years. He was also an outstanding baseball player, an excellent fielding first baseman whom major league scouts were observing.[29] Bush also made Phi Beta Kappa and advanced his contacts by being tapped for the Skull and Bones Club, a supersecret society whose members (one of whom had been his father) remained close for the rest of their lives.

In June 1948, just before his graduation from Yale, Bush wrote a friend:

> I have thought of teaching. . . . I could work for [uncle] Herby Walker in St. Louis. . . . [But] I am not sure I want to capitalize completely on the benefits I received at birth. . . . I have this chance to go with Neil Mallon's Dresser Industries—perhaps to Texas. . . . at the moment [the job] has great appeal. I would be seeing new people, learning something of basic importance.[30]

Given his background, as well as his experience in World War II, one should not be surprised, as are many of Bush's biographers and political contemporaries, that he gravitated toward an adventurous rather than a "safe" career choice. Having been weaned on self-sufficiency since his youth, Bush went his own way after his June 1948 graduation from Yale, entering an occupation that was loaded with the possibility of failure. He chose the oil business and moved his young family to Texas.

However, the Bushes did not go into these volatile hinterlands without a safety net; their way was made much easier by his father's contacts. Prescott had been a member of the board of Dresser Industries and was a friend of the company's president, Neil Mallon, who agreed to take George on as the company's only trainee in 1948.

That summer Bush moved to Odessa, on the Permian Basin in western Texas (Bush: "I had no idea where it was. Had to look it up on a road map").[31] A Saharan backwater, Odessa was a stagnant town of 25,000 that had not yet been transformed by the oil boom. Bush started at Ideco (International Derrick and Equipment Company), a subsidy of Dresser, in a job that paid $375 a month and where he became a member of the United Steelworkers Union.[32] It was hardly the lap of luxury. Living in a town dominated by warehouses and hard-fighting and hard-drinking roustabouts and pipelayers, the Bushes lived in a tiny apartment where they shared a bathroom with their neighbors—several prostitutes. Bush's job included such menial tasks as sweeping warehouses and hand painting pump jacks. He took the first opportunity to escape. In April 1949, Dresser moved Bush to Pacific Pumps, one of its subsidiaries based in Huntington Park, California, where he worked as a salesman. It was hardly a step up—the family "lived in a motel in Whittier, the Pierpont Inn in Ventura, a rented house in Bakersfield, and finally an apartment in Compton."[33] Bush described his work to a friend as being much like what he had done in Odessa: "I am a laborer . . . and a dues paying CIO steelworker."[34]

But Bush did not come west to lead a blue-collar life. He wanted to become a part of the oil boom that was making independent investors wealthy men. He wanted to "wildcat"; he wanted to make his fortune. He was hardly alone. Thousands of Americans moved to the South and West in the years immediately following the war. By 1948, some 3,000 wells were being drilled deep into the substrata of the Permian Basin by men with big dreams. Everyone wanted in: Bob Hope and Bing Crosby invested $160,000 in a well in Scurry County—they made $5 million each in profit.[35]

The next step toward this dream was a move from Odessa to Midland in April 1950. As historian Burton I. Kaufman has noted, although Midland was only thirteen miles from Odessa, the two towns might as well have been "separate worlds." Oil was growing Midland—its population had jumped from 25,000 in 1940 to 60,000 in 1950. It had 215 oil company offices, and, unlike in Odessa, Bush did not toil in anonymity as a college man—Midland boasted Yale, Harvard, and Princeton clubs.[36] Bush did not wait long to make his move. In 1950, with friend and University of Texas graduate John Overbey, Bush formed an oil development company, and again his eastern contacts were useful. Bush-Overbey Oil Development Company was partly bankrolled by Brown Brothers (Prescott invested $50,000) and by Bush's grandfather, who invested $500,000 of his own money.[37] The business model was risky—Bush-Overbey bought the mineral rights on land that was close to other pieces of property where another wildcatter was preparing to drill. If the other guy struck oil, Bush-Overbey's land would immediately appreciate in value.[38]

Two years later, Overbey and Bush merged their firm with one run by Hugh Liedke, a Harvard-educated lawyer from Midland who, like Bush, was a navy veteran. They formed Zapata Petroleum, named for the Mexican revolutionary who recently had been played in the movies by Marlon Brando. Zapata bought 8,000 acres seventy-five miles east of Midland in Coke County for $850,000.[39] Then they drilled. Bush and Liedke struck it rich; indeed, Zapata struck oil on the first hole they drilled.[40] By the end of 1954, Zapata assets included 8,100 acres of property and seventy-one active wells, which produced an average of 1,250 barrels a day. Not one of them was dry, and the oil that was pumped netted Zapata $1.2 million per year.[41]

Liedke and Bush were complementary spirits—Liedke enjoyed the management of Zapata's assets, while Bush was a natural-born risk taker.[42] As a result, Bush became interested in the new technology—and high rewards—of offshore oil drilling. To accommodate the dreams of its founders, in 1958 Zapata split in half. Liedke's half would eventually merge into South Penn Oil Company, later changing its name to Pennzoil.[43] Bush took over the presidency of the new half, Zapata Offshore. Needing to be near the action in the Gulf of Mexico, in 1959 Bush moved his family from Midland to Houston.

For a businessman of the 1950s, Bush was unusually devoted to his young family. Barbara developed into something of a frontier wife, quickly adapting to life in Texas. They soon had three children—George W. (born in 1946), Pauline Robinson (Robin, 1949), and John Ellis (Jeb, 1953). Soon after the birth of Jeb, tragedy struck. Robin, who had been born while the Bushes were in Compton, was diagnosed with an advanced case of leukemia. The child's torture lasted seven months, as George and Barbara shuttled back and forth between Midland and New York's Sloan-Kettering Hospital, where Robin received her treatment.

Robin died on Columbus Day 1953, two months before her fourth birthday, with both her parents at her bedside.[44] For forty years Bush carried three good-luck charms in his wallet—a ripped clipping of Barbara's engagement photo, a four-leaf clover, and a small gold medallion, on which was inscribed "For the Love of Robin."[45] Despite their tragedy, the Bush family continued to grow, with the addition of Neil (named after Neil Mallon, 1955), Marvin (named after Barbara's father, 1956), and Dorothy Walker (Doro, named after Barbara's mother, 1959).

For Prescott Bush, elective office was a natural corollary to his view of public service. As would his son, Prescott first made his money, then he entered politics. As the elected moderator of the Greenwich Town Meeting, Prescott was, in the words of one observer, "taking care of the public schools his children would never attend."[46] In 1950, Prescott Bush lost by only 1,102 votes in the race for the U.S. Senate from Connecticut to incumbent William Benton. In 1952, he worked to nominate Dwight D. Eisenhower as the presidential nominee of the Republican Party. Later that year, in his second try, Prescott defeated Abraham Ribicoff and was elected to the Senate, where he would serve until 1963. A moderate Republican in the Eisenhower-Dewey mold, Bush was fiscally conservative but socially progressive, speaking out in favor of both civil rights and legalized abortion. He was also an outspoken opponent of Joseph McCarthy (R-WI), denouncing him from the floor of the Senate ("Either you must follow Senator McCarthy blindly, not daring to express any doubts or disagreements about any of his actions, or, in his eyes, you must be a communist, a communist sympathizer, or a fool who has been duped by the communist line").[47] In 1964, Prescott would work in vain to keep ultraconservative Barry Goldwater from winning his party's nomination for president.[48]

The son shared his father's dream of political glory and service. But Texas was not Connecticut. Postwar Texas was the scene of a vibrant, often violent, political transition. The state had voted Democratic in every presidential election since 1948, save for 1928, when it went for Herbert Hoover. But Dwight Eisenhower gained a foothold in the state for the Republican Party when he carried Texas in 1952 (thanks primarily to the state's Democratic governor, Allen Shivers, who bolted his party to support Eisenhower, largely over Eisenhower's support of state ownership of Tidelands Oil—an issue close to an oilman's heart). Eisenhower would be reelected in 1956, and he would carry Texas as well as several other southern states. But Eisenhower's victories in Texas were personal ones. The Democrats held such a numerical advantage in the state that in 1960 the state Republican Party could not hold regular primary elections. Against these numbers, and without Ike running, the "Shivercrats" could not hold. In 1960, with favorite son Lyndon B. Johnson on the Democratic ticket, John F. Kennedy narrowly won Texas—one of the keys to his presidential victory.

The state was back in the Democratic column, but Texas Democrats were split, with a conservative faction, led by governor John Connally, and a liberal faction, led by Senator Ralph Yarborough. The Republicans sensed an opportunity, and in May 1961, John Tower, a former college professor, exploited the split by openly courting conservative Democrats and tarring the Yarborough Democrats with the brush of Kennedy liberalism. Tower's victory gave Texas its first Republican senator since Reconstruction, but the Republicans were as divided as were the Democrats. The moderate, anti-McCarthy, internationalist Republicanism of Prescott Bush found few takers in Texas, and the party found itself increasingly under the wing of the archconservative John Birchers. While this appalled the few moderate businessmen who called themselves Republican, the fact of the matter was that the Texas Republican Party was becoming more and more conservative by the day.

George Bush's first foray into politics inserted him into the eye of the hurricane that was this divided Texas Republican Party. One of the most hopeful areas for Texas Republicans was Harris County, the center of which was the city of Houston—the largest metropolitan area to go for Nixon in 1960.[49] In 1962, the chairman of the Harris County (Houston) Republican Party moved to Florida, thus creating a vacancy that the Birchers were threatening to exploit. Moderate Republican businessmen begged Bush to run for the chairmanship. Bush was willing, but he faced the problem of being branded an eastern liberal in oilman's clothing (one GOP member put it succinctly: "I'm not votin' for another country club asshole").[50] To overcome this handicap, Bush began to make his own political contacts, pulling close to him people who could help him overcome the carpetbagger image. Chief among them was James A. Baker III. As circumspect as Bush was gregarious, Baker possessed an undisputed Texas pedigree. A classics major at Princeton and a University of Texas Law School graduate, he was an associate in Baker and Botts, the second-oldest law firm in Texas. He was also a Democrat. But the bond between the two men went far beyond politics. Since Bush's early days as a Texas oilman, Baker had been his closest friend—Bush was godfather to one of Baker's daughters. Bush was also close to Robert A. Mosbacher, of Houston's Mosbacher Energy Company. Tied to the Texas establishment as well as to the Newport yachting set, Mosbacher had served as the chair of the national finance committee of the President Ford Committee in 1975; he had also served on the Republican National Finance Committee and as chairman of the Texas Congressional Boosters.[51] Bush had offered Mosbacher, a fund-raiser without peer, a partnership in Zapata Offshore, but Mosbacher turned it down.[52] With Baker's and Mosbacher's help, Bush easily won the position of Harris County Republican chair—his 34,337 votes made him to that point the top Republican vote getter in Texas history.[53]

Bush was a resounding success as head of the Harris County Republican Party. He raised a lot of money, led the charge to computerize the voter rolls, and even engineered the election of Houston's first Republican city councilman.[54] But Bush disappointed many of his business supporters when, rather than turn the Birchers out, he gave them positions within the party. While some argued that Bush was showing his true, ultraconservative colors, Bush positioned himself as a uniter, arguing that he needed the Birchers in the party coalition in order to defeat Democrats.[55]

Bush's first shot at statewide office came in 1964, when he ran for the U.S. Senate seat then held by Yarborough. Bush's landslide victory in the Harris County election, and Yarborough's avowed liberal tendencies, gave Bush hope. So did Kennedy's decision to speak out in favor of a civil rights bill in June 1963—a decision that sent thousands of conservative Democrats flocking to the GOP. Bush also stood to benefit from the feud between Yarborough and Connally, which by 1963 had reached a fever pitch. Indeed, Kennedy went to Dallas on 22 November 1963 to try to patch up the feud between Connally and Yarborough and to try to make some inroads in Texas against Goldwater. Some optimistic Republicans, remembering Tower's upset victory of a divided Democratic Party, dared hope for another Republican senator.

It was not to be. Kennedy's assassination completely changed the political landscape, both nationally and in Texas. Now Johnson was at the head of the national ticket in 1964, running with a unified Democratic Party and poised to destroy Goldwater's candidacy. Old feuds were forgotten; Johnson came to Texas and stumped the state with Yarborough by his side. This would probably have been enough to defeat Bush, or any Texas Republican in 1964. But Bush's competitive juices were flowing. He let himself believe that the state had tired of Yarborough, and he also believed that having Goldwater at the top of the ticket would help any Republican who ran as far to the right as did Goldwater. So Bush ran hard, and he ran to the right. Indeed, in 1964, Bush ran to the *far* right. He attacked the Johnson administration for being soft on Vietnam, he opposed the Civil Rights Act of 1964,[56] he denounced the United Nations, and he criticized the nuclear test ban treaty that had been passed in July 1963. Yarborough's answer was simple and devastating. He charged that Bush had become the "darling of the John Birch Society," thus scaring any moderate Democrats who might be inclined to vote Republican.[57] He told his supporters that Bush "ought to pick up his baggage and go back where he came from";[58] told voters that the state should "elect a senator from Texas, and not the Connecticut investment bankers"; and painted Bush as the tool of a big international firm—Liedke's Pennzoil—instead of being a good ol' Texas independent oil man.[59]

Along with almost every Republican challenger that fall, Bush was handily defeated, earning only 43 percent of the vote (Johnson carried Texas with 63 percent of the vote). He responded after learning of his defeat to Yarborough, "I guess I have a lot to learn about."[60] He certainly learned that running a part-time campaign—Bush continued to work at Zapata Offshore throughout the campaign—was no way to get elected. He might also have learned that running so far to the right did him little good—African Americans voted 98.5 percent to 1.5 percent against him,[61] and the Birchers gave Bush little to no help in the election.[62]

In 1966, Bush tried again. First, in an admission that his work schedule had held him back in his previous campaign, he sold his interest in Zapata. Then rather than attempt a statewide campaign again, he stayed close to home—he declared his candidacy for the congressional seat in Texas's Seventh District, located on the well-heeled west side of Houston. This time, the deck was stacked in his favor. In 1963, Harris County Republican chairman Bush had filed a suit under the Supreme Court decision in *Baker v. Carr*,[63] and he succeeded in having the district's lines redrawn in his favor—the district was now 90 percent white.[64] In this district, Bush had little to fear from the Birchers, and he was able to run on a platform of moderate Republicanism. Indeed, at several stops he made a point of saying that he was pro-choice on the abortion issue. Tutored by Harry Treleaven, a New York City adman hired by Bush to streamline his campaign, Bush was an exciting candidate, full of energy and indefatigable on the stump.[65] Unopposed in the primary, Bush defeated his Democratic foe, Harris County district attorney Frank Briscoe, with 57.6 percent of the vote.[66]

Bush served two terms in Congress (he was reelected in 1968 without opposition) during a time of unprecedented conflict in the nation's history. The Republicans, in the minority in both houses of Congress, struggled to find a response to Johnson's Great Society policies that did not make them look like troglodytes. Bush biographer Timothy Naftali is not far from the mark when he claims that Bush had "few, if any, settled policy ideas. What he had were tendencies."[67] Bush supported the Vietnam War, a stand that said less about political philosophy (by 1966, both support and opposition to the war cut across party lines) or, one could argue, political expediency (virtually everyone in his district supported the war) than about his feelings of duty. His work on the House Republican Research Committee Task Force on Earth Resources and Population featured a dogged advocacy for family planning—thus earning him the nickname "Rubbers." These efforts earned for Bush the criticism of many of his party's conservatives, many of them fundamentalist Christians who were beginning to coalesce around the pro-life banner. For example, in April 1970, the conservative group Young Americans for Freedom (YAF) published an article excoriating Bush for his stand, branding him "the leading life-prevention henchman for the administration and the House."[68] Bush did not publicly respond to the criticism at the time; later he argued that his critics did not see that he was in favor of family planning as an alternative to abortion, which at the time he publicly opposed.[69]

These were hardly stances that would separate Bush from the pack of Republican backbenchers. But it was his startling stand on civil rights that branded him as a moderate, infuriated his constituents, and jeopardized his political future. In June 1968, six days after the assassination of Martin Luther King Jr., Bush voted in favor of the administration-sponsored Civil Rights Act of 1968, which addressed the issue of discrimination in housing—an extension of the Civil Rights Act of 1964 that he had opposed in previous campaigns. In 1999, in an edited volume of his letters, Bush explained his flip-flop: "I still had some constitutional concerns about the Bill, just as I did in 1964, but the problem of discrimination troubled me deeply."[70] But Bush no longer needed the Birchers as much as he had four years earlier, and it was now easier to vote his conscience; when he wrote that "almost all" of his constituents were against the bill, he was not exaggerating.[71] After telling his friend Bob

Mosbacher that he was "being fitted for my lead underwear,"[72] Bush went home.

On 17 April, in what many present described later as the tensest political meeting they would ever attend, Bush came back to Houston, faced down the boos and vicious catcalls, and explained his vote to an audience of furious constituents: "One hundred out of 184 Republicans in the House voted for it. . . . I voted from conviction . . . not out of intimidation or fear, not stampeded by riots, but because of a feeling deep in my heart that this was the right thing for me to do." This, the audience refused to buy, and the boos grew louder. But Bush would not be heckled down. He showed a true skill for thinking on his feet at this meeting, as he won over the audience by playing to their patriotism: "If you're good enough to fight for your country [in Vietnam], you ought to be able to buy a decent house when you get back." By the end of the speech, the audience was on their feet, cheering for their congressman.[73] He had broken out of the Republican pack.

Richard Nixon publicly placed Bush on the shortlist of vice presidential candidates in 1968. This, however, was a token for services rendered—Nixon had already decided on Maryland governor Spiro Agnew as his running mate early that spring.[74] Indeed, neither Nixon nor National Security Advisor Henry Kissinger had much respect for Bush: indications of this can be found in a recorded telephone conversation between Nixon and Kissinger, where Nixon called Bush "soft and unsophisticated,"[75] as well as a later Kissinger conversation with historian Arthur M. Schlesinger Jr. where Kissinger called Bush a "very weak man."[76] Nixon did, however, admire Bush's loyalty, as did Nixon's aides-de-camp. In the margins of a memorandum requesting an appointment for Bush with Nixon, chief of staff H. R. Haldeman scribbled, "We need more congressmen like Bush!"[77]

That loyalty was tested in 1970, when, at the request of Nixon, Bush gave up his safe House seat to run for the Senate. Initially, Nixon was not asking Bush to fight a lost cause. Bush's opponent, for a second time, started out as Ralph Yarborough, whose liberalism had long since begun to grate on Texans. But Yarborough was unexpectedly defeated in the Democratic primary by Lloyd Bentsen. Bentsen had founded the Consolidated American Life Insurance Company and was a decidedly more conservative Democrat than Yarborough; unlike Yarborough, Bentsen ran knowing he had a united Democratic Party behind him. Despite the fact that Bush tried to cut into Bentsen's liberal base by reminding the state of his vote in favor of Johnson's civil rights bill; despite the fact that

Nixon, Agnew, and five other cabinet officers campaigned in Texas for Bush; and despite the fact that Nixon's staff both dug up dirt on Bentsen and sent Bush some $106,000 from a secret campaign fund (the "Townhouse Operation"), the race was lost for Bush as soon as Bentsen had won the primary. Bush lost the general election, winning only 46 percent of the vote. He was devastated. After the results were announced, he told Mosbacher, "I feel like General Custer."[78] Bush's daughter Doro cried after learning of his defeat—"I'll be the only girl in the fifth grade whose dad doesn't have a job."[79]

Hardly. Bush would later remember that Nixon had "subtly made it clear that should I lose, I'd have a job."[80] On 11 December 1970, Nixon made good. After offering Bush a staff position, then the chair of the Republican National Committee—both positions that Bush turned down[81]—Nixon nominated him as ambassador to the United Nations. Lud Ashley, an old friend of Bush's, gently put his finger on why his friend's confirmation hearings were so tough: "George, what the fuck do you know about foreign affairs?"[82] Very little at that point, but once Bush was nominated, the administration never wavered in its support. The reason was simple enough—as Nixon adviser Charles Colson noted in a July 1971 memo, Bush "takes our line beautifully."[83] This assessment remained true of the new ambassador even when he was double-crossed by the administration over the issue of the expulsion of Taiwan from the UN, to be replaced with the communist People's Republic of China (PRC). As the Security Council debated the measure, Nixon instructed Bush to "hold the line" against Taiwan's expulsion. This Bush did, giving a stirring pro-Taiwan speech the night before the vote. However, Nixon had not told Bush that the administration was actually courting the PRC and covertly campaigning for that nation's acceptance into the UN at the expense of Taiwan. Taiwan was finally expelled by a 75-to-35 vote—the outcome that the administration wanted. Bush was furious over how he had been used, but he kept his own counsel.[84]

Bush's career path changed once again on 17 June 1972. On that evening, five burglars were arrested after breaking into the headquarters of the Democratic National Committee (DNC) at Washington's Watergate Hotel. The botched operation—an attempt to fix defective telephone taps that had earlier been placed in the offices of DNC chairman Lawrence O'Brien—began the final chapter in a five-year story of abuse of power by the Nixon administration. As the press, prosecutors, and congressional investigators began to unravel the story, Nixon came to believe that he needed a steadier hand leading his defense from within the Republican Party. Kansas senator Bob Dole was serving as the head of the Republican National Committee (RNC) at the time of the break-in, but his well-known penchant for angry outbursts promised to make an already volatile situation even more troublesome for the White House. After his 1972 reelection, Nixon offered Bush the party chairmanship, and Bush accepted.[85]

Until the final weeks of the Nixon administration, Bush believed Nixon's protestations of innocence and remained a tireless defender of the president. While RNC chair, Bush visited thirty-five states and made 190 appearances, the vast majority of which were speeches defending the president.[86] Chase Untermeyer, who had worked in Bush's campaigns, believes that this discipleship was the most important of Bush's pre-presidential jobs, as it allowed Bush to make valuable contacts around the nation, contacts he would both recall and reuse in his presidential campaign.[87] But that was for another day. The crisis of 1973–1974 was an intensely personal one for Bush, who turned down an offer to run for governor of Texas because he felt a loyalty to Nixon, then found himself "sickened" by the "amoral tone" of what he read in the transcripts of office tape recordings released by the White House to the special pros-ecutor.[88] When the final batch of tapes was released in August, tapes that clearly showed Nixon to be guilty of an obstruction of justice, Bush finally gave up. On 7 August, during Nixon's last cabinet meeting, the president steered the conversation away from Watergate and onto the economy. Several of those present, including Bush, tried to shift the talk back to the possibility of impeachment, but Nixon would hear none of it. The following day, a seething Bush sent Nixon a letter, telling him that his base of support in the Republican Party had vanished and that he should resign. The next day, Nixon did so.[89] Bush's diary reveals that he saw Nixon's resignation as a personal betrayal: "The man is amoral. He has a different sense than the rest of the people."[90]

Under the terms of the Twenty-Fifth Amendment, the new presi-dent, Gerald Ford, was required to nominate for congressional approval a person to serve as vice president. Bush was asked to submit names from Republican state chairmen, and House and Senate leaders were re-quested to canvass their membership. The tally from the combined polls showed Bush with 255 votes, followed by former New York governor Nelson Rockefeller with 181. But Ford, aware of the donations to Bush's 1970 campaign from the Townhouse Operation, was afraid that if they were made public, a future Vice President Bush would be tainted by scandal. Ford chose Rockefeller.[91] Bush clearly believed that he was going to be chosen, and he was confounded by the news. In a letter to Jim Baker written on 21 August 1974, Bush commiserated: "Yesterday was an enormous personal disappointment. For valid reasons we made the finals . . . and so the defeat was more intense."[92] One of his biographers would observe with accuracy: "No American politician had ever tried so hard to be vice president and failed."[93]

As a consolation prize, Ford offered Bush the ambassadorships to Britain or France; Bush asked instead for the PRC. Ford agreed.[94] Perhaps wishing to distance himself from Washington after the travails of Watergate, Bush spent a largely uneventful year as the American envoy to the PRC (the United States not yet having full diplomatic relations with that nation, he did not have ambassadorial rank). The Bushes' informal style was a strange but welcome sight to their hosts—they bicycled almost everywhere they went, and their dog, a cocker spaniel named C. Fred after a family friend, was a rarity in China. The closest Bush came to having an active role in foreign policy was his encouraging the leadership of the PRC to exert pressure on the Khmer Rouge captors of the crew of the merchant vessel USS *Mayaguez*; a Government Accounting Office report following that crisis concluded that that pressure from the PRC may well have led to the eventual release of the crew.[95]

Despite the seeming paucity of policy decisions in which Bush participated, China was far from being merely a rest after Watergate. In an interpretive essay in an edition of Bush's diary, kept while he was in China, editor Jeffrey A. Engel makes the salient point that the China posting "reveals [Bush's] core foreign policy principles." Here, according to Engel, Bush developed his "gentlemanly diplomatic style—equal parts personal, genial, pragmatic and conservative—that became his hallmark." To Engel, what was created in China was "a man committed to American values yet cognizant of the limits of American power; a leader dedicated to personal diplomacy . . . and a strategist committed to balancing Washington's interests with those of its allies. They demonstrate his overriding belief in stability over radical change. . . . The Bush presidency was in this sense made in China."[96] Although one could argue the importance of Bush's time at the UN in much the same light, as well as argue that the future president often embraced and pushed for "radical change," Engel's argument about Bush the man is persuasive—George Bush went to China a politician; while in China, he became a statesman. And after one year, he wanted to come home.

17

Bush's desire to come home coincided with a political problem that Ford needed to neutralize before the upcoming presidential election. Early in 1975, allegations against the Central Intelligence Agency (CIA) had led to a series of investigations. The resulting reports made it clear that the CIA had been involved in abuses of its power that went far beyond the mandate of its charter. The administration was looking to clean house at the agency, and at the RNC Bush had already proved his ability to rein in a wildcat organization. Bush's name was floated to Ford as a possible replacement for director of central intelligence (DCI) William Colby. Donald Rumsfeld, then Ford's chief of staff, provided the president with a list of fifteen "candidates worthy of consideration," and Bush's name made the list. The pros Rumsfeld listed in favor of Bush's nomination were "experience in government and diplomacy, generally familiar with components of the intelligence community and their missions; [and] high integrity and proven adaptability." But the one con almost cost Bush the appointment: "RNC post lends undesirable political cast."[97] Bush was ultimately favored by only three of eight Ford advisers.[98] Ford's first choice was Washington lawyer Edward Bennett Williams, but Williams refused the offer, and the president turned to Bush.[99] Kissinger cabled him on 1 November 1975, offering him the position. Bush's response, cabled the next day, is a fascinating and candid document, not only serving to reveal how shocked he was to receive the offer but also showing in microcosm his sense of duty to the president:

> Your message came as a total and complete shock....Here are my heartfelt views....I do not have politics out of my system entirely and I see this as the total end of any political future....I sure wish I had time to think and sort things out. Henry, you did not know my father. The President did. My Dad inculcated into his sons a set of values that have served me well in my own short public life. One of these values quite simply is that one should serve his country and his President. And so if this is what the President wants me to do the answer is a firm "Yes." In all candor I would not have selected this controversial position if the decision had been mine, but I serve at the pleasure of our President and I do not believe in complicating his already enormously difficult job.

In contradiction to views of Bush that he had articulated in the past, Kissinger responded obsequiously to Bush: "The president was deeply moved—as was I—by your message. He is deeply appreciative of the nobility of your decision.... You are indeed a fine man."[100] Yet the nomination was not a cinch. After a discussion with Mike Mansfield (D-MT), Ford scribbled a note to himself: "Geo[rge] Bush—for him, but he must say no to politics."[101] In order to get Bush through the confirmation process, on 18 December 1975, Ford wrote John Stennis (D-MS) that if Bush was confirmed by the Senate, "I will not consider him as my vice-presidential running mate" in 1976, a promise that Bush reiterated during his committee testimony.[102] It was this promise that won Bush the approval of the Armed Services Committee as well as of the full Senate.

In several letters to friends, as well as in his diary, Bush initially referred to the DCI position as a "graveyard" for his political ambitions.[103] But only three months after his confirmation, he wrote a friend that "this is the most interesting job I've ever had."[104] As DCI, Bush inherited an agency that was cutting back on its human intelligence assets. But Bush had a great faith in spies on the ground, and he decided not to implement a recommendation from his own covert-action chief that the agency cut 2,000 more agents.[105] This trust in human assets endeared Bush to the employees at the agency at a time when both their loyalty and their usefulness were under fire. Six months into his new job, he outlined his successes in a memo to Ford. According to Bush, "Morale at CIA is improving.... our recruitment is up. Our people are willing to serve abroad and take the risks involved." And in a harbinger of things to come, Bush told Ford that "on the personal side, I get total cooperation from Brent Scowcroft, for whom I have the highest personal regard."[106] Nonetheless, when Jimmy Carter was elected in 1976, Bush became the first DCI in the history of the agency to be dismissed by an incoming president-elect.

Bush now found himself out of government for the first time since 1966. To the chairman of Chase Bank, he wrote, "I don't know if I can write a book or not";[107] he wrote plaintively to a friend, "How do I stay alive?"[108] But thanks largely to the contacts of Baker and Mosbacher, he was quickly embraced by corporate America, although he had never been a part of it. He joined the executive committee of the First International Bank in Houston and sat on the boards of several other banks.[109] He served as the chairman of the American Heart Fund, as cochair of national fund-raising for Yale, and as a member of the Board of Trustees of Trinity University, Andover, and the Baylor University School of Medicine.[110] Financier Ross Perot asked Bush to run his Houston-based oil business; Bush turned him down.[111] Bush also watched as his son George W. ran his first political race—in 1978, for Congress—and lost.

Yet Bush's sabbatical from government was never meant to be permanent. In 1978, two political action committees—the Fund for Limited Government[112] and the Congressional Leadership Committee—were created to raise money for a Bush presidential run.[113] By the turn of 1980, Bush for President committees had been set up in nine of the first eleven primary states, a finance chairman had been chosen for forty of the states, and $825,000 had been raised.[114] Nevertheless, Bush knew what he was up against. On 31 January 1979, he wrote Nixon: "I start with no name identification. . . . I am travelling with no press secretary, no advance text, and no fanfare." But Bush was, in his words, "determined to make an all out effort."[115] On 1 May 1979, Bush announced that he was a candidate for the Republican nomination for the presidency. His early campaign slogan: "A President We Won't Have to Train."

Former California governor Ronald Reagan, making his third run for the White House, had spent two decades co-opting the conservative wing of the Republican Party. Thus, Bush assiduously courted the moderates. Indeed, Bob Mosbacher would later remember that most of Bush's support in the primaries came from former supporters of Gerald Ford, many of whom thought that if Bush could knock out Reagan, then Ford might be convinced to step in and run again.[116] Thanks to their early support, the well-prepared Bush was fast out of the gate. His upset win in a November 1979 Maine straw poll and a strong showing in a Florida straw poll raised the eyebrows of the political establishment. In the 21 January 1980 Iowa caucuses, Bush took the Reagan campaign by surprise, eking out a victory with a margin of 2,182 votes.[117] The reason for Bush's victory was simple enough; the energized Bush had personally traveled to *each* of Iowa's 99 counties—Reagan had not even bothered to visit the state.[118]

However, Bush himself sowed the seeds for future troubles when, following his Iowa victory, he jubilantly announced, "I've got the momentum. . . . I'm on my way." When a reporter pressed for a more concrete statement of the candidate's beliefs, Bush replied, "I'm just going to keep going. I've got Big Mo."[119] "Big Mo" sounded childish; instead of gaining more momentum from the victory, the Bush campaign was forced to respond to charges that their candidate was a juvenile preppy—a criticism that would later become known as the "wimp factor." It was a powerful weapon for Bush's opponents in conservative New Hampshire: the *Manchester Union-Leader*, the state's reactionary paper, proclaimed that Bush was no more than a "spoon-fed little rich

kid."[120] As important was the fact that Reagan, furious at his poor showing in Iowa, stepped up what had been a complacent campaign and
came roaring into New Hampshire with a vengeance.

Any hopes for Bush riding to victory on the shoulders of "Big Mo"
were dashed during a debate in Manchester on 23 February. Bush had
agreed to a one-on-one debate with Reagan, but when the sponsor
backed out, the better-financed Reagan campaign agreed to pick up the
tab. As a condition of his financial largesse, however, Reagan demanded
that the other four Republican candidates—Philip Crane, Howard
Baker, John Anderson, and John Connally—be allowed to participate.
The Bush campaign saw the trap; Reagan had more to gain if five candidates ganged up on Bush. With Reagan footing the bill for the debate,
Bush had no choice in the matter. Yet instead of facing the inevitable,
Bush dug in and continued to voice his opposition to a panel debate (he
told a supporter, "I've worked too hard for this and they're not going
to take it away from me").[121] Always quick to sense a dramatic moment,
on the night of the debate Reagan marched into the hall, followed by
the other contenders. Rather than standing his ground, Bush sat meekly
on stage, looking as if he had been hit by a steamroller—which, indeed,
he had. When the moderator of the debate, a Bush supporter, tried to
call attention to the fact that Reagan had changed the rules on Bush,
a sanctimonious Reagan declared, "I am paying for this microphone,
Mr. Green."[122] Reagan looked in command, as indeed he was.[123] On 25
February, Reagan swept New Hampshire, 49 percent to 23 percent for
Bush.[124]

From that point on, nothing could save the Bush campaign. After
the embarrassment of the Nashua debate, Baker, Dole, Anderson, and
Crane pledged together that they would work to deny Bush the nomination.[125] Bush also made other gaffes, such as the interview with the
Los Angeles Times where he asserted that "you can have a winner" in a
nuclear exchange (despite Bush's attempts to explain the comment by
citing projected survival statistics, it made for an ugly headline).[126] More
important was the fact that Bush was out of money. Baker told Bush that
if he stayed in the race, he would only further anger an already piqued
Reagan, thus losing all hope of getting the vice presidential nod.[127] On
Memorial Day, Bush withdrew from the race. To his friend Hank Knoche
he wrote: "No one died but it feels like it."[128]

For the long run, even more important than the loss to Reagan was
that 1980 saw a return of a dynamic that had plagued Bush in his Texas
elections—the fact that he was distrusted by the right wing of his party.

Social conservatives pointed to a meeting Bush held with a group of pastors at Chicago's O'Hare Airport Hilton. There, he was quizzed regarding his faith. He stumbled through his answers, finally committing the cardinal sin to the group of admitting he had not yet been "born again."[129] Bush had also taken swings at Reagan's support for supply-side economics—the theory that argued that lower taxes would lead to an increase in a desire to invest those savings back into the economy, the dividends from which would "trickle down" to help the less fortunate. Bush called such ideas "voodoo economics," which were sure to cause widened deficits; this apostasy infuriated those Reaganites who had an unshakable faith in the theory. Bush had helped to create the modern, ultraconservative Republican Party in 1962 as Harris County chair; now, running as a Ford moderate, he was left in the dust of a conservative movement that was gathering more steam with every Reagan speech.

As a result of this, Bush's choice as Reagan's running mate confounded even his closest advisers. The polls showed that Reagan would have to balance his ticket with a moderate as his running mate.[130] Bush clearly wanted the position, and Mosbacher and other Bush supporters worked hard in Detroit, spreading what Mosbacher called a "mini-campaign" for Bush.[131] But because of the Manchester debate and the charge of "voodoo economics," Reagan's advisers, particularly his wife, Nancy, were adamantly against having Bush on the ticket (Ed Rollins, a Republican political operative who worked for Reagan, remembered that the First Lady privately called Bush "Whiny" and made fun of his speaking style to friends).[132] Their moderate of choice was Gerald Ford, and Reagan quickly became entranced with the thought of a "dream ticket"—if it could be arranged, it would be the first time that a former president ran for the vice presidency. Ford was clearly in favor of the idea, but he publicly communicated his eagerness to CBS's Walter Cronkite in a televised interview. Furious with Ford for destroying the surprise announcement he had planned for the convention, Reagan abruptly rescinded his offer and called Bush. Conservatives almost balked—the Texas delegation, holding a lot of anti-Bush feelings, almost bolted.[133] But in the end, the logic of a seemingly ideologically balanced ticket prevailed. Nancy Reagan was livid, and many of Reagan's closest advisers grumbled that Bush would hurt the ticket in the conservative Midwest. But Reagan knew his man. Already showing the loyalty to Reagan that would mark his vice presidency, Bush acceded to a Reagan demand, reversing his stand on abortion, agreeing to support the ticket's pro-life stand. Yet Bush campaigned doggedly, and the ticket swept to victory against Carter that fall.

Between 1981 and 1989, Vice President George Bush put in 1.3 million miles of travel, visiting all fifty states and sixty-five different countries. In 1982 he met the PRC's Deng Xiaoping; in 1983 he visited the bombed marine barracks in Lebanon; at the 1984 funeral of Soviet premier Yuri Andropov, he first met Mikhail Gorbachev. Quite aside from his travels, Bush was able to accomplish the one goal necessary for a successful vice presidency: by all accounts, he and the president got along remarkably well. At regular Thursday luncheons, which had been arranged by Bush confidant and new Reagan chief of staff James Baker (Baker had impressed the Reagan team with his attention to detail, as well as his loyalty to Bush), Bush and Reagan eschewed a formal agenda and simply chatted for an hour.[134]

The close relationship between the two men was cemented after the 30 March 1981 assassination attempt against Reagan. At the time of the attack, Bush was flying in Air Force Two, returning from a trip to Texas. On learning of the attempt on Reagan's life, Bush immediately began jotting down his thoughts on the first piece of paper he could find: "Enormity of it comes upon me twenty minutes out of Austin. Pray—literally—that RR recovers. Element of *friend* not just in C[ommander] in C[hief] president. Decent, warm, and kind."[135] An obviously over-wrought Alexander Haig, then secretary of state, had proclaimed to the nation that he was "in charge"—an unfortunate misrepresentation of the constitutional line of succession, as well as a statement of just how frenzied the situation was in the White House in the hours after the attack. When Bush arrived, he put things aright with his equilibrium and sense of purpose. The Secret Service wanted him to return directly to the White House, but the vice president refused, saying that "only the president lands on the South Lawn."[136] He also refused to take the president's seat at the cabinet table in the days after the near tragedy. One Reagan operative paid Bush the ultimate compliment: "George Bush is too much of a gentleman to be reminded how to behave at a time like that."[137]

After Reagan's recovery, the level of trust between Bush and both the president and his acolytes grew. Bush's influence in the foreign affairs of the first Reagan term also grew. C. Boyden Gray, then serving as Bush's personal counsel, argues that Bush was "really the de facto national security adviser."[138] This observation is borne out by events.

President Ronald Reagan and Vice President George H. W. Bush in the Oval Office of the White House, 20 July 1984. (Courtesy of the George Bush Presidential Library and Museum)

Reagan appointed Bush to conduct meetings of the National Security Council (NSC) when he was not present and put the vice president in charge of the NSC's Planning Group. Bush was made chairman of the Crisis Council, a position that had, in the past, gone to the national security adviser. These moves angered Haig and may have played a part in his resignation early in Reagan's first term and his replacement with George Shultz. Bush was personally responsible for reversing the view of several European leaders on the deployment of U.S. Pershing missiles in Europe, particularly Margaret Thatcher's and Helmut Kohl's—two leaders who would become especially important in the subsequent Bush administration.[139] Bush's private discussions with Deng Xiaoping also helped the administration win an agreement with the PRC that governed arms sales to Taiwan.[140]

Bush was also put in charge of the administration's Task Force on Regulatory Relief, a role that was completely compatible with his belief, shared by moderate and conservative Republicans alike, that government had become too intrusive in the lives of businessmen. Moreover, it gave Bush the opportunity to win over some of the same conservative economists who had castigated him for his "voodoo economics" remark.[141] Gray, himself a specialist in regulatory legislation, served as Bush's assistant on this task force, which recommended that hundreds of federal regulations be scrapped or changed.[142] In 1983 Bush worked on "reducing the growth of federal regulations by more than 25 percent and cutting over three-hundred million hours of government-required paperwork annually."[143] However, one area where Bush refused to cut back on government regulation was in the area of aid to those with disabilities; it would lead to his signing of the Americans with Disabilities Act as president in 1990.

More important for his later career was Bush's involvement with the plan that became known as Iran-Contra. With the much more than tacit approval of their president, White House aides had sold arms to Iran—a nation that only months before had been an American enemy. The purpose of the sales was to obtain the support of Iran in the release of American hostages held in Lebanon, although such releases never occurred. The excess profits from the sale were secretly laundered through Israel, then given to anti-Marxist freedom fighters in Nicaragua—the Contras—in direct violation of American law. Administration critics saw these dealings as evidence of the continuation of a Nixonian "imperial presidency," with the chief executive reserving for himself the power to make foreign policy decisions despite laws intended to restrict his actions.

As the Iran-Contra scandal dominated the final two years of the Reagan presidency, so too did it threaten to hurt Bush's chances to win the presidency for himself. The press demanded to know of the presumptive front-runner for the 1988 Republican nomination what the extent of his involvement was. Bush dug in. On 6 August 1987, David Broder of the *Washington Post* quoted Bush as claiming that he had been "out of the loop" on the whole affair: "If I had sat there and heard [secretary of state] George Shultz and [secretary of defense Caspar] Weinberger express it strongly, maybe I would have had a stronger view. But when you don't know something, it's hard to react."[144]

For his part, Shultz remembered being "astonished" at Bush's claims.[145] This was with good reason. Bush definitely attended a meeting on 6 August 1985 where national security adviser Robert McFarlane floated the first part of his master plan—if Iran received 100 TOW missiles, it would pressure Lebanon to release four of the seven American hostages.[146] Exactly five months later, on 6 January 1986, Bush was present at another meeting, where Admiral John Poindexter, who had succeeded McFarlane as national security adviser to the president, briefed Reagan on an expanded scheme—the Israelis would give Iran 4,000 TOWs in exchange for their influence in gaining the release of *all* the American hostages.[147] The next day, a second meeting was called to discuss the idea—Bush was again present. Shultz, who was vehemently against the plan, would later write: "It was clear to me by the time we went out [of the meeting] that the president, the vice president [and others present] all had the opinion and I had a different opinion and [Weinberger] and I shared it."[148] Clearly, Bush was well "in the loop" about the arms-for-hostages plan. It is just as clear that there is no evidence that ties Bush to the second part of the scheme—the diversion of funds to the Contras—a point that was clearly made in the report of the congressional committee that investigated the affair.[149] But the evidence tying Bush to the plan would not be made available until many years later; as he geared up to run for the presidency, his strenuous denials, save any other evidence, would serve to keep Iran-Contra from hurting his chances.

Bush's performance concerning Iran-Contra was totally in character with how he viewed his vice presidency. Loyalty was his byword. To Nixon, Bush wrote: "I don't believe a President should have to be looking over his shoulder wondering if the Vice President was out carving him up or undermining his programs."[150] The vice president did, however, differ with Reagan on a matter that would ultimately affect Bush's presidency. An intelligence operative would later observe to veteran investigative reporter Seymour Hersh that General Manuel Noriega, the de facto ruler of Panama, "was always scum, but you use scum like him."[151] The Panamanian strongman had been a paid informant of American intelligence since his college years. He sent information on the leftist opinions of his teachers, and for that information he was well paid. The *New York Times* reported that throughout the years, the CIA and the Pentagon had paid Noriega some $322,000 in cash and gifts. A huge operative in the Latin American drug trade, Noriega was also being used by the Americans as a conduit to get arms to the Contra rebels in Nicaragua. He had also worked every conceivable side of the street, dealing as often with Cuba as he did with the Americans. In May 1988, Reagan's Justice Department indicted Noriega for drug trafficking. But by 1988 Noriega was incredibly powerful, incredibly wealthy, and well insulated. There was no way he was going to allow himself to come to the United States and stand trial.[152]

In an effort to rid himself of the Noriega problem, Reagan decided to offer him a deal. Reagan proposed that on 12 August 1988 Noriega retire as commander of the Panamanian military and, in Reagan's words, "shortly thereafter" leave Panama until after the 1992 election. Bush strenuously voiced his opposition to the deal in a meeting called to discuss that issue; Reagan remembered that Bush's reasoning was "because of politics—how it will look giving in to a drug dealer." In his diary, Bush fumed: "The Noriega deal is terrible. . . . It's wrong for our country. It sends the wrong signals to the drug pushers."[153] Shultz, however, supported the president.[154] The next day, after hearing once again from his advisers and finding no minds changed, Reagan decided to offer the deal to Noriega.[155] Noriega took the deal, the indictment was lifted—and nothing happened. Noriega stayed in Panama and in command of the armed forces; he would soon be George Bush's problem.

On 12 October 1987, at Houston's Hyatt Regency Hotel, George Bush announced his second candidacy for the presidency (in a poignant entry in his diary, Bush remembered that "thirty-four years ago today, Robin died").[156] When he said that his campaign would not travel in "radical new directions" but would give "steady, experienced leadership," Bush sounded for all intents and purposes as if he would run his campaign as a defense of Reaganism. The presidential campaign of 1988 had many facets—but that was not one of them.

2

★ ★ ★ ★ ★

"JUGULAR POLITICS"

In a diary entry dated 4 November 1986, Bush considered the problem at hand:

> The great question WHY DO YOU WANT TO BE PRESIDENT? And, I've tried to write it down. Believe me, even though I know, it's not easy. I know I've got the leadership ability. I know I've got the experience. I want to see an educated America. I want to see a literate America. . . . I want to use our abilities to bring peace, to continue the discussions with the Soviet Union. . . . But, how do you say all these things and get it into a slogan or a formula—a catch-all? I don't know.[1]

Bush understood that he had yet to package himself—or allow himself to be packaged—in a manner that allowed the nation to understand his beliefs and his goals. Put another way, in a term that would haunt Bush throughout his succeeding years in public life, he had yet to corral "the vision thing." For all his experience, his loyalty to other leaders had subsumed him. Few people knew what he stood for, and Bush was not sure how to fix that. Even Ronald Reagan, who privately backed Bush and would give him wholehearted support after he ultimately gained the nomination, was quoted during the primary season as saying that Bush "doesn't stand for anything."[2]

This went a long way toward explaining why, as the election season kicked into high gear, the sitting vice president of the United States was running behind in the polls. Smelling blood, challengers from within the Republican Party jumped in. One exploratory candidacy was brief: Lee Iacocca, chairman of Chrysler Motors and one of the business icons of the early Reagan years, let it be known that he was interested in the nomination. However, when he was fired as head of the advisory commission on the restoration of the Statue of Liberty and Ellis Island (a move that Iacocca attributed to Bush), he grumbled that he would never enter politics again and that the people in Washington were "schizos."[3] Before 1987 was over, Illinois governor James Thompson, former Delaware governor Pierre S. (Pete) DuPont, former Nixon and Ford staffer and Reagan's secretary of state Alexander Haig, former secretary of defense Donald Rumsfeld, and Reagan chief of staff and former senator Howard Baker had made trips to Iowa and New Hampshire. Yet none of these men, accomplished politicians but neophytes in the presidential arena, was considered strong enough to go the distance.

Bush had three serious opponents for the nomination, however. Two came from Congress. Kansas senator Bob Dole could bask in the reflected glory of the Reagan Revolution—as majority leader, it was he who had shepherded most of its measures through Congress. Many Republicans worried about the "dark side" of Dole, who was grouchy and sarcastic on a good day. Few could forget his blaming World War II on the Democratic Party when campaigning as Gerald Ford's running mate in 1976, but he had a strong base in the Midwest. If he could win the Iowa caucuses in January, and if that victory brought more donations to his campaign, he could pose a threat to Bush in conservative New Hampshire. However, many disillusioned movement conservatives, rightfully sensing that neither Dole nor Bush was one of their own, turned to New York congressman Jack Kemp, an indefatigable speaker and party fundraiser with indisputable conservative credentials, being one half of the congressional sponsorship of the signature domestic achievement of the Reagan presidency, the 1981 Kemp-Roth Bill, which cut the marginal income tax rates by some 23 percent over three years. Kemp had become the poster child for supply-side economics, and his party's right wing loved him for it.

Throughout 1986 Dole hammered at the vagaries of Bush's role in Iran-Contra, and Kemp hammered at the need for even further tax cuts. But a more gut-level message, sent by the Reverend Pat Robertson, appealed to the party's evangelical conservatives—a group that had cast its lot with Ronald Reagan and had reaped the benefits during the Reagan years of an increased influence. Both an originator and a beneficiary of televangelism in the 1980s, Robertson was the host of *The 700 Club*, one of the most watched shows on cable television. In a party where 20 percent of the membership listed themselves as born-again Christians, Robertson had a natural constituency, one that an NBC reporter assessed as "not wide, but deep," and one that had proved willing to donate heavily for its causes.[4] Throughout 1986, Robertson went around the country, telling audiences that he was waiting for his "call" to the nomination. His strong showing in the Michigan selection choice in late May 1986 was treated as a shocking upset by much of the press. The early success of Robertson's candidacy revealed that there was a morally identifiable constituency in the Republican Party that could not be counted upon to support the vice president.

At best, Bush faced a grueling primary campaign, and party insiders remembered that he had not survived the process in 1980. Members of Reagan's staff, who had never completely trusted Bush, leaked that if Bush imploded early in the primary scene, they would support Reagan's friend Nevada senator Paul Laxalt over the vice president.[5] There was even some talk in summer 1986 that made the papers about a plan afoot to amend the Constitution so that Reagan could run for a third term. It was clear that Bush needed help.

Harvey LeRoy Atwater would provide that help. Born in 1951 in Atlanta, Atwater was a born clown, ladies' man, and hell-raiser. Always looking for the spotlight (quipping to a reporter, "I never really became an adult. . . . I made my own [rules] up"),[6] he naturally gravitated to politics, serving as an intern in the office of Senator Strom Thurmond (R-SC) before he set out to become a political kingmaker. Between 1974 and 1978, Atwater had worked in or directed twenty-eight winning campaigns. In so doing, he showed himself to be a master of negative campaigning. In one campaign, Atwater got a reporter to ask him about an opponent's mental illness; Atwater quipped that the candidate had been "hooked up to jumper cables"—Atwater's candidate won. Atwater was also one of the first users of "push-polling," a process where poll questions were worded in order to guarantee a certain answer, such as one used in the 1978 campaign that Atwater ran in South Carolina for Carroll Campbell against Max Heller, a Jew, with questions such as: "Would you vote for a

Jew who did not believe in the Lord Jesus Christ?" Campbell won. One reporter who observed Atwater during this period likened him to "a wolverine chewing through plywood."[7]

In 1980 Atwater ran Ronald Reagan's winning primary and general election operation in the pivotal state of South Carolina. During the primary campaign, Atwater leaked a story that former Texas governor John Connally was trying to buy the black vote in the state. The story, and Connally's response, forced him out of the race. When Reagan won the presidency, Thurmond recommended Atwater for a low-level job in the White House Office of Political Affairs. Atwater became a deputy to Edward Rollins, then special assistant to the president for political affairs. From that vantage point, Atwater's star shot into the political heavens. He was honored in 1982 by the Jaycees as one of the nation's Ten Outstanding Young Men (one of the other ten was the freshman senator from Indiana, Dan Quayle).[8] Yet Atwater's refusal to allow himself to be encumbered by moral scruples when it came to political strategy was the key to his advancement. In 1984 Atwater leaked that Rollins was running a black-ops-type deal against the Democrats; the resulting bad publicity led to Rollins's being eased out of the inner circle of the campaign.[9] Indefatigable, and an incredible organizer and fund-raiser, by 1988 Atwater was chomping at the bit to run a national campaign.

Atwater's biographer, John Brady, quips that the pairing of Atwater and George Bush was the "odd coupling."[10] On its surface, this seemed to be an understatement. The two men met in 1973, and their relationship survived even the bitter primary campaign of 1980 when Atwater had cast his lot with Reagan. Temperamentally, the juvenile Atwater and the aristocratic Bush could not have been less alike. Yet in 1988, Bush knew that he needed Atwater's special political talents. Atwater was a superb practitioner of the type of negative campaigning that George Bush had, to that point, avoided throughout his political career. In 1987 Bush wrote that "jugular politics—going for the opposition's throat—wasn't my style."[11] This was true enough. Yet despite his proclivities to run a more gentlemanly campaign, Bush instinctively knew that he needed a wolverine, someone who could force his opponents onto the defensive. Most observers have concluded that Bush came to the decision to go negative with a heavy heart, as if he wanted to run a positive campaign and was moved to the negative by Atwater against his will.[12] There is absolutely no evidence of this, and much to the contrary. For one example, former New Jersey senator Nicholas Brady, who prior to the convention was serving as chair of the Bush campaign, remembered that "it wasn't like making him take a drink of castor oil. He knew exactly what had to be done in the long run."[13] There would not be another 1980 for Bush. Negative politics was Atwater's specialty, and Atwater was allowed room to create.

But not without some supervision. For Bush, Atwater was always a curiosity—the political genius as prodigal son. Bush's family and staff never fully trusted Atwater's loyalty or accepted his compulsive womanizing. Into this dynamic came Bush's eldest son, George W. Bush, then trying his hand in the oil industry but readying himself for a role in his father's campaign. He met with Atwater and point-blank asked him, "How do we know we can trust you?" Atwater was quick with his response: "If you're so worried about my loyalty, why don't you come to Washington and help with the campaign?"[14] This George W. did, and the two became good friends. Indeed, as it turned out, George W. needed some supervision of his own. Taking it upon himself to defend his father from all slights—perceived and real—George W. earned a justifiable reputation as being, in his own words, "a loyalty enforcer,"[15] and in the words of prescient reporter Richard Ben Cramer "a roman candle . . . bright, hot, a sparkler—and likeliest to burn the fingers."[16] In April 1986 George W. was in a Dallas restaurant when he saw journalist Al Hunt, who had had the temerity to predict that Jack Kemp would win the 1988 nomination. George W. went over to Hunt's table, screaming: "Ya no good fucking sonofabitch! I will never fucking forget what you wrote!"[17] Despite his temper, George W. was also entrusted by the campaign as a link to the evangelical community,[18] and with a particularly delicate task—that of crushing campaign rumors about his father's marital infidelity.[19] He did so with a directness that surprised some observers—he reportedly asked his father point-blank about the rumors (response: "They're not true"). Then he met with Howard Fineman of *Newsweek* and in the course of the interview offered the following quote: "The answer to the 'Big-A' question is N-O."[20]

To Atwater, the problem with the nascent Bush campaign was twofold. First, in many circles, the perception of Bush, born of the 1980 campaign, was that of an effete eastern snob. Second was the belief held by many who remembered his flip-flop on abortion in 1980 that Bush would say or do just about anything to court Reagan supporters and win the nomination. These perceptions led to several unflattering portrayals in the press as Bush began his campaign. In his wildly popular comic strip *Doonesbury*, cartoonist Garry Trudeau created a Bush character who, in order to be elected, "put his manhood in a blind trust." Conservative columnist George Will called Bush a "lapdog" for his seeming obsequious acceptance of all of Reagan's policies ("the unpleasant sound Bush is emitting as he traipses from one conservative gathering to another is a thin, tiny 'arf'").[21] Most devastating, however, was an October 1987 story for *Newsweek*. Having had good success with the magazine, Atwater had set reporter Margaret Warner up for an interview with Bush,[22] and on its own, the resulting story was innocuous enough. But the cover photo, with its bold caption "Fighting the Wimp Factor," incensed Bush and his family (ever the hothead, George W. accosted Warner, accused her of a "political ambush," and told her, "You ought to quit if that's the kind of journalistic integrity you have").[23] Regardless, Bush had now been labeled as a wimp, just as he entered into the knock-down-drag-out of another presidential campaign. Indeed, in a 1987 debate, Al Haig, when asked about a 1982 arms control treaty when he was secretary of state, shot at Bush: "I never heard a wimp out of you."[24]

On 25 January 1988, only a few days before the Iowa caucuses, an opportunity presented itself to attack the wimp factor head-on. Bush had agreed to do a live satellite interview with CBS News anchor Dan Rather. Roger Ailes, who had started as a prop boy in Cleveland, moved up to producer of the *Mike Douglas Show*, and coordinated the media campaign for Richard Nixon's successful 1968 campaign, had been recruited by Atwater the previous fall. As senior director of marketing for the Bush campaign, Ailes was put in charge of getting Bush ready for Rather. For both Ailes and Atwater, it was simple—Bush had to see Rather as the enemy and be prepared to take the offensive as quickly as possible. This was drilled into Bush in the preinterview preparation, and by all accounts he went into the interview ill-tempered and ready to pounce. When Rather opened with a taped piece that emphasized Iran-Contra, Bush immediately charged Rather with changing the ground rules for their interview. Bush remembered in his diary: "I tried to keep my cool. In fact, I think I did. But, I'd be damned if I was going to let this guy walk all over me."[25] What followed has gone down in political lore:

RATHER: I don't want to be argumentative, Mr. Vice President.
BUSH: You do, Dan.
RATHER: No—no sir, I don't.
BUSH: This is not a great night because I want to talk about why I want to be president, why those 41 percent of the people are supporting me. And I don't think it's fair—

RATHER: Mr. Vice President, these questions are designed—
BUSH: . . . to judge a whole career, it's not fair to judge my whole career by a rehash on Iran. How would you like it if I judged your career by those seven minutes when you walked off the set in New York?[26]

Bush's reference to the night six months earlier when Rather, in a fit of pique because a U.S. Open Tennis match had delayed the start of his newscast, had stalked off the set, leaving seven minutes of dead air, was seen by many viewers to be in poor taste. But Atwater loved it. Bush had been tough—certainly no wimp—and he had been able to avoid talking about Iran-Contra (after the interview, the microphone was still on, and it picked up Bush mumbling "that bastard didn't lay a glove on me").[27] Atwater later claimed that the Rather interview "was the most important event of the primary campaign."[28] While this is a wild over-statement, it certainly lifted the gloom that had been hanging over both Bush and his campaign.

It was, however, too little too late for any one event to help Bush in Iowa. Not only did Bush lose to Dole, but as Atwater had predicted, he came in third behind Robertson, winning 17,000 fewer votes than he had won in 1980.[29] The defeat was total—Bush did not carry a single county in the state.[30] Bush adviser Roger Stone remembered that Atwater became physically ill, vomiting for several days after the loss.[31]

Had it not been for the steadying hand of New Hampshire governor John Sununu, it is likely that Bush would have lost in that state as well, thus effectively ending his candidacy. Sununu remembered that Atwater had come to him as early as 1986, and the fire-breathing governor, with the help of Andrew Card, formerly Reagan's liaison to local governments and then the Bush campaign manager in New Hampshire, had helped Atwater put together a strategy for that state.[32] The plan called for Bush to yank his campaign onto the offensive. Ailes and Sig Rogich, the campaign's director of advertising, created a series of half-hour shows, "Ask George Bush," designed to exploit the antitax feelings held by the fiercely independent New Hampshirites. Ignoring an earlier Bush moment (in 1986, both Bush and Dole had refused to sign the no-new-taxes pledge circulated by the Americans for Tax Reform and signed by some 140 congressmen) and ignoring the fact that, as vice president, Bush had never been vocal in either direction on the issue of tax cuts, one of Ailes and Rogich's shows implied that Dole would raise taxes, a charge Dole flatly denied. Brushing aside Dole's denials, Ailes and his wife created an ad that portrayed Dole as a two-faced "Senator Straddle," accusing him of taking both sides on Pentagon spending as well as secretly favoring a tax increase.[33] The ads were a complete misrepresentation of Dole's position; nevertheless, everyone in the Bush camp—including George W., Atwater, and Barbara—was in favor of using them.[34] Sununu saw to it that the ads were carried by both local and Boston stations. The ads found their mark, and Dole began to slip in the polls. Quick to seize the initiative, Bush pledged never to raise taxes.[35]

Along with the fact that the Dole campaign was more poorly financed and organized in the Granite State than it had been in Iowa, the "Straddle" ads and Bush's tax pledge sealed the deal. On 16 February, Bush won 38 percent of the vote to Dole's 28 percent (Kemp won 13 percent, DuPont 10, and Robertson 9). The evening of the primary, after Bush had been declared the victor, NBC's Tom Brokaw interviewed both Bush and Dole. Appearing on the screen together, they answered a few questions. Then both candidates were asked if they had anything to say to the other. Bush was gracious in his praise of Dole; when it was his turn, a sullen, exhausted Dole looked into the camera and growled, "Yeah. Tell him to quit lying about my record."

It was not a good time for Dole's famous temper to show itself. The first chance for the candidates to prove their strength in the South would come in five days in South Carolina. Three days later would be the first "Super Tuesday" primary day, when seventeen states—fourteen of them southern and border states—would hold their primaries on the same day. But Bush had long been ready for a southern campaign. Since 1984 he had been courting the conservative vote, so important to success in the South. Although he often professed his disgust with the need to court the conservatives—his gentlemanly tendencies led him to disagree with the recent revelations of sex and financial scandal in the big televangelist empires—he had learned that particular part of the game in his Texas campaigns, and he courted them with no particular subtlety. His open fawning upon leaders like televangelist Jerry Falwell, who eventually gave Bush his support, earned Bush the derision of the more liberal press. But as an observer told two *Time* correspondents, "It had the effect of putting enough deposits in those accounts so that we didn't have to worry about them anymore."[36] Just as important was the money that Bush had been pouring into the South, creating what Atwater aptly called a "firewall," designed to pick Bush up from the expected loss in Iowa and what had once been a probable loss in New Hampshire.

With that money, Bush was able to saturation buy his advertising in the South. Some of the most effective ads were Rogich-produced spots in South Carolina that featured Barry Goldwater proclaiming his support of Bush.[37] Robertson, who was expected to do well in the South, was neutralized after his campaign was caught misrepresenting his marine service in Korea as combat service, when in reality he was a liquor officer.[38] Three days before Super Tuesday, in Atwater's home state of South Carolina, Bush won half the vote. On Super Tuesday, he swept every state but Washington.

The New Hampshire comeback, based as it was on attack politics, the courting of the Christian conservatives, and the southern "firewall strategy" had won Bush the nomination. It did not take much longer for a philosophical Kemp, a chastised Robertson, and an embittered Dole to drop out of the race. Yet Bush could not rest easy. He continued to be hampered by problems from within the Reagan administration. The president had vetoed a civil rights bill; Attorney General Edwin Meese was linked to a scandal revolving around defense contracts; charges had been levied against former Reagan aide-turned-lobbyist Michael Deaver that he had been improperly profiting from his White House connections; and the press was harping on revelations that First Lady Nancy Reagan consulted an astrologer about political and social decisions. Moreover, the congressional and presidential investigations into Iran-Contra were satisfying no one with their nondescript findings and recommendations. These predicaments chipped away at the popularity of the Republican Party in general, and of Bush in particular. At the Democratic convention held in Atlanta in mid-July, Edward Kennedy (D-MA) harassed Bush with a litany of charges, followed by a chorus of "Where was George?" hooted by the delegates. When that convention ended, its nominee, Massachusetts governor Michael Dukakis, led Bush by as many as seventeen points.

In retrospect, the two strongest hopes for the Democratic Party in 1988 were the two men who refused to run. In 1985 Edward Kennedy told the *Washington Post* that he was "personally convinced that [I] can gain the Democratic nomination"; one month later, he took himself out of the race.[39] New York governor Mario Cuomo then began a yearlong flirtation with a candidacy, refusing to say whether or not he was running. But his coyness tried the patience of both his party and the nation (*Washington Post* reporter David Broder spoke for many when he wrote that "the Democrats . . . will not waste their time trying to decipher an enigma").[40]

On 19 February 1987, at the end of a New York City radio talk show, Cuomo announced that he was not running.

With Kennedy and Cuomo out of the race, the road to the Democratic nomination was littered with lesser political lights, all of whom had trouble raising funds and many of whom watched their campaigns self-destruct. Former Colorado senator Gary Hart, who had nearly bested former vice president Walter Mondale for the presidential nomination four years earlier, was in the race for only a few weeks when it was revealed that he was involved in a questionable relationship with a young model. Hart angrily suspended his campaign, blaming the media for intruding in his personal life. Senator Joseph Biden of Delaware watched his candidacy implode when it was revealed that he had publicly misrepresented his Syracuse University law school grades and that he had been regularly quoting a British Labour leader in his speeches without proper attribution. None of the other candidates—Congresswoman Patricia Schroeder of Colorado, former governor of Arizona Bruce Babbitt, Congressman Richard Gephardt of Missouri, and Senators Paul Simon of Illinois and Albert Gore Jr. of Tennessee—had any depth of support (collectively numbering seven candidates at one point in the early campaign, the field was derisively called the "Seven Dwarfs" by the press). Only the Reverend Jesse Jackson stuck out the campaign all the way through to the convention. He scored several impressive early victories, and at the end of the race, he had won a majority of the total popular vote in the Democratic primaries. But a key loss in New York, where memories of his 1984 labeling of New York City as "Hymietown" still ran deep, helped to scuttle his campaign. One other lesser-known leader, Arkansas governor Bill Clinton, seriously considered entering the race but ultimately decided to wait.[41]

The eventual Democratic nominee, Governor Michael Dukakis of Massachusetts, had a life experience and a personality that were the exact opposites of George Bush's. His father had immigrated to the United States at age sixteen; by age twenty-eight, he had become the first Greek immigrant to graduate from Harvard Medical School. His mother came to the United States from Greece at age nine; she became the first Greek immigrant to graduate Phi Beta Kappa from Bates College. Michael, the second of two boys, excelled at sports and academics (his yearbook picture was labeled "Chief Big Brain in the Face"). After graduating Phi Beta Kappa from Swarthmore College in 1955, then spending two years in the army as a clerk-typist, Dukakis graduated from Harvard Law School in 1960. But practicing the law was never his passion. In 1962 he won the first of four terms in the Massachusetts legislature, where he earned a reputation as a maverick, supporting rules reform and fronting an organization that one close observer labeled a "throw the bums out organization."[42] After an unsuccessful run for Massachusetts attorney general, he was elected that state's governor in 1974. Four years later, after taking his challenger too lightly, Dukakis was defeated for renomination in the Democratic primary. Stunned, he spent the next four years planning his comeback; he recaptured the statehouse in 1982.

During the next two terms, Dukakis was generally given credit for turning his state around from the recession of the early Reagan years. Trumpeted as the "Massachusetts Miracle," Dukakis was whisked into contention for the Democratic nomination for the presidency, where a well-planned campaign, virtually devoid of reference to divisive issues, allowed him to emerge at the end of the primary process as the only candidate left standing. His personality—distant and intense, with an air of superiority (Andrew Card, who knew Dukakis from his days in Massachusetts politics, remembered that the governor often acted as if "'people should do what I want because I'm smart'")—promised to contrast unfavorably with that of the more garrulous Bush.[43] But Dukakis was the beneficiary of the troubles at the end of the Reagan presidency, and after the Democratic nomination, he was leading.

As it had against Dole in the primary season, the Bush campaign went on the attack against Dukakis, even before Bush had been formally nominated. The first decision led to the unveiling of a new ad campaign. Sig Rogich went to Atwater with the idea for a series of ads to run in between the two national conventions that would castigate the Democrats but name no specific candidate. As such, the ads could be paid for by the Republican National Committee from its "soft money" funds, an expenditure that did not have to be debited to the Bush campaign. Atwater approved the idea, and Robert Mosbacher raised some $6 million to fund the ads. The ads reminded viewers of how things had been before Ronald Reagan, asking, "Why go back seven years?" They were a huge success, helping to bring Bush some nine points closer to Dukakis before the opening of the Republican convention in New Orleans.[44]

The second decision designed to help close the gap with Dukakis would become much more problematic. The Friday before the Republican convention opened, Bush met with his senior staff to discuss the vice presidential selection. The result of that meeting was the development of a short list that included Bob Dole (Jim Baker remembered that "Bob made no secret about wanting the nod")[45] and his wife, Elizabeth, who had served in the Reagan cabinet; Jack Kemp; and Senators Pete Domenici of New Mexico, John Danforth of Missouri, Alan Simpson of Wyoming, and Dan Quayle of Indiana. Quayle was first on the list of Craig Fuller, Bush's chief of staff, and of Roger Ailes, who had worked on Quayle's 1986 reelection campaign to the Senate. He was a bit lower on others' (Atwater wanted Libby Dole), but the consensus was that Quayle would be a strong choice.

For many observers, the vice presidential choice was their first opportunity to notice an important Bush trait—that of letting virtually no one in on important decisions until the last minute. In his study of military decision making in the Bush presidency, Bob Woodward explained this trait as being that "of an intelligence agent," noting that Bush would "'compartment' information, dividing it into pieces so that only he himself knew the whole."[46] On the day that Bush flew to the convention, he told several of his aides that he had made up his mind, but he would not tell them whom he had chosen. On his arrival in New Orleans, he met Reagan at the airport and whispered his choice to him.[47]

James Danforth Quayle, the junior senator from Indiana, had graduated from DePauw University in 1969, and he joined the National Guard rather than risk being drafted, according to him because he wanted to immediately go into the law. He graduated from the law school of Indiana University at Indianapolis, but he never practiced. Instead, he went to work as the associate publisher of the *Huntington Herald-Press*, a local newspaper owned by his father. It took only a year for Quayle to abandon journalism and enter politics. In 1976 he was elected to the first of two terms in the House, where he was the second-youngest member. In 1980 Quayle rode Reagan's coattails to a Senate seat, defeating eighteen-year incumbent Birch Bayh.[48]

Quayle did not find his way onto Bush's short list by accident. Nor was his final choice as Bush's running mate a hasty, overnight decision by a harried presidential candidate. As reported by Bob Woodward and David Broder, who interviewed both Quayle and his wife, Marilyn, for a 1992 series of articles in the *Washington Post*, the Quayles had launched "an unofficial, sub rosa campaign to become Bush's choice" immediately after the New Hampshire primary. Quayle lobbied to be chosen as the convention's keynote speaker so that he could prove himself on national television. He also pushed for more visibility in the Senate, backing off from issues that were near and dear to the Reagan conservatives, so that he could get closer to the Bush campaign.[49]

As Bush pondered his short list, Quayle's negatives were notable. His attendance record as both congressman and senator was well below average, and his one major piece of sponsored legislation, the Job Training Partnership Act of 1982, probably would not have passed had it not been cosponsored by Ted Kennedy. He had also had a brush with scandal, appearing at a Florida golf resort in 1980 at the same time as did Paula Parkinson, a former lobbyist who had posed nude for *Playboy* (Quayle claimed that he had played a round of golf, then left the day after she arrived).[50] Moreover, his choice was certain to upset Richard Lugar, the senior senator from Indiana, who had entertained the possibility of running for president in 1988, and who, his staff believed, wanted the vice presidential nod.[51]

In other ways, however, Quayle was the perfect choice. Although his father was a far-right conservative and a member of the John Birch Society, Quayle was no ideologue. In 1980 Quayle was quoted as arguing that "conservatives have very different ideas than the New Right where we ought to go. Some of the New Right people really want to turn the clock back . . . on affirmative action and all the civil rights gains. . . . We won't let them."[52] Like Bush, Quayle had a deep loathing for government bureaucracy. He also had shown the type of political loyalty that so impressed Bush; he had voted against his party an average of only 10 percent of the time in all his years in Congress.[53]

Indeed, what has been completely missed by virtually every observer is that on paper, the choice of Dan Quayle as George Bush's running mate was an inspired one. He complemented Bush in every way and brought to the ticket many strengths that Bush lacked. His youth would play well in the eighteen- to twenty-nine-year-old voting bracket so coveted by Bush. His family values would appeal to the movement conservatives and the Robertson Right; even the Parkinson flap could not stop Broder and Woodward from concluding that "family comes first for the Quayles, not just rhetorically in the speeches they both give, but in the ordering of their daily lives."[54] He tested well as a potential candidate between the Rockies and the Mississippi, a part of the country that still distrusted George Bush as an elitist yuppie. And although he was not an accomplished speaker, Quayle possessed an energy behind the podium that Bush often lacked.

One is left to wonder how Bush ultimately felt about his choice, as the evidence offers an interesting discrepancy. Bush biographer Herbert

S. Parmet quotes Bush's 21 August diary entry on the subject: "[Quayle] was my decision and I blew it, but I'm not about to say that I blew it!"[55] Bush was rarely introspective about such matters, and it is surprising to find out that he was so about his choice for the vice presidency. Yet in his edited compendium of letters, *All the Best* (1999), Bush includes that selection from his diary, but the line "I blew it" is missing. Instead, Bush added a footnote to the entry: "I had picked Indiana senator Dan Quayle as my running mate. The press were hard on him from the beginning, first by unfairly accusing him of avoiding the draft by joining the National Guard. He kept his head high and was loyal to me, and I never regretted my choice."[56]

Regardless of how he ultimately felt, Bush did not "blow" the choice. The choice was a home run. However, how it was *handled* by Bush and his campaign was little short of disastrous. The first problem lay in Bush's management of the announcement. He held his cards close to his vest for too long, and his staff was completely unprepared to deal with the inevitable press questions surrounding the appointment. No one other than Bush and Robert Kimmitt, a lawyer and former staff member on Reagan's National Security Council, saw the background checks on the members of the short list, so none of Bush's political advisers were able to weigh in on what was found about the candidates.[57] One member of Jim Baker's staff was so caught off guard that he had to race to find biographies of Quayle in *Congressional Quarterly* and the *Almanac of American Politics*.[58] This measure of surprise kept Bush's staff from planning for possible damage control when the press began to delve into Quayle's background. As a result, when the press ran with the stories on the National Guard, Paula Parkinson, and a rumor that his father had bought Quayle's way into law school, the Bush campaign learned about these problems at virtually the same time as the public.

The second problem turned out to be Quayle himself. When Bush introduced his choice to the public, Quayle turned to an obviously stunned Bush, jabbed at the vice president, and with a wide grin shouted, "Go get 'em!" It looked sophomoric, and the press pounced on the young man with obvious glee. During the invocation on the last day of the convention, just before Quayle was confirmed by the delegates, the speaker intoned, "How can we thank thee for this electrifying young giant from Indiana?" The television cameras caught several of the delegates repressing a snicker. But an even bigger problem was that Quayle had become an overnight laughingstock on the late-night talk shows (Johnny Carson one-lined: "Do you get the feeling that Dan Quayle's golf bag doesn't have a full set of irons?"). Literally overnight, Quayle had gone from young Republican-conservative superstar to being the campaign's new "wimp." For several weeks, he became what no presidential candidate wants his or her running mate to become—*the* story. Then he disappeared from sight, as the Bush campaign took over his schedule, sending him to parts of the country where he could do little damage.

Thanks to the flap over Quayle, Bush's acceptance speech to the convention took on a whole new level of importance. Democrats were already beginning to charge that Bush's choice for his running mate said less about Quayle than it did about Bush's penchant for secret decision making. They also claimed that Quayle's flaws would put the country in danger if something should happen to President Bush. More so than ever, it was imperative that George Bush look and sound presidential when he faced his party for the first time as its nominee.

The speech, as crafted by Peggy Noonan, was up to the task. Noonan, who had recently left a position as a speechwriter for Reagan to raise a family, had reluctantly agreed to join the Bush campaign. In her witty memoir of the period, Noonan takes her readers through her decisions regarding some of the speech's most memorable phrases. Bush called for a "kinder, gentler nation" based on individual acts of volunteerism (Noonan remembered that the phrase came to her after reading a note from Bush in which he described his motivation in politics: "I know what drives me . . . everyone matters"). Those volunteers would become "a thousand points of light." (Noonan: "Why stars for communities? I don't know, it was right.")[59]

On 18 August, at the Louisiana Superdome, Bush delivered the speech with an energy and air of certainty that surprised even his closest supporters. The most memorable line, delivered with theatrical pauses that would have made Reagan proud, brought the convention to its feet: "The Congress will push me to raise taxes, and I'll say no, and they'll push, and I'll say no, and they'll push again. And all I can say to them is: *read my lips*. No new taxes." According to later published reports, Richard Darman crossed that line out of an early draft of the speech, pronouncing it "stupid and irresponsible." Angling for a position in the administration, perhaps at the Office of Management and Budget (OMB), Darman panicked at the thought of being backed into a corner on taxes. But Ailes and Noonan were adamant; the phrase offered *the* sound bite of the speech, a line that Noonan later defended as "definite.

It's not subject to misinterpretation. It means, I mean this." In the short run, Ailes's and Noonan's instincts were correct. Immediately following the speech, Mosbacher found Noonan in the pandemonium of the convention hall and yelled, "Out of the park! Out of the damned ball park!"[60] He was right. Despite what it later cost Bush when he proved incapable of keeping his promise, it was the best speech of his political career. And he had cut Dukakis's lead in half.

Biographer Herbert Parmet has called the 1988 campaign "one of the dirtiest campaigns in American history."[61] It is impossible to dispute this assessment; indeed, one poll taken right after the election showed that the vast majority of the public felt the campaign had been filthy.[62] After the Quayle flap, Bush's campaign structure was revamped; Nicholas Brady became Reagan's secretary of the Treasury, and Jim Baker was brought in from Treasury to formally chair the campaign. The campaign's strategy for that fall was to paint Dukakis as a stark raving liberal by highlighting his stand on specific, red-meat issues that would resonate with the core of voters who had long supported Ronald Reagan. Yet Dukakis was not merely castigated as a liberal; the Atwater-led assault portrayed him as a man whose very patriotism was open to debate.

One should not fault Bush's patriotism—to do so would be to ignore both his military heroism and his public service. Bush said the Pledge of Allegiance with almost religious fervor: he would write to his friend A. Bartlett Giamatti in 1982: "The journalists slouch through it . . . but Bart it feels good to go to some Rotary meetings in Iowa and say the Pledge—it really does—especially that part 'one nation under God.'"[63] But in 1988, Bush and his campaign called Dukakis's patriotism into open question. As part of this strategy, Bush attacked Dukakis as a "card-carrying member" of the American Civil Liberties Union (ACLU), a charge that was true enough. But he also co-opted the American flag as a virtual symbol of his campaign. In 1977 Dukakis had vetoed a bill passed by the Massachusetts state legislature that would have required teachers to lead their class in the Pledge of Allegiance. The timing was right for such a charge; on 17 October, the Supreme Court agreed to hear the case of a man who had violated Texas law by burning a flag during a protest at the Republican convention in 1984.[64] With a flag in his lapel, Bush hammered at this point and drew wild responses from crowds throughout the country, as he asked, "What is it about the Pledge of Allegiance that upsets him so?"[65]

If Bush did not revel in such a campaign, as some of his advisers have later claimed, he was nonetheless very good at it. He seemed both natural and comfortable in attack situations, as when he invaded Dukakis's home state and rode around Boston Harbor in a skiff while delivering a mocking litany on the governor's unwillingness to clean up the sludge (Bush snidely claimed that Dukakis would probably get his naval advice from the rubber ducky in his bathtub).[66] Garry Trudeau now created a *Doonesbury* character named "Skippy," who was Bush's evil twin and enjoyed getting into mud on the campaign trail. As a result of this—and as a result of the complete ineffectiveness of the Dukakis campaign to turn the attention away from attacks on his personality and toward the issues that Dukakis was prepared to debate—the 1988 campaign thus became one of symbols rather than issues.

And the most memorable symbol was that of an African American murderer. Though many states had programs to allow their prisoners time away from their incarceration to reward good behavior (the first governor to institute such a program was California's Ronald Reagan),[67] only Massachusetts extended that privilege to men and women who were serving life sentences for murder.[68] While on a furlough from a Massachusetts prison in 1987, convicted murderer Willie Horton made his way to Maryland, broke into a home, pistol-whipped the owner, cut him twenty-two times across the midsection, and then raped his wife. In February 1988, Dukakis announced that he would no longer oppose—as he had done in the past—a ban on the furlough program for convicted killers. In the New York Democratic primary that April, Al Gore had tried to use the furlough issue against Dukakis, but it did not catch on.[69] Now, James Pinkerton, Bush's director of opposition research, came across the issue and passed it along to Andrew Card, then serving as the Bush campaign manager in New Hampshire. Card, who knew the victim's family, recalled that he researched the issue and passed it on to Atwater. From that point, Card remembered that the furlough issue became "very attractive."[70] Reportedly, Atwater became fond of saying, "If I can make Willie Horton a household name, we'll win the election."[71]

Both things happened. Although the Bush campaign never technically produced an advertisement that showed Willie Horton (that was done by the National Security Political Action Committee, and the ads were pulled from the air after a short period of time),[72] the campaign team *did* create an ad that became a classic of attack advertising. Titled "Revolving Door," the ad showed prisoners (who were actually members of the Young Republican Group at Brigham Young University, acting in real prison uniforms loaned them by the state prison in Utah, where the ad was shot) walking through a turnstile as they moved in and out of prison.[73] The copy was devastating:

> As governor, Michael Dukakis vetoed mandatory sentences for drug dealers. He vetoed the death penalty. His revolving-door prison policy gave weekend furloughs to first-degree murderers not eligible for parole. While out, many committed other crimes like kidnapping and rape. And many are still at large. Now Michael Dukakis says he wants to do for America what he's done for Massachusetts. America can't afford that risk.[74]

But it wasn't just the copy. Only one African American came through that "revolving door," and he was the only character in the ad who looked directly at the camera, thus exaggerating his presence in the ad. Clearly, the ad was designed to emphasize the black face, thus drawing a link to Willie Horton. As one Republican quipped, the ad was "a wonderful mix of liberalism and a big black rapist."[75]

Dukakis foolishly decided not to respond to the ad. Bush, however, jumped at the opportunity. Bush not only refused to distance himself from the racially charged ads but actually embraced them. Bush referred to Willie Horton by name more than once in his speeches and alluded to him in many more. For example, on 2 September in New Jersey, he said: "We need a president who believes in family values, like saying the Pledge of Allegiance. . . . We need a president who is not going to offer some kind of program to furlough a murderer so he can go out and rape and pillage again. We need a president who will support our law enforcement community in going after these drug traffickers. . . . I am that man."[76]

Whether or not these ads swayed undecided voters—the purpose of any well-planned advertising campaign—is still an open question. The authoritative study of Bush's 1988 ad campaign concludes, "We lack evidence that shows conclusively how many voters were actually influenced by these spots."[77] But despite the argument of James Baker in his memoir *"Work Hard, Study . . . and Keep Out of Politics!"*—that the Bush campaign did not "go negative" but instead showed "the 'contrasts' between the candidates, a fair tactic as long as the ads were factual, and ours were"[78]—Bush's was, by any objective assessment, a negative campaign. It is difficult to think otherwise when Atwater tried to leak to journalist Robert Novak that Dukakis had psychological problems, or when he floated the falsehood that Kitty Dukakis had once burned an American flag at a demonstration.[79] In a very real sense, as observed by Atwater biographer John Brady, the Bush campaign created a negative "record" for Dukakis and forced him to defend it, as would an incumbent, running for reelection.[80]

While the Bush juggernaut of 1988 offered one of the most effective negative campaigns in modern memory,[81] it is also true, as Atwater later quipped, "We couldn't have done it without them."[82] Dukakis and his campaign were clearly caught off guard by the effectiveness of the venom coming from the Bush camp. Early in the campaign, Dukakis made the same mistake he had made in his gubernatorial campaign of 1978: he took his opponent for granted. Reminiscent of the 1948 campaign of Thomas Dewey, which had as its basic assumption that the brash Harry Truman was unelectable, the Dukakis campaign was haughty and overconfident, refusing to counterattack. Dukakis seemed to be waiting for Bush to self-destruct or to tire of his attack campaign. To the governor's surprise, neither happened. His own feeble attempts to create a favorable image of himself usually backfired, as was the case during a visit to a General Dynamics plant in Michigan, when he took a ride in an M1 tank while wearing a helmet that made him look like the cartoon character Snoopy. Baker was correct when he wrote, "There is no kind or gentle way to say this: Dukakis looked goofy"[83]—a point noted by the attendant press corps, which could not contain its laughter.[84] The Bush campaign pounced quickly on the gaffe. Sig Rogich, who remembers first seeing the footage of Dukakis's ride while in his hotel room, quickly realized that it would make a good ad. However, it was difficult to get the footage, protected as it was by the networks. Rogich was finally able to buy it from an ABC News archive, and he used it as the background of an ad that rolled a list of the defense initiatives that Dukakis opposed: "And now he wants to be our commander-in-chief. . . . America can't afford that risk."[85]

Perhaps the most devastating moment in the Dukakis campaign came during the second presidential debate, held at the Pauley Pavilion on the campus of the University of California at Los Angeles on 13 October. The moderator, Bernard Shaw of the Cable News Network (CNN), had the first question, which went to Dukakis: "Governor, if Kitty Dukakis were raped and murdered, would you favor an irrevocable death penalty for the murderer?" The question, which had been born of the

George Bush and Michael Dukakis, second presidential debate, 13 October 1988. Pauley Pavilion, UCLA. (Courtesy of the George Bush Presidential Library and Museum)

furlough issue, and which was at best on the ethical borderline, was made to order for Bush. Either Dukakis would say no, thus showing him once again to be soft on crime, or he would say yes, thus opening himself up to charges of flip-flopping on the issue. In the end, few people remembered what Dukakis said, but everyone remembered how he said it—matter-of-factly, with no passion or outrage in his voice, as if he was merely producing a pat answer from his briefing book. Former Texas senator John Tower, then advising the Bush campaign, remembered going into the pressroom following the debate and saying "what the reporters themselves had been thinking: whatever Michael Dukakis's qualifications for the job might have been, his coldness and detachment were appalling."[86] The Bush campaign had not only succeeded in burying the wimp factor for Bush but also painted Dukakis as one.

The nastiness of the campaign had grasped the attention of the American people, but it did not propel them to the polls; the turnout on 8 November 1988 was only 54.2 percent of eligible voters—the lowest since 1924.[87] Although the results were hardly of landslide proportions, Bush's victory was convincing. He won 54 percent of the popular vote and 426 electoral votes to Dukakis's 112.[88] Bush swept the South, Midwest, and Southwest; Dukakis won only ten scattered states and the District of Columbia.

One month before the election, *Reader's Digest* held separate interviews with Bush and Dukakis, ultimately asking, "In the final analysis, what is going to decide this election?" Bush replied, "The economy and foreign affairs—it has ever been thus." Dukakis replied, "Strength and values."[89] Both men were wrong, as was political scientist Steven Wayne, who in 1997 assessed that in 1988 "Reagan won again. . . . Bush was the carry-on candidate for the future that Ronald Reagan had prepared for us, and for him."[90] The reasons for Bush's victory in 1988 were not as grand as these explanations would have it. Issues were downplayed in 1988; instead, the negative Bush campaign kept Dukakis on the defensive and kept any serious foreign or domestic policy issues from being discussed. And rather than run as Reagan's heir, Bush effectively ignored his connection with Reagan for the whole campaign—a point that did not go unnoticed by many of the conservatives who were only begrudgingly supporting their nominee. Closer to the mark was Dukakis's more distanced reflection, as he admitted in a later interview: "Look, there's no question that the negative campaigning hurt us. . . . I think that one of the lessons of the campaign is you have to . . . respond quickly."[91]

Dukakis's self-flagellation has some merit; his campaign was poorly run. The press also bore some responsibility. A prescient study of the campaign by William Boot concluded that the press turned away from tough scrutiny of the conduct of the candidates and was satisfied instead with airing the sound bites that the campaigns provided—and the Bush campaign provided better sound bites (in the words of one ABC News reporter: "George Bush wanted some free advertising. We gave it to him").[92] But the main reason for Bush's victory was the ability of his handlers to understand that a new form of political campaigning—one based on quickly identifiable symbols and sound bites—was the way to get to an electorate that had stopped reading and started watching music videos on television. They saw Dukakis as being ultraliberal, a man who released rapists to prey on the public, indecisive about foreign policy, and unpatriotic. No less an observer than Bill Clinton nailed the reason for Dukakis's defeat: "The Republicans had defined him right out of the race."[93] Dukakis clung to the old style of politics and paid the price. The most incisive assessment of how Bush won came from Gerald Boyd of the *New York Times*, who observed that Bush "pick[ed] the right fights and [got] the right opponent."[94]

Nevertheless, a closer look at the 1988 electoral results bode ill for both the Bush administration and the future of the Republican Party. Bush's victory was hardly a mandate. He had won a smaller percentage of Republican votes than had Reagan in either 1980 or 1984.[95] For the first time in twenty-eight years, the Democrats gained seats in both houses of Congress while losing the presidency. Indeed, the Democrats now controlled both houses: in the Senate they outnumbered the Republicans 55 to 45; in the House, 262 to 173. The phrase "divided government" was now in every observer's political lexicon. Equally important was the fact that Bush had not won his victory as emphatically as had Ronald Reagan in 1984. Bush had received 5.4 million fewer Republican votes than had Reagan in 1984, lost 500 counties that Reagan had won, and received less support from Independents and "Reagan Democrats." Indeed, in virtually every category of voter, Bush's share of the vote had dropped from that won by Reagan.[96]

More important was the extent—quite aside from the fact, as George Will observed, that the Bush campaign had been "unattractive but effective"[97]—to which many of the same voters who had voted for Bush were beginning to grumble about the state of American political campaigns. In his prescient study, *The Governing Crisis: Media, Money and Marketing in American Elections* (1996), W. Lance Bennett argued that the 1988 election began a political era "in which electoral choices are of little consequence. . . . The best hopes for creative leadership are effectively screened out by political and economic forces that are only dimly understood. . . . Our national politics have created a system in which the worst tendencies of the political culture . . . have been elevated to the norm in elections."[98]

3

"THE UNTOUCHABLES"

Within twelve hours of his election, Bush announced that he would nominate James Baker as his secretary of state. The choice, as Bush remembered in his memoirs, "was what we call in golf a 'gimmie.'"[1] Bush's closest friend, Baker had run Bush's campaign for the Senate in 1970 and had served as his campaign manager in the 1980 and 1988 presidential campaigns. Moreover, his tenure as Reagan's chief of staff and secretary of the Treasury served as a bridge to the party's conservative wing. Baker later characterized their bond as a "big brother–little brother relationship"; to the president-elect he was "Jimmy," a man who could be turned to for personal as well as political aid (Baker reportedly called his friend "Bushie" in private).[2]

Bush's choices for his transition team, announced the same day as Baker's appointment, also contained no surprises. Craig Fuller, Bush's chief of staff as vice president, and Robert Teeter, a Republican pollster who had served Nixon, Ford, Reagan, and Bush, were chosen cochairmen. Joining them on the transition team were two Bush aides who were reprising their roles from the campaign: C. Boyden Gray as the transition's general counsel and Sheila Tate as press secretary. Tate was soon replaced by Marlin Fitzwater, who had served since January 1987 as Reagan's press secretary (feeling a loyalty to both Reagan and Bush, Fitzwater refused the requests of reporters to photograph the changing of the presidential photos on the walls of the West Wing of the White

House).[3] Chase Untermeyer, a Bush family intimate, was named personnel director. The team would oversee an operation with 125 paid staff members, which would be covered by $3.5 million of congressionally appropriated funds. Their task was to recommend appointments to the president and then to clear them through the vetting process. Not a formal member of the transition team, but seminal to the process nevertheless, was Bush's eldest son, George W. Bush. He chaired an internal group, which included Untermeyer, Lee Atwater, and Baker aide Margaret Tutweiler. Dubbed the "Scrub Team" by insiders, it was responsible for "scrubbing" all potential appointments to make sure that their loyalties were to Bush.[4]

It was the influence of the "Scrub Team" that led Bush to choose neither Fuller nor Teeter to be his White House chief of staff. Teeter's lack of administrative skills was well known. Fuller, however, had been with Bush since the vice presidential days. He was also Baker's candidate for the job.[5] But Fuller had long been suspected of leaking to *Washington Post* reporter David Hoffman, a sin Bush could not forgive.[6] Moreover, as Untermeyer later recalled, Fuller had "run quite afoul of George W. Bush" by being "insufficiently attentive" to the family and friends around the vice president, pushing them aside in an effort to get ahead. Untermeyer remembered that George W. started the "drumbeat" that ended in Fuller's being passed over for chief of staff.[7]

If a lack of loyalty cost Fuller the job, it played a major role in winning it for John Sununu. Bush's political debt to him was immense. In his victory speech in November 1988, an exultant Bush had shouted "Thank you, New Hampshire!" He had not forgotten that that primary victory, in which Sununu played a pivotal role, had helped to turn his electoral fortunes around. But Sununu also had other strengths for the position. He came with government and administrative experience that neither Fuller nor Teeter could match. He had served as a New Hampshire state representative from 1973 to 1974 and as governor of that state from 1983 to 1988, leading Bush to quip that "you want someone who's run for sheriff" as chief of staff.[8] Sununu also appealed to conservatives, who approved of his anti-Soviet leanings.[9] His appointment may well have solved another problem for Bush: adding a strong presence at chief of staff would help to blunt fears that Baker was going to dominate Bush, much like a "deputy president."[10]

But most important was the fact that Sununu filled a gap in Bush's managerial style. Teeter's experience was as a pollster; Fuller, as one reporter put it, "preferred a low-key devotion to process rather than the rough and tumble of political combat."[11] Neither was the best choice to rein in what could often be an unruly White House staff. Sununu, on the other hand, had a reputation for being the type of manager who would complement Bush's often paternalistic approach to his subordinates. Andrew Card, who became Sununu's deputy, remembered that the governor's appointment would "give George Bush something that he needed in the White House—a little bit of bite...and John Sununu has a lot of bite."[12] Tough, blunt to a fault, Sununu provided the nasty edge to Bush's "kinder, gentler" persona. In a 1997 interview, Sununu observed that "the president was smart enough to complement his style"; he was much more blunt with the press in 1989, telling the *New York Times*, "I don't know what they expect me to do. I don't have a reputation for assault and battery. What do they think I will do to the system, break it?"[13] Sununu was thus chosen for the same reason as had been Atwater—they both brought something to the table that Bush needed, and did not, in his character and personality, possess.

Bush had two tasks that he felt had to be accomplished before beginning a new administration. The first was to bind the wounds caused by the recent campaign by showing the American people a nicer George Bush. This effort began immediately, with a campaign of kindness toward the press. After a Reagan presidency that had angered journalists with its deception and lack of access, the press was pleased to see the president-elect inviting reporters to attend a background interview or—the plum prize—to join Bush on his morning jog. During the three months of the transition, Bush gave more press conferences than had Reagan over the past two and a half years.[14] He also met with members of the political opposition, who proclaimed to the press a new warmth of relations that had long been absent (after a meeting with the president-elect, Jesse Jackson marveled, "Reagan had a closed door policy for eight years. You couldn't get an audience with him").[15] In the immediate run, it worked. Bush received generally high marks from the press; the *Washington Post*, for example, described his style as "unscripted...a more free-wheeling, self-confident style than the choreographed Reagan."[16] There was talk of an end to the imperial presidency; the bile of the recent campaign seemed forgotten.

But Bush also wanted to make it clear that he did not intend to operate in the shadow of a Reagan presidency. This desire was never hidden from the public view, but most observers dismissed Bush's promise to choose a "brand new team" as no more than necessary postelection rhetoric. A joke was making the rounds in Washington at the time that even with the advent of a new administration, no one was going to have to change their Rolodexes. Certainly it seemed probable that, because the Republican Party had retained the executive branch, there would be few startling changes and that, as under Reagan, conservative groups could continue to expect their share of the spoils.

The observers were soon proved wrong. The word came down that all Reagan holdovers had to be out of their offices by 20 January—no exceptions.[17] If they did not leave, there were reports that Reaganites would be threatened with having their taxes audited.[18] Bush also made it clear that his style of governing was different from his predecessor's. He announced to the press that he was going to be a "shake me, wake me kind of president" and volunteered that he was going to "personally read" the morning intelligence report.[19] He also announced that all his appointments would be completely screened for ethical and financial irregularities and that he would institute a code of conduct for his administration—all less-than-subtle digs at his predecessor. Far from the "friendly takeover" that many members of the press and, later, one influential scholarly book viewed it to be, Bush sounded as if he were taking the office away from a president of the other party.[20]

The composition of the cabinet, on its surface, seemed to contradict this observation. Indeed, it looked like Reagan redux. Seven Reagan cabinet members were asked to continue in the Bush administration, being either retained in their old department or reassigned. Baker's move from Treasury to State was a sign to most observers that foreign policy would dominate the new administration.[21] Bush also kept his friend Nicholas Brady at Treasury and retained Lauro Cavazos at Education and Richard Thornburgh as attorney general. Two other former Reagan cabinet members were given new assignments under Bush: Elizabeth Dole, who had been secretary of transportation from 1983 to 1987, was made secretary of labor, and Clayton Yeutter was moved from U.S. Trade Representative (USTR) to Agriculture. The Thornburgh appointment can be seen also as a paean to the party's conservatives, as was the appointment of New York congressman Jack Kemp at Housing and Urban Development.

Bush's sense of loyalty led to other cabinet appointments. He paid back two enormous political debts by naming his Texas ally John Tower as secretary of defense and longtime friend Robert Mosbacher

The first Bush cabinet, 23 January 1989. *Back Row, left to right:* Dr. Lauro Cavazos, Clayton Yeutter, Dr. Louis Sullivan, Richard Darman, Samuel Skinner, Adm. James Watkins, Carla Hills, Robert Mosbacher, Jack Kemp, Edward Derwinski. *Front row, left to right*: Elizabeth Dole, John Tower, James A. Baker III, Bush, Dan Quayle, Nicholas Brady, Richard Thornburgh, Manuel Lujan Jr. (Courtesy of the George Bush Presidential Library and Museum)

to Commerce. He also paid back governor of Illinois James Thompson, who had made an early withdrawal from the 1988 presidential race, by naming Samuel Skinner, the former chairman of the Northern Illinois Regional Transportation Authority and the chairman of the Bush campaign in Illinois, to Transportation. Edward Derwinski, also of Illinois, was no crony of Thompson, but he had had a long relationship with Bush, serving with him in the House and by his side again in 1971 as a delegate to the General Assembly of the United Nations; he was named secretary of veterans affairs. Minorities and ethnic Americans got four slots—Cavazos was the first Hispanic to be named to the cabinet, and Derwinski was the first Polish American to be named to a Republican cabinet in the nation's history. African American Louis Sullivan, president of Morehouse College of Medicine, was named secretary of health and human services, and Manuel Lujan, a former congressman from New Mexico and a Hispanic American, was named to Interior. The second woman appointed to the cabinet was Carla Hills as USTR; she had been secretary of labor under Ford. Retired admiral James D. Watkins, a former nuclear submarine commander, rounded out the cabinet as secretary of energy.

Yet those who judge (or judged) the Bush administration by the makeup of its cabinet know little about the cabinet's relative power in the modern presidency. In short, it has none. Richard Nixon began the practice of centering policy decisions at the White House, leaving the departments with little power, save whatever advisory role the president deigned to assign specific cabinet members. Nixon's successors had kept that paradigm intact. With the exception of Baker at State, and often Thornburgh at Justice, Bush had absolutely no intentions of dispersing power back to the departments. Bush kept the two cabinet councils that had been formed under Reagan—the Domestic Policy Council and the Economic Policy Council—both of which will be discussed in more detail in the next chapter, but little policy flowed from them. As the administration carried on, cabinet meetings became more infrequent. Though he made it clear to his staff that any member of his cabinet could see him at any time, Bush reserved the policy-making role for his White House staff.[22]

On that level, Bush wanted to clean house, as the appointment of two of the members of his team most responsible for policy decisions bears out. Richard Darman had been a presidential assistant and deputy secretary of the Treasury under Reagan, but he had infuriated Reagan conservatives by his behind-the-scenes engineering of the administration's retreat from the 1981 tax cut. Thus his appointment as Bush's director of the Office of Management and Budget, with cabinet rank, sent up flares to the press, suggesting that Bush might not be truly wedded to his "no new taxes" pledge. That assessment would soon be shown to be correct, and Darman's role in effecting the reversal in Bush's declaration was substantial. But the forty-three-year-old Darman was never an intimate of Bush; indeed, rumor had it that the two men did not really like each other. Perhaps this was because of Darman's consistent self-promotion in the press; perhaps it was because of his corrosive personality. Darman himself remembered that he hoped that Sununu's reputation for irritating people would become "less notable. Unfortunately, it didn't. Soon, we were *both* said to be arrogant and abrasive."[23]

The choice of Brent Scowcroft as national security adviser was indicative of an even greater policy split between the incoming administration and the outgoing Reagan conservatives. The son of a Utah grocer, the sixty-three-year-old retired air force general and Russian history professor at West Point had served in the U.S. embassy in Belgrade, as a National Security Council (NSC) aide under Nixon, and as Gerald Ford's national security adviser. Scowcroft had been a consistent critic of Reagan's foreign policy. He had supported neither Reagan's labeling of the Soviet Union as the "evil empire" nor the sprint at the end of the Reagan administration to achieve a form of détente with Mikhail Gorbachev. Scowcroft had also publicly differed from the administration on arms control, calling the 1986 Reykjavik plan to eliminate all ballistic missiles "insane."[24] To CBS News reporter Lesley Stahl, Scowcroft grumbled that Reagan was "much worse in foreign policy. We'll be damned lucky if we pull ourselves out of the mess he created for us in Europe. He gave up weapons we need and kept the ones we didn't."[25] He continually warned of the "clever bear syndrome"—the penchant of the Soviets to lull the Americans to sleep while maintaining their own imperialist aspirations.[26] At the press conference announcing his appointment to the NSC, Scowcroft was clear: "I want to have a new look. We're going to formulate *our* policies."[27]

Scowcroft's appointment also sent a clear signal that Bush's NSC would be a far sight different than Reagan's NSC. The fact that the dysfunction of Reagan's NSC had been a major reason for the catastrophe that became Iran-Contra was high on the minds of the transition team, as well as Bush, who had been a member of that NSC. Scowcroft, who had with John Tower cochaired the commission that investigated Iran-Contra, and had concluded in part that Reagan's NSC was largely responsible for the debacle, wholeheartedly agreed. Bush's NSC would have to be as clean as a hound's tooth. It would also be, as Bush remembered it, retooled so that unlike Reagan's NSC, it would become "critical in the decision-making process."[28]

The initial step in this direction was the issuance of a National Security Directive (NSD-1) on the day of Bush's inauguration. This order, the genesis of which could be traced back to advice that Scowcroft had given his predecessors on the NSC immediately after Iran-Contra,[29] restructured the NSC by creating two subcommittees of that statutory body. The first, the Principals Committee, designed to review national security policy, included the members of the NSC plus the chief of staff; as a result, Sununu had a much greater impact on, and input into, foreign and security policy than any of his predecessors. The second one, the Deputies Committee, consisted of the deputies of each of the principal members of the NSC and was charged with the development of policy options. Here Scowcroft's deputy Robert M. Gates—a former air force officer, NSC staffer, and CIA analyst—quickly became the first among supposed equals on this committee as he controlled the paper flow in the committee.[30]

In this organizational paradigm, while the deputies performed the day-to-day tasks of running the NSC, Scowcroft was to be, in the words of analyst John P. Burke, an "honest broker"—an adviser who offered the president guidance but did not actively pursue his own policy agenda.[31] Burke believes that Scowcroft began his second stint as national security adviser in this manner. He observes that every day, after the president's intelligence briefing, Scowcroft would meet with the president, and that Scowcroft "took special care that these [meetings] *not* be occasions for presidential decision making without the knowledge and participation of the other principals."[32] Other students of the NSC have joined in calling Scowcroft a broker rather than a promoter of his own policy; one team of scholars notes Scowcroft was so meticulous in maintaining that role that when he traveled abroad, he took assistant secretary of state Lawrence Eagleburger with him so that Baker would be fully informed.[33] A born consensus builder with a quiet, self-effacing demeanor, Scowcroft certainly looked the part of the neutral broker, and there is ample evidence to support that assessment of his role—at least at the beginning of the administration. But, as will be seen, it didn't stay that way. By the end of the first year of Bush's presidency, Scowcroft was clearly advocating his own point of view with a president who trusted him explicitly; by the end of the administration, Scowcroft was unquestionably George Bush's most important foreign policy adviser.

Had there not been a Democratic majority in both houses of Congress, which would have to confirm Bush's major appointments, the transition from the Reagan administration to the Bush administration might have gone off without major incident. As it was, only two of Bush's early appointments met with any significant opposition on Capitol Hill. Louis Sullivan was criticized for his pro-choice stance, but that condemnation was muted by the time of his hearings, largely because no one in Congress had the stomach to turn down Bush's only African American nominee. But the Democrats were champing at the bit for a chance to exact their pound of flesh for the nastiness of the previous campaign. In that climate, allowing the name of John Tower to be placed in nomination for any position, much less that of secretary of defense, was like dangling a red flag in front of a bull.

Born in 1926, John Tower left Southwestern University in June 1943, joined the navy, and served during World War II on a landing craft in the Pacific. After the war, he taught political science, sold insurance, and was a radio announcer. He was persuaded to run against Lyndon Johnson for the Senate in 1960, the same year that Johnson concurrently ran for the vice presidency. Tower lost that election, but the following year, after Vice President Johnson was forced to give up his Senate seat, Tower ran again and won. As discussed in chapter 1, his victory helped put life back into a Texas Republican Party that to that point had been moribund. It also encouraged young Republicans like George Bush to run for office.

Bush soon found himself in Tower's debt. In 1970, when Bush was running for the Senate, Tower was the chairman of the Republican Senate Campaign Committee. He gave Bush monies that amounted to nearly twice as much as that given to any other senatorial candidate.[34] Tower supported Bush in each of his congressional races and stuck with him during the 1980 presidential primaries. As chairman of the President's Special Review Board on Iran-Contra, he later wrote in his memoirs that "the working assumption was—and indeed had to be if we were going to conduct an honorable, credible inquiry—that George Bush was directly involved. That assumption was *never* borne out by our investigation."[35] After the report was released, Atwater recruited Tower, who had introduced Bush at the 1987 Houston rally where he announced his candidacy for the presidency, as a surrogate campaigner. Tireless on the stump, Tower gave credence to the campaign's claim that Bush was innocent of any wrongdoing in the scandal. He also accompanied Quayle on several legs of the campaign, making sure that there were no more major flare-ups. Clearly, Tower was a man who had to be rewarded.

However, several members of the Bush team objected to Tower's being named to Defense. Their reasons were legion. Rumors of Tower's womanizing and excessive drinking had floated around Washington for more than two decades. Only days after the election, a story surfaced in the *Atlanta Constitution* claiming that his second marriage had ended because of "marital misconduct," a charge that was soon carried on national television.[36] Many of those on Bush's team professed to have firsthand knowledge of his undisciplined behavior. They argued against his being given a position that called for being alert and available at all times.

But Tower's troubles went deeper than his personal life. Treasury secretary–designate Nicholas Brady, who had witnessed Tower's behavior while serving as an appointed senator from New Jersey, reported to the president-elect that despite their statements of support, Tower was far from beloved by his former colleagues on the Hill.[37] Napoleonic in bearing, Tower eschewed compromise for confrontation; he simply had few friends in the Senate, and many members on both sides of the aisle wanted to see him "get what was coming to him." One individual close to the process remembered that during the confirmation hearings, he heard that Tower was visiting the Pentagon and having his picture taken. The individual's response was, "I've spent enough time in the Senate to know there's nothing they resent more than presumptuousness."[38]

The new chairman of the Senate Armed Services Committee, which would examine Tower's credentials and make a recommendation to the full Senate, was Sam Nunn (D-GA), who was hardly a Tower supporter. He met with Bush and told him that this was not the job for Tower—a job where one would "have to be with it" twenty-four hours a day.[39] There were also concerns about Tower's connections to defense contractors, some of which he had worked for as a consultant after his 1987 resignation from the Senate (administration documents suggest that between 1986 and 1988, Tower had earned $1,028,777 from his consulting services).[40] And there were rumors that Tower had improperly used leftover funds from his previous Senate campaigns for his personal benefit following his retirement. Added to this was the resentment among congressional Democrats regarding Tower's role in the Iran-Contra investigation (William Webster, then Bush's director of central intelligence, recalled that Congress was "just full of bitterness as to how they had been hustled").[41]

Brady, Fuller, and Teeter reportedly tried to come up with a "consensus alternative" to Tower at Defense but failed. It hardly mattered. Bush wrote in his memoirs that he held "some slight reservations" about Tower.[42] If so, he never let them show. Despite the lengthy list of allegations, Bush stayed loyal to his friend. After a delay in announcing the nomination—a delay that many advisers told Bush would weaken Tower's chances—Bush named Tower to Defense on 16 December. Bush told the press, "I am totally satisfied...because the investigation was extensive....I believe this matter is now totally concluded."

On 11 January 1989, Ronald Reagan gave his televised farewell address to the nation. In a wistful tone, Reagan ticked off what he considered to be the accomplishments of his administration, paying particular attention to the new, close relationship with Mikhail Gorbachev and the Soviet Union that the two men had brokered during the last two years of Reagan's tenure. When referring to the domestic scene, he modestly claimed that "they called it the 'Reagan Revolution,' and I'll accept that, but for me it always seemed more like the 'Great Rediscovery'—a rediscovery of our values." Yet one theme contained a rather ironic warning, given the tone of his presidency—that simple patriotism was not enough to guarantee the survival of the American nation, and that Americans also had to depend on their history: "If we forget what we did, we won't know who we are....I am warning of an...eradication of...the American memory that could result, ultimately, in an erosion of the American spirit." Reagan left office with the highest approval rating of any American president since World War II.[43]

The Bush administration formally began on Friday, 20 January 1989. It was the 200th anniversary of the inauguration of George Washington. To celebrate that milestone, Bush rested his hand on the Bible used by Washington, as well as on the Bush family Bible, as he was sworn in as the nation's forty-first president. Wearing a business suit (a small flap occurred when he announced he would not wear the formal morning coat that had been worn during each of Reagan's two inaugurations), Bush had trouble repressing a smile of satisfaction as he read the oath. Surrounded on the dais at the West Front of the Capitol by friends and family, the effusive Bush could not resist saying hello to them; even as the twenty-one-gun salute blasted in the background, the audio feed of the ceremony picked up the new president shouting, "Hey, Jack! Hey, Danny!"

Bush's inaugural address was, for the most part, a labored affair. His delivery was halting, as he often paused for what he seemed to think would bring applause, and when none came, he hesitatingly plowed on. But the speech was a rather well-written piece that highlighted the themes of the transition. After announcing that he was pleased to be talking to the nation on "democracy's front porch—a good place to talk as neighbors and friends," Bush announced that "my first act as president is a prayer," which he read word for word and which had as its chief message the hope that he could "use power to help people...help us remember, Lord, Amen." This, and his slow conversational style, helped to emphasize a departure from the Bush of the recent campaign, as he announced that a purpose of his administration would be "to make kinder the face of the nation and gentler the face of the world."

After perfunctory comments on the successes of the Reagan years (including what soon became a highly ironic observation—that "the day of the dictator is over"), the speech became a thinly veiled criticism of Reagan's legacy, to the point where one observer claimed that Nancy Reagan had to be nudged because her face was betraying so much anger. Bush repeated the phrases "a new breeze is blowing" and "there is much to do" several times, which brought applause. Specifically, he reminded Americans that "we have a deficit to bring down. We have more will than wallet, but will is what we need. We will make the hard choices." He warned that "America is not the sum of her possessions. They are not the measure of our lives." He promised to help the "homeless, lost and roaming" and that his administration would have a "new engagement in the lives of others—a new activism." As part of this engagement, Bush called for a "new bipartisanship" with Congress. In fact, the most boisterous applause came when he observed that his presidency would usher in the "age of the offered hand . . . the American people await action; they didn't send us here to bicker."

Yet for the first weeks of the administration, bickering from Washington was what the American public got. Although the Tower nomination had been in trouble from the start, it nevertheless needs to be seen in the light of Bush's inaugural promise to make his administration more ethical than had been Ronald Reagan's. The *New York Times* nicknamed the Bush administration "The Untouchables" after the incorruptible team of federal agents who chased gangsters during Prohibition.[44] In one of his first acts as president, Bush issued an executive order creating a bipartisan commission chaired by ambassador to Uruguay Malcolm R. Willey to examine the laws that governed executive appointees and members of Congress. The committee's report, issued on 10 March 1989, recommended the tightening of federal ethics laws. But the report also warned that "laws alone will not do the job. Officials must emphasize ethics and lead by example."[45] And only a few days after the inauguration, Bush had declared a National Ethics Week.[46] There was considerable discussion among Bush's aides as to whether the issue of ethics had been hammered home too hard, thus creating the impression that the administration was challenging the press to find anything wrong.

Problems close to home seemed to confirm that assessment. First, press reports claimed that White House counsel C. Boyden Gray, who had played a role in appointing Timothy Muris to the Federal Communications Commission, had nonetheless kept a financially lucrative chairmanship of the Summit Communication Group, which owned sixteen radio stations and had some 130,000 cable television subscribers throughout the South. Gray, son of a Bush friend who had been a member of the Eisenhower cabinet, had been one of Bush's closest personal aides since the vice presidency. Given the stridency of his position on the subject, however, Bush could ill afford to be seen as tolerating any ethical impropriety, no matter how small, on his staff. When the possible conflict of interest was made public, Gray resigned his chair and put his assets in a blind trust.[47] Not even Jim Baker was immune to scrutiny; after charges of a conflict of interest similar to Gray's emerged in the press, Baker sold all his stock holdings.[48] Maureen Dowd of the *New York Times* wryly observed that the White House was so worried about its ethical image that an aide had told her in all seriousness that the president never cheated at tennis.[49]

Such a climate hardly would be charitable to the Tower nomination. The early part of the confirmation hearings bears out Tower's desire to present himself as a moderate alternative to Reagan's defense secretaries, each of whom had pushed for the administration's record defense expenditures. Tower testified that he would counsel the new president to abandon the Strategic Defense Initiative (an expensive Reagan-supported plan for a nuclear missile interceptor system that had been dismissively dubbed "Star Wars" and had long been mired in controversy), noting that it would be impossible to build a shield that "can protect the entire American people from nuclear incineration." He also promised to pare the Pentagon's budget: "I am not such a mindless hawk that I would come to you and ask for a substantial increase in defense expenditures when I know that is not going to happen."[50]

But Tower's stand on defense policy simply did not interest the Armed Services Committee. Despite the fact that he no longer had any equity interest in any of his former clients, the committee pressed for an accounting of his dealings with defense contractors. In this, Tower did not help his own cause any. At one point, he professed to having trouble remembering whether he had advised a unit of British Aerospace on the sales of military systems to the Pentagon, even though during a 1987 divorce deposition, he claimed that he had.[51] Nunn and other members of the Armed Services Committee claimed that Tower had "crossed the line on the revolving door" between government and the private sector.[52]

It was, however, the issue of his personal behavior that was the most damaging. On 31 January, Paul Weyrich, a conservative activist, testified that he had seen Tower drunk on several recent occasions. The next day, in open session, Tower responded to a question from Chairman Nunn as to whether he had a problem with alcohol with a flat denial: "I have none, Senator. I am a man of some discipline."[53] Perhaps. But the committee was holding up the investigation for another key reason—on 10 February, Nunn informed FBI director William Sessions that the committee was investigating allegations that while he was in Geneva, Tower had "cavorted with a woman who, unknown to him [was] a KGB 'swallow'—an agent whose specialty is pillow talk."[54] One week later, on 16 February, a much more benign version of Tower's escapades appeared in the Knight-Ridder newspapers; citing an Office of Personnel Management investigation, the story claimed that in 1986, Tower had quit the U.S. Arms Control delegation in Geneva after his then-wife threw him out of their home because he was keeping secretaries as mistresses.[55]

Several of Bush's aides—including, according to one report, Boyden Gray—counseled him at this point to withdraw Tower's nomination. House minority whip Richard Cheney (R-WY) unequivocally told Vice President Dan Quayle, "Tower's down the tubes. You've got to find someone to work with Congress."[56] But Bush would not budge. The day after Nunn's announcement, the president met informally with reporters in the Oval Office. One reporter described him as "fired up" and quoted the president as saying, "I have seen nothing, not one substantive fact that makes me change my mind about John Tower's ability to be secretary of defense." Bush also remarked, "I'm not mad. I'm calm and content. I don't get mad."[57] On 21 February, Bush wrote a friend in Washington, "I'm going to stand with Tower all the way, and I am confident he will make it. I have never seen such a campaign of innuendo, vicious rumor, and gossip in my entire life... [but] I am not considering alternatives."[58] Indeed, Bush had already begun his counterattack. A White House aide went before the press to claim that Tower was limiting his intake of wine on doctor's orders, and Tower's own doctor announced that he had seen no signs of alcohol damage during a recent operation on Tower for cancer.[59]

Nevertheless, on 23 February, by a straight party-line vote, Nunn's Armed Services Committee voted 11 to 9 to give the nomination a negative recommendation.[60] The majority report admitted that Tower "has a substantial understanding of national security policy and international security affairs." However, the committee believed that his "excessive use of alcohol would disqualify him from being assigned to many sensitive positions in the Department of Defense" and that his work as a consultant "created the appearance of using inside information for private gain." Although it had unearthed "no findings of liaisons with female foreign nationals, and hence, no security violations that such activities would entail," the committee claimed that it did discover "some examples of personal conduct which the committee found indiscreet and which call into question Senator Tower's judgment."[61]

Bush, however, continued to show no signs of withdrawing the nomination. After the committee vote, he told the press: "I stand strongly with John Tower. I know of nobody else whose knowledge in defense matters can equal his." Bush's unshakable loyalty to Tower was certainly one explanation for his stubbornness, as was his desire not to surrender to the Democratic Congress on their first test of strength. And this was not a passive commitment—once the committee recommendation had been sent to the Senate, Bush actively lobbied Capitol Hill in favor of Tower. As one example of Bush's faithfulness, on 28 February, his entire day—from 8:30 a.m. to 6:00 p.m.—was filled with a series of appointments with eleven senators to try to persuade them to vote for Tower.[62] For his part, Tower decided to take his case to the people, but it did not help. On Sunday, 3 March, in appearances on all three major Sunday morning television political talk shows, Tower promised that if confirmed, he would not take a drink while on the cabinet.[63] Virtually no one believed him. Tower had now become a national joke, but Bush still refused to withdraw the nomination.

The brawl then shifted to the floor of the Senate, where minority leader Bob Dole decided that if the nomination was going to be defeated, the Democrats would have to pay. The day of the vote on the Armed Services Committee, Dole threw down the gauntlet: "If you want to kill somebody around here, just start piling up the garbage...eventually it begins to smell."[64] For the Democrats, the vote was the first test of the leadership of new Senate majority leader George Mitchell. The Maine native, a former federal judge and former federal prosecutor, had been elected to the leadership post three months earlier. Bush later called him "as fierce a partisan as I've come up against."[65] But for all the rhetoric—and it was as ugly as had been seen in Congress in many a day—the issue was never really in doubt. Mitchell only had to hold his lines. Of the Democratic senators, only Howell Heflin of Alabama, Christopher Dodd of Connecticut (Tower had voted against Dodd's father's 1967 censure by the Senate), and Lloyd Bentsen of Texas broke ranks to support Tower. On the Republican side, Nancy Kassebaum of Kansas voted against the confirmation. Thus, on 9 March, the final vote against confirmation was 53 to 47; it was the first time that the Congress had rejected a cabinet nomination since 1959.[66]

Attention now turned to finding an immediate replacement for Tower. Within hours of Tower's nomination being voted down, Scowcroft asked Dick Cheney to come to the White House. Bush, Baker, and Scowcroft had both known the forty-nine-year-old Cheney from their days in the Ford White House, where he had served as chief of staff. More hawkish than Tower, Cheney had been a consistent supporter of the Reagan arms buildup and was an outspoken supporter of the Nicaraguan Contras. He had served as the ranking Republican on the House committee that had investigated the Iran-Contra affair and had recently been promoted to a leadership role as House minority whip. A complete contrast to the voluble Tower, Cheney stood out for his lack of pretension (when his press secretary saw the nameplate "Richard B. Cheney" on the door to the secretary's new office, he remembered thinking that it would have to be changed, because "he's not a 'Richard B.' kind of guy. It would have to be 'Dick'").[67] A careful politician—Colin Powell remembered that he "never show[ed] more surface than necessary"[68]— he was well liked on both sides of the aisle, and quick confirmability was now the number one priority. When Scowcroft asked Cheney for his thoughts on the situation, Cheney remembers asking, "How about [former secretary of defense under Ford Donald B.] Rumsfeld?" Sununu rejected that suggestion, and Scowcroft offered Cheney the nomination. Cheney, who remembers that he "wasn't completely surprised," jumped at the chance. He later remembered that his choices were simple: "[Did I want] four more years in the minority in the House, or did I want to go downtown and run the Department of Defense?"[69] The only serious question at Cheney's confirmation hearings was about the state of his health; since 1978 he had had three heart attacks and quadruple bypass surgery. Convinced of Cheney's overall health despite his coronary episodes, and unwilling to undertake another bruising confirmation battle, the Armed Services Committee voted unanimously to confirm, and on 17 March the full Senate followed suit, 92 to 0. Cheney was sworn in that day.

Cheney was uniformly accepted as a good choice, but this made the pill that Bush had to swallow no less bitter. One week after the defeat, Bush sent Tower an autographed photo of his original cabinet choices, including Tower, with the inscription: "John: This is the way it should have been."[70]

Thus had the "character issue" become the business of the day. Members of the administration stumbled over each other in a race to show that they had divested themselves of any financial conflict of interest, and every major politician pontificated for the camera on the importance of protecting "ethics in government."[71] But for the Republicans, ethics paled in comparison to the need to exact political revenge for the Tower defeat. In the attacks that followed, the nation was treated to a mud-wrestling match on Capitol Hill—a bloodletting of accusation, innuendo, and pious condemnation that had not been witnessed since the days when McCarthyism reigned supreme in the early 1950s. The attack was led by the abrasive and brilliant Newt Gingrich of Georgia. The former history professor and conservative Republican tied his considerable ambition to the issue of ethics. He was particularly interested in ferreting out Democratic violators, declaring that "to do nothing is to surrender."[72]

As the newly, and narrowly, elected replacement for Cheney as House minority whip, Gingrich led the charge against the Republican's first target: "We are going to ask Nunn, 'If you couldn't stomach Tower at the Department of Defense, how do you feel about Jim Wright being second in line to the president?'"[73] Like Tower, Speaker of the House James Wright (D-TX) was quite vulnerable to attack. In the words of the most complete chronicler of Wright's fall from political grace, "One thread connected all of Wright's life—hubris."[74] Among other accusations, Wright was charged with evading limits on outside income by persuading people who heard him speak to buy copies of his autobiography instead of paying him an honorarium. He was also charged with taking $145,000 in improper gifts from a Texas businessman, listing them instead as gifts to his wife. Wright's defense lasted through the spring (one Republican staffer gloated that "the only thing better than a dead speaker is a weak speaker"), until he finally resigned on 31 May. In a defiant final speech to the House, Wright urged an end to the "mindless cannibalism" that was taking place on Capitol Hill in the name of ethics.

But no immediate end was in sight, as both parties attempted to corner the market on ethical purity in time for the 1990 midterm elections. The new Speaker of the House, Thomas Foley (D-WA), had to defend himself against charges of homosexuality, charges that were brought into the public eye by a memo from the Republican National Committee entitled "Tom Foley: Out of the Liberal Closet." The memo had been approved by Mark Goodin, communications director at the

RNC; many people also believed that Lee Atwater, the new chairman of the RNC, had approved its release. After the memo was made public, a furious Bush, who wanted to maintain good relations with Foley, reprimanded Atwater, and Goodin was forced to resign.[75]

Before the end of the summer, Gingrich found himself in the crosshairs, charged with improperly benefiting from the sales of a videotaped teaching package. In August, Congressman Barney Frank (D-MA) admitted to a reported dalliance with a male prostitute; he was formally reprimanded by the House the following July.[76] In November, as part of the fallout from the savings and loan scandal (see chapter 5), five senators were investigated for giving preferential-treatment aid to Charles Keating, the head of the doomed Lincoln Savings and Loan. In May 1990, Senator David Durenburger (D-MN) faced charges that included exceeding the honoraria limits set by the Senate (in any one year, 40 percent of a senator's salary), converting campaign contributions for personal use, and violating Senate rules on personal travel; he was formally denounced by the Senate by a vote of 96 to 0 that July.[77]

The ethics frenzy of 1989–1990 was much more than the usual Washington tempest in a teapot. It was another part of the saga of the grassroots anger directed at all politicians at all levels that would feed support for the candidacy of Ross Perot only two years later. Several observers pinpoint the Tower nomination and the subsequent ethics brawl as the moment when all civility ended in the Senate, and any civility that was left in the press went out the window.[78] But the immediate problem for the Bush administration was that the ethics battle threatened to obscure the president's attempts to develop a coherent set of domestic and foreign policies. Certainly Bush did not want to continue reading such critics as the *Washington Post* writers David Hoffman and Ann Devroy, who in March 1989 concluded that his administration was a ship without a rudder.[79]

4

★ ★ ★ ★ ★

DOMESTIC POLICIES

There were three significant obstacles in the way of White House success with its domestic and economic policies. The first was relatively simple—Bush could not afford much. Ronald Reagan had traded the problems of an inherited inflation and a program of high taxes for the equally vexing problem of an unbalanced budget. Reagan expected that the savings from his tax cuts would by themselves be enough to stimulate the economy. Not so. He refused to offset his tax cuts with corresponding cuts in entitlement programs—indeed, federal outlays for Medicaid were exactly the same in 1987 as they had been in 1981, and Social Security and Medicare outlays had actually increased.[1] Reagan also refused to cut defense spending. Indeed, during his first term, defense spending increased from $171 billion to $229 billion.[2] Those combined costs led to gaping deficits. Despite preaching a balanced budget (from his 1981 inaugural address: "You and I, as individuals can, by borrowing, live beyond our means, but only for a limited time. Why, then, should we think that collectively, as a nation, we're not bound by the same limitation?"), Reagan would never submit one. One of the most elusive facts in the Reagan literature is the size of the deficits he would bequeath his successor—they were simply so large that the sources are at odds over their size. The figure most often quoted is a tripling of the budget deficit during Reagan's tenure, to more than $2.7 trillion a year—the highest in American history.[3] By 1988 the payment on the interest alone was $140 billion a year. Bush had been right: what he called "voodoo economics" had not worked. But now, Bush had to find a way to pay the bills.

The second obstacle was the president himself. George H. W. Bush is the least introspective of men, never comfortable with articulating any abstract idea, much less talking to the nation about what he stood for. As president, Bush consistently scorned the press's attempt to pin him down on what he derisively called the "vision thing." There was to be no domestic or social package even remotely comparable to a New Frontier, a Great Society, or even a New Federalism in the Bush administration.[4] Bush simply did not see "vision" in terms of grand, integrated sets of programs. As he told two *New York Times* reporters in 1990, "Having vision does not necessarily mean having a fixed blueprint. It means having a general direction and an ability to redefine strategy as events require."[5] Bush bluntly told me in 1998, "[I] never tried to pigeonhole myself" when it came to articulating his positions for the public.[6] A little bit of pigeonholing, however, might have gone a long way in making the public see how Bush stood on his policy priorities. Quite clearly, the post-Reagan public, now used to a "great communicator," expected their president to be both willing and able to articulate a long-term philosophy for his administration. Bush was neither, and it ultimately cost him much support for his domestic and economic policies.

The third hurdle involved simple arithmetic. The Democrats had a ten-vote majority in the Senate and an eighty-nine-vote majority in the House. And even those numbers were soft; many congressional Republicans felt themselves to be less beholden to George Bush than to Ronald Reagan, and conservative Republicans, who had never fully trusted Bush, lay in wait to make sure that his agenda did not betray the gains of the "Reagan Revolution"—particularly when it came to Bush's promise not to raise taxes. Even had he wished to articulate a "vision" for his domestic and economic policies—which he did not—it would have been foolish to do so; it would simply have offered the Democrats a large target to shoot at.

The question asked in these next two chapters, then, is whether or not Bush was able to overcome these rather significant obstacles, and have passed by Congress a successful domestic and economic policy that was true to his political philosophy—and if so, how.

In a situation where Democrats outnumbered the Republicans on Capitol Hill, the veto was the most formidable weapon in the White House legislative arsenal. In 1989 the majority Democrats needed to have 218 of 262 of their number vote in favor of a measure to pass a bill in the House; in the Senate, they needed 51 of their 57 votes. But Bush needed to keep only 34 of his 43 Republican votes to sustain a veto in the Senate. Thus was born a "veto strategy." Given the political arithmetic, Bush's vetoes were most likely to be sustained—in four years, Bush vetoed forty-four bills (twenty-nine regular vetoes and fifteen pocket vetoes), and his veto was upheld forty-three times.[7] Whenever it found itself opposed to a piece of legislation, the White House quickly sent a memo to the Congress threatening a veto—as opposed to making a speech on the subject to which the Democrats would have to issue a public rebuttal, thus starting a chain of legislative acrimony[8]—so that there was time to amend the legislation toward a point of view more acceptable to the administration.[9] Bush was certain that this strategy would work. He was not only a former congressman, but he had also watched a veto strategy work during the Ford administration, when Ford faced much the same numbers as Bush did in 1989.[10]

There are many examples of the threat of a Bush veto being successful in allowing the administration to put his own cast on legislation that was, in its original form at least, marked by the liberal slant of the Democratic Congress.[11] One of the best examples was the fight over the minimum wage. In early March 1989, the Senate Labor and Human Resources Committee, chaired by Edward Kennedy (D-MA), approved a plan to raise the minimum wage from $3.35 an hour to $4.65 an hour.[12] Bush told a *Washington Post* reporter, "There will be no compromise with me on the amount of the minimum wage," and he threatened a veto of any figure over $4.25 an hour.[13] On 23 March, the House voted to raise the minimum wage to $4.55; the Senate followed suit in May. Tony Coehlo (D-CA), the Democratic whip, threw down the gauntlet: "If he vetoes this, the American people will have to judge whether he is being kinder and gentler toward working people or some other group of Americans."[14] Bush picked up the gauntlet. On 13 June 1989, in his first veto as president, Bush sent the legislation back to Congress. The next day, the veto was sustained, falling thirty-seven votes short of the two-thirds necessary to override.[15] The following November, Bush and the Senate agreed on a compromise; the minimum wage would rise to $3.80 in 1990 and to $4.25 in 1991.[16]

There will be other examples of the success of this strategy later in this chapter. But on other, much testier social issues, the veto was not enough. Thus Bush took a road not often traveled by a president—he demanded, and fought vigorously for, constitutional change.

One cartoon published during the 1988 campaign depicted Bush so tightly wrapped in the American flag that he was gasping for air. Unquestionably, Bush and Lee Atwater magnified the Pledge of Allegiance issue so as to paint Michael Dukakis as a liberal, but no one ever needed to exaggerate George Bush's patriotism, or his visceral love of the American flag. At his Presidential Museum in College Station, Texas, visitors can listen to a tape-recorded message from Bush, which gives them a guided tour of a mock-up of his Camp David study. During that tour, the study's flag is bathed in a spotlight, as Bush, with obvious passion in his voice, tells his audience, "I feel emotional when I see it.... This flag symbolizes a lot of wonderful things about the United States of America."[17]

Gregory Lee Johnson did not agree. A member of the Maoist Revolutionary Communist Party, Johnson and about a hundred other demonstrators went to Dallas, Texas, on 22 August 1984 with the intent of protesting as near to the site of the Republican National Convention as they could get. After a march of more than a mile that included numerous acts of larceny and vandalism (acts for which the ever-present security and police decided not to arrest the group), they arrived at Dallas City Hall. Forming a circle, members of the group burned an American flag, chanting as they did so: "Red, white, and blue, we spit on you / You stand for plunder, you will go under." After the flag had been destroyed, many of the demonstrators jumped into a nearby fountain. It was there that within half an hour, all of them were arrested on a myriad of charges, but four of them, including Johnson, were charged with violating a 1973 Texas law that made illegal the "desecration of a venerated object." Three others paid their fine, but Johnson, arguing that his First Amendment rights had been violated, took his case all the way to the Supreme Court.[18]

On 21 June 1989, the Supreme Court issued its ruling in *Texas v. Johnson*. In its 5-to-4 decision, the justices declared that burning an American flag during protest is a form of symbolic speech protected by the First Amendment. The ruling invalidated all state flag-desecration laws (all states besides Alaska and Wyoming had one). For the majority, Justice William Brennan wrote that "the government may not prohibit the expression of an idea simply because society finds the idea itself offensive or disagreeable." The case had touched a particularly raw nerve; Justice John Paul Stevens took the highly unusual step of reading his dissent from the bench: with tears in his eyes, Stevens argued that the flag "is a symbol of freedom, of equal opportunity, of religious tolerance, and of good will for other peoples who share our aspirations. . . . The value of the flag as a symbol cannot be measured."[19]

When he was informed of the *Texas* decision, Bush reportedly "responded with blunt words" and "simmered" for a week.[20] He was then galvanized into action. After hearing that Senate minority leader Bob Dole and House majority leader Robert Michel (R-IL) were planning to introduce to the Congress an amendment to the Constitution protecting the American flag, Bush beat them to it, announcing at a 27 June press conference that he would introduce such an amendment.[21] Three days later, with all the media power that the presidency can muster, Bush reannounced his plan, with the Iwo Jima monument as his backdrop. After the White House staff smoothed out the ruffled congressional feathers, and after Bush agreed that the bill be called the Dole-Michel Amendment, the proposed amendment read in its entirety: "The Congress and the States shall have the power to prohibit the physical desecration of the flag of the United States."

With memories of the 1988 election still fresh, many observers were dubious about Bush's intent and charged that he was trying to turn the amendment into an issue for the upcoming 1990 congressional campaign. Regardless, Bush seemed to be on solid political ground: a poll showed that 78 percent of the public agreed with him, despite the fact that Speaker of the House Thomas Foley (D-WA) called the amendment "unnecessary."[22] But Foley could ill-afford to have his party be seen as antiflag or antipatriotic. Foley instead supported the Flag Protection Act of 1989, which called for essentially the same thing as Bush's proposed amendment. Despite the fact that there is a great deal of controversy as to whether a *statute*, not an *amendment*, can reverse a Supreme Court decision,[23] on 15 October the bill passed the Senate, 91 to 9. The Senate then voted down the constitutional amendment, leaving it fifteen votes short of the required two-thirds majority. The Flag Protection Act, however, was not long on the books. The following February, a federal judge ruled it unconstitutional.[24] The administration immediately had its solicitor general, Kenneth Starr, appeal the decision to the Supreme Court. On 11 June 1990 in *U.S. v. Eichman*,[25] the Court upheld the decision of the federal court, thus declaring the Flag Protection Act unconstitutional.

The Court's decision in *Eichman* led to a renewed public outcry for a constitutional amendment, but Foley continued to oppose the step. As a result of Foley's personal engagement on the issue, and his argument that the passage of time would defuse the issue without the need to change the Constitution, the proposed amendment fell to defeat for a second time on 21 June, 254 to 177—or 34 votes short of the two-thirds needed to send it to the state legislatures. Five days later, in its final gasp, the amendment went down to defeat in the Senate, 58 to 42. The only bright spot for the administration was the continued belief that in a replay of 1988, the Republicans would be able to use the flag-burning issue against the Democrats in the upcoming congressional elections. They hoped that the abortion issue would afford them the same opportunity.

A desire to reverse the 1973 finding of the Supreme Court in *Roe v. Wade*[26] had long been the litmus test for the conservative wing of the Republican Party. Yet despite the heat of the rhetoric, the rate of abortions did not significantly decline during the Reagan years, and abortion foes privately grumbled that on this issue, Reagan was not really one of them. Conservatives were not sure what to expect from Bush. Early on in his career he had been outspokenly pro-choice, but as noted in chapter 1, he had reversed himself on the issue in 1980 at the explicit request of Reagan (Erica Jong quipped that "Mr. Bush apparently changed his views on abortion once, for political reasons, when he joined the Reagan team. He can change them again, and join the human race").[27] Since that time, through his presidency, and into his postpresidential years, Bush was absolutely consistent on the topic—as he opened into the margins of a 1990 letter: "I do oppose abortion. I do _favor_ and support family planning."[28] Moreover, he made it clear in several letters that he was of a big-tent mind-set on the issue. To one correspondent: "I recognize that this subject is a very personal, often painful one for most Americans. Difficult though this issue may be, however, I believe that the Republican party is inclusive enough to allow differing views on hard moral questions."[29] He was even blunter to another: "I will . . . continue to support Republican candidates, regardless of their position on abortion."[30] But Bush had long been thinking about how he might end the issue once and for all. In a 1986 letter to John Lofton of the *Washington Times*, Bush protested, "Frankly, while I have long opposed abortion, there has been an evolution in my thinking on the legal means by which we protect the sanctity of human life." His solution was the "adoption of a constitutional amendment to overturn *Roe v. Wade* and the effort for a human life amendment."[31]

Yet while the 1988 Republican platform was firmly pro-life and Bush's statements on the issue during the campaign were also, there was a nagging doubt in the conservative community that, like Reagan,

Bush was not wedded to the cause. Those fears seemed to become reality when Bush appointed Dr. Louis Sullivan, a pro-choice advocate, as secretary of health and human services. Only after Sullivan publicly reversed his position was he confirmed by the Senate, but his nomination seemed to be a sign that Bush could not be trusted on the issue of abortion. Bush attempted to allay conservative fears by contacting leading pro-life members of Congress, telling them that he supported the Mexico City policy, which allowed federal funding for organizations that agreed to provide contraceptive services but refrained from promoting abortion. He also declared that he would not agree to fund the United Nations Fund for Population Activities (UNFPA) as long as those monies continued to support programs involving compulsory abortion.[32]

On 3 July 1989, in one of the most anxiously awaited decisions in modern memory, the Supreme Court ruled in *Webster v. Reproductive Health Services of Missouri*.[33] The case dealt with several Missouri laws that had placed limits on a woman's right to obtain an abortion under the three-trimester paradigm decided in *Roe*. One law stated that life began at conception; another barred the use of state property for abortions; another required physicians to perform tests to determine the viability of the fetus if it was twenty weeks or older in gestational age. In deciding to hear *Webster*, the Court had its opportunity to reverse *Roe*. It did not do so. In a 5-to-4 decision, the Court found the Missouri laws to be constitutional, but it reaffirmed a woman's right to choose an abortion to be a liberty that was protected by the due process clause of the Constitution. This was a shock to the conservative community, made all the more troubling because two usually conservative votes on the bench made it clear that they saw no need to overturn *Roe*. Justice Sandra Day O'Connor, the swing vote in the majority, wrote in her concurring opinion that the Court saw "no necessity to accept the state's invitation to reexamine the validity of *Roe v. Wade*." And Chief Justice William Rehnquist argued that "nothing in the Constitution requires states to enter or remain in the business of performing abortions." Nevertheless, *Webster* did open up the very real possibility that the impact of *Roe* would be moderated on a state-by-state basis; *U.S. News & World Report* reported that twenty-seven states were likely to enact more restrictions on abortions.[34]

The official White House reaction to *Webster* was a positive one: "The Court appears to have begun to restore to the people the ability to protect the unborn."[35] But in reality, the Court had rebuffed the administration, which had presented a significant and detailed amicus curiae brief in favor of using *Webster* to overturn *Roe*. The *Webster* defeat prompted Bush to publicly announce his support of an antiabortion amendment to the Constitution.[36] But there was little hope of the Democratic Congress sending such an amendment to the states, and it did not happen.

Indeed, quite the opposite occurred, as Congress began to bombard Bush with legislation designed, within the federal guidelines set by *Webster*, to loosen federal restrictions on legislation. Bush vetoed them all—ten of his forty-four vetoes were of abortion-related bills—and he threatened to veto many more. For Bush, his yardstick was both a moral and a financial one, as he explained in a 4 June 1991 letter to Bob Dole:

> Given the importance of this issue, I am writing to make sure there is no misunderstanding of my views or convictions. I have not reached these decisions easily or lightly. Abortion is a difficult, deeply emotional and very personal decision for all Americans. It is made even more difficult when the underlying issue is whether the government—and ultimately the American taxpayer—is asked to pay for abortions. . . . I will veto any legislation that weakens current law or existing regulations.[37]

His vetoes included the August 1989 bill that would have allowed abortions for poor women whose pregnancies resulted from rape or incest and the District of Columbia appropriations bill for 1990, which contained a clause whereby appropriated funds would pay for abortions other than those where the life of the mother would be endangered if the fetus was carried to full term. *Ms.* magazine responded on the cover of its August 1989 issue, printing in big red letters, "It's War!" But from the point of view of legislation, Bush won; although he did not get his constitutional amendment, all his abortion-related vetoes were upheld.

Observers of the Bush administration are often surprised to find that for a Republican president, Bush's initial support among black Americans was quite strong. Through 1989 and into 1990, his approval rating among blacks was little less than astounding for a Republican president. By March 1990, it had reached 63 percent, the highest level of approval for any Republican president in thirty years.[38] John Berlau attributes this support to the measures taken by Bush to reach out to black Americans. He cites Bush's appointment of Jack Kemp, well respected in black communities, as secretary of housing and urban development, the appointment of Colin Powell as the first African American to head the Joint Chiefs of Staff, and symbolic gestures such as Bush's celebrating Christmas at a black church in 1989.[39] There was also Bush's support of Louis Sullivan, despite pressure to drop him as the nominee to head the Department of Health and Human Services, and Bush's public courtship of Jesse Jackson (Bush invited Jackson to the White House for a second visit in March 1989 and instructed his cabinet members to make themselves accessible to him).[40]

This would all change, as the Supreme Court ruled in a series of cases dealing with the thorny issue of job discrimination. In 1989 the court handed down six decisions that severely restricted the ability of employees to control their own destinies on the job. Two of these cases were of particular importance. In *Patterson v. McLean Credit Union*,[41] the Court limited how the Civil Rights Act of 1866 could be used to sue for private acts of racial discrimination. And in *Wards Cove Packing Co. v. Atonio*,[42] the Court overturned an eighteen-year-old decision that allowed plaintiffs to charge discrimination by claiming that a business work group did not represent the demographics of the local workforce. This time, the Court's opinion reflected the beliefs of the Bush administration. But the Democratic Congress struck back by passing the Civil Rights Act of 1990, sponsored by Edward Kennedy, which called for the protection of employees from job discrimination by forcing employers who practiced it to pay significant monetary penalties. Businesses opposed the bill, arguing that it would lead to expensive lawsuits. Even many black leaders opposed it, seeing it as a step back from the civil rights laws of the 1970s.

Unlike the Civil Rights Bill of 1968, which Bush had defended at the town hall meeting in Houston at the risk of his political career, he was willing to neither defend nor sign Kennedy's 1990 bill. Bush argued that the threat of lawsuits from big business would lead, de facto, to businesses having to set hiring and promotion quotas for themselves so as to escape litigation. An attempt to broker a compromise measure in time for a state visit from South Africa's Nelson Mandela failed. To no one's surprise, the Civil Rights Act of 1990 passed the Senate on 17 October; five days later, also to no one's surprise, it was vetoed by Bush, who stated that it would "introduce the destructive force of quotas into our Nation's employment system."

The issue of job discrimination in general, and the vetoed civil rights bill in particular, was a white-hot issue in the congressional elections of 1990. Republican Senate incumbent Jesse Helms used it to stave off a strong challenge to his bid for reelection in North Carolina from Democrat Harvey Gantt, the African American mayor of Charlotte. Helms ran an ad that showed a white man ripping up a job rejection letter ("You needed that job and you were the best qualified, but they had to give it to a minority because of a racial quota"). Also that fall, former Ku Klux Klansman David Duke lost his bid for a Louisiana Senate seat but won 60 percent of the white vote by playing to the quota issue, and Republican Pete Wilson used the same issue in his successful race for governor of California.[43]

Thanks to the message sent by the voters in 1990, as well as furious White House lobbying, Bush was able to defeat an attempt to override his veto, mustering the minimum of thirty-four senators in its support.[44] But the issue was still on the table, and Bush was getting pressure to sign some sort of a civil rights bill before the 1992 election. Lee Atwater, then gravely ill from the brain tumor that would soon take his life, pleaded with Bush in a letter: "I urge you to try to work something out. My gut tells me this may be the straw that breaks the camel's back. . . . Mr. President, please try to roll as much as you morally can on this one. . . . It's an idea whose time has come, and it's going to pass one way or another."[45] Bush took the hint, from Atwater and others; he had also endured the scathing nomination process of Clarence Thomas to the Supreme Court (discussed in chapter 10) and had watched his support among blacks plummet. On 21 November 1991, Bush signed the Civil Rights Act of 1991—for all intents and purposes, the same bill he had vetoed the year before.[46]

On 20 July 1990, noting that "the strenuous demands of Court work and its related duties...appear at this time to be incompatible with my advancing age and medical condition," Justice William Brennan resigned from the Supreme Court, giving Bush his first opportunity to appoint an associate justice to the nation's highest bench.[47] For an administration that had already been rebuffed by the Supreme Court on several major issues, the choice took on an unusual amount of importance. At the time that Brennan retired, Bush was also in the midst of battles that angered the right wing of his party, particularly the battle over the budget that would lead to his reversal on his pledge to have "no new taxes" (see chapter 5). But Bush remembered the last fight over a Supreme Court nomination, when Reagan had put forward conservative jurist Robert

Bork, and his nomination was picked clean by the Democratic-controlled Senate Judiciary Committee. Thus Bush was torn: while he would never bring himself to nominate a Brennan-like liberal to the Court, he did not relish the thought of the reception that another conservative jurist would receive on the Judiciary Committee.

As the vetting process began, White House counsel Boyden Gray liked Kenneth Starr, who had been Bush's solicitor general for less than a year. At the time, Starr was well known in Washington for being, in the words of Jan Crawford Greenburg, a "first rate intellectual who valued hard work and collegiality."[48] However, Attorney General Richard Thornburgh's advisers opposed Starr, believing him to be both easily distracted and not conservative enough.[49] At a breakfast meeting called to discuss the nomination, Thornburgh made it clear that he would never support Starr, and Gray chose not to challenge the attorney general. Next, they considered Judge Lawrence Silberman of the Federal Appeals Court. All involved in the process liked him, but he was tainted goods. Only the day before Brennan's resignation, Silberman had been a part of a three-judge panel that had thrown out the Iran-Contra-related convictions of former National Security Council aide Oliver North. Thus, any Silberman nomination would seem like political payback.[50] Bush put forward the name of Clarence Thomas, a member of the DC Court of Appeals and an African American, but Gray later remembered that "both Thornburgh and I thought Thomas wasn't ready. . . . Bush was very disappointed."[51] Gray next floated the name of Edith Jones, then sitting on the Fifth Circuit Court of Appeals in New Orleans. Jones had been a partner in Jim Baker's law firm and had been active in Texas Republican politics (serving for a time as general counsel to the Texas GOP);[52] Bush showed interest.

Into the fray stepped chief of staff John Sununu, who put forth the name of fellow New Hampshirite David Souter. Souter had graduated from Harvard Law School in 1966. He was appointed assistant attorney general for New Hampshire in 1968, then promoted to deputy attorney general by the then attorney general of that state, Warren Rudman. In 1976 Souter replaced Rudman and served as attorney general until his appointment to the Superior Court of New Hampshire in 1978. In 1983 he was once again promoted, becoming an associate justice of the New Hampshire Supreme Court. Souter was well liked by the Reagan administration; indeed, he had been thoroughly vetted for the Supreme Court appointment that eventually had gone in 1988 to Anthony Kennedy.[53]

On 30 April 1990, Bush appointed Souter to the U.S. Court of Appeals for the First Circuit, where he was unanimously confirmed by the Senate, and he compiled a record that was clean of controversy.

Souter, a bachelor, living the life of a scholarly recluse, displayed a reticence that made him the perfect nominee to face the grilling of the Senate Judiciary Committee. Rob Portman, then an associate counsel to the president, remembered that the White House did indeed view Souter as more confirmable because his personal life was so dull.[54] Rudman, now a Republican member of the Senate from New Hampshire, helped in this regard, writing Bush, "I can guarantee he has no skeletons in his closet."[55] And, as Chase Untermeyer wrote in his congratulatory note to Souter, Sununu's active and focused lobbying turned out to be an important factor: "OK, being from New Hampshire helped."[56]

Both Souter and Jones were invited to Washington for interviews with the president. Bush liked Jones, but she was young, not an Ivy Leaguer (she had graduated from the University of Texas Law School), and had impeccable conservative credentials—which would make her a Bork-like target on the Senate Judiciary Committee.[57] Bush decided to go with Souter.

The White House geared itself up for battle. Edward Kennedy told the *Boston Globe* that he would be sure to question Souter "to determine whether he possesses a strong commitment to the fundamental values of the Constitution and the Bill of Rights."[58] Kennedy's Democratic colleague on the committee, Patrick Leahy of Vermont, was more forthcoming in his comments to the *Washington Times*: "There will be a lot more to know about him, I guarantee you that."[59] Leahy was wrong. In his testimony before the Judiciary Committee, Souter was everything the administration could have hoped for. Greenberg concludes that "Souter wowed Senate Democrats with a performance so flawless that, years later, a Democratic administration would ask its own Supreme Court nominee to watch a videotape of it as an example of 'what to do.'"[60] Branded the "stealth candidate" in the press, Souter simply refused to offer the committee any specifics on any question. Most notably, he declined to state his stand on abortion, saying only that he had not yet made up his mind about whether or not he would vote to overturn *Roe v. Wade*. Supporters of abortion rights asked the Senate Judiciary Committee to reject Souter, but their pleas fell largely on deaf ears. To Democrats, Souter sounded moderate, not an ideologue, the best they could get; to Republicans, they could only hope that Souter's refusal to sound conservative was simply playing to the Democrats. All were impressed.

Judiciary Committee chairman Joseph Biden (D-DE) told Souter that his testimony had been a "tour de force," and Souter was easily blessed by the committee, then confirmed by the whole Senate by a vote of 90 to 9.

Yet Souter did not come as advertised. Within the first year of his tenure, Souter stunned the administration by siding with the liberal bloc on the Court in several key decisions. In his memoir, George W. Bush speaks for his father, who has never voiced such a view, when he says that Bush was "disappointed" in Souter, who had "evolved into a different kind of judge than he expected."[61] The right wing of his party was disappointed too, and it anticipated that the next opening on the court would be filled with a doctrinaire conservative.

In 1983, the National Commission on Excellence in Education, formed by Reagan's first secretary of education Dr. Terrel Bell, issued its required report. Entitled *A Nation at Risk: The Imperative for Educational Reform,* the report shocked the administration and the nation with its harsh view of the nation's public education system, which, the report made clear, was now lagging far behind those of other industrialized nations when it came to children's performances on key tests. *A Nation at Risk* caused a firestorm of criticism, led most eloquently by conservatives who demanded a reduced federal role in education. Reagan's second secretary of education, William Bennett, became an evangelist for school reform and helped to position the situation of America's public schools as a national crisis.[62] It is hard to argue with this assessment, or with Reagan's third secretary of education—and Bush's first—Lauro F. Cavazos, who in May 1989 labeled education in the United States as "stagnant." The figures were telling: 33.5 percent of the nation's youth did not finish four years of high school; between 1980 and 1985, spending for K–12 education, when seen in comparison to other industrialized nations, had declined. During the same period, the United States had fallen from twelfth to fourteenth place among the sixteen industrialized nations.[63]

As Bush considered how best to position himself as the "education president" he had promised in his 1988 campaign that he would be, he faced a conundrum. In the campaign, Bush broke with a Reagan administration that had tried to abolish the Department of Education; failing that, he had refused to increase the budget of that department in its final budget cycle. It was not just campaign talk. In a speech to the joint session of Congress on 9 February 1989, Bush used the bully pulpit to charge that "when some of our students actually have trouble locating

America on a map of the world, it is time for us to map a new approach to education." Two months later, Bush sent the Educational Excellence Act of 1989 to the Hill. In it, he called for a $500 million program to reward America's best schools, those he called "merit schools." He also called for the creation of presidential awards for the best teachers in every state, the establishment of the National Science Scholars Program, and the use of magnet schools to allow parents more choice in deciding which schools their children would attend.[64] However, despite intense administration lobbying, the act died on Capitol Hill.

In an interview ten years later, Bush could only sigh as he blamed the Democrats: "We thought we were pioneering on education—but we couldn't get it through the Congress."[65] True enough—but there were other reasons for the death of the Educational Excellence Act. Conservative Republicans who had supported Reagan's plan to get rid of the Department of Education balked at Bush's expensive proposals, all of which would increase the role of the federal government in education. Gary Bauer, who had served as Reagan's undersecretary of education, spoke for many: "Without an emphasis on choice, merit pay, values, school discipline, it's going to be hard to win conservatives' support."[66] For their part, educators faulted Bush for not spending money on a real solution to the problem. They had a point, but thanks to the budget deficit, there was precious little money to be had.

In an attempt to reinvigorate the discussion, Bush made good on his promise to consult the states. In a 31 July speech to the National Governors' Association, Bush invited the state executives to meet with him in Charlottesville, Virginia, to discuss educational policy. Only twice before in this country's history had the nation's governors met as a group with a president to address an issue.[67] The summit, held on 27 and 28 September, was at best a first step. No formal policy plans emanated from their deliberations. Nevertheless, Bush saw the meeting as a triumph. At the end of the conference, he wrote to one of its attendees, Governor Bill Clinton of Arkansas: "Well done—oh, so well done. You were a joy to work with on the summit and all our folks feel the same way. I guess partisan politics will strain some relationships in '90 but I really want to keep education reform out there above the fray. I'll try to do that and I know you will continue to do so as well. Great Job. George."[68]

But education reform was also held hostage by the White House's stand on affirmative action. Early in December 1989, the Department of Education ruled that scholarships guaranteed only to minorities were

The President's Education Summit with Governors, University of Virginia, 28 September 1989. *Left to right*: Booth Gardner (Washington), Terry Branstad (Iowa), Bush, Secretary of Education Dr. Lauro Cavazos, and Bill Clinton (Arkansas). (Courtesy of the George Bush Presidential Library and Museum)

illegal. An explosion occurred in the press, and Cavazos was forced to resign. He was replaced by Lamar Alexander, a former governor of Tennessee who had championed education reform in that state and then gone on to serve as president of the University of Tennessee system. Alexander's appointment was supported by professional educators, who were impressed with his credentials. The appointment seemed to signal a new phase of Bush's education program, but such hopes were premature. Despite reports to the contrary, the White House refused to back down on its decision to curb college aid that was linked to race.[69]

Just as important was the fact that Bush's retooled education plan, announced in April 1991, marked a major change in direction for the administration. "America 2000" placed the burden of school improvement not on new federal programs but squarely on the backs of the localities, which could pledge their desire to reform and be designated an "America 2000 Community." The plan called for voluntary national tests (American Achievement Tests) to enforce higher standards and a request to business leaders to raise $150 million to help create at least 535 "break the mold" schools. It also offered several private school choice demonstration projects.[70]

In presenting "America 2000," Bush tried to address the concerns that the right wing of his party had voiced about the Educational Excellence Act. "America 2000" was largely voluntary and clearly cheaper, and it tinkered gingerly with school choice, but it did little to address the concerns of educators or the deep issues of segregation and poverty in inner-city schools. In retrospect, it can be seen that these were not areas that the Bush education plan was designed to address. Again, it was not backed by funds; in virtually every area, the proposed fiscal year 1992 budget cut education spending.[71] Indeed, the letter that Alexander sent to the Senate Appropriations Committee outlining "America 2000," a plan he called a "bold, comprehensive, and a long-term strategy," included a footnote: "No additional amounts are added to the total Department of Education budget to fund America 2000."[72] With no monies at his disposal, Alexander was forced to take to the road to convince Americans that only they could fix their local schools. Alexander claimed that he was leading a "populist crusade"; one critic termed it an "empty public relations exercise."[73]

George H. W. Bush was the first president to specifically address the drug problem in his inaugural address.[74] He was also the first president, under the terms of the Anti-Drug Abuse Act of 1988 (signed by Reagan on 18 November 1988), to appoint a director of the newly created Office of National Drug Control Policy. His choice as the nation's "drug czar," William Bennett, was, in a public forum, the exact opposite of Bush. Loquacious to a fault and eminently quotable, Bennett actively sought out the press, with what many observers at the time felt to be an eye toward a future presidential run of his own. Bennett was also impatient for an instant solution to the drug problem. One reporter remembered that when Bennett was serving as Reagan's secretary of education, he stunned a meeting of the National Drug Policy Board by growling, "Let's send the helicopters into Bolivia again" to destroy any drug sources. An aide called him a "tornado in a wheatfield."[75] Bennett had been chosen by Bush because, as Reagan's evangelizing secretary of education, he had become the darling of the conservative Right. He brought the same zeal and hard-line approach to the drug problem that he had brought to education reform. This fervor appealed to many conservatives who had long felt that Washington—even Reagan—had been too soft on drugs. Also, Bush fundamentally agreed with his czar that the drug problem had been mishandled under Reagan and needed a different approach. What followed was not only the announcement of a new way of dealing with the drug problem but also a public relations crisis of the first order.

In his *White House Ghosts,* Robert Schlesinger has sketched a detailed inside view of the genesis, writing, and delivery of Bush's drug speech. According to Schlesinger, as the Bush team brainstormed for ideas, speechwriter Chriss Winston asked if anyone in the room had ever actually seen crack cocaine. Thus was born the idea of obtaining some cocaine and having Bush use it as a prop in his speech. Drug Enforcement Administration (DEA) agents approached their mark, eighteen-year-old Keith Jackson. His response: "Where the [expletive] is the White House?" Regardless of Jackson's poor geographic skills, he was lured by the DEA to Lafayette Park, directly across the street from the White House, where, on 1 September, he sold the agents three ounces of crack cocaine for $2,400. That same day, two new drafts of the speech were written, both of which referenced drugs purchased "just blocks" from the White House. In those drafts, however, Schlesinger noticed that "someone crossed out 'just ten blocks' and wrote in 'just across the street.'"[76]

On 5 September 1989, in his first address to the nation from the Oval Office, Bush outlined the details of his first drug plan. Midway through the speech, he held up a small plastic bag: "This is crack cocaine. [It was] seized a few days ago in a park across the street from the White House.... It could easily have been heroin or PCP." The bag did indeed contain the three ounces of crack. But when Michael Isikoff of the *Washington Post* broke the story of how the drug had been obtained by the White House, the press had a field day. When reporters quizzed him on the story, an obviously perturbed Bush, believing that the press felt sorry for the confused and manipulated drug dealer, shot back, "Has somebody got some advocates for this guy?"[77]

Almost lost in the press field day that followed the exposé of the drug bust speech was the substance of the drug policy that Bush had outlined. Three areas of Bush's first National Drug Control Strategy represented a significant break from Reagan's more passive "Just Say No" policy. The first was an expansion of the criminal justice system by providing funds for larger police forces and increased jail space. Second, the plan called for federal funding to the states for developing alternative sentencing programs for nonviolent drug offenders, including one of Bennett's favorite programs—"boot camps." Third, it advocated a "fresh approach to interdiction"—enhancing border interdiction systems and targeting key individuals and high-value shipments.[78]

Bush addressing the nation on his drug policy, 5 September 1989. (Courtesy of the George Bush Presidential Library and Museum)

The idea of military interdiction particularly appealed to Bush. It is telling that even before his Oval Office address, Bush had spoken on the drug problem in early March, before the national convention of the Veterans of Foreign Wars in Washington. There he told his audience, "I mean to mobilize all our resources, wage this war on all fronts. We're going to combat drug abuse with education, treatment, enforcement, and, yes, interdiction and yes, with our nation's armed services." In late March, he approved the use of the National Guard in twelve southern and western states to help local law enforcement officials battle the drug trade.[79] Bush even floated a trial balloon when Attorney General Richard Thornburgh publicly suggested that the administration was considering sending troops to Colombia to interdict the drug traffic. However, Bush backed down after it became clear that neither the public nor his drug czar supported such a plan.[80]

Bush's drug policies drew immediate fire from those who believed that the administration should be more concerned with funds for treatment than with funds for enforcement. The administration countered with pleas that there simply was not enough money in the budget to significantly expand both theaters of the drug war. For his part, Bennett agreed with the emphasis placed on enforcement, but he believed that the administration was unwilling to commit the resources necessary for victory. His attendance on the nation's talk shows became ubiquitous, and his outspoken devotion to the cause soon put him at odds with many members of the administration.

In January 1990 Bush asked for a 50 percent increase in funds for the military to control drugs, and the following month he attended a drug conference in Colombia, where he promised to consider the request of the Latin American leaders for the United States to subsidize the coca farmers for limiting production.[81] By the end of 1990, the administration had won passage of a bill that offered duty-free treatment for certain articles from Bolivia, Ecuador, Colombia, and Peru.[82] But the drug problem did not disappear. This was hammered home to the public by the January 1990 arrest of Marion Barry, mayor of the District of Columbia, for narcotics possession, and the subsequent public release of FBI videotapes showing Barry smoking crack cocaine in a hotel room with a female acquaintance. In April 1991 the administration declared that the war on drugs had failed in the District of Columbia, an assessment with which Bennett took public issue.[83] In November 1990, Bennett left the administration and was replaced by former Florida governor Bob

Martinez. Bush announced the new National Drug Strategy in February 1991, which included a proposed 11 percent increase in the budget for health incentives.[84] However, the appropriation was soon taken out of the budget.

The nation's disabled (classified by the government as individuals who have a physical or mental impairment that "substantially limits one or more of [their] major life activities")[85] had not been explicitly covered by the Civil Rights Act of 1964. Of the estimated 43 million Americans with disabilities, a congressional study estimated that the vast majority had faced either segregation or discriminatory actions.[86] In the late 1960s through 1970s, disability advocates added their points of view to the civil rights movements. Their first victory, Section 504 of the Rehabilitation Act of 1973 "prohibit[ed] discrimination in federally assisted programs on the basis of race and sex, respectively."[87] But by the 1980s, the disabled community was losing its foothold, as the Reagan administration largely turned a deaf ear to their demands. Vice President George Bush's Task Force on Regulatory Relief was to review the 1973 act; most expected the task force to gut it. However, while he was a congressman, Bush had become friends with disability advocate Evan J. Kemp Jr. Diagnosed at age twelve with Wohlfart-Kugelberg-Welander syndrome (a disease related to polio), Kemp began using a wheelchair after an accident as an adult. Reagan had appointed Kemp, a member of the conservative Federalist Society, as a commissioner to the Equal Employment Opportunity Commission (EEOC); he became the chair of the EEOC when his predecessor, future Supreme Court justice Clarence Thomas, was named to the federal bench.[88] Kemp was instrumental in taking Bush's natural empathy toward those with disabilities (his daughter Robin had died of leukemia; his son Neil suffered from dyslexia and had endured bullying in school as a result) and channeling it toward a vocal support for federal legislation to help the disabled. In 1983, Bush surprised many by announcing that his regulatory task force would leave the 1973 act intact.[89]

In the mid-1980s, despite the expected opposition of the Reagan administration, the National Council on the Handicapped began to push for the Americans with Disabilities Act (ADA); on 28 April 1988, Lowell Weicker (D-CT) introduced the ADA into the Senate; the next day, Tony Coelho (D-CA) introduced the bill into the House. The four-part bill forbade employers from discriminating against qualified people with disabilities and required employers to provide adequate access to their businesses for patrons with disabilities. It also called for expanded access to transportation services and required the Federal Communication Commission to provide equivalent telephone services for those with speech and hearing impairments.[90] The bill's supporters hoped that by introducing the measure during the presidential campaign—and banking on the residual support of candidate Bush's commitment of support for the bill in his convention acceptance address—it would pass. They were half right: the bill passed the Senate but died in the House.[91] Moreover, Weicker was defeated for reelection, and Coelho left the House after stories emerged that he had received a questionable loan from a bank manager. But others picked up the standard. In the House, Steny Hoyer (D-MD) voiced his support for the ADA; in the Senate, it was championed by Tom Harkin (D-IA) and Ted Kennedy. In May 1989, the bill was reintroduced. The reinvigorated debate centered around the overall cost of the program, and what the ADA would cost business owners—both red meat issues for conservatives. All amendments that would limit costs were defeated, but there was also opposition, led by William Dannemeyer (R-CA), who proposed an amendment excluding "homosexuals regarded as having AIDS or HIV." While Dannemeyer's amendment was eventually defeated, the Chapman Amendment— which would have allowed a food service establishment "to refuse to assign an employee with an infectious or communicable disease of public health significance to a job involving food handling"—had the strong support of conservative firebrand Jesse Helms.[92]

Despite the opposition of the right wing of his party—opposition that included his own chief of staff, John Sununu[93]—Bush was unwavering in his support of the ADA. He spoke out in favor of the act in his inaugural address, telling the assembled staff of the Department of Health and Human Services that it was one of his highest domestic priorities.[94] Bush was particularly incensed by the Chapman Amendment, and he lobbied hard for its defeat, and told a group of business leaders that "our goal is to turn irrational fear into rational acts."[95] The Chapman Amendment was defeated, and on 26 July 1990, Bush signed the ADA into law.

Boyden Gray has often called the ADA "in a sense, the first welfare reform," in that disabled individuals were empowered to make their own living.[96] Certainly there is a point to be made here, and it bears noting that the bill stood to make more active consumers of America's disabled by giving them unfettered access to businesses. Yet the act can also be seen as the first real civil rights reform (as courts were put at the middle of the ADA's implementation procedure)—in the face of business opposition—supported by a Republican administration since the successful desegregation of southern public schools under Nixon.

John Turner, the president of the Conservation Fund, claimed that "no president since Teddy Roosevelt has done more to protect the wild heritage of America than George Bush,"[97] and the claim is justifiable. Bush was a sportsman and a member of the National Rifle Association who was deeply committed to environmental issues. Many times during the 1988 campaign he voiced a desire to be the "environmental president," and one of his first acts as president-elect was to call a working meeting of thirty of the nation's leading environmental experts.[98] Bush appointed William Reilly as the first professional conservationist to head the Environmental Protection Agency (EPA). In 1989 the agency announced an almost total phase-out of all uses of asbestos by 1991. Bush set aside ninety-three new national wildlife refuges; protected or restored 1.7 billion acres of wetlands; doubled funding for parks, wildlife, and outdoor recreation; and tripled funds to the states under the Land and Water Conservation Fund. His support was the driving force behind the omnibus water bill of 1992 to protect the Grand Canyon. And without the support of the Bush White House, the most important piece of environmental legislation of the postwar period—the Clean Air Amendments of 1990—would most likely have stayed mired on Capitol Hill.

Richard Nixon had created the EPA in 1970. Not to be outdone, Senator Edmund Muskie (D-ME), long a supporter of environmental reform and himself eyeing the 1972 Democratic nomination for the presidency, called for a bill that would require the automobile industry to make a 90 percent reduction in its total emissions by 1 January 1975 and that would direct the EPA to set air-quality standards for industry and limits on toxic pollutants. Muskie's Clean Air Act of 1970 was passed, but there were immediate concerns, not the least of which came from industries worried that they could not meet the government's timetable. Muskie's act was initially swept aside by Watergate, but with the support of the Carter administration and the newly elected Democratic Congress, those requirements were extended in 1977, as automobile manufacturers were mandated to reduce nitrogen-oxide emissions in cars to a minuscule one gram per mile.

But virtually no major urban community or industry was able to meet the deadlines, which were first extended to 1982 and then to 1987. As Richard Cohen, author of the standard book on the subject, points out, there were several attempts during the Reagan years to amend the 1970 act once again. But these attempts were opposed by John Dingell (D-MI), whose constituents in the Detroit auto business stood to lose millions of dollars if any further restrictions were placed on emissions, and by Robert Byrd (D-WV), whose constituents feared that any further restrictions on factory emissions would reduce the demand for West Virginia bituminous coal. By 1988 a bill had been crafted in committee, but there seemed to be little hope of its passage, except, perhaps, in a severely gutted form.

In his confirmation hearings, Reilly made it clear that the first item on the administration's agenda was legislation to strengthen the Clean Air Act.[99] The administration's desire was inadvertently helped by an environmental tragedy. On 24 March 1989, more than 10 million gallons of oil spilled into Alaska's Prince William Sound when the oil tanker *Exxon Valdez* went aground. The spill affected 6,000 square miles of ocean, stained 800 miles of shoreline, and killed countless seabirds, sea otters, and deer. Bush designated secretary of transportation Samuel Skinner as his personal liaison to the cleanup efforts. Skinner's involvement was heavy, as he traveled to and from the disaster site many times in spring 1989. *U.S. News & World Report* dubbed him the "firefighter in chief . . . [Bush's] unlikely star."[100] Skinner kept the pressure on Exxon to hold to its responsibilities for the cleanup, which led to criminal charges being brought against the company for its complicity in the accident. Although some environmentalists criticized the administration's role as being too slow and deliberate—a criticism it would face again three years later during Hurricane Andrew—the cleanup was terminated on 15 September 1989. It had employed some 11,000 people, 1,400 vessels, and more than 100 aircraft and treated some 1,000 miles of shoreline.[101]

The *Exxon Valdez* disaster thus contributed to a climate more favorable to environmental legislation. Sig Rogich wrote Bush that the "public response to the assistance in Alaska has been outstanding here in the West. I think it is setting a broad environmental tone for the administration."[102] Looking to take advantage of the momentum, Bush charged a small working group, which included domestic policy adviser Roger Porter, Boyden Gray, William Rosenberg of the EPA, and Robert Grady, the associate director for resources at the Office of Management and Budget, with crafting a bill that would break the congressional logjam on the Clean Air Act. On 12 June 1989, the administration announced its proposal to the public.

Largely because of the expense, the bill's passage was not guaranteed. However, George Mitchell, Bush's nemesis from the Tower nomination, this time worked with the administration. When he became majority leader in 1988, amendments to the Clean Air Act were just as much a priority for Mitchell as they were for Bush. Cohen contends that Mitchell's shepherding the bill to passage was "a personal tour de force rarely matched in Senate history."[103] In the House, much of the credit belonged to New York Republican Sherwood Boehlert, who brokered the compromise measure.[104] Bush was particularly active in pushing the bill through the committee structure, and threats of a veto sped that process along.[105] The committee compromise passed the House on 22 October and the Senate on 1 November; Bush signed it into law two weeks later. The Clean Air Act Amendments of 1990 were a landmark piece of legislation. In a tribute to the administration's lobbying efforts, the legislation as it was passed by the House and the Senate contained the central features of Bush's June 1989 proposal. It detailed provisions to bring all cities into compliance with the National Air Quality Standards for ozone, carbon monoxide, and other pollutants; called for an acid rain control program that would achieve a permanent reduction in sulfur dioxide emissions of 10 million tons by the year 2000; and called for a program to reduce industrial emissions of hazardous air pollutants by 75 to 90 percent in the first phase, using technology-based controls. It boasted advances in tailpipe emissions, controls on local air, and the first constraints on midwestern industrial pollution from coal-fire burners that emitted acid rain. It also cataloged 189 toxic chemicals for which the EPA had to set public health standards to decrease their pollution of the air and offered the first steps for dealing with global warming and the depletion of the ozone layer.[106] It also included a cap-and-trade system, which allowed companies to sell ("trade") the unused portion of their emissions limits to other companies that were having problems complying with the letter of the law. Al Gore, who worked on the bill, remembered that this "gave a market incentive to those companies that were the most efficient in limiting emissions."[107]

5

★ ★ ★ ★ ★

PAYING FOR REAGANOMICS

By 1989 the bills of the Reagan years had come due with a vengeance. The budget deficit was $2.7 trillion; service on the debt itself was $200 billion a year.[1] As Robin Toner wrote in the *New York Times* in January 1989, "The business of the 101st Congress is, in a way, painfully simple: the Federal budget and its deficit will drive nearly every issue this year, from the modernization of the land-based leg of the nuclear triad to child care to the savings and loan troubles."[2] The budget deficit hovered as a pall over any attempts by the Bush administration to articulate a domestic and social agenda. Bush's early proposals for narrowing the budget gap offered little hope of success. During the campaign, he had called for a "flexible freeze"—letting spending increase, but only at the inflation rate; then, when the economy began to grow faster than inflation, the budget would naturally balance itself. Few people, if any, truly believed that it would work. Most believed that the budget could not be balanced unless Bush reneged on his promise not to raise taxes. Both Gerald Ford and Jimmy Carter, during separate meetings with the president-elect in November, told him as much.[3] Three weeks after the elections, the General Accounting Office publicly stated that new taxes would be needed as a part of any "credible" effort to lower the deficit; one House Democrat referred to Bush's policies as "deja voodoo."[4]

Publicly, at least, Bush refused to discuss the possibility of a tax hike. In fact, in the early months of 1989 he argued for a 50 percent cut in the capital gains tax—taxes levied on the profits made by the sale of stock and other assets—down to 15 percent, a measure that would only have widened the deficit. Yet at the same time, like his predecessor, he could not bring himself to slash discretionary federal spending to make the deficit more manageable. Thus, the prospect for an imbalanced budget into 1990 was quite real. However, thanks to the Gramm-Rudman-Hollings Act of 1985, there was a catch: if the White House and Congress could not agree on a budget that kept to deficit reduction targets aimed at a balanced budget by 1993, there would be a mandatory sequester—a general cut in government spending—beginning on 1 October 1990, which would require a shutdown of many government services. Thus, Bush's allies began to soften the ground for a possible presidential reversal. As New Hampshire senator Warren Rudman observed in February of that year when a reporter asked him if he thought there would be a tax hike: "Obviously no promise is forever, none that I know of."[5]

Bush later remembered that he "didn't really want to" abandon his pledge not to raise taxes and that he did so only because he felt he had to in order to balance the budget.[6] Many administration alumni ascribe Bush's eventual willingness to accept a tax hike to the influence of Richard Darman, his director of the Office of Management and Budget. Darman's belief that spending cuts alone would not balance the budget was demonstrated by his actions during the Reagan administration, when he reportedly helped convince the president to abandon the 1981 tax cut and to adopt "revenue enhancements" to bring the deficit into line. It is likely that Darman gave the same advice to Bush. But Bush wanted to get through at least the first year's budget cycle without raising taxes. On 24 April 1989, Michael Boskin, the chairman of the White House Council of Economic Advisers, hinted at the president's plan to the press:

> We're going to see what happens when we get into negotiations for 1991.... We have said all along that we don't see the merits of a tax increase. We're willing to hear that case made in negotiations and discuss it on its merits. The president has said he wanted to make sure he kept that pledge the first year and he is hoping to be able to keep it over a longer period, to the extent that's possible.[7]

President Bush was, indeed, successful in keeping his pledge for the first year, thanks to his calling in of a political marker. After a private meeting with Bush, chairman of the House Ways and Means Committee and Bush friend Dan Rostenkowski (D-IL) promised to wait a year before he pressed for a tax hike.[8] As a result, Bush's first budget was completed and passed by the Congress in record time. Abandoning the "flexible freeze," the budget for the 1990 fiscal year, as it was finally approved by Congress, estimated federal spending at $1.16 trillion, with a deficit of $91.1 billion. But analysts immediately began to look forward to the next budget cycle. Don Feder of the *Boston Herald* asked Bush in May 1989 if his no-new-taxes pledge was only good for one year or, "as many of us expected, the life of the administration." Bush replied, "It was just a flat pledge, is what I'd say. And I don't think—the way this budget agreement worked out, we don't need a tax increase."[9]

But the battle was far from over. The economic picture continued to darken, making Bush's hopes for a second brokered budget compromise seem very difficult to attain in 1990. By year's end, the Democrats were trying to paint Bush into a corner. Senate majority leader George Mitchell (D-ME) made it clear that he would not agree to any cuts in the capital gains tax; New York senator Daniel Patrick Moynihan called for eliminating Social Security from the budget and reducing the Social Security tax, thus making a balanced budget all but impossible.[10] Moreover, Bush was about to face the prospect of a particularly expensive bailout of the nation's badly mismanaged banking system.

Savings and loans (S&Ls), or thrifts, are financial institutions that, like banks, accept deposits and pay interest on them. Unlike most banks, however, S&Ls invest most of their funds in home mortgages. As the market in real estate, especially in the Southwest, boomed throughout the late 1970s and early 1980s, the S&Ls made huge profits for their depositors. However, when the real estate market faltered, as it began to do by 1985, both inflation and interest rates began to creep up. As borrowing slowed, the smaller banks, like the S&Ls, were the first to feel the pinch to their assets. But it was not just the free market that doomed the thrifts. Reagan's solution to the oncoming crisis was to deregulate the S&Ls, arguing with Hooverian logic that without government interference they would be able to save themselves. However, this left them at the mercy of unscrupulous directors and managers who invested depositors' money in get-rich-quick real estate schemes.[11]

Congress—many members of which were intimately involved with S&Ls in their home districts—must also share in the blame for the debacle. The Garn–St. Germain Act (1982) allowed the S&Ls to expand their lending capabilities beyond home mortgages. It also increased the

Federal Deposit Insurance limit from $40,000 to $100,000. Thus, when the banks began to fail, the Congress had made the government a full 150 percent more responsible for the bailout of depositors. Thanks to Garn–St. Germain, in the words of L. William Seidman, head of the Federal Deposit Insurance Corporation (FDIC) under Reagan, the government was now "a full partner in a nationwide casino."[12]

By the end of the Reagan administration, the scope of the crisis was astounding. By 1989 a total of 350 S&Ls had already gone under. The majority were located in New England, where the real estate market had taken a particularly hard beating since 1980, and in the Southwest—147 of the failed S&Ls in 1989 were in Texas alone. Some observers were predicting that the problem would be solved only by massive infusions of federal monies, perhaps between $50 billion and $100 billion. Of course, these figures could be counted on to widen the already cavernous budget deficit.[13]

Bush's initial steps toward dealing with the problem showed that his tax pledge had become disposable. Just before his inauguration, he proposed an annual fee of twenty-five cents for every $100 of insured deposits placed in the custody of an S&L. Chief of staff John Sununu and Treasury secretary Nicholas Brady stressed that these fees were not taxes, but their arguments lacked credibility. The proposal not only violated Bush's no-new-taxes pledge but clearly would not generate the amount of revenue needed to resolve the problem. Facing bipartisan opposition to the plan, Bush backed quietly away from it.[14]

A more complex plan, one that Bush hoped would lead to the banks themselves paying for most of the bailout, was announced by the president during a press conference on 6 February 1989. The plan called for raising $50 billion in thirty-year government bonds to help the failing thrifts. The interest on the bonds—estimated in February at some $36.4 billion over the first ten years—would be paid both by the public and by increasing the insurance premiums paid by banks. The Federal Home Loan Bank Board (FHLBB), which had been the rather ineffective regulator and insurer of the thrifts, was dissolved. The FHLBB's role as insurer was transferred to the FDIC; its regulatory role was given to a new agency, the Office of Thrift Supervision (OTS). For the remaining insolvents, a new Resolution Trust Corporation (RTC) was created; it would perform triage on the insolvents during the resolution process and, according to the White House, "complete the resolution or other disposition of all institutions and their assets over a period of five years."[15]

Bush's plan for saving the S&Ls involved no new taxes. But it created a massive layer of new federal regulatory agencies: this from a president who had both chaired a committee on deregulation as vice president and campaigned in favor of deregulation in 1988, and was facing criticism from the right wing of his party, which was sure to have a problem with his addition of a new layer to the federal government. And the expense was astronomical; the RTC itself required $50 billion in funding. Within only two weeks' time, the administration was forced to admit that the cost of the bailout would exceed $39.9 billion over the next ten years, and it announced that the federal government would soon have to spend an additional $24 billion to shut down all the S&Ls that the RTC would close in the 1990s. Brady informed Bush that more than 722 banks and 1,037 thrifts were in danger of closing; by summer, private projections given Bush for the bailout were exceeding $200 billion.[16] Moreover, it would take time. Seidman, the chair of both the RTC and the FDIC, claimed that if the RTC sold off $1 million of assets a day, it would take 300 years to sell them all.[17] Faced with a disaster of unprecedented proportions, Congress passed the Financial Institutions Reform, Recovery, and Enforcement Act in August 1989, but not before it had stripped Bush's original proposal of its bonding plan, thus requiring that the monies come straight from the Treasury. As a result, the bailout plan increased the deficit by $50 billion over three years.[18]

For Bush, the S&L crisis was not an abstract economic issue. Since 1985, Bush's son Neil had been an outside director of Denver's Silverado Savings and Loan. Silverado had issued bad loans to clients, among whom were Bush family friends and campaign donors who had invested in Neil's oil exploration company. These bad loans and many others had been responsible for Silverado's closing in the summer of 1988; the collapse of Silverado would, according to one reporter, end up costing taxpayers in the neighborhood of $1 billion. Although Neil's relationship with Silverado was not a major issue in the 1988 presidential campaign, his troubles became a national punch line when his father began the S&L bailout; at one point, Neil was called the "poster boy of bunko banking." But he fought back. In a 19 January 1990 press release, Neil was emphatic: "I have done nothing wrong. The regulators acknowledge that I did not violate any bank regulations, did not act dishonestly, did not derive any personal gain or benefit and did not cause any loss to the bank by my actions." Neil protested that he was being singled out for persecution because of his family lineage, and he refused to sign an agreement that would lead to his being banned from banking forever. Neil appeared before the House Banking Committee, and the OTS accused him of various conflicts of interest, but he was not charged with any crime. A civil suit brought against Bush and other Silverado officials by the FDIC was later settled out of court for $2.65 million.[19]

By the end of 1989, the talk around Washington had turned to the oncoming recession, with its resulting high prices and high unemployment. Constrained by a Federal Reserve System that continued to pursue a tight-money policy, the economy was starting to falter. Inflation was creeping up; by 1989 it had reached 5 percent, up from 4.8 percent in 1988, 3.7 percent in 1987, and 1.9 percent in 1986, the lowest rate in the decade.[20] Bush and Darman blamed the administration's economic woes on the Fed, which was, in the words of its chairman, Alan Greenspan, "supposedly" keeping the money supply too tight.[21] But the country was beginning to blame Bush, and the congressional Democrats, smelling blood, attempted to turn the situation to their advantage. They refused to meet with Bush to discuss the budget until he put forth his proposals for fiscal year 1991—the cycle that would see the deadline mandated by the Gramm-Rudman-Hollings act for sequester and a government shutdown if the budget was not significantly reduced.

The situation was made even more urgent by a grim reminder of how shaky the economy had become. On Friday, 13 October 1989, investors in the stock market finally reacted to the unstable economic climate. The Dow Jones Industrial Average plunged 190 points, its worst nosedive since 1987. The following Monday, the market recovered about half of its losses in heavy volume, as the Dow rose by 88.12 points, only to go down another 30 points the next day.[22]

Bush submitted his fiscal year 1991 budget to Congress on 29 January 1990, in the wake of the stock market crash. It called for total expenditures of $1.23 trillion—roughly the size of the entire West German economy. It also called for the reduction of the deficit to $64 billion, the target mandated by the Gramm-Rudman-Hollings Act. Bush proposed to accomplish this without cutting Social Security, with a 2.6 percent reduction in defense spending, and with a reduction in the capital gains tax. However, the administration had quietly included as potential income some $14 billion in "user's fees."[23] Though these fees were technically not taxes, it was clear that Bush was willing to consider some sort of income enhancement in order to get the budget closer to the deficit level required by law. On 11 March, Rostenkowski put forth his

Meeting on the budget, 6 May 1990. *Left to right*: John Sununu, Richard Darman, Sen. Robert Dole, Sen. George Mitchell, Rep. Robert Michel, Speaker Thomas Foley, Secretary of the Treasury Nicholas Brady, and Bush. (Courtesy of the George Bush Presidential Library and Museum)

promised counterproposal: a freeze on all cost-of-living increases in all spending categories, and a fifteen-cent-per-gallon tax hike on gasoline.[24] Talks droned on, and Bush seethed. To his diary on 4 May: "We need a deal. I'm willing to eat crow, but the others are going to have to eat crow. I'll have to yield on 'Read My Lips,' and they're going to have to yield on some of their rhetoric on taxes and entitlements."[25]

Two days later, Bush personally intervened in the negotiations. On 6 May the congressional principals in the budget negotiations—Speaker of the House Thomas Foley, House minority leader Robert Michel, Senate majority leader George Mitchell, and Senate minority leader Bob Dole—as well as Darman, Sununu, and Brady, attended a talk at the White House given by presidential historian David McCullough. At a prearranged time after the conclusion of the lecture, they quietly retired upstairs to the president's living quarters. The subject was the impasse on the budget. Darman tried to impress upon the group the problems that would be caused by a sequester. Mitchell asked Bush if he was prepared to negotiate on taxes; Bush said yes. Mitchell requested that Bush release a statement to that effect, and the president agreed. The White

House press release declared that the budget talks would begin "with no preconditions." Bush made this point even clearer after a 26 June meeting with the congressional leadership, when he agreed to the need for "tax revenue increases."[26]

In a 1998 interview, Bush was certainly correct when he told me that breaking his promise on taxes "played right into the hands of the opposition, as well as those critics" on the right in his own party.[27] Budget negotiations could now begin—Bush had broken the logjam. But he did so by reversing himself on a public promise, a flip-flop that was costly. The reaction was both immediate and hostile. On 5 July 1990, the *New York Post* ran the headline "Read My Lips: I Lied." Conservatives were furious, treating the announcement as the ultimate denial of Reaganism. When he was informed of the decision by Sununu, House majority whip Newt Gingrich angrily hung up on him.[28]

Thus, the Democrats actually entered the last phase of the budget negotiations with a stronger hand than if Bush had *not*, at least at that moment, backed off his no-new-taxes pledge. With the 1 October deadline—and, as important, the November congressional elections—fast approaching, the Democrats dug in. For the better part of two months, the negotiations dragged on with no movement on either side. Not surprisingly, it was Sununu who served as the administration's lightning rod. The day after the White House announced that a tax hike was on the table, the *Washington Post* reported that a "senior White House official traveling on a plane from Costa Rica to Washington"—Sununu—claimed that while Bush's announcement allowed for the Democrats to propose new tax increases, Bush would simply veto them.[29] Press secretary Marlin Fitzwater hastened to assure the press that there were no preconditions to any negotiations, and the congressional leadership wailed about the breach of trust. But none of this seemed to matter to Sununu. He reportedly threatened Republican members of Congress, hinting that Bush would campaign against fellow Republicans if they did not get into line. For example, after Trent Lott (R-MS) questioned the president's decision on taxes, only to be upbraided by the negotiating team, Sununu declared, "Trent Lott has become an insignificant figure in this process." Democrats privately referred to Bush's negotiating team as "Nick, Dick, and Prick."[30] Moreover, the rank and file of both parties were angry at the manner in which the deal was being negotiated; it smacked of a smoke-filled room, and they felt left out.

Clearly, Bush's decision to back off on his no-new-taxes pledge had gained him little. Observers of the process, the vast majority of whom disagree with Bush's decision, also disagree over what he *should* have done. Roger Porter, an assistant to the president for economic and domestic policy, believes that the "tax card was played far too quickly. It should only have been played after securing the entitlement and budget process reforms that were on the table."[31] For his part, Darman believed that had Bush moved *earlier*, he might well have been better able to deal with the inevitable political fallout. Darman suggests that the way that the release was worded hurt the administration's case. He concedes that "we allowed the president to make his biggest possible concession publicly without, at the same time, announcing a complete substantive compromise."[32] James Cicconi, then serving as White House staff secretary, believes that Bush should have let the Gramm-Rudman-Hollings mandatory sequester kick in, thus putting the burden on the Democratic Congress.[33] One thing is certain—the president of the United States had allowed himself to go into budget negotiations having already taken the full public blame for the new taxes. Richard N. Haass, a special adviser to Bush on Near East and South Asian affairs, put it succinctly: "[After the policy reversal], the president should have gone out and sold lemonade. He would have convinced at least some of the critics and earned points for being presidential. By not presenting the package himself, he let his critics put their face on the deal, which made him look weak and unprincipled."[34]

Then things changed. On 2 August 1990, Saddam Hussein invaded Kuwait. Over the next week, the budget negotiations ground to a halt, as Bush dealt with the crisis (see chapter 7). It is quite possible that this experience drove Bush to appeal to the public on the budget fight. On 6 August, Bush told Foley that he was "going to have to go forward and get out from behind the rock"—meaning that Bush was not going to put up any longer with the criticism from the Democrats, and he was going to hit back publicly. Foley warned Bush that using the bully pulpit on the budget might well "undermine [his] leadership in this important Iraq crisis."[35] Foley was right to be worried, as Bush's plan was to link the passage of the budget to patriotism in a time of impending war. He indicated his strategy in his diary on 7 September: "I just hope that Iraq and the country's unity can now be parlayed into support for the budget agreement."[36]

On 10 September, Bush spoke to the Congress regarding the 2 August invasion of Kuwait by Iraq, and the status of the American buildup in the region, by this point code-named Desert Shield. After reporting on the status of American forces in the Persian Gulf, Bush shifted gears, proclaiming that domestic policy was inexorably tied to foreign affairs—"a woven piece, strongly bound as Old Glory"—and declared, "We must address our budget deficit—not after election day, not next year, but *now.*" He continued, "The Gulf situation helps us realize that we are more economically vulnerable than we ever should be....It is high time we pull together and get the job done right....This is no time to risk America's ability to defend her vital interests." But Bush was to find that it would take more than an appeal to patriotism to break the impasse on the budget. Although this section of the speech was met with sporadic applause from the assembled legislators, close observers noticed that Foley, sitting behind Bush in the Speaker's chair, did not applaud once. It did not take Bush long to change tactics yet again. On 25 September, Bush told reporters that if there was no budget agreement "with real spending reduction and real process reform by the end of the week, I will have to veto it."[37] The next day, the summiteers presented Bush with a plan that Bush was quick to announce he could live with.

On 26 September, the budget summiteers gathered in the Rose Garden to announce the fruit of their labors. The proposed budget agreement would, they claimed, cut $119 billion from entitlement and mandatory programs and $182 billion from discretionary programs (taken primarily from defense, which would be reduced by $67 billion over three years). It also called for a cap on all discretionary spending and a "pay as you go" system that required new programs to be paid for at the time that they were initiated. But the plan also called for an increase in tax revenues of $134 billion; the largest portion would be raised by a phased-in increase in gasoline taxes, starting with a five-cent-per-gallon hike in the first year. Bush protested, "I do not welcome any such tax measure....However, this one does have the virtue not only of contributing to deficit reduction, but also, over time, of decreasing America's dependence on foreign oil—an objective whose importance has been made increasingly evident in the face of the Iraqi invasion of Kuwait." The next day, Bush signed a continuing resolution to keep the government going past 1 October, pending the passage of a budget resolution that reflected the summit agreement.

Bush would later write: "We did get a budget deal, one that included a tax increase but also accomplished my number one goal of getting spending under control."[38] Darman later pointed out that the tax increase called for in the 1990 budget agreement was less than one-half of Reagan's 1982 tax increase.[39] This was true enough, but it was hardly the point, because they would not get that deal from Congress. Liberals didn't like the program cuts; conservatives didn't like the tax hike. The conservatives jumped first. After promising Sununu in a phone call that while he "wasn't thrilled" with the deal he would nonetheless support it, Gingrich stunned his colleagues by refusing to come out to the Rose Garden and stand with the rest of the leadership when the agreement was announced to the press. He then began to actively construct a coalition against the package.[40] Embittered, Bush recalled in his memoirs: "Years later [Gingrich] told me that his decision was one of the most difficult he had made in his life. Maybe so, but it sure hurt me. His support could have eliminated the flak I took on the tax question and on my credibility."[41] Led by Gingrich, conservative Republicans flocked en masse to join House Democrats in opposing the measure. On 5 October, the Congress formally rejected the budget plan. The next day, the House passed a second continuing resolution, and Bush immediately vetoed it, telling the press: "Three dozen continuing resolutions—business as usual—and we can't have it."

It was five days past the 1 October deadline set by the Gramm-Rudman-Hollings Act, and Bush's veto kicked in the mandatory sequester. For three days the government was shut down. This affected mostly tourist attractions such as the national parks; the military buildup in the Persian Gulf was specifically exempted. Nevertheless, the public was furious, and it directed its anger—not entirely fairly, since the process was then in congressional hands—at the White House. Despite his promise to the contrary, on 9 October Bush signed a second continuing resolution, providing the funds for the government to operate through 19 October.

Over that two-week period, the star of the final act of this budget drama was Dan Rostenkowski, who had become sick and tired of trying to steer a middle course on the budget. Knowing he had Bush over a barrel, Rostenkowski proposed a completely new plan, one with a decidedly liberal slant, and one that he was now in a position to demand of the president. It called for jettisoning most of the gasoline tax provided for in the summit agreement and replacing it with a 10 percent tax hike for millionaires, and a hike in income taxes for the most wealthy Americans (from the 28 percent that had been set in 1986 to 31.5 percent). It also trimmed the cuts in Medicare and spending programs for the poor that had been part of the initial agreement.[42] Congress passed this budget—the Omnibus Budget Reconciliation Act of 1990—in late October. But even with these changes, the Gingrich-led conservatives were not placated; only one-quarter of the Republicans in both houses backed the measure.[43] Left with literally no choice, on 27 October Bush signed it.

Bush tried to put the best face on what had clearly been a defeat. He told the press, "It was a good plan. It got done what I wanted done, which was a $500 billion reduction over five years—real enforcement. Didn't get everything I wanted. Had to compromise." A White House Fact Sheet claimed that the "only thing that went right" in the process was Bush's determination to "hold the line." It noted that the $500 billion in deficit reduction included $355 billion in spending cuts—"the largest cut in history"—and that Congress "agree[d] to put itself on a pay-as-you-go plan, and reduce the rate of spending growth with the first five-year curb on spending *ever*." Most analysts have agreed with this assessment and have treated the 1990 budget deal quite kindly, noting most often that the pay-as-you-go provision kept deficits from rising to what would surely have been greater heights. Thus, they give the deal much of the credit for the budget surplus that, by 1998, the Clinton administration enjoyed.[44] But in fall 1990, the American people only knew that their taxes were being raised: despite the patriotic fervor that was enveloping the country as it geared up for war, they were about to take it out on Bush.

As the nation went to the polls in the off-year congressional elections of 1990, it faced the very real possibility of war in the Persian Gulf. That fall, however, it was the tax hike that mattered most to the voters. Ed Rollins, the cochair of the Republican National Committee, called the budget deal a "disaster" and counseled congressional candidates to "take the pledge" not to vote for higher taxes (writing in a memo, "do not hesitate to distance yourself from the President").[45] Bush was so incensed by this act of political treason that after the election, he had Rollins fired.[46] But the public needed little coaxing from Rollins, or anyone else, as they resisted the temptation to validate Bush's actions in the Persian Gulf and instead sent him a clear message on how they felt about higher taxes. The Republicans lost ten Senate seats, twenty-five House seats, and two governorships; in Georgia, Gingrich almost lost. Bush had targeted his own campaigning on sixty-two close races; thirty-five of those candidates lost.[47] It had been an experience that conservative Republicans would not forget.

6

★ ★ ★ ★ ★

"ENLIGHTENED REALISM" AND THE END OF THE COLD WAR

On 7 December 1988, Ronald Reagan and George Bush met with Soviet president Mikhail Gorbachev on Governor's Island in New York Harbor. The press, long smitten by Gorbachev's charm and media savvy, reported that the meeting was a pleasant one, with both the president and the president-elect assuring Gorbachev of their support for perestroika and glasnost.[1] But insider reports of the meeting point to far testier exchanges. In his memoirs, Bush writes that Gorbachev "genuinely flared up when Reagan innocently asked him about progress in reform and perestroika" and responded, "Have *you* completed all the reforms you need to complete?"[2] Michael Beschloss and Strobe Talbott, in their book on the relationship between the United States and the Soviet Union between 1989 and 1991, paint the same story of conflict, but between different combatants. According to their version, it was Bush who became defensive during the meeting, demanding of Gorbachev, "What assurance can you give me that perestroika and glasnost will succeed?" Gorbachev snapped in response, "Not even Jesus Christ knows the answer to that question!" Then Gorbachev lectured the president-elect: "You'll see soon enough that I'm *not* doing this for show....I'm engaged in real politics....It's going to be a revolution nonetheless....Don't misread me, Mr. Vice President."[3]

Gorbachev was a bit calmer when Henry Kissinger met with him at the Kremlin on 17 January 1989—three days before Bush's inauguration.

Kissinger's memo to Bush claims that Gorbachev "eagerly welcomed a confidential dialogue with the new administration." When he was about to leave, Kissinger observed that Gorbachev "grew pensive. He said, 'I lead a strange country. I am trying to take my people in a direction they do not understand and many do not want to go. . . . But one thing is sure—whatever happens to perestroika this country will never be the same again." Kissinger's conclusion: "In my view Gorbachev is treading water with perestroika. He is looking to foreign policy as a way out. He will pay a reasonable price to that end."[4]

Students of American foreign policy tend to place presidents into one of two diametrically opposed philosophical camps. Those who are called idealists support the active spread of democracy wherever they feel it to be wanting, and this belief is often accompanied by more than a dab of hyperpatriotism. Convinced in the righteousness of their cause, idealists are normally evangelists for their policies and are notoriously inflexible in their demands—of other nations, of Congress, and of themselves—as they attempt to make the world, in the oft-quoted phrase of the quintessential idealist, Woodrow Wilson, "safe for democracy." For the majority of his administration, Ronald Reagan behaved decidedly as an idealist as he applied economic, covert, and public pressure to hasten the end of the "evil empire" of the Soviet Union ("Mr. Gorbachev: Tear down this wall"). In the other camp are those who call themselves realists. To them, the ideological rigidity of the idealists leads to their undoing; the calling card of the realist is flexibility in a world of active power sharing. More so than the idealists, realists are willing to compromise, deal, and broker. Most scholars treat Richard Nixon and Henry Kissinger—and less so, but including, Gerald Ford—as the quintessential modern-day realists, constructing a flexible détente with the Soviet Union that was brokered through largely secret negotiations. It has also been noted that Reagan shifted in his last two years from a rigid idealism to a more fluid realism, as he began his courtship of Mikhail Gorbachev in the hopes of ending the nuclear arms race, thus ending the Cold War.

George Bush had been tutored by both the realists and the idealists. He had apprenticed at Richard Nixon and Gerald Ford's training table for realists—at the UN he had seen how the administration shifted American policy away from Taiwan and toward the People's Republic of China (PRC); as envoy to the PRC he had seen how the Ford administration had continued that policy, and as head of Ford's CIA he had seen, and been a player in, practical realism on a full-world scale. He then watched as Ronald Reagan crafted a foreign policy, most notably in Latin America, based on a nostalgic patriotism that blinded the administration to any alternative course of action, and continued to watch as Reagan shifted to a realist as he moved his policy toward a new détente with the Soviet Union.

It was this background, mixed in the tradition of Wilsonian idealism and Nixon-Ford realism, that shaped George Bush into an infinitely more complex practitioner of diplomacy than any of his postwar predecessors. In his foreign policy, Bush showed signs of being a consummate realist, as he looked for balance, shaped coalitions out of erstwhile enemies, and negotiated with the skill of a power poker player, having more success in this regard than many of his predecessors—and none of his successors. And yet there are signs of the evangelist in the diplomacy of George Bush as well. His experience in World War II, forged in battle, led to a belief that tyrants must be eradicated from the face of the earth; this led to policies that were driven by a zeal that often smacked of righteousness.

Few, if any, serious students of the Bush presidency would agree with Richard Clarke, who assessed Bush's foreign policy as one that "looked for the simple solution, the bumper-sticker description of the problem."[5] Even a surface study of Bush's foreign policy shows a vibrant decision-making process, joined with well-thought-out goals and strategies on the world stage. Nevertheless, to date, few scholars have given Bush the credit he clearly deserves for the complexity of his philosophy. Most tend to settle for calling him—as they do secretary of state James A. Baker III and national security adviser Brent Scowcroft—a realist, pointing to Bush's successful brokerage of the end of communism in Eastern Europe and the reunification of East and West Germany, then to his creation of the international coalition that won the Gulf War.[6] Indeed, political scientist Jeffrey Engel has taken this one step further and labeled Bush's foreign policy an example of "hypochondriac realism."[7] Political scientist Stephen Skowronek calls Bush an "orthodox innovator."[8] Few, if any, have spent appreciable time looking at the evangelistic fervor that fired Bush, and even fewer have explored how this mixed philosophical background may have turned Bush into a unique twentieth-century diplomat. However, Brent Scowcroft recognized this mix in his boss's thinking and dubbed it "enlightened realism."[9] This label will do as well as any other moniker.[10]

It was this foreign policy view of enlightened realism that was necessary in the waning years of the Cold War. The realism of the Nixon-Ford years, and its détente, had offered a paradigm for improved relations. But with the implosion of the Soviet economy, a window of opportunity presented itself for destroying communism in Europe. It was Ronald Reagan's idealism that pushed the Soviet Union and its satellites until they were ready to break. Break they did in 1989. Recognizing that this breakup could bring with it unprecedented violence and reprisals, George Bush backed off from Reagan's rigid idealism, replacing it with a more flexible response to events. It was this type of foreign policy that was needed to guide the end of the Cold War to a peaceful conclusion.

Much was expected of George Bush in foreign policy. He was, after all, the "résumé candidate" who had represented the United States in China, headed the CIA, and traveled the world as vice president. A *New York Times*–CBS poll taken immediately after the 1988 election showed that 82 percent of those asked believed that Bush would be able to improve relations with the Soviet Union. And by 1989 those relations were already significantly warmer. Reagan had come to office as the proverbial idealistic lion, proclaiming the evils of the Soviet Union and demanding an arms buildup; he was leaving office a comparative lamb, working toward détente with Gorbachev and having achieved a treaty banning intermediate-range nuclear missiles. Many members of the press observed that Reagan's legacy as a peacemaker was assured; most assumed that Bush would continue his predecessor's courtship of Gorbachev.

In his memoirs, Bush claims that the day after the Governor's Island meeting, he told Brent Scowcroft that he "wanted to come up with something dramatic to move the relationship with Moscow forward."[11] But this did not mean that Bush would be rushed into making that move public. He had agreed with little of Reagan's foreign policy, and he was nowhere near as smitten with Gorbachev as had been his predecessor. He had opposed both Reagan's hard-line position toward the Soviets during his first term and his abrupt about-face toward Gorbachev and acceptance of disarmament in the second term. Unquestionably, Bush would have to deal with the Soviets. Yet in an effort to avoid making a blunder from which he could not recover—or to avoid backing a Soviet leader whose radical ideas might any day cause his downfall—Bush initially chose, in the words of Beschloss and Talbott, "to apply the brakes to the Soviet-American relationship, pull over to the side of the road, and study the map for a while."[12] The centerpiece of this strategy was an internal policy review that was not fully completed until the Malta

Summit of December 1989. Bush explained it in a letter to Gorbachev, sent a week before his inauguration:

> My new national security team and I will need time to reflect on the range of issues—particularly those relating to arms control—central to our bilateral relationship, and to formulate our own thoughts on how best to move that relationship forward. Our purpose is to assure a sound and coherent American approach; it is in no way an attempt to delay or reverse the positive progress that has marked the past year or two.[13]

This put the brakes on Reagan's new détente; the Soviets derisively called it the *pauza*—the pause. For Jack Matlock, then the American ambassador to the Soviet Union, "Our marching orders are clear: Don't do something, *stand there!*"[14]

In his desire for a cooling-off period with the Soviets, Bush had the support of his closest foreign policy advisers. In a 1997 interview, James Baker protested that "my political experience pretty much ended" after his service as Reagan's chief of staff, but this view is somewhat disingenuous.[15] Self-described as "more of a man of action than reflection," and once quoted as saying "I'm more interested in the game than in philosophy," Baker kept Bush's political future in mind throughout his tenure.[16] Baker knew that Bush could ill afford to be seen as being "soft" toward the Soviet Union and still hope to keep the support of his party's right wing; its members had already criticized Reagan for his policy of détente with Gorbachev. Moreover, Baker thought that Reagan and George Shultz, his secretary of state, had given too much away in their negotiations; waiting out Gorbachev would bring a better deal.[17] In this view Baker was joined by his deputy, Lawrence Eagleburger, who became an important administration envoy to the Middle East.

Bush's national security team also agreed with the *pauza*, although on the whole they were more pessimistic about its chances for success than was the State Department. As noted in chapter 3, Brent Scowcroft, the administration's national security adviser, had long established himself as an opponent of Reagan's foreign policy. He remembered in a 1997 interview that the Reagan administration had gone "from a posture of extreme hostility . . . to the point that they were virtually declaring by 1988 that the Cold War was over. . . . [But] the fundamentals hadn't gone near as far as the rhetoric."[18] In his memoirs, Scowcroft implied that the *pauza* was the "bold move" that Bush was looking for.[19]

Yet Scowcroft also saw it as an opportunity to plan a strategy that would entail a harsher line toward Moscow. He was supported in this view by secretary of defense Richard Cheney, chief of staff John Sununu, and Robert Gates, Scowcroft's deputy at the National Security Council and his representative on the Deputies Committee, who was even more anti-Gorbachev than was his boss.[20] Thanks largely to this unanimity of approach, there was little of the infighting that had so typified Reagan's national security team. Baker's later assessment—that Bush "made the national security apparatus work the way it was supposed to work"—is an accurate one.[21]

In a speech delivered in 1997, Gorbachev claimed that he was "surprised" at the initiation of the *pauza*. If that was indeed the case, he should not have been, given the combative tone of his exchange with Bush on Governor's Island. Nevertheless, Gorbachev remembered that he expressed his concern about the situation to British prime minister Margaret Thatcher "in rather stark terms," and his concern found its way to the White House.[22] Gorbachev tried to push the United States back toward Reagan's détente by unilaterally cutting his missile stockpile and making large cuts in his defense spending.[23] But Bush and his advisers suspected that these moves were as much a result of the pressure caused by the imploding Soviet economy as of Gorbachev's desire to continue warm relations with the United States. Bush believed that as the Soviet Union continued toward internal weakness, the United States could negotiate from strength. There was, in his mind, no need to be rushed.

However, the go-slow policy was fraught with dangers of its own. With no great foreign policy statements coming from the White House, Bush opened himself up to further criticisms of his lack of "vision" (an editorial in the *New York Times*: "The leader of the free world can become a leader of the whole planet; but he has to try").[24] He also had to endure the stories in the press that lauded Gorbachev's personal popularity (again, the *New York Times*: "Imagine that an alien spaceship approached the Earth and sent this message: 'Take me to your Leader.' Who would that be? Without doubt, Mikhail Sergeyevich Gorbachev").[25] Moreover, he was under pressure from both his Western allies, particularly Thatcher, and the right wing of his own party, to use this moment of weakness and instability in the Soviet Union to press Gorbachev for concessions that he might not otherwise have been willing to make.

On 14 March 1989, Bush's advisers sent him the report of their deliberations during the *pauza*. It was, in the words of one student of Bush's foreign policy, a "big picture document" that did not give any specific initiatives and took no discernible stand as to whether or not Gorbachev would succeed or fail.[26] This frustrated Bush, who had hoped for a paper that would give his administration immediate direction in terms of his relationship with the USSR. Therefore, it was gently discarded. It was mid-1989, and Bush still did not have a plan.

Bush must have had this in mind as he prepared for the commencement speech at Texas A&M University on 12 May. Billed as his first major statement on foreign policy, the speech was a particularly important one for Bush; in his markup of the seventh draft, he referred to the quotable author of phrases like "a thousand points of light" and "read my lips" when he wrote, "I think we need a Noonanism or two more. Perhaps we can salute the Soviet people a little." Then he added the line, "I stand ready to hold out my hand, our hands, to the people of the Soviet Union."[27] But it was another phrase, already in the draft, that members of the press latched onto when they heard the speech: "Containment worked. And now it is time to move *beyond containment* to a new policy for the 1990s." While warning that America's foreign policy "must be based on deeds," he nevertheless articulated what he called a "sweeping vision" of the Soviet Union—with drastically cut troop strength in Europe, serious economic and political reforms, and a commitment to human rights—as a part of the world community of nations. In an attempt to demonstrate his seriousness, Bush floated a plan he called "Open Skies." First suggested by Dwight Eisenhower in 1955, it called for both the Soviet Union and the United States to allow each other the freedom to fly over the other's territory to observe defense capabilities. Scowcroft remembered that the Open Skies proposal "smacked of gimmickry"; Bush, more accurately, observed that it was a "no-lose proposition from our side. Gorbachev, committed to glasnost, would find it hard from a public-relations standpoint to reject it."[28]

Bush took another small step toward Gorbachev during the fortieth anniversary meeting of the North Atlantic Treaty Alliance (NATO), held on 28 May in Brussels. Since March, Bush had been considering a Scowcroft recommendation designed to counter Gorbachev's announcement at the United Nations of significant Soviet troop withdrawals: the unilateral withdrawal of U.S. and Soviet ground forces in Europe. As the recommendation was staffed out, it was scaled down. Cheney was leery of the proposal, and Baker recommended initially limiting such cuts to the removal of weaponry rather than troops. At the summit, Bush proposed that both the Warsaw Pact and NATO limit their conventional ground forces to about 275,000 for each side, a total cut in combat manpower for NATO of some 350,000 men. Perhaps more important was Bush's use of the word "partnership" in describing the relationship.[29] As a result, Bush unnerved many of his European allies, particularly hardline cold warrior Margaret Thatcher, prime minister of Great Britain. Bush later remembered that at the summit Thatcher was "a little tense. [She] kept telling me not to negotiate. . . . 'We must not give in on this,' and 'You're not going to give, are you?' she asked me plaintively over and over again."[30]

Bush was moving forward, but at his own pace. However, world events conspired in a way that forced him to move much more quickly. Bush was better prepared for the intrigue that underlay policy with the PRC than had been any president since Richard Nixon. While serving as the American envoy to the PRC, Bush had come to know Deng Xiaoping, then serving as the first vice premier. They had visited each other several times since then; Deng even made a pilgrimage to Houston in 1979. James Lilley, who became the American ambassador to the PRC in April 1989, remembered that "both [Bush and Deng were] practical men . . . down to earth . . . human beings who enjoyed each other."[31] In 1989 Deng was the premier of the PRC; Bush believed him to be a man with whom he could deal.

When he came to office, one of Bush's priorities was to strengthen U.S.-PRC relations. The rapidly Westernizing nation was now exporting everything from students to electronics, and Bush wanted America's share. As a result, Bush pursued a policy that treated the PRC as a more important partner than either Japan or Taiwan—a policy that fed the nervousness of his European allies and angered Republican conservatives who had sworn protection of Taiwan throughout the Cold War.[32] Bush traveled to the PRC in March 1989, but Lilley remembered that the trip was "quite negative. . . . [Bush] was quite disappointed." A large measure of his disappointment resulted from the case of Fang Li Zhi, a noted dissident who was hated by the Chinese leadership, particularly by Deng. Fang had been invited to the banquet held for Bush, but the Chinese leadership announced that they would not attend if Fang did. When Fang arrived, guards stopped him, and the leadership did not come in until they were sure that Fang had left the building. Recognizing that his life was clearly in danger, Fang asked for and received refugee status in the American embassy.[33] The situation did not stop Bush from approving a one-year extension of most favored nation (MFN) status for the PRC.[34]

Nevertheless, the episode involving Fang clearly indicated how worried the Chinese were over the burgeoning dissident movement in their country. Made up mostly of students, the Chinese reformers wished to be freed from the yoke of communist rule. Their anger peaked on 15 April 1989 with the death of Hu Yaobang, a former general secretary of the Communist Party who had been sympathetic to the dissidents. In a mass outpouring of grief, thousands of students occupied Tiananmen Square, in the heart of Beijing's government district. On 26 April, Deng delivered an address, branding the students as "counterrevolutionary." His words only inflamed the situation; in full view of the world press, hundreds of students began a hunger strike.[35]

One explanation of the timing of the protests is that Gorbachev's promise of perestroika and glasnost had inadvertently opened a window for the Chinese opposition.[36] On 15 May, Gorbachev arrived in China on a state visit; because of the large number of students, his welcome had to be changed from the Great Hall of the People to the Beijing airport. By late that night, students all over China were out on strike, rallying and demanding democracy. The next day, hundreds of thousands of students marched in Tiananmen Square, carrying Gorbachev's picture and shouting their support for perestroika. Gorbachev's wreath-laying ceremony at the Monument to the People's Heroes had to be postponed because of the student unrest. By 17 May, the crowd in Tiananmen Square was well in excess of 100,000; by that afternoon, the American embassy estimated that "as many as a million people marched and gathered in Beijing."[37] As he was being driven around the streets to a meeting with Deng, Gorbachev saw the turbulence in the streets and muttered, "Who the hell is in charge here?"[38]

After Gorbachev left for Shanghai on 18 May, the students stayed in Tiananmen Square; indeed, they erected a plaster "Goddess of Liberty" statue right in front of the portrait of Mao Zedong hanging above the entrance to the Forbidden City.[39] The next day, the government declared martial law to deal with the situation. In the last days of May, the American embassy either deluded itself or misunderstood the situation, as it cabled the White House on 26 May that "the possibility of violence is remote," and the next day that "everyone is convinced that the PLA [the People's Liberation Army; the Chinese military] cannot and will not move against the demonstrators."[40] The embassy was wrong. On 4 June the PLA answered Gorbachev's question, as it moved in to clear the square, emptying their submachine guns on those who refused to move. In the ensuing bloodshed, some 3,000 protesters were killed and 10,000 more were wounded. Broadcast live on television, the picture of a single student dissident, standing with an upraised hand in front of an oncoming PRC tank, became a worldwide symbol of nationalist resistance.[41]

Baker remembered that "in considering our response to the massacre, there was simply no dispute that we had to strike a delicate balance between the need for decisive steps and the need to safeguard the underlying strategic relationship to the fullest extent possible."[42] The Chinese did not help much; their parading of arrested students, with shaved heads, in front of a kangaroo court only inflamed world opinion. Perhaps more important, as Lilley remembered, was that after the massacre, the Chinese had cut off communication with the United States: "When the Chinese get into a situation like this, they don't talk to you....They hunkered down."[43]

The former liaison to the PRC agonized over Tiananmen. Three days after the massacre, Baker met with Han Xu, the PRC ambassador to the United States. Baker's notes show that he communicated the president's distress to the Chinese: "You know the president. He's distressed. No intent to interfere in internal affairs. But the carnage overwhelming [sic]. Terrible things have happened. Pres.[ident] had to speak out. Strong reaction from other democratic countries. Trying to hold this relationship together, Enormous pressure on him."[44] Scowcroft later remembered that Bush was "determined that a single incident, no matter how horrible," would not destroy the relationship between the two nations.[45] To do so, Bush told his advisers that "we must walk our way through this."[46] As he walked, Bush mixed sanction with appeasement. On 5 June Bush ordered the suspension of all government-to-government sales and commercial exports of weapons, a suspension of visits between Chinese and U.S. military leaders, a "sympathetic review" of requests by Chinese students in the United States to extend their stay, the offer of humanitarian aid to China, and "a review of other aspects of our bilateral relationship as events in China continue to unfold." Bush also cut off the military relationship between the two nations and delayed loans to the PRC from the World Bank.[47] But he also kept the lines of communication open with Deng. In a 20 June letter to the chairman, Bush wrote "in a spirit of genuine friendship" and requested clemency for the student leaders, noting that "the clamor for stronger action [on the part of the United States] is intense. I have resisted that clamor, making clear that I did not want to see destroyed this relationship that you and I have worked hard to build."[48] The next day, Bush wrote to "Dear Chairman Deng, Dear Friend" regarding the chairman's anger with Bush's suspension of military sales and contracts to China: "Please do not be angry with me if I have crossed the invisible threshold lying between constructive suggestion and internal interference."[49]

Bush's deference was designed to sprinkle water on the fire; in his memoirs, he wrote that "while angry rhetoric might be temporarily satisfying to some, I believed it would deeply hurt our efforts in the long run."[50] But he did not sit idly by and hope that the Chinese would take the bait. Bush turned to a time-tested tool of the realist—secret diplomacy. On 30 June Scowcroft and assistant secretary of state Lawrence Eagleburger were dispatched on a secret trip to Beijing. The reason for the trip, as Baker remembered, was that "the Chinese had to be made to realize...that progress was impossible until they ceased their repression."[51] As Eagleburger later told Baker, "They never said so directly, but I think the smarter ones absorbed the message that we can do a lot more for them when they aren't killing their own people."[52] The following December, Scowcroft and Eagleburger returned to Beijing. In a dinner toast, Scowcroft referred to the "negative forces" in both countries that "seek to frustrate our cooperation."[53] Scowcroft later remembered that he "made a mess of it"—largely because the Cable News Network (CNN) taped the toast, and the moment it was played back on the national news it became instant ammunition for administration critics.[54]

But no one saw these secret negotiations, and Bush was pilloried for placating the Chinese. Many of Bush's critics thought that he was so afraid of losing Chinese trade that he was being callous toward the memory of the Tiananmen martyrs. A. M. Rosenthal of the *New York Times*, one of Bush's severest critics in the press, grumbled that "at a moment of passion in the story of democracy, [Bush] has been pale and thin."[55] Soviet dissident Andrei Sakharov chided Bush in a letter: "This is the very case where a normal, careful, and pragmatic attitude is out of place. The responsibility is with you."[56]

Bush also had congressional critics. He ignored Representative Olympia Snowe (R-ME), who had asked for consideration of a period of mourning, by sending her a form letter.[57] But other voices, more prominent, were impossible to avoid. He recorded in his diary: "[Representative Stephen] Solarz [D-NY] on the left and [Senator Jesse] Helms on the right want to move much more radically. Helms has always detested this relationship."⁵⁸ On 28 June the House voted 418 to 0 to impose additional sanctions against the PRC. In November 1989, Representative Nancy Pelosi introduced legislation that would protect Chinese students in the United States from deportation after the expiration of their visas. The bill passed 403 to 0 in the House and without a recorded vote in the Senate. On 30 November, Bush pocket vetoed the bill, saying that he would take care of the problem administratively. A furious House of Representatives overrode Bush's veto on 24 January 1990, 390 to 25, but the next day the Senate sustained the veto, by a vote of 62 to 37—five votes short of the two-thirds needed to override.⁵⁹

Bush absorbed the criticism and continued with his strategy of private pressure on the Chinese sprinkled with a small amount of public approval. Despite Eagleburger and Scowcroft's shuttle diplomacy, the Chinese were still obstinate about releasing the dissidents from their prisons. But Bush still held several financial trump cards. By 1990 Bush had informed the Chinese through diplomatic back channels that he would not extend MFN status to them unless they gave him something in return. The Japanese also threatened to withhold a loan package unless the Chinese improved their relationship with the United States. Both moves worked; the Chinese privately promised that their position would soon be moderated. On 24 May 1990, Bush extended China's MFN status. Soon after, the Chinese started to release dissidents from their prisons.⁶⁰

Despite the horrific loss of life, Bush was not willing to rub the noses of the Chinese in the ashes of Tiananmen. He had allowed the Chinese to save face, and although it had taken a year, the relationship between the two nations creaked back toward normalcy. By 1991 the dissidents were freed, the loans were flowing, and there had even been a new initiative toward mutual scientific and technological development. By the end of 1989, Bush was faced with the same dilemma, but this time in eastern Europe. As communism imploded in the lands behind the Iron Curtain, Bush's post-*pauza* attitude of a world "beyond containment" would face a key test—like Deng, would Gorbachev respond with violence as he faced, one by one, the loss of Soviet satellites?

Mikhail Gorbachev was frank as he spoke to the Soviet Politburo on the day that that body nominated him to be the general secretary of the Communist Party: "We can't go on like this."⁶¹ Gorbachev was referring to the deteriorating condition of life in the Soviet Union, which by 1988 had hit crisis proportions. The Soviet economy was dropping like a stone, worker morale was down and alcoholism was up, and there was a reported rise in corruption within the Communist Party.[62] Many observers give Ronald Reagan the credit for this development; they argue that his massive defense expenditures were designed, at least in part, so that the Soviets would have to try to keep up—in other words, that Reagan was trying to spend them into oblivion.[63] But as Reagan left office, Gorbachev doubled down. Before the UN General Assembly on 7 December 1988, Gorbachev announced what many interpreted as a form of economic cutback—a unilateral cut of 500,000 troops in the Soviet armed forces,[64] a decision that caught the U.S. off guard.[65]

The Soviet bear was clearly wounded, and the wounded bear was being challenged by its satellites. As George Bush took the presidency, several Warsaw Pact nations were striking back at their Soviet patron. What followed would be a test of the Brezhnev Doctrine—that 1968 pronouncement that made it clear that if a leader of a communist satellite was under fire, Moscow was pledged to come to its aid. With the Soviet Union on the economic ropes, it was anyone's guess how Gorbachev would react to the freedom movements now bubbling to the fore in his satellites, and everyone's fear was that he would react as the Chinese had reacted in Tiananmen Square.

Poland led the way. In 1981 there had been a series of violent clashes between the Polish government and nationalist dissidents. But by 1989, thanks in equal measure to the bravery of Lech Wałęsa, the leader of Solidarity (the first independent trade union in the Soviet bloc), the election of John Paul II as the first pope of Polish origin, and the agreement of the communist leader, General Wojciech Jaruzelski, to lift the official ban on Solidarity, the situation had greatly improved.[66] Taking advantage of the situation, the Bush administration set up roundtable talks between Jaruzelski and Solidarity. On 6 April 1989, the two groups agreed to open and free parliamentary elections, a new second house in the parliament (the Senate), the election of a state president who could nominate a prime minister, and the relegalization of Solidarity.[67] Bush called the agreement a "watershed" and announced a package of trade and financial aid for Poland.[68] On 4 June—the same day as the massacre in Tiananmen Square—the promised parliamentary elections were held. In the lower house, Solidarity took every seat it contested; in the upper house, even though the Communist Party kept a majority that was mandated by law, Solidarity won all but one of the seats it contested.[69] In the wake of Solidarity's successes, Hungary creaked its door open toward freedom. On 16 June 1989, Hungarian rebels reburied Imre Nagy, who had led the unsuccessful 1958 rebellion against the Soviet Union, and whom Nikita Khrushchev had ordered executed. Some 100,000 people attended the reinternment.[70] The symbolism of these events was apparent to all. Poland had voted against its communist leadership, and Hungary had thumbed its nose at Moscow.

To a gathering of scholars in 1997, Scowcroft put it bluntly: "We supported any satellite that . . . made it difficult for the Russians."[71] In July 1989, on his way to economic talks in Paris, Bush scheduled a trip to Poland. He made it clear to his speechwriters that he would not be giving a "victory speech."[72] Far from it. Indeed, Bush stopped in Warsaw and personally persuaded Jaruzelski to run for the presidency. As Bush remembered, "It was ironic: here was an American president trying to persuade a senior communist leader to run for office. But I felt that Jaruzelski's experience was the best hope for a smooth transition in Poland."[73] Jaruzelski was easier for Bush to accept, since he was also Solidarity's choice for the presidency, Wałęsa being ineligible to seek the office. Jaruzelski would win the election but ultimately was unable to form a government.[74] Bush then went to Gdansk to meet with Wałęsa, who asked for a massive aid package totaling some $10 billion, but Bush promised only $100 million. Thanks to the budget deficit at home, Bush simply could not afford the kind of money that Wałęsa was requesting. But according to one close student of the situation, there was more: Bush "was suspicious of Wałęsa. . . . He tended to view [him] as someone who could cause more trouble than his reforms were worth, possibly by provoking the Kremlin."[75] After his trip to Poland, Bush stopped in Hungary—the first American president to visit that nation. After a moving gesture at the Budapest airport, where Bush gave his coat to a woman in the rain-soaked crowd, Bush spoke at that city's Karl Marx University. There, along with promising that nation a package of American aid, he made it clear where his sympathies lay: "For the first time the Iron Curtain has begun to part. And Hungary, your great country, is leading the way."[76]

Changes in Poland and Hungary were contemporaneous with upheaval within the Soviet Union itself. Several of the Soviet republics had witnessed nationalistic uprisings, and unlike the movements in Poland and Hungary, where Gorbachev had essentially turned a deaf ear, each of the movements in the Baltic States had been met with Soviet military force. In April, at the request of the government of the Republic of Georgia, Soviet troops used spades and gas against a nationalist rally in the city of Tbilisi; twenty-one Georgian civilians were killed.[77] Nevertheless, on 18 May 1989, Estonia reaffirmed its declaration of independence from the Soviet Union. Lithuania declared its own independence on the same day; Latvia followed suit on 18 August. These Baltic states demonstrated their resolve—the "Baltic Way"—with an unbroken human chain that went through the capitals of the three nations; it represented a turnout of some 40 percent of the total population of those three states.[78]

The rumblings for reform soon made their way to Russia, the largest Soviet republic. The centerpiece of that fervor was Boris Yeltsin, then a member of the Soviet Parliament but, in perhaps the greatest irony of glasnost, already a formidable critic of Gorbachev's policies, and soon to be the most important agent of Gorbachev's undoing. Bush's desire not to provoke Gorbachev necessitated that the administration ignore Yeltsin, relegating the 12 September 1989 visit of the Russian leader to second-class status. Brought to the side entrance of the White House instead of the front, where diplomats are usually met, and told by NSC staffer Condoleezza Rice that he had a meeting with Scowcroft and not with the president, Yeltsin threw a fit ("I am not used to this kind of treatment! I am an important man in my country! I can see the general secretary any time I want!" Offered a visitor tag, Yeltsin refused, muttering, "I am Yeltsin"). Rice finally convinced Yeltsin that it was Scowcroft or nothing. Yeltsin begrudgingly agreed. He went to Scowcroft's office, where the two men had a brief discussion. In the midst of that discussion, Bush dropped in unannounced. He and Yeltsin exchanged pleasantries, and sixteen minutes later, Bush left. However, when he met the press afterward, Yeltsin boasted that he had presented a "Ten Point Plan" to Bush to "rescue perestroika." Bush and Scowcroft were furious with Yeltsin's grandstanding; Scowcroft called him a "two-bit headline grabber"; Baker's reaction after meeting him later that day: "What a flake!"[79]

Yeltsin may well have been a flake, but it was Gorbachev who had the power to react to the upheavals in the republics with violence. As troublesome for the United States was what might happen if Gorbachev did *not* attempt to quash the freedom movements—his hard-line military advisers might interpret such a policy as soft, thus throwing the Soviet Union into a coup-induced chaos. Bush believed that the time had come to meet with Gorbachev.[80] On 21 July 1989, flying back from his visit to Poland and Hungary, Bush penned a note to Gorbachev, proposing that the two men "sit down soon and talk . . . without thousands of assistants hovering over our shoulders."[81] Gorbachev quickly agreed, and after some wrangling over time and place, they agreed to hold the

121

summit in December 1989 at a neutral site, the island of Malta, located fifty miles south of Sicily in the Mediterranean Sea.[82] Immediately trying to downplay expectations, the White House began to refer to the upcoming meeting as the "little summit."

But the forces of history would not wait for a summit. In early October, coinciding with the fortieth anniversary of East Germany's (formally the German Democratic Republic) endorsement of communism, thousands of demonstrators took to the streets of East Berlin and began to flood embassies with demands for asylum. Thousands more attempted to leave the country for Poland, Czechoslovakia, or Hungary, where they were already permitted to travel freely. But the decision by the government to seal off its borders only caused more rioting. The East German government of Erich Honecker—who in 1961 had supervised the building of the Berlin Wall—was one of the most reactionary in the Soviet sphere, and he was defended by Kremlin hard-liners, who pressed Gorbachev to step in and save East Germany.

Gorbachev would not. During a 7 October visit to East Germany, Gorbachev shocked many observers—and further angered his own cold warriors—by announcing that policy for East Germany was made "not in Moscow, but in Berlin." Gorbachev had written off Honecker, effectively sealing the doom of communism in East Germany.[83] On 18 October, Honecker resigned and was replaced by Egon Krenz, then Honecker's deputy on the Council of State. Gorbachev reacted to Honecker's resignation by announcing that the Soviet Union had "no right to interfere" in Eastern European affairs.[84] The Brezhnev Doctrine had been repudiated; Soviet satellites had been told that they could now expect to fend for themselves. It was the end of the Cold War.

Without Soviet support, Krenz fared little better than his predecessor; on 7 November his entire cabinet quit. Two days later, the Krenz government threw its hands into the air, announcing its intent to end its travel ban and to open East Germany's borders in the near future.[85] But the promise was no longer enough; it took only a few minutes from the time of the government's announcement for a crowd of East Berliners to gather at the Berlin Wall and demand that the guards open the gates to the West. The crowds quickly grew in both size and volume, with many people climbing on the wall and openly taunting the guards at the gates, who had been given no orders on how to deal with the situation. As night fell, the guards made the only decision they could make—at 10:30 p.m. they opened the gates. The crowds rushed madly into West

Berlin, many of them singing "We Shall Overcome," and the Krenz government released an "order" that effectively affirmed the decision made by the guards. Within days, the world saw pictures of German youths scaling the wall, chipping off pieces for souvenirs and East Germany had announced that it was relaxing its border-control policy with West Germany (formally known as the Federal Republic of Germany).[86]

The opening of the Berlin Wall set loose the freedom movements in the Warsaw Pact satellites. In early December the communist governments in Yugoslavia and Bulgaria fell. In Czechoslovakia, poet Václav Havel succeeded Gustav Husak, one of the most entrenched of the communist leaders. These seismic events were largely peaceful and were quickly dubbed the "Velvet Revolution." The one exception was in Romania, where hard-line communist Nicolae Ceauşescu, who had publicly praised the Chinese for their actions at Tiananmen, was executed by a firing squad on Christmas Day. Virtually all of Eastern Europe was now free of Soviet control. And in all cases, Gorbachev had done little to nothing to stop it.

Why did Gorbachev refuse to intercede? Historian Vladislav M. Zubok attributed it to Gorbachev's "deep aversion to the use of force," stemming from the bloody crushing of the Czechoslovak revolt in 1968—Gorbachev and other like-minded reformers resolved after that debacle that they would never send Soviet troops to defend a satellite nation, and no blood would ever be on their hands.[87] Bush's diary entry the day after the fall of the Berlin Wall supports this view: "We got a message from Gorbachev yesterday urging that we not overreact. He worries about demonstrations in Germany that might get out of control, and he asked for understanding."[88] There were other minds besides Gorbachev's thinking this way. In September 1989, Baker invited Soviet foreign minister Eduard Shevardnadze to his vacation home in Jackson Hole, Wyoming. On the flight there, Shevardnadze mused on the East German situation: "It is not up to us to solve this problem; it is up to them. If I were in their shoes, I'd let everyone who wants to go, leave."[89]

But it was Gorbachev's decision, and in his 1995 memoir, he puts a decidedly egalitarian spin on his actions: "We had no right to interfere in the affairs of our 'satellites,' to defend and preserve some and punish and 'excommunicate' others without reckoning with the people's will. Such procedures were against the principles of equality, independence, non-interference in each other's internal affairs, and full responsibility of the leadership of each country before its own people."[90] For whatever reason, Gorbachev's resolve in not sending troops to defend East Germany was one of the key decisions in the events of 1990. Bush could only have been ecstatic when he learned that Baker had been told through an East German official: "There will be no Tiananmen Square solution here."[91]

Relieved that Gorbachev had not intervened with troops but still wary of the instability of the situation, Bush responded to the crumbling of the Berlin Wall in a characteristically muted way. The day before the wall fell, Bush confided to his diary: "If we mishandle this and get way out [in front] looking like [the rebellions are] an American project—you would invite crackdown, and invite negative reaction that could result in bloodshed. The longer I'm in this job, the more I think prudence is a value and experience matters."[92] Bush also understood that despite the opening of the wall, the Soviet Union remained intact, and Germany was still divided. Put another way—despite the rather frantic proclamations of the media, Bush knew that the Cold War was far from over. Thus, Bush did his level best not to gloat, take credit, or rub Gorbachev's face in the events at the Berlin Wall. Meeting with the press in the Oval Office on 9 November, the president looked very calm, almost matter-of-fact, as he mused: "I don't think any single event is the end of what you might call the Iron Curtain....I didn't foresee it, but imagining it? Yes." Lesley Stahl of CBS News observed that he did not sound "elated"; Bush responded, "I'm not an emotional kind of guy....I'm very pleased."[93] Bush's response met with criticism from all quarters. Dick Gephardt (D-MO) responded for the Democrats: "Even as the walls of the modern Jericho come tumbling down, we have a president who is inadequate to the moment."[94] Bush's later response to Gephardt's criticism: "Absolutely absurd."[95]

It was certainly absurd from the point of view of a president who was about to ask a Soviet leader to acquiesce in the peaceful devolution of what many saw as the most significant portion of the Soviet empire. Bush had turned his sights to what he viewed to be the ultimate prize: the reunification of East and West Germany, and the welcoming of that reunified Germany as a member of NATO. On 10 November, Bush spoke to West German chancellor Helmut Kohl on the telephone.[96] When the call was reported in the press, along with mention that the two leaders had made plans to speak again, Gorbachev instantly demanded a meeting of the Four Powers to address the situation. His request was

President Bush talks to the press in the Oval Office regarding the developments in East Germany, 9 November 1989. *Left to right around the desk:* James A. Baker III, General Brent Scowcroft, and John Sununu. CBS reporter Lesley Stahl is standing in front of the grandfather clock. (Courtesy of the George Bush Presidential Library and Museum)

denied, and Bush tried to alleviate his concerns by arguing that he was pursuing a "passive" policy. This was hogwash. Bush wanted a reunified Germany, but he hoped to proceed deliberately, taking the needs of both Germanys and the Soviet Union into account.[97]

Kohl did not help. On 28 November, in a speech to the German Bundestag on "German-German politics" that caught all his allies off guard, Kohl announced a ten-point plan for a closer relationship between the two Germanys. Not a call for complete reunification (he called for "unhindered travel," "technological cooperation," and a "contractual community"), it nevertheless threw down a gauntlet, as Kohl announced, "We, in the free part of Germany, stand in solidarity side by side with our fellow countrymen."[98] Thatcher, French president François Mitterrand, and Gorbachev were all furious with Kohl,[99] but the speech had served its purpose. Bush had been yanked out of his German *pauza*, and Kohl had put reunification on the world's front burner.

George Bush and Mikhail Gorbachev at the Malta Summit, 3 December 1989.
(Courtesy of the George Bush Presidential Library and Museum)

The possible reunification of Germany dominated the Malta Summit, held on 1 through 3 December 1989. As the two leaders met on board the cruise ship *Maxim Gorky* in the storm-tossed Mediterranean (the winds were so bad that the press dubbed it the "Seasick Summit"; Bush recorded in his diary that he had "a patch behind my ear—the things really work"),[100] Bush made it clear that he was willing to help perestroika succeed. Gorbachev told Bush, "We accept your role in Europe. It is very important that you be there.... We shouldn't do anything to undermine it—and we should work together and not lose an opportunity."[101] On the issue of reunification, Gorbachev expressed serious reservations to Kohl's plan, labeling his 28 November speech a "pre-election game." Bush disagreed, telling Gorbachev that he believed Kohl felt "an enormous emotional response" to what had happened over the past six months. Nevertheless, Bush promised, "We will do nothing to recklessly try to speed up reunification. When you talk to Kohl, I think you will see he agrees."[102]

When reacting to Tiananmen and the opening of the Berlin Wall, as well as to the early stages of the process of German reunification, Bush clearly showed himself to be a diplomatic realist. But there was another side to George Bush. Fundamental to his understanding of world events was the experience of World War II. He had risked his life to liberate the world from the grip of Nazi and Japanese dictatorships. This war was not fought against a faceless enemy; it had been personalized. Bush and his comrades were fighting against Hitler, against Mussolini, and against Hirohito. For President Bush to act precipitously against a nation or its leader, he had to see him in the same light as he had seen the dictators of the 1940s—as sinister threats to Western society. If the leaders were not this personification of evil, then Bush was more willing to test the diplomatic waters. If they were, then he was more than ready to throw the entire force of American power behind an effort to unseat them. Not Deng, not Gorbachev, not Honecker, not any other Eastern European leader fit this description of malevolence; thus the president was willing to allow events to take a more deliberate course. But for Bush, Saddam Hussein certainly fit that description. And so, too, did Manuel Noriega.

As noted in chapter 1, Reagan had offered Noriega a deal—step down, leave the country, and the Justice Department indictment would be quashed. Noriega took the deal but ultimately reneged, refusing to leave Panama. As vice president, Bush had strenuously opposed Reagan's decision and had accurately predicted its outcome. As president, Bush ordered $10 million to the CIA to back the opposition against Noriega in Panama's 7 May 1989 election,[103] but there was little hope that Noriega would lose, or, if he did, step down. At a meeting with Bush on 5 May, Baker recommended a series of steps, including the recall of the U.S. ambassador and an increased U.S. military presence, once it was clear that the election had been stolen.[104] On 7 May, Noriega's opposition won the election. In a surprise to no one, however, that same day Noriega publicly nullified the results of elections that had effectively ousted him as leader. Bush protested that "the Panamanian people have spoken. And I call on General Noriega to respect the will of the people." Not only did Noriega ignore Bush, but his personal police force, the Dignity Battalions, publicly beat Guillermo Endara, the victorious vice presidential candidate, with an iron bar until his white shirt was soaked in blood. The grizzly scene was witnessed by former president Jimmy Carter, who had flown to Panama to observe the election for the Carter Center, and was replayed over and over on American television and published in virtually every major newsmagazine. It clearly had an effect on Bush, who ordered an additional 2,000 troops to the Canal

Zone.[105] Bush ordered Admiral William Crowe, head of the Joint Chiefs of Staff (JCS), to put together a plan to oust Noriega and to assist the Panamanians with the task of setting up a new government. The plan, code-named Blue Spoon, also included a scheme to retrieve Kurt Muse, a captured CIA operative, from a Panamanian prison. On 11 May, Crowe and Cheney presented the plan to the president; on the same day, Bush sent 1,881 more troops to Panama.[106]

All connected with the Panamanian incursion are quick to note that the main goal was the protection of transit rights through the canal, as well as the protection of the 12,000 American troops stationed there.[107] But Bush was clearly obsessed with getting rid of Noriega; the situation reminds the historian of the fixation that the Kennedy brothers had with disposing of Fidel Castro. Bush thundered in a 14 May speech at Mississippi State University: "The will of the people should not be thwarted by this man and his Doberman thugs."[108] The next day, in an interview with Arnaud De Borchgrave of the *Washington Times*, Bush's idealistic outrage continued to flame:

> You've had an election that was stolen right out from under the eyes of the people and under the eyes of the world....You have 40,000 American citizens and quite a few American troops in Panama. And we have the vital interests of the Canal.... Now, those ingredients are different than what you have in Nicaragua in terms of the abuse of people's rights.... That's why we are going to make sure we exercise our rights under the treaty. And that's why I've augmented U.S. force. Because when you see an elected president denied his mandate, and when you see an elected vice president beaten and bloodied by thugs that clearly come under the direction of Mr. Noriega, you have an alarming situation, and one where an American president has to act promptly and prudently.[109]

The situation in Panama offered the first test of Bush's national security team. Dick Cheney, chosen as secretary of defense in the wake of the rejection of John Tower, had quickly exerted more civilian control over the Pentagon than had been seen since the days of Robert McNamara. He had shown himself to be an independent, take-charge leader, but in so doing he had ruffled more than a few feathers. Only days after taking over at the Pentagon, he had publicly censured air force chief Larry Welch for lobbying Congress with his own plan to upgrade the air force's missile system. In an answer to a direct question on this, Cheney snapped: "General Welch was freelancing. . . . No, I'm not happy about it. . . . Everybody's entitled to one mistake."[110] Cheney himself had been reprimanded for a 29 April comment on CNN that Gorbachev would "ultimately fail."[111] The comment threatened the placidity of the *pauza*, and Bush immediately disassociated himself from his secretary's remarks.[112] Not yet a member of the Bush inner circle, Cheney nevertheless radiated the cool confidence that had initially drawn the administration to appoint him. Jim Baker paid Cheney a high compliment when he recalled, "It's hard to keep your sense of equilibrium in Washington, but the power game has never gone to his head."[113]

Cheney's reproach of Welch was one factor in Crowe's decision not to seek reappointment as head of the JCS, despite support from Scowcroft.[114] In his place, Bush appointed army general Colin L. Powell. A decorated veteran of Vietnam, Powell had served as Reagan's national security adviser. During the transition, Bush offered Powell either the post of director of the Central Intelligence Agency or deputy secretary of state; Powell opted instead to become the commander of U.S. Forces Command, responsible for all field forces based in the United States.[115] Bush remembered that he had some reservations about promoting Powell, the most junior of the four-star generals who were eligible, to the chairmanship and wondered if it was "actually the right step for Colin at this stage of his service."[116] But Cheney lobbied for Powell, and Bush ultimately agreed.[117] In promoting Powell, an African American, Bush had sent a powerful message to the black community, one that was met with overwhelming approval. But Bush had also gained a valuable adviser who was as politically agile as was Cheney. And Powell had a stronger base from which to work. He was the first full-term appointment as chief under the terms of the Goldwater-Nichols Act of 1986, which made the chief the "principal military adviser" to the president.[118] Powell would soon use this pulpit to its fullest extent.

Cheney and Powell faced different dilemmas in their different Pentagon offices. One of the most pronounced legacies of the Reagan years was that of increased defense expenditures. As Bush began his administration, the press announced that the Pentagon was entering an "era of lowered expectations," and it was Cheney who would be expected to make the cuts in military spending that reflected not only the realities of the post–Cold War world but also the political reality of the budget deficit.[119] Powell, in contrast, had inherited a military that had been largely demoralized by the experience of Vietnam. The oft-cited "Vietnam Syndrome" was the belief that that war had been lost because the government had refused to commit the proper amount of American military force to the battle. Privately, Powell vowed that the next battle would be fought with overwhelming force. But given the prospect of Cheney's budget cuts, it was a promise he could not guarantee.

On 3 October, less than a day after Powell was sworn in as chairman, Major Moises Giroldi Vega, an officer in the Panamanian Defense Force (PDF), put in motion a coup against Noriega. He asked the Americans to support the coup by blocking the exit from Fort Amador and the Bridge of the Americas across the canal. This they did, but no more. Although the administration was aware that Giroldi was planning something, it simply did not know enough about his intentions; in any case, it was too late to give him any substantial help.[120]

Not that American aid at any hour would have made much of a difference. William Webster, Bush's director of central intelligence, was charitable when he noted, "It was not what you would call your best planned coup."[121] Giroldi had indeed captured Noriega, but he did not have a clue as to what to do with him. Despite being told by General Max Thurman, the commander in chief of the U.S. Southern Command, that if Giroldi brought Noriega to a U.S. military base he would be accepted as a prisoner, Giroldi refused.[122] Indeed, in his book *The Commanders*, a penetrating study of American military decision making during the first two years of the Bush administration, Bob Woodward reports that the conspirators floated to Noriega the possibility of his retiring with a full pension.[123] Incredibly, Giroldi even allowed the captured Noriega to use the telephone.[124] He called the PDF, which stormed Giroldi's hideout and reclaimed the Panamanian dictator. Within forty-eight hours, Giroldi had been tortured and killed.

The question of how the administration reacted to the Giroldi coup is still open to debate. One scholar concluded that although Bush was "tempted to move" on the coup, he "hesitated."[125] If there was such hesitation, the principals ascribe it to poor crisis communication. Webster remembered that at the time the coup took place, there was a "senior foreign official" being squired around the White House, and many of the key players were away from their desks. When they finally dealt with the emergency, Webster remembers that they did so by "huddling" rather than through formal strategy sessions. As a result, Webster remembers more "grousing" than crisp decision making.[126] Bush's team agreed. In Baker's assessment, "It was apparent that a prime opportunity to remove Noriega had been squandered. Our reaction had been wholly defensive....It's an understatement to say that administration decision making was less than crisp."[127]

Powell, however, offers another point of view on administrative decision making in his memoirs. He suggests that there was no indecision regarding the Giroldi coup in the administration. Indeed, it was quite the opposite. He remembers that Thurman believed the coup to be destined to failure; Woodward reported Thurman as saying to Powell: "This is ill motivated, ill conceived—they are going to talk this guy into retirement.... Stay out of it big time." Powell recalls that "Cheney, Thurman, and I... agreed that the United States should not get involved" and that Scowcroft agreed. As for Bush, Powell remembers that the president never had any intention of giving serious aid to the coup because "Giroldi had said nothing about democracy. And we would not support him unless he had made a commitment to restore civilian rule."[128]

Whether or not the administration had acted decisively, the perception of indecision had become reality. As noted by Bush biographer Herbert Parmet, "The most unfortunate part of the Giroldi affair was the notoriety, which gave it a momentum of its own."[129] Thanks to comments such as those made by Representative David McCurdy (D-OK) that Bush's failure to help the Giroldi coup "makes Jimmy Carter look like a man of resolve,"[130] the press had rediscovered the "wimp factor," and Noriega was publicly berating the masculinity of the president of the United States as he bragged about his near escape. After the affair, columnist George Will, whom Bush despised, accused the president of having an "unserious presidency" and wrote that its symbol "should be a wetted finger held up to the breezes."[131] Bush was also attacked by many members of Congress on both sides of the aisle; Republican Jesse Helms called the administration a bunch of "Keystone Cops." Publicly, the administration admitted only to "bad handling" of the affair, but a furious Bush told his staff that "amateur hour is over."[132] The administration heightened its planning for the moment of retribution. One of the first steps was to enhance the power of the NSC's Deputies Committee—unless time did not allow, crisis decisions would now go to the Deputies Committee, chaired by Scowcroft's deputy Robert Gates, before going to the full NSC.[133]

The administration had an opportunity to fine-tune its crisis response on 30 November 1989, when word came to the White House of a coup attempt against Corazon Aquino of the Philippines. Bush was at the Malta Summit, and Cheney was in bed with what was later called the flu (Bush remembered that Cheney "refused to come to the White

House on the grounds that the vice president was not in the chain of command and such a meeting could not validly take place").[134] In their memoirs, Vice President Dan Quayle and Colin Powell both take credit for assuming control of the crisis;[135] both Cheney and Bob Woodward side with Powell, reporting that he decided to have U.S. planes fly low and buzz the rebel planes on the ground, thus keeping them from taking off—a show of force with a small chance of loss of life—a plan that Bush approved. To most of those close to the process, it was Powell who had proved himself to be a confident crisis manager.[136]

Two weeks later, on 16 December, four American soldiers were heading for a restaurant in Panama City. They got lost and unintentionally drove to the PDF headquarters. As they were stopped by five uniformed PDF soldiers, their car was stormed by a crowd that had gathered there. Fearing for their lives, the soldiers sped away. The PDF fired at the car and hit two of the soldiers. One, Lieutenant Robert Paz, died fifteen minutes after arriving at Gorgas Army Hospital. Half an hour before the four men were ambushed, navy lieutenant Adam J. Curtis and his wife were stopped at the same PDF checkpoint; they too were lost. They were told to pull over and wait by the curb. As they did so, they witnessed the shooting of Paz and his friend. When the PDF realized that they had inadvertently provided witnesses to their deed, they blindfolded the couple and drove them to another location. Over the next four hours, Curtis was beaten, was kicked in the groin and the head, and had his life threatened. His wife was slammed into the wall with such force that her head was bleeding; she was also sexually threatened. After four hours, they were released.[137]

When the story broke, Cheney was quick to respond: "Ultimately it is General Noriega who has encouraged this lawlessness." Although there was a token debate at the White House on 17 December as to whether the incident was enough provocation for a military strike, Thurman, Cheney, Powell, and Baker all recommended that Blue Spoon commence.[138] For his part, Bush needed no convincing (Scowcroft later claimed that Paz and Curtis were "the excuse" for the invasion).[139] Bush gave it his approval (Powell remembered Bush's order: "Okay, let's do it. The hell with it"),[140] along with the approval for troop reinforcements requested by Thurman to give the plan better odds of success. There had been one small change to the plan, however. Noting that men would not be properly motivated to fight and die for a spoon, Thurman changed the name of the plan to Operation Just Cause.

At 12:39 a.m. on 20 December, Guillermo Endara was sworn in as Panama's new president. Fifteen minutes later, American paratroopers descended upon Panama City. Throughout the night, Baker was in close touch with John Bushnell, the embassy's charge in Panama City. At 2:00 a.m. Bushnell wired that everything was on schedule—in less than an hour, Kurt Muse had been freed from his prison; by 2:40 a.m., Noriega's headquarters, the Commandancia Building, was in flames. By 9:00 a.m., the military action was over.[141] There later were some questions about the performance of U.S. military hardware, particularly the much-maligned Stealth bomber, which mistakenly bombed a basketball court and a saloon.[142] But on the whole, the Pentagon could breathe a sigh of relief. American losses were comparatively light: 23 dead and 394 wounded.[143]

But the Americans had not yet captured Noriega. Despite Powell's protests to the press ("He's not running anything because we own all the bases he owned eight hours ago"), the mission as planned was not complete without what the military called the "snatch": having Noriega in American hands. (This was quite unlike Operation Desert Storm, which as we will see never had capturing Saddam Hussein as a goal, stated or otherwise.) On Christmas Eve, a disguised and frightened Noriega showed up at the home of Monsignor Sebastian Laboa, the papal nuncio—the pope's representative in Panama City—where he was granted asylum. The Americans responded by both blasting rock music at the building at earsplitting volume and landing and unloading troops where Noriega could see. It was not until 3 January 1990 that Noriega finally surrendered, apparently convinced by the nuncio. He was brought by helicopter to the United States to stand trial. On 9 April 1992, Noriega was found guilty on eight of ten charges, including cocaine trafficking, money laundering, and racketeering.

The Panamanian episode was both a military and a political victory for Bush. For the moment, at least, the wimp label had disappeared. R. W. "Johnny" Apple of the *New York Times* wrote, "Whatever the other results of this roll of the dice in Panama, it has shown [Bush] as a man capable of bold action."[144] Bush's approval polls shot up. At the end of 1989, his 76 percent approval rating was second only to John Kennedy's among modern presidents at the end of a first year in office.[145]

At Malta, Bush had made it clear to Gorbachev that he wanted a reunited Germany. If anything, the Panamanian episode reinforced to the world the president's resolve. In early 1990, in a worldwide climate that

133

favored the Americans, Gorbachev moved to try to get as good a deal on reunification as he could. On 1 February, the Soviets announced their support of a plan for a neutral confederation between East and West Germany, with both keeping their sovereignty.[146] The plan was unacceptable to both the Americans and the West Germans: the next day, Baker met with his West German counterpart, vice chancellor and foreign minister Hans-Dietrich Genscher, who told him that "neutrality for a unified Germany is out of the question. The new Germany would remain in NATO because NATO is an essential building block to a new Europe."[147] On 7 February, Baker offered the Soviets a counterproposal. In a meeting with Soviet foreign minister Eduard Shevardnadze, Baker proposed that East and West Germany would begin negotiations about the internal facets of unification, and at the same time the four World War II victors (the United States, the Soviet Union, Great Britain, and France) would begin discussions of the international facets of unification—but all would agree that the eventual goal of what would be called the "Two-Plus-Four" talks was a permanent reunification. The inclusion of both East and West Germany in the talks meant, de facto, that the four postwar powers were terminating their rights to control over the two Germanys.

When the plan was pitched to Gorbachev on 9 February, he balked—he wanted to wait until after the German elections, to be held in March, and he continued to be opposed to the inclusion of a new, larger Germany in NATO.[148] But Gorbachev came to realize that the need to keep open the hope for loans from the United States to his beleaguered nation far outweighed the anger he would face from his hard-liners if he agreed to talks that might bring an end to East Germany. In late February, at a meeting held in Ottawa, NATO and Warsaw Pact foreign ministers agreed that the "Two-Plus-Four" format was acceptable. On 24 February, after meeting at Camp David, Bush and Kohl reaffirmed that a reunified Germany would be a member of NATO. On 18 March, Kohl's Alliance for Germany Party won 48 percent of the vote in his elections; the Bush-Kohl plan for reunification had been accepted at the German polls, and "Two-Plus-Four" talks soon commenced in Bonn.[149]

As Gorbachev struggled with reunification, so too did he struggle with continued unrest in his nation. On his right flank, the hard-liners were castigating him for being soft on Germany; on his left flank, on 4 February, some 300,000 protesters marched to the Kremlin to demand that the Communist Party relinquish its power.[150] Moreover, the republics were yet aflame. As the new year began, Gorbachev faced increased

West German Chancellor Helmut Kohl and President Bush, 16 September 1991. (Courtesy of the George Bush Presidential Library and Museum)

trouble in Lithuania and in the Caucasus republics of Armenia and Azerbaijan. To the Soviets, the republics were not satellites; they were a part of the Union of Soviet Socialistic Republics, submitting themselves to central party control. To lose them would be tantamount to the United States losing Texas. On 11 March, Lithuania reaffirmed its declaration of independence from the Soviet Union. This was more than Gorbachev was prepared to accept; he vowed not to negotiate with the Lithuanians until they revoked their declaration. In April, in an attempt to force the issue, Gorbachev placed an economic embargo around the republic and cut off its oil supply.

Bush was walking a tightrope. On the one hand, many in the press and in Congress were pushing the administration to intervene and to recognize a free Lithuania. However, Bush needed to keep Gorbachev inside the tent, as negotiations for a reunified Germany as a member of NATO progressed. Thus, in public, the administration was, in the words of the *New York Times*, "artfully silent" on the issue of the republics,[151] accepting only, in the words of Marlin Fitzwater, "the need to restore order where order has broken down."[152] But in a series of blunt letters to Gorbachev, Bush made it clear that Soviet intransigence—regarding both unification and the Baltics—would not be tolerated much longer. Bush hit Gorbachev where it hurt the most, writing, "I may be forced very soon to state publicly that under existing conditions there can be no trade agreement."[153] Gorbachev responded angrily to Bush's letter by accusing him of going back on the Malta agreement that had labeled Lithuania an internal Soviet problem and stressing that threats to stop the trade agreement could be "detrimental to the relations between the US and the USSR."[154]

But Bush clearly held all the cards, and Gorbachev now faced up to the inevitable. On 1 June, Gorbachev was in Washington for his second summit meeting with Bush. The afternoon session brought one of the most startling moments in modern world history. As they discussed reunification, Gorbachev asked Bush: "Do you and I agree that a united Germany has the right to be non-aligned, or a member of NATO, in the final document?" Bush replied: "I agree with that, but the German public wants to be in NATO. But if they want out of NATO, we will respect that. They are a democracy." Gorbachev replied: "I agree to say so publicly, that the United States and the USSR are in favor of seeing a united Germany, with final settlement leaving it up to where a united Germany can choose." While this was a repeat of what Gorbachev had decided regarding the opening of the East German border, to hear it said regarding reunification—and in front of the Americans—made Gorbachev's advisers visually apoplectic. Gorbachev tried to calm them by suddenly demanding a long transition period for reunification, a demand that Bush simply ignored. Bush accepted Gorbachev's promise; in return, Bush agreed to sign a trade bill, despite congressional protest over his handling of the Lithuanian situation, so that Gorbachev could bring home a victory. (Gorbachev, beaming, told the Americans, "This really matters to me.")[155] But in secret, Bush made it clear that he would not send the trade package to Capitol Hill until Gorbachev had lifted his embargo on Lithuania, which Gorbachev did immediately upon his arrival back in Moscow.[156] Kohl came quickly on board, agreeing on 14 July to a $3 billion line of credit for the Soviet Union.[157] After the meeting with Kohl, Gorbachev announced that he would withdraw his objections to a unified Germany, whose troops could remain in NATO without a corresponding role for the East Germans in the Warsaw Pact.

On 23 August, East Germany's House of Representatives, the Volkskammer, voted its fealty to the West German constitution; terms of the reunification were demarcated in a treaty signed in Berlin on 31 August. The treaty was signed at Moscow on 12 September by the four victorious powers; in it, France, Great Britain, the United States, and the USSR "hereby terminate their rights and responsibilities relating to Berlin and to Germany as a whole."[158] Both German parliaments ratified the treaty on 20 September, and formal reunification of East and West Germany into a nation now known as Germany, took place on 3 October, with elections scheduled for 3 December.

Even as seasoned a diplomat as George Bush marveled at the events of 1990: "I am not sure why Gorbachev did what he did. Perhaps he realized that our position would prevail and this was the best way to manage it within his own team. In any event, it was an amazing performance."[159]

In a diary entry written five days after the formal reunification of Germany, George Kennan, a key architect of the Cold War, wrote: "The unification of [Germany] . . . was not the result of anyone's foresight or of an agreed upon policy on the part of the powers that were allied in the Second World War. It was the result of spontaneous action on the parts of several tens of thousands of young East Germans, motivated by the hope of getting better jobs."[160] Kennan could not have been more wrong. Yet to claim, as did Gorbachev before an academic audience in 1997, that "the unification of Germany was inevitable" is equally wrong.[161] Nothing was inevitable about the reunification of East and West Germany into a nation now known as Germany, and it was simply not accomplished by the citizenry in the streets. The fact that the reunification of Germany came about bloodlessly was largely due to the decisions of Mikhail Gorbachev. But it would never have come about at all had it not been for the commitment of George Bush. With James Baker, Bush created a framework for the talks; it was he who kept them moving forward—he would modestly call his role "shepherding reunification."[162] But Baker was absolutely correct when he wrote: "This would never have occurred without U.S. leadership. We framed the talks, kept them on course."[163] It was coalition building of the highest order.

There would be a united Germany in NATO. It would be done peacefully, with the complete support of the USSR. George Bush had won his greatest victory as president.

7

DESERT SHIELD

Iraq, a nation approximately the size of the state of California, had in 1990 a population of 16.5 million. It also had the fourth-largest army in the world, the personal property of the nation's president for life, Saddam Hussein. Saddam had been a fixture in the bloody and unpredictable politics of Iraq since the early 1960s. His brutality and self-confidence had long been legendary. Of the many examples available, one will suffice: in 1969, he added a law degree to his pantheon of honors simply by showing up in the examination room with a pistol in his belt and flanked by two armed bodyguards. He immediately passed the exam.[1] Leader of the Ba'ath Party and the nation's military strongman throughout the 1970s, he was named president of Iraq in July 1979. Later that year the shah of Iran was overthrown; Saddam invaded Iran in fall 1980. The war lasted eight years and completely destroyed both nations' economic infrastructures. The war had cost Iraq several hundred thousand of its citizens (as opposed to about half a million Iranians) and about $250 billion, and Saddam faced a foreign debt of about $80 billion.[2] Moreover, he could no longer count on oil exports, which once made up 95 percent of Iraq's postwar income, to help pay the debt, since the price of oil was falling precipitously at the end of the 1980s, thus putting the macrostructure of the Iraqi economy on even shakier ground.[3]

This situation led Saddam to court moderate Arab nations such as Egypt, European nations such as France, and the United States. The

Reagan administration was particularly receptive to Saddam's entreaties. Brent Scowcroft was blunt in a 1997 interview: the Reagan policy was to "aid the weaker [nation], which was Iraq."[4] Richard Haass, one of Bush's foreign policy advisers, was even blunter, noting that the outcome of the Iran-Iraq War "lulled many American analysts and policy makers into concluding that Iraq would opt for years of tranquility in order to regain strength."[5] Hoping that Iraq would provide a check to Iran in the region, by 1987 Iraq had been given $1 billion in agricultural commodity credit guarantees by the United States—the largest loan of its kind to any nation in the world.[6] The Reagan administration had also approved export licenses for Saddam so that he might buy "dual use items"—products not including arms that could have either a military or a nonmilitary use.[7]

To put it mildly, Saddam was a troublesome business partner. Immediately following the end of the war with Iran, he turned his attention toward ridding himself of the Kurds, an ethnic minority in the north of Iraq, and he enforced his desires with chemical weapons—in March 1988, in the Kurdish village of Halabja, chemical weapons killed 5,000 Kurds in one day.[8] There was also evidence that American money borrowed by Saddam for food had actually gone toward the purchase of the weaponry that had been used against the Kurds.

Loath to rock the boat in the Middle East by openly criticizing Saddam, the Bush administration initially kept the policy of the Reagan administration largely in place. In October 1989 the Bush administration increased the number of agricultural credits to Iraq but protested Saddam's use of the money for military purposes, limiting the extent of its objections to Saddam's methods. Indeed, the administration consistently opposed congressional attempts to impose sanctions on Iraq, the last time coming only two days before Saddam's attack on Kuwait.[9] All in all, Saddam received some $400 million in U.S. aid.[10]

If the Americans truly believed that agricultural credits would buy stability in the Persian Gulf, they were sorely mistaken.[11] Obsessed with a fear of assassination, Saddam reacted to the fall of communism in Eastern Europe—particularly to the bloody execution of Romania's Nicolae Ceausescu—with paranoia regarding the intentions of his neighbors. This may well have led him toward developing a nuclear ability for Iraq, which was, by late 1989, in its earliest stages.[12] Saddam was especially terrified of Israel. Early in March 1989, he began to construct six fixed launchers for Scud missiles at a point on the Jordanian border within range of Israel, a fact that the *Washington Post* later reported to be known by American intelligence.[13] Always believing that the best defense was a good offense, Saddam raged in a 1 April 1989 address to his armed forces, "By God, we will make fire eat half of Israel if it tries to do anything to Iraq."[14] Despite such bluster, Saddam was well aware, as he reportedly told the Saudi ambassador to Washington, Prince Bandar bin Sultan, that if Israel attacked Iraq, "I would not last six hours."[15]

Saddam's "eat fire" speech caused considerable concern within the Bush administration; Baker remembered that after the speech, "our strategic calculation changed irrevocably."[16] Recognizing that fact, Saddam summoned Prince Bandar to Baghdad for the express purpose of asking him to convey to Bush that he would never attack Israel. According to one report, Bush was skeptical, remarking to Bandar (who delivered Saddam's message personally), "If he doesn't intend it, why on earth does he have to say it?"[17] The following month, the administration decided not to go through with the next installment of the commodities credit loan to Iraq. With the end of the loans, Saddam had to look elsewhere for the money to rebuild his war-ravaged economy.

He saw the solution to his dilemma in his neighbor to the south. Oil was discovered in the emirate of Kuwait, a nation roughly the size of New York State with a population of approximately 1.7 million, in 1938, and by 1953 it had become the largest exporter of oil in the Persian Gulf. Kuwait had gained its independence from Great Britain in 1961; immediately upon that announcement, Iraq moved troops to the Kuwaiti border, only to be stopped when the British, following a Kuwaiti request, sent troops to the area. Facing the inevitable, Iraq tacitly recognized Kuwait's right to exist in 1963 by acquiescing in its membership in the Arab League—but only after receiving a sizable cash payment from the emir of Kuwait in return.[18] While Kuwait had been a financial supporter of Iraq in its war against Iran, the cold war between the two nations continued unabated. Saddam had long demanded access to the oil fields on the islands of Warba and Bubiyan. This demand was then joined with charges that the Kuwaitis had been "slant-drilling" into the Rumaylah oil field, the majority of which lay in Iraqi territory.[19] Then came the issue of oil prices. When most of the member nations of the Organization of Petroleum Exporting Countries (OPEC), including Iraq, agreed to cut back production of oil so as to force prices up, Kuwait refused to do so. This action perturbed many of the nations in the oil cartel; to them, the Kuwaitis were seen as little more than mercenaries who were more concerned with lining their own pockets than they were with the welfare or the stability of their nation. For his part, Saddam saw their action simply as, in his words, "a kind of war against Iraq."[20] Add to this perceived affront the fact that Iraq owed Kuwait some $10 billion that it had borrowed during the war with Iran, and there was more than enough reason, from Saddam's point of view, for a military solution.

On 15 July 1990, the U.S. Defense Intelligence Agency (DIA) learned that a division of the select Iraqi Republican Guard had begun to move southeast toward Kuwait. Within four days, some 35,000 Iraqi soldiers from three divisions were within ten miles of the border. General Colin Powell, chairman of the Joint Chiefs of Staff, remembers that this action prompted him to order General Norman Schwarzkopf, the commander in chief of the Central Command (CENTCOM), to prepare a military response to a possible Iraqi invasion of Kuwait.

In the words of Rick Atkinson, one of the most thoughtful reporters of the Gulf War, "H. Norman Schwarzkopf was the most theatrical American in uniform since Douglas MacArthur."[21] The recipient of three Silver Stars in Vietnam, Schwarzkopf was equal parts prima donna (described by Atkinson as a man who could "swagger sitting down"),[22] tyrant, and master motivator. For many, the general came to personify American heroics in the Gulf War. It might not have been so. Atkinson reports that because of Schwarzkopf's unpredictable tirades against his staff and his "yen for imperial trappings," secretary of defense Dick Cheney considered firing him, and Powell hints in his memoirs that he had "a replacement in the back of his mind."[23]

Despite this tension, Schwarzkopf stayed in command, and in response to Powell's order he produced a plan that addressed two possible levels of Iraqi aggression. One tier would provide a retaliatory option if Saddam committed what Powell called a "minor border infraction"; the second tier was a response in case of a full-fledged invasion of Kuwait.[24] The second-tier plan, code-named Operations Plan 1002-90, called for an expeditionary force of between 100,000 and 200,000 military personnel, and it was estimated that it would take about a year to establish that force in such a manner that it had a chance of expelling Saddam from Kuwait.[25]

But Operations Plan 1002-90 was to be held in reserve. Virtually no one in the administration believed that Saddam would use his troops for anything more than a brief surgical strike and withdrawal, if that. Schwarzkopf told the Joint Chiefs of Staff as much when he briefed them on 1 August.[26] Baker was told this by Soviet foreign minister

Eduard Shevardnadze ("Don't worry. Nothing's going to happen. Saddam would not be so foolish");[27] Bush was told this by Egypt's Hosni Mubarak ("Let us handle it within the Arab family"), Jordan's King Hussein ("There is no possibility for this"), and American ambassador to Iraq April Glaspie, all of whom had met with Saddam in July. They all believed that Saddam was most likely looking for more bribe monies from the emir and that then he would stand his forces down. (William Webster remembered that at the height of the crisis, the White House was concerned that the Kuwaitis "were ready to write checks over there...sometimes an Arabian solution").[28] Indeed, the Kuwaitis themselves seemed unconcerned, as they had yet to mobilize their own forces. So it was difficult for the Americans to show any alarm.[29]

Everyone was wrong. By the time that Saddam moved his troops into a clearly offensive position on the morning of 1 August, there was nothing that the 10,000 CENTCOM troops stationed in the region could do, except watch events unfold. As Scowcroft remembered, "Our approach to averting conflict—to warn against belligerent behavior, to make clear we would stand by our friends, yet continue to offer good relations for good behavior—had failed."[30]

On 2 August 1990, with Saddam announcing that Iraq was responding to calls from a revolutionary government working for the overthrow of the emir, some 140,000 Iraqi troops and 18,000 tanks rolled into Kuwait. The 16,000-man Kuwaiti army was hopelessly outmatched. Within three and a half hours, the invaders had reached the capital of the emirate at Kuwait City; within twelve hours, Kuwait City had fallen to Saddam. Although the Iraqis failed to capture the emir, who had fled to Saudi Arabia (Saddam hoped to put him on trial as a war criminal), the Iraqi leader controlled not only Kuwait but also 21 percent of the world's oil supply. Saddam proclaimed that Kuwait had ceased to exist and that it had become the "Nineteenth Province, an eternal part of Iraq."

On the morning of 2 August, Brent Scowcroft went to the residence of the first family in the East Wing of the White House. He found the Bushes still in bed, reading the morning papers. There, Scowcroft informed the president of the Iraqi invasion of Kuwait. Scowcroft had brought with him an executive order, drafted by the National Security Council Deputies Committee, freezing the approximately $100 billion in Iraqi property and assets in the United States and overseas (an action somewhat offset, as it were, by the fact that the Iraqis were able to plunder Kuwait at will and by all reports did so). Bush immediately signed it; he also moved the USS *Independence* Carrier Battle Group (two carriers, one guided missile destroyer, two frigates, and one ammunition ship) into the Persian Gulf from the Indian Ocean.[31]

Later that morning, Bush himself chaired the first NSC meeting to address the emergency. Scowcroft remembered being "appalled" at the number of his colleagues who were treating the invasion either as "a *fait accompli* . . . [or] as the crisis *du jour*."[32] Not everyone was thinking that way, however. Following the meeting, Scowcroft asked NSC staffer Richard Haass to write an "overview memo from me to the President as background for the next meeting." In it, Haass argued that evicting Iraq would "likely require the use of military force on our part."[33]

Immediately following the meeting, Bush boarded Air Force One to travel to a long-standing appearance with British prime minister Margaret Thatcher, where they were both to speak on Cold War diplomacy at the Aspen Institute in Colorado. Bringing his predilection for personal diplomacy front and center, Bush worked the phones from the plane and spoke to every leader of the Western alliance, building a coalition of world leaders against Iraqi aggression. Great Britain, France, West Germany, Japan, and seven other nations quickly joined the United States in freezing Iraqi assets. Bush also spoke with Egypt's Mubarak and Jordan's King Hussein, both of whom apologized for inadvertently misleading Bush regarding Saddam's intentions and both of whom urged him not to act precipitously, still holding out hope for an Arab solution. Eventually, thirty-five nations would join the coalition; Egypt would join Bush's alliance against Saddam—Jordan would not.[34] To suggest, as has one scholar, that "without strong pressure from [Scowcroft], Bush's reaction [to the invasion of Kuwait] would probably have been more hesitant" is simply absurd.[35] Bush built the coalition on his own; he needed no prodding from anyone. As the crisis progressed, Bush could feel comfortable that from the earliest moments, the world had his back.

It had been only twenty-four hours since the invasion. Saddam undoubtedly was stunned by the surprising unity in the international community against his actions. He also must have been stunned at how quickly Bush was able to get the United Nations to act. Thanks to a timely shove by an American president who had also served as UN ambassador, the UN lurched forward and gave the strongest show of unanimity in its forty-five-year history. The Security Council met within hours of the invasion; by the end of that evening, UN Resolution 660—denouncing Iraq's invasion, calling for its immediate withdrawal, and promising sanctions if it did not comply—had been unanimously passed (with one abstention: Yemen). It was only the fifth time in its history that the Security Council had issued such a threat.

While in Aspen, Bush met privately with Margaret Thatcher, whose respect for Bush had, in her words, "soared" in the hours since the invasion. She made her feelings plain to Bush: "If Iraq wins, no small state is safe."[36] She was hardly alone in her feelings. Later that day, from the home of his Colorado host, Bush spoke with King Fahd of Saudi Arabia, who spoke with the concern of a man staring down the barrel of a gun: "I believe nothing will work with Saddam but the use of force."[37]

The next day, 3 August, the president returned to Washington. In the Oval Office before the second NSC meeting on the crisis, Scowcroft convinced Bush to allow Scowcroft to give the opening remarks. In those remarks, Scowcroft plainly stated his position: "My personal judgment is that the stakes in this for the United States are such that to accommodate Iraq should not be a policy option." While no decision was yet made, both Eagleburger and Cheney agreed with Scowcroft.[38] Bush closed the meeting with a warning: "We should tell Saddam this would be a new ballgame, and give him our bottom line. . . . American deaths and hostages will not be tolerated."[39]

But Bush's thinking was moving beyond the issuance of rhetorical threats. On the afternoon of 3 August, Bush told Scowcroft to invite Prince Bandar to the White House to make a case for allowing American troops to deploy in Saudi Arabia. During that meeting Bandar reminded Scowcroft about Jimmy Carter's reneging on a promise to send F-15 jets to Saudi Arabia; Cheney responded, "We're serious this time."[40]After the meeting had progressed for a bit, Bush entered Scowcroft's office. The president told Bandar that the Kuwaitis had not asked for help until it was too late, and that Fahd should not wait until the last minute. Bush then ordered Colin Powell to fully brief Bandar on Schwarzkopf's two-tiered plan. Powell did so, and he also showed the Saudi ambassador secret satellite photos that demonstrated that Saddam had increased his military strength in Kuwait to the point where an attack against the Saudis was a real possibility. When Bandar asked how many men the Americans were thinking of placing in Saudi Arabia, Powell replied "about one hundred thousand," an understatement of Schwarzkopf's estimate.

Still, Bandar was stunned by the force that Bush had in mind; he smiled and replied to Powell, "Well, at least it shows you're serious."[41] Bandar then excused himself to dispatch the news to his uncle, King Fahd.

Later that day, the world received the news that a rather unexpected partner had joined Bush's coalition. Bush needed the Soviet Union either on his side or scrupulously neutral, if for no other reason than to ensure that there would be no trouble in the UN Security Council. For his part, Mikhail Gorbachev was reluctantly creaking into line with the rest of the international community against his former client in Iraq. But he was facing mounting opposition. Despite the promise of a trade pact with the United States, Gorbachev's hard-line opponents, particularly in the Soviet military, were still seething over what he had conceded to get that pact: an agreement to end the Lithuanian embargo, and an agreement to tolerate a unified Germany. Gorbachev's cold warriors were also concerned about the possibility that the Kuwaiti crisis would lead to a permanent American presence in the Middle East. Thus, they pressured Gorbachev to send Soviet aid to Saddam.

But by the end of 1990, the Soviet economy had crumbled into further disarray. The food situation was getting close to desperate, and Gorbachev was forced to once again ask Bush for aid. He knew that if he was ever to hope for any further American economic support, he would have to join Bush's coalition against Iraq. Besides, he and his closest advisers saw Saddam's invasion as both foolhardy and a violation of international law. Thus, Gorbachev had to walk a tightrope during the crisis, torn as he was by his own belief in the necessity of joining the coalition and the demands of his military hard-liners to help Saddam.

Again, Gorbachev sided with Bush. On the day of the invasion, Baker had just left the Soviet Union after a visit with Shevardnadze and was on his way to Mongolia for a previously scheduled state visit. While in Mongolia, Baker worked out the details of a joint statement with Shevardnadze. On 3 August, Baker joined the foreign minister on the tarmac of Vnukovo II airport, just outside Moscow. In its statement, the Soviet Union took the unprecedented step of joining with the United States in calling for "an international cutoff of all arms supplies to Iraq."[42]

Shevardnadze's announcement was a critical, if not the most important, moment in the whole of the Persian Gulf crisis. It was now clear to the world that Saddam could not count on the normal U.S.-Soviet catfighting over Middle East policy to help him quietly consolidate his gains. For the first time since 1945, the United States and the Soviet Union were fighting on the same side.

On 4 August, during an NSC meeting at Camp David, Bush was more fully briefed on an expanded version of Schwarzkopf's plan. He was also informed that intelligence reports strongly suggested that the Saudis continued to be disinclined to accept any long-term American presence on their soil. As Scowcroft's notes of the meeting show, Bush was clear: "Our first objective is to keep Saddam out of Saudi Arabia. Our second is to protect the Saudis against retaliation when we shut down Iraq's export capability. We have a problem if Saddam does not invade Saudi Arabia but holds on to Kuwait." The meeting led to Bush's approval of the plan, subject to the approval of the Saudis.[43] After the meeting, according to journalist Bob Woodward, Bush met with Scowcroft alone and decided to immediately send Cheney and Schwarzkopf to present the Pentagon's plan to Fahd and to personally request his approval of sending coalition troops to his country.[44]

But the Saudis had every reason to be skeptical of American promises of protection; they had heard it all before. They remembered Carter's flip-flop on the F-15s. And there were concerns about a long-term American presence in Saudi Arabia, particularly around their holy sites. But Bush held some cards of his own. Saddam had lied to King Fahd about his plans for Kuwait, as he had lied to Jordan's Hussein and Egypt's Mubarak. Further, Bush had built up a close relationship with Fahd during his years as CIA director. Perhaps most important was that military intelligence showed the distinct possibility that Saddam's next move would indeed be against Saudi Arabia. Later on the afternoon of 4 August, Bush spoke to Fahd by telephone, making the case for sending coalition troops to Saudi Arabia and sharing with the king that he was sending Cheney and Schwarzkopf.[45]

To this point, the administration had emphasized that any involvement on the part of the coalition would be to protect Saudi Arabia; it had been careful not to sound as if it was going to push into Kuwait to remove the Iraqis. That all changed on the afternoon of 5 August. Returning from Camp David, an obviously agitated Bush nearly leapt off the stairs of his helicopter and made a beeline for the press. Whether the next event was a result of Scowcroft's convincing Bush, as Woodward's reporting implies, or of Thatcher's prompting, as Powell implies, remains an open question.[46] But Bush stunned the crowd with a phrase that would be borrowed by his son a decade later: "I'm not going to discuss what we're doing in terms of moving forces, anything of that nature. But I view it very seriously . . . and please believe me, there are an awful lot of countries that are in total accord with what I've just said. . . . This will not stand, this aggression against Kuwait."

Powell was astonished; Bush's statement clearly changed the focus of the American response from protecting Saudi Arabia to evicting the Iraqis from Kuwait.[47] It is, of course, highly possible that Bush's statement was designed primarily to impress the Saudis with the irreversibility of the American commitment. If that was one of the goals of Bush's statement, it worked. The next day, 6 August, Cheney and Schwarzkopf arrived in Riyadh to explain the extent of the American commitment to Fahd. The delegation was astounded at the king's immediate positive reply.[48] That same day, the UN passed Resolution 661, calling for a complete prohibition of trade with Iraq and authorizing nonmilitary measures to enforce the sanctions. Had the UN not acted, the developing scenario might well have been the same. Schwarzkopf's plan was in place, it had been approved by Bush, it was supported by the overwhelming majority of his administration and the world community—including the Soviet Union—and Fahd had given his permission. Scowcroft was clear in his memoirs: "Never did we think that without [the UN's] blessing we could not or would not intervene."[49] But the UN had provided Bush with significant political cover; on both votes, the United States was supported by the Soviet Union.

On Wednesday, 8 August, Bush addressed the nation, announcing the deployment of the Eighty-Second Airborne Division as well as two squadrons of F-15 fighters to Saudi Arabia. He later remembered that as he prepared his speech, he wanted to make it clear to the American people that "this time I wanted no appeasement."[50] Proclaiming that "a line has been drawn in the sand," Bush said that what the Americans sought was nothing less—or more—than "the immediate, unconditional, and complete withdrawal of all Iraqi forces from Kuwait." Addressing his proclamation that Saddam's invasion "would not stand," Bush left the door open for a military action that would expel Iraq from Kuwait: "The mission of our troops is wholly defensive . . . [but] they will defend themselves, the Kingdom of Saudi Arabia, and other friends in the Persian Gulf." By the end of August, there were 80,000 coalition troops in Saudi Arabia, part of what was by then code-named Operation Desert Shield. Saddam immediately reinforced his own army to a strength of some 200,000; on 21 August, Bush responded by calling up 40,000 reservists to help transport troops, the first call-up of the reserves since the Tet Offensive of 1968. On 19 November, Saddam added 250,000 more troops, giving him a ground contingent of approximately 680,000 men.[51] This was a time of peaked anxiety for the White House. Had Saddam chosen to move against the Americans while their relatively small force was deploying, the result might have been catastrophic; Cheney mused that "we couldn't have done much had Saddam decided to keep right on rolling into the Saudi oil fields."[52] The *Washington Post* severely understated the case when it noted that "a happy ending does not appear imminent."[53]

In the weeks that followed Bush's announcement of Desert Shield, the allied coalition became both larger and more fully committed to the American cause. Much of this was thanks to Saddam, who had embarked on a program of "Zionizing" the conflict. In an attempt to win Arab support, he intimated that he would withdraw from Kuwait only if Israel would withdraw from its occupied Palestinian territories. But Saddam had worn out his welcome with his Arab neighbors. After a 10 August meeting of the Arab League, both Syria and Egypt joined forces against Iraq. In fact, it was Mubarak, who felt personally betrayed by Saddam, who made the first reference to the Iraqi leader as "the new Hitler, since he has become a danger to the region, to the Arabs, and to the world."[54]

Yet the key to keeping Arab support on the side of the budding alliance against Saddam—and the most difficult task that Bush had in the entire war—was keeping Israel out of the coalition. There had never been any love lost between Bush and the Likud government of Yitzhak Shamir. Baker and Bush held the prime minister responsible for holding up the Middle East peace process by continuing to build settlements on the disputed territory of the West Bank, even as the Palestine Liberation Organization (PLO) had taken a major step in 1989 by acknowledging Israel's right to exist.[55] By the time of the Gulf War, U.S.-Israeli relations were on the rocks—something that Saddam felt he could exploit. However, from the point of view of Washington, Israel could not become a formal member of the coalition. If it entered the war, neighboring Arab states would be forced to decide whether or not to declare war on the hated Israel, a quandary that Saddam hoped would present itself. But Shamir turned out to be the voice of reason within his cabinet. In the days after the invasion, he promised that Israel would restrain itself unless attacked.

Bush was also shrewd enough to understand that he needed to win commitments of financial support from the coalition, if for no other reason than that the cost of American intervention was incredibly expensive; one estimate suggests that by the end of August, the Americans were spending $28.9 million a day to keep U.S. troops in Saudi Arabia.[56] There were also early warning signs of the recession to come, not only in the United States but also abroad. In terms of financial underwriting, Bush concentrated his efforts on Germany and Japan. Neither nation could be expected to commit troops; both had constitutions, drafted by the United States after World War II, that severely constrained what they could do with their troops outside of their own borders. Moreover, there were domestic political considerations. Germany was only weeks away from its first elections as a unified nation since 1945, and in Japan leaders of several of the minority parties argued against sending aid of any kind. But the two countries could afford a financial commitment, and German chancellor Helmut Kohl owed Bush for the latter's unswerving support of German reunification. Kohl and Japanese prime minister Toshiki Kaifu eventually convinced their respective governments to send money.[57] By no means were these the only two nations that helped to foot the bill. Baker and treasury secretary Nicholas Brady flew all over the world on what was called "tin cup missions."[58] By the end of the operation, Kuwait, Saudi Arabia, and the United Arab Emirates (UAE) paid for 62 percent of the costs; Germany, Japan, and South Korea another 26 percent. More than 70 percent of the foreign commitment came in cash.[59] In addition, Bush asked for, and on 10 April 1991 received, a supplemental defense appropriation from his own Congress of $15 billion in budget authority to support Desert Shield.[60]

If persuading the world community to support American intervention in the Gulf financially was an act of political legerdemain—and it was—convincing the other members of the coalition to send troops for the purpose of ousting Saddam from Kuwait was actually much easier. The hawkish Thatcher's support came effortlessly (in the words of Sir Lawrence Freedman and Efraim Karsh, "Fighting aggressors can appear as almost a national calling in Britain").[61] Squadrons of Tornado fighters and the Seventh Armored Brigade were sent to Saudi Arabia. Even France, which had been closest to Iraq of any Western nation, eventually sent 4,200 troops.

As coalition troops began to arrive on Saudi soil, they were particularly vulnerable to Iraqi attack. One estimate suggested that it would take until the end of September for the troops to be ready to withstand an assault. Yet, on 22 August, war almost came. Saddam challenged the UN embargo policy by sending an Iraqi tanker, the *Khaneqan*, toward Yemen, one of Saddam's few remaining allies. An American frigate fired warning shots across the bow of the tanker; Saddam warned of "grave consequences" if any more shots were fired. Bush originally favored an immediate retaliation, and Powell, Cheney, and Scowcroft agreed. Baker protested, however, pointing out that the Soviet Union made it clear that it was not in favor of an attack on the tanker. Baker won. He called Shevardnadze and said that Bush would not fire on the ship, but only if the Soviets agreed to a new UN resolution that would allow the coalition to enforce the embargo—by force, if necessary. Gorbachev agreed.[62] Bush allowed the tanker to pass and pressed the UN to be more definitive in its statement on the embargo (an angry Thatcher told the president on the phone, "This is no time to go wobbly"). On 25 August that body passed UN Resolution 665, giving the coalition the right to search, and if necessary disable, ships that were suspected of attempting to run the embargo.[63] Thatcher supported it; Gorbachev supported it, but only if the United States would extend diplomatic overtures to Saddam Hussein.[64]

Terrified at the prospect of completely losing the support of the Soviet Union just as the Americans were threatening a counterstrike, Saddam sent his foreign minister, Tariq Aziz, to Moscow to try to soften up Gorbachev. It was to no avail. Out of gratitude to Gorbachev's response, as well as from a desire to keep the coalition together, Bush agreed to travel to Helsinki on 5 September for a third summit.. Bush was even willing to appear as the supplicant, and during the summit he agreed to an international conference on the Middle East, an implicit admission that after the conflict, in a stunning reversal of more than forty years of policy, America would agree to a Soviet presence in the Middle East.[65] At Helsinki, Bush and Gorbachev issued a joint statement: the two nations would act "individually and in concert" to see to it that Saddam unconditionally withdrew from Kuwait, "even if that cannot be accomplished by peaceful means." With the Soviets on board, it would be impossible for Saddam to find any European allies. The *New York Times* called it "Bush and Gorbachev, Inc."[66]

Some analysts of the Gulf Crisis have contended that Bush and Scowcroft worked alone, set policy on their own, and, in the words of one such team of analysts, "defined the nature of the problem, the goals the United States would pursue, and the policy it would implement, with very little input from the other senior foreign-policy advisors. . . .

"The Gang of Eight," 15 January 1991. *Left to right*: Robert Gates, John Sununu, Dick Cheney, Dan Quayle, Bush, James A. Baker III, Gen. Brent Scowcroft, and Gen. Colin Powell. (Courtesy of the George Bush Presidential Library and Museum)

[There was an] absence of a systematic analysis."[67] The evidence flies in the face of this conclusion. Since the beginning of the crisis, Bush had been meeting regularly with a group of his close advisers outside the regular membership of the NSC. The "Gang of Eight"—Dan Quayle, James Baker, John Sununu, Brent Scowcroft, Robert Gates, Dick Cheney, and Colin Powell—was where Bush heard the most pointed debate over whether or not he should use military force to expel Saddam Hussein from Kuwait. Baker and Powell urged the president to continue the containment route, at least until that time when economic sanctions and diplomacy had been given enough time to work.[68] But Scowcroft, Gates, and Cheney doubted that the economic sanctions would ever work; they clearly advocated an offensive option that would expel Saddam from Kuwait. The arguments were often sharp. At one meeting, Powell remembered raising the question of whether or not "it was worth going to war to liberate Kuwait." In Powell's telling, following the meeting he was upbraided by Cheney: "You're not the Secretary of State. You're not the National Security Advisor anymore. And you're not Secretary of Defense. So stick to military matters." Powell's later reflection on the incident: "I was not sorry."[69]

In the end, whether or not to go to war was, given the byzantine and extraconstitutional development of the presidential war-making power since 1945, Bush's decision. In his memoirs, Bush claims, "I don't know exactly when I became resigned to the fact that it would come to war."[70] Observers of the Bush administration, both contemporary and historical, have also struggled with this question, trying to decide when Bush's intentions turned from a defense of Saudi Arabia and toward a plan for expelling Saddam Hussein from Kuwait in Operation Desert Storm. Many have claimed that Bush had not made up his mind until late into the fall, well beyond the implementation of Operation Desert Shield.[71] Others argue that while he was ready to use force, Bush was playing a waiting game, waiting until all other options had been exhausted and the coalition had coalesced before he took the country to war.[72]

From within the administration, Powell believed that at least from the "This will not stand" comment, Bush had made his mind up to go to war. But in his memoirs, James Baker offers an alternate point of view on this question, one that deserves to be quoted at length:

> Some critics have fixed on this statement ["This will not stand"]—and the resolute manner in which the President issued it—as an indication of the President's intention from the very beginning to go to war. That, however, would be a serious misreading, both of George Bush the man and of the situation in which the United States . . . found itself that August. The President's statement reflected his instinctive sense, very early on, that this was no ordinary crisis. . . . His statement also showed his determination to undo Iraq's aggression. . . . And with every decision, the world community would be one step closer to ejecting Iraq from Kuwait. What the President's statement did not reveal was how he would go about doing that.[73]

A careful reading of the available evidence strongly suggests that while he publicly wedded his administration to the economic sanctions, Bush never really thought they would work. The most outspoken proponent of this view is Colin Powell. In his memoir, Powell cites an instance in mid-August when Bush turned to him and said, "I don't know if sanctions are going to work in an acceptable time frame"; Powell concluded that Bush "did not sound like a man willing to wait long for sanctions to work."[74] Indeed, throughout Powell's account, Bush is depicted as a person who is simply waiting for the right moment to launch an offensive attack. But we have more than Powell's word on this subject. Bob Woodward reports a meeting where Baker and Powell argued for diplomacy, and, after hearing from them, Bush interjected: "Don't you realize that if [Saddam] pulls out, it will be impossible for us to stay? . . . We have to have a war."[75] Bush himself remembers that as early as 23 August, when he was fishing with Scowcroft at Kennebunkport, he "asked impatiently when we could strike."[76] Indeed, Bush admitted as much to the American people on 10 September, in a speech to a joint session of Congress, when he quietly but pointedly said, "Iraq will not be permitted to annex Kuwait. That's not a threat or a boast. That's just the way it's going to be."[77] On 22 September, Bush wrote in his diary: "I am wondering if we need to speed up the timetable."[78]

Whenever it was that Bush decided to expel Saddam Hussein from Kuwait, the president had an offensive military strategy at his disposal. That plan, developed by Schwarzkopf and code-named Operation Instant Thunder, called for the targeting of key Iraqi military and technological installations for air bombardment. It also called for an intensive air bombardment of Iraqi command and communications, followed by a ground war straight into the teeth of the Republican Guard. Nevertheless, the prediction of the planner was succinct: "National leadership and command and control destroyed. Iraq's strategic offense and defense eliminated for extended period."[79] Powell was briefed on the plan on 11 August, and he ordered it to be expanded to include options for expelling Hussein from Kuwait, should it come to that.

The plan was presented to Bush and his advisers in early October, but it satisfied no one. Calling for a one-pronged, straight-on attack into the middle of Saddam's forces, Instant Thunder virtually guaranteed high losses (one aide quipped that the plan was "the charge of the Light Brigade into the *wadi* of death").[80] The military felt that they were being pressured into providing an offensive option too soon, before the Desert Shield troops were even safely in place; the civilians in the room saw only poor planning. Ordered to present a new offensive strategy that would guarantee success, Schwarzkopf returned with a bolder plan, one that called for the doubling of the Desert Shield troop commitment so that the army might execute both an initial attack against the heart of Saddam's forces and then a strike against the Iraqi flank to the west—a "left hook"—that would encircle the fleeing Iraqi army.[81]

The revamped Instant Thunder plan provided the rapid, daring strategy that the administration was searching for. But Bush recognized that he could not immediately send reinforcements to Saudi Arabia; congressional elections were coming up, and Bush did not want to bring the word "escalation" into the political debate. Thus, while he approved the doubling of forces on 31 October, he did not announce it until after the election.[82] On 8 November, Bush revealed that he was doubling the American force in Saudi Arabia from 230,000 to more than 500,000 troops in order to create an "offensive military option." Bush also added more than 1,200 M1 tanks to those already in Saudi Arabia. Democrats were furious. Dubbing the announcement the "November Surprise," they accused Bush of playing politics by holding back on the escalation of forces until after the election. It seems that they were right, but it did not matter much. The reinforcements, in numbers approximately equal to those stationed in Europe at the height of the Cold War, represented the largest American military deployment since the Vietnam War. Schwarzkopf would have enough men to do the job. In Cheney's words, Bush was an adherent of the post-Vietnam "don't-screw-around school of military strategy."[83]

Bush justified his decision to move toward an offensive option on the grounds that he was saving the world from a brutal bully. As the administration prepared to expel Saddam from Kuwait, no one helped cement that image in the court of worldwide public opinion more than did Saddam himself. Foremost was his taking of hostages. Saddam's treatment of the thousands of Western civilians (including more than 3,000 Americans) living in Kuwait or Iraq whom, according to his announcement of 17 August, he would not allow to leave Iraq can only be described as bizarre. Although they were called "human shields," they were nonetheless treated well, housed in hotels in Baghdad, and then paraded in front of television cameras with Saddam so that they might testify to the humaneness of their treatment. The strategy, if it was one, backfired. Initially, remembering the damage the Iran Hostage Crisis had done to the Carter administration, Bush recoiled at using the word "hostage" in public. But Westerners were quickly appalled at pictures of five-year-old British hostage Stuart Lockwood, riveted with fear, standing next to Saddam as the Iraqi leader patted his head and asked him, "Are you getting your milk, Stuart, and your corn flakes, too?" Thatcher mocked Saddam for "hiding behind women's skirts."[84] On 20 August, in a speech to the Veterans of Foreign Wars in Baltimore, Bush finally called the detainees "hostages"; from that point on, he used the term frequently, and with great effect.

For his part, Saddam ignored the rumbling of world opinion against him, and on 22 September he issued a statement urging all Iraqi citizens to prepare for "the mother of all battles."[85] Bush responded by making regular comparisons between Saddam (whose name he continually mispronounced, a serious slight to an Arabic male and one that it is possible Bush did deliberately) and Adolf Hitler.[86] The reference to Hitler was particularly resonant. Bush's speechwriters liked the idea, but the NSC continually cut the reference from Bush's speeches. It didn't matter—Bush would continually ad lib the reference back into his talk.[87] He also frequently used terms like "rapist," "evil," and "madman" to describe the Iraqi leader. Continuing to use the Wilsonian rhetoric of idealistic righteousness in his 1991 State of the Union address, Bush bluntly asserted, "Our cause is just. Our cause is moral. Our cause is right."

Yet Bush's most impassioned utterance in this regard was part of an interview, first broadcast to the American people on 2 January 1991. British journalist David Frost had been given access to Bush for a program analyzing the first two years of his presidency. Not surprisingly, the crisis in the Gulf dominated the program—particularly since on the day he was interviewed, Bush had read an Amnesty International report that outlined a host of Iraqi atrocities. Bush told Frost that the report "should be compulsory reading [for] anyone who thinks we have all the time in the world." He then listed several examples from the report, the most gruesome of which was the torture and rape of a handicapped child. As he continued, Bush's lips tightened and his face flushed with anger. He called Saddam "primeval" and "the rapist of Kuwait" and promised, "We will prevail. There's no question about it."[88]

Bush was completely sincere in his hatred of Saddam; it was easy for him to equate the Iraqi dictator's actions to those of the dictators of the 1940s whom he had risked his life to defeat. But there was an equally important national security reason for Bush's actions, one that James Baker highlights in his memoirs: "We *had* responded to a clear violation of international law . . . and we *were* dealing with a megalomaniacal personality. But it was also true that we had vital interests at stake. . . . We had to make sure we could maintain a secure supply of energy."[89] For half a century, the United States had clearly stated that keeping the Middle Eastern oil pipeline flowing—and keeping the price of crude as low as possible—was in its vested national security interests. Indeed, on 2

October 1989, Bush issued National Security Directive 26 (NSD-26), entitled "U.S. Policy toward the Persian Gulf," which stated that "access to Persian Gulf oil and the security of key friendly states in the area are vital to national security."[90] Yet Bush did not articulate the economic ramifications of Saddam's actions nearly as well, or as passionately, as he expressed his belief that Saddam was basically an evil man. Bush left the oil argument up to Baker to explain, which the secretary of state did on several occasions. The most notable came after a 13 November press conference, when Baker declared, "We cannot permit a dictator such as this to sit astride that economic lifeline. And to bring it down to the level of the average American citizen, let me say that means jobs."[91] Baker later argued that it was the "rhetorical confusion" of the administration—sending too many mixed messages in an attempt to justify the military actions—that played into the hands of a growing movement in opposition to Desert Shield.[92] Just as likely is the explanation that Baker never should have mentioned the oil issue publicly, for that was the aspect the antiwar activists pounced on.

The announcement of troop reinforcements, as well as the belief that Bush was taking the nation to war for oil, brought a wave of antiwar protests both in the United States and around the world. In New York City, a parade of marchers six blocks long rallied at Times Square, chanting, "Hell, no, we won't go—we won't fight for Texaco."[93] A group that called itself "Out Now" ran an advertisement in the liberal magazine the *Nation,* asking for contributions for future ads so that it might continue to broadcast its message: "Must We Trade Body Bags for Oil? Why Not Give Peace a Chance? Speak Out Now—Remember Vietnam....Out Now—Bring Our Troops Home."[94]

Bush's actions were also opposed by one of his predecessors. In January 1980, in his final State of the Union address, Jimmy Carter spoke to the ongoing hostage crisis in Iran by enunciating a doctrine that was to bear his name: "Let our position be absolutely clear: an attempt by any outside force to gain control of the Persian Gulf region will be regarded as an assault on the vital interests of the United States of America, and such an assault will be repelled by any means necessary, including military force." Apparently, Carter did not see the Gulf Crisis as "an assault on the vital interests of the United States." In 1990, he secretly lobbied the UN Security Council to reject Bush's resolutions to authorize force to expel Saddam. When that did not work, Carter went to the newspapers, and then sent personal letters to all the countries then sitting on the Security Council. Carter's efforts were in vain, and from that point on, he was cut off from the Bush White House.[95]

More troubling from a political point of view was the fact that many Republican conservatives, who presumably would support the president's actions, were instead opposing the move toward war, claiming that Bush was involving the nation in another Vietnam-like morass for no real purpose. Chief among these critics was conservative columnist and television talk show host Patrick J. Buchanan. In August 1990 the former Nixon speechwriter wrote an editorial titled "How the Gulf Crisis Is Rupturing the Right." In it, he claimed that "neoconservatives" like Bush supported a war "that has quagmire written all over it....Saddam Hussein is not a madman; he is no Adolf Hitler; while a ruthless menace to his neighbors, he is no threat to us....Have the neocons thought this through?"[96] And Buchanan was by no means the only conservative critical of Bush's policies. In January 1991, the Cato Institute sponsored a conference "America in the Gulf: Vital Interests or Pointless Entanglement?" The papers presented make it clear that the participants overwhelmingly sided with the latter interpretation.[97]

Public support for Bush's actions, which had been high at the beginning of the crisis, slowly ebbed throughout the fall. In August Bush's popularity rating had been at 75 percent in favor of the job he was doing as president; by October it had fallen to 59 percent.[98] This drop was caused not only by his moves toward an offensive option but also by his reversal of his promise not to raise taxes, discussed in chapter 5. With this tumble in the polls, the opportunity presented itself for the Democratic Congress to make some political hay before the November election. The Senate Armed Services Committee, chaired by Sam Nunn (D-GA), began a series of hearings on the Gulf crisis. They gained instant notoriety because of the testimony of a young girl who claimed to have seen Iraqi soldiers snatch Kuwaiti babies from the incubators in the hospital where she worked, leaving them to die on the floor. The witness, however, was the daughter of the Kuwaiti ambassador to the United States who had been prepared for her testimony by an American public relations firm.[99]

Looking to stabilize its position in the court of public opinion, in early November the administration pursued a UN resolution that demanded that Iraq comply with all the earlier resolutions. Baker exhaustively lobbied Security Council members; China expressed concerns; so did

France and Great Britain (both Thatcher and French president François Mitterrand were sick of UN resolutions) and the USSR (Gorbachev had not seen enough diplomatic overtures from the United States to Iraq). But in the end they came around. On 29 November Security Council Resolution 678 was passed, giving Saddam Hussein a hard deadline: it agreed to support the use of "all necessary means" by the coalition forces to expel Saddam from Kuwait if he did not "fully comply" with previous UN resolutions and withdraw his forces by 15 January 1991. The vote passed 12 to 2, with Cuba and Yemen in opposition and China abstaining.

The day after the UN vote, Bush surprised many observers when he announced that he was willing to go the "extra mile for peace," and he offered to send Baker to Baghdad and to receive Tariq Aziz in Washington. The decision stemmed from both diplomatic and political necessity. On the diplomatic front, Bush had to neuter Gorbachev's consistent demand for—and secret initiatives for—a negotiated peace, linked to promises of a Middle East peace conference. Baker's political radar also told him not only that there was a great deal of support in the country for the idea but also that even if Saddam spurned the invitation, as the administration seems to have assumed, then the mere act of extending the olive branch would help defuse the rapidly growing antiwar feeling at home. As Baker recalled, it would show that "we weren't cowboying this."[100]

Saddam tried to blunt this effort by releasing his hostages on 13 December. Bush, however, would have none of it. When asked if the United States would give something in return, Bush snarled, "Hell no! Not one thing! You don't reward a kidnapper." On 14 December, in remarks to the press on his way to Camp David, Bush chided his adversary: "It is simply not credible that he cannot, over a two-week period, make a couple of hours available for the secretary of state on an issue of this importance—unless, of course, he is seeking to circumvent the United Nations deadline." Eventually, Saddam agreed to a meeting between Baker and Aziz in Geneva on 9 January 1991.

The meeting was both tense and confrontational. Baker presented Aziz with a letter from Bush, to be delivered to Saddam. Dated 5 January, it was stark and blunt. Bush told Saddam, "We stand today at the brink of war between Iraq and the world," a war that "can only be ended by Iraq's full and unconditional compliance" with UN Security Council Resolution 678. Bush also made it clear that the time for negotiating was over and that if Saddam used chemical or biological weapons—which he had done against Iran—or if he destroyed any of the Kuwaiti oil fields, "the American people would demand the strongest possible response." Bush closed the letter by saying that he had written not "to threaten, but to inform."[101] Aziz, who apparently believed that the meeting was for the purposes of negotiation, refused to accept the letter from Baker. Clearly, Baker had not come to negotiate but to deliver Bush's ultimatum. Baker wanted to make sure that Saddam understood the gravity of the situation; he looked at Aziz and quietly declared, "Don't let your military commanders convince you that your strategy against Iran will work against us. You are facing an entirely different kind of force.... Because of the superiority of our forces, we will dictate the terms of the battle, not you." Aziz responded, "We accept war." After the meeting broke up, Baker told the press, "Regrettably, I heard nothing today that suggested to me any Iraqi flexibility,"[102] an outcome which the administration might not have "regretted" quite so much as Baker suggested.[103]

The final hurdle to war was on Capitol Hill. Bush firmly believed that "the constitution gave me the authority to send our troops into battle without Congress officially declaring war."[104] The Congress stood opposed to that assertion and was prepared, if not to force a congressional declaration of war, then to claim authority given it under the War Powers Act and to debate Bush's authority to send troops into combat. Bush decided to co-opt the process and to formally ask Congress for its support before such a debate could begin. This decision was made despite the advice of White House counsel C. Boyden Gray, who believed that "as a question of international law, we were on solid ground deploying the troops" (a conclusion heartily shared by Bush),[105] and of Cheney, who did not want to take the risk that Congress would reject the measure.[106] But Bush was adamant; as he later remembered, he wanted "to send a signal to Saddam Hussein that [he] wasn't just a trigger-happy president" but that he had the American nation behind him.[107] And there was another consideration; as Gray remembered, "If it went sour, [Bush] wanted Democrats with him.... He wanted a unified government.... It's a military, constitutional, moral, and political thing."[108]

The debate was surprisingly civil, but lines had been drawn. Antiwar resolutions were introduced in both houses of Congress, and for most of 10 and 11 January, the debate on the issue was nonstop. Senate majority leader George Mitchell (D-ME), who with Nunn had sponsored the antiwar resolution in the Senate, argued that although "it may become necessary to use force to expel Iraq from Kuwait...because war is such a grave undertaking, with such serious consequences, we must make certain that war is employed only as a last resort." Edward Kennedy proclaimed that "there is still time to save the president from himself." In the House, minority leader Robert Michel argued, "Either we stop [Saddam] now, and stop him permanently, or we won't stop him at all."[109] Several times, debate had to be suspended because visitors in the gallery were shouting antiwar slogans. The vote in both chambers promised to be close.

But Baker's gamble in Geneva paid off, and as a result the administration was able to say that it had gone the extra mile and been spurned. Both the House and the Senate voted on 12 January. In the House, the conservatives who had abandoned Bush on the budget only weeks before returned to the fold; the vote was 250 in favor to 183 against an antiwar resolution. In the Senate, the vote was closer. Mitchell and Nunn worked hard to hold the Democratic ranks together. However, minority leader Bob Dole (R-KS) did a better job of holding the Republican feet to the fire. The final vote was a razor-thin 52-to-47 defeat of the antiwar resolution. Nine Democrats, including Al Gore Jr. of Tennessee, had defected to support the president; only two Republicans, Charles Grassley of Iowa and Mark Hatfield of Oregon, voted no. Following the defeat of the antiwar proposals, both houses voted, by the same tally, in favor of House Joint Resolution 77, the Authorization for Use of Military Force against Iraq. Cheney remembered in his memoir that after the vote, he called Bush and told him: "Mr. President, you were right."[110]

However, as had been the case with the earlier support of the UN, the vote of Congress was, while welcome, not deemed by the White House to be absolutely necessary. Bush and Baker both believed that Article 51 of the UN Charter—containing as it did the right of member nations to engage in their own self-defense—gave him every right to act.[111] Indeed, in a later interview, Bush stressed to me, "I know I would have" ordered troops into combat, even without a resolution of support from Congress.[112]

Three days after the congressional vote of support, Bush signed National Security Directive 54, which read: "Pursuant to my responsibility under the Constitution as President and Commander in Chief, and under the laws and treaties of the United States, and pursuant to H[ouse] J[oint] Resolution 77 and in accordance with the rights and obligations of the United States under international law," the president was initiating military hostilities against Iraq. The directive was clear in its statement of war aims:

a. To effect the immediate, complete, and unconditional withdrawal of all Iraqi forces from Kuwait.
b. To restore Kuwait's legitimate government.
c. To protect the lives of American citizens abroad, and
d. To promote the security and stability of the Persian Gulf.

Bush was also clear about when those military operations would end: "Only when I have determined that the objectives set forth . . . above have been met."[113]

8

DESERT STORM

On 31 December 1990, after he left a family celebration at Camp David, Bush wrote a letter to his children:

> I hope I didn't seem moody. I tried not to....I have thought long and hard about what might have to be done. As I write this letter at year's end there is still some hope that Iraq's dictator will pull out of Kuwait. I vary on this. Sometimes I think he might; at others I think he is simply too unrealistic—too ignorant of what he might face. I have the peace of mind that comes from knowing that we have tried hard for peace.
>
> I look at today's crisis as "good vs. evil"—yes, it is that clear....Principle must be adhered to—Saddam cannot profit in any way at all from his aggression...and sometimes in your life you have to act as you think best—you can't compromise, you can't give in.
>
> So, dear kids, better batten down the hatches.[1]

At 3:00 a.m. Iraqi time, 17 January 1991 (7:00 p.m. eastern standard time, 16 January, in the United States), one day after the deadline set in United Nations Resolution 678, Operation Desert Shield turned into Operation Desert Storm. The first strikes came from AH-64A Apache antiarmor attack helicopters, which flew into Iraq and knocked out key early warning radar systems. They were followed by attacks by F-117 bombers—the "stealth fighter"—and F-15E fighter-bombers, which struck at targets in the heart of the city of Baghdad. Within the first fourteen hours of the war, more than 1,000 sorties were flown, and forty-five key targets in the capital city were hit.[2] The bombing runs were supported by Tomahawk missile attacks from destroyers in the Persian Gulf—one of the support carriers was Bush's old ship, the USS *San Jacinto*. That first night, Americans were glued to their television screens, as the Cable News Network (CNN), which had three reporters holed up in a hotel in Baghdad, broadcast terrifying live shots of Tomahawk missiles descending upon the city, then exploding only yards from where the reporters were stationed. In a televised address to the American people, Bush put the war on an idealistic, Wilsonian scale: "We have before us the opportunity to forge for ourselves and for future generations a new world order—a world where the rule of law, not the law of the jungle, governs the conduct of nations."

After five and a half weeks of near-constant air bombardment, and several attempts by Saddam to end the war without withdrawing from Kuwait, the land war began on 24 February. Feinting an amphibious marine landing just outside Kuwait City, the First and Second Marine Divisions and the Tiger Brigade of the Twenty-Second Armored—already some ten miles inside Kuwait before the attack order was given—smashed into the teeth of the Iraqi frontline defenses. However, the marines moved so quickly that they engaged the Iraqis in Kuwait City before they could be joined by the Twenty-Eighth Corps and the Seventh Corps advancing from the west (neither General Norman Schwarzkopf in the field nor General Colin Powell at the Pentagon thought that the army was advancing anywhere near fast enough).

As a result, within twenty-four hours Iraqi troops poured out of Kuwait City in a disorganized retreat, taking the road north to Basra—a road soon nicknamed the "Highway of Death." On the afternoon of 26 February, in the half-hour Battle of 73 Easting, thirty Iraqi tanks, twenty armored vehicles, and thirty trucks were lost at the cost of one coalition Bradley tank.[3] On 27 February, more than 1,500 coalition tanks, led by the Seventh Corps, shattered the heart of the Republican Guard defensive position at the Battle of Medina Ridge (tank commander to his forward positions: "Understand we are engaging the Medina Division?" Response: "Negative sir. We are *destroying* the Medina Division").[4] In about forty minutes, 300 Iraqi tanks were lost, at a cost of one American killed. That evening, press secretary Marlin Fitzwater told the press, "The war [is] essentially over."[5] He was right. The next day—six weeks after the beginning of the air war, and exactly 100 hours after the beginning of the ground war—a cease-fire was declared.

On 3 March at Safwan, Iraq, Schwarzkopf met with the Iraqi military leadership and dictated the terms of the cease-fire.[6] During the course of the meeting, Schwarzkopf exhibited a rather advanced case of generosity. He not only promised the Iraqis that American forces would not long remain in Iraq but went even further. Through his generals at Safwan, Saddam claimed that he needed to keep his armed helicopters because the Americans had destroyed most of the bridges and roads. Without obtaining the permission of Washington, Schwarzkopf acquiesced and, according to a transcript of the meetings quoted in Thomas Ricks's compelling book *The Generals*, agreed "not to shoot any helicopters that are flying over the territory of Iraq where we are not located."[7] Thus, the Safwan cease-fire allowed the Iraqis to continue to fly armed helicopters over their territory, an arrangement that soon came back to haunt other Iraqi opponents. After the war, Scowcroft claimed that he wanted to reverse Schwarzkopf's decision, remembering in a later interview, "I didn't care whether the country was administered that way or not and it gave [Saddam] a great loophole." If that was the case, however, Scowcroft was overruled.[8]

The United States lost 148 killed in action and suffered 458 wounded (by way of comparison, more Americans were murdered in the United States during that 100-hour period than were lost in combat in Iraq). The rest of the coalition lost some 92 soldiers. Iraqi reports, although still disputed, suggest some 22,000 Iraqi dead.[9] On 2 April, the UN Security Council passed Resolution 687, which required Iraq to accept the decision of an international commission regarding its border with Kuwait, as well as accept a peacekeeping force in the demilitarized zone between Iraq and Kuwait. Iraq also had to publicly admit that it had been developing weapons of mass destruction (WMDs) and agree that the oil embargo would remain in place until the UN decided it was no longer needed. This was followed by Resolution 688, which attempted to address one of the glaring oversights at Safwan by providing no-fly zones in the north and the south of Iraq, designed to protect the minority populations there.[10]

My purpose here is not to offer a full military history of the Persian Gulf War. Indeed, the literature on the subject is vast and, beginning with Rick Atkinson's exceptional *Crusade: The Untold Story of the Persian Gulf War*, and Ricks's probing account *The Generals*, surprisingly good, given that at this writing much of the government material on the war continues to be classified. My goal, rather, is to look at the impact of the war on the nation as a whole and on the Bush administration in particular.

With that in mind, several points do need to be made. First, the point that is the most often mentioned in connection with the Gulf War: the outcome was never in doubt. Outnumbered and with no air support, Saddam knew that he could not win. The only strategy open to him was to dig in his lines and hope that he could repel the coalition advance long enough for the American people to tire of the war, just as they had during the Vietnam War. However, this strategy played right into the coalition's hands. With superb intelligence, the coalition knew that the Iraqi forces were dug in and knew exactly where they were; thus, the Iraqis were sitting ducks. When the bombardment began, it was so easy for the coalition forces that airmen christened a new sport: "tank plinking."[11] Moreover, this entrenched Iraqi army was so chained to its eastern trenches that when the ground assault came, they had no chance. After the left hook began, reports circulated of American tanks simply rolling over and burying Iraqi soldiers who had no way out of their trenches.

Over the five and a half weeks of the air bombardment, the coalition flew more than 100,000 sorties. Saddam's tiny air force was both unable (most of the 800-plane air force was destroyed on the ground early in the offensive; during the entirety of the conflict, a total of 76 American planes were shot down) and ultimately unwilling to respond. Few Iraqi sorties—toward the end of the bombardment, virtually none—were flown to meet the allied offensive. American stealth fighters were never touched by Iraqi defenses, and they operated at will over Baghdad. During the ground war, the marines advanced so quickly against only token opposition that they reached Kuwait City before the flanking attack could catch up with them. When the left hook finally met the Republican Guard, there was absolutely no contest. Iraqi T-72s were simply no match for the new American M1A1s; coalition soldiers called it a "turkey shoot."

Added to this was the fact that the Iraqi military leadership was completely incompetent. Let one example suffice: the Iraqis marked their way through their own minefields with concertina wire in a path that was clear to the invading coalition tanks. As one tank commander put it, "Once we found that, the only thing missing was a neon sign saying 'start here.'"[12] Iraqis surrendered by the thousands, chanting

"M–R–E" (the American serviceman's slang for "meals ready to eat") and flashing victory signs rather than white flags (final military guesstimates say that the coalition captured some 80,000 Iraqi prisoners of war). Bush's Office of Communications was so optimistic about a quick victory that on 14 January, a full three days before the war began, it sent chief of staff John Sununu a full plan—including the setup for lights and teleprompters, the length of the address, and sequencing—for the "presidential announcement of the liberation of Kuwait."[13] The staff was overly confident, but not wrong. For the coalition, Operation Desert Storm was always a no-lose proposition.

Another key point that had long-lasting effects was the role that Israel played during the Gulf War. The Iraqi's only real offensive weapons were Scud missiles, which were 14,000-pound liquid-fueled rockets with an approximate range of one mile (to improve its range, the Iraqis welded two rockets together). For all intents and purposes, the Scud was useless as a tactical weapon and useful only for inflicting civilian terror.[14] On the second night of the war, Saddam began to indiscriminately lob Scud missiles into Israel. Property damage occurred, but initially there were no fatalities. The Iraqi missile attack was caused rather directly by Schwarzkopf, who during the air war had refused, despite Israeli entreaties, to divert resources from bombing Baghdad to hunting for Scuds. While Cheney made it clear that that had to stop, and the knowledge that the Americans were now spending part of their time hunting for Scuds made some Israelis more comfortable, it did not solve the pressing question—would the Israelis retaliate?[15]

So far, Bush had been surprisingly successful at keeping the Israelis out of the conflict. With the launching of the Scuds, however, he had to up the ante. The Delta Force, a counterterrorist commando unit, was infiltrated into Iraq to try to ferret out and destroy any Scuds as well as their launchers.[16] Bush also sent two Patriot missile batteries to Israel, the largest airlift of American military weaponry to Israel since the 1973 Yom Kippur War. Assistant secretary of state Lawrence Eagleburger and undersecretary of defense Paul Wolfowitz went to Tel Aviv to personally reassure the Israelis.[17] And Bush agreed to inform prime minister Yitzhak Shamir in real time, by way of the newly installed secure satellite line between the White House and Tel Aviv, code-named Hammer Rick, of any confirmed Scud launchings toward Israel. Iraq continued to fling Scuds into Israel; a total of forty were fired at Israel and forty-six at Saudi Arabia. The total death toll from this counterattack was 31 dead and 400 injured.[18] Israelis lived with gas masks within their reach: puppet performers on the children's television program *Kippy of Rechov Sumsum* also wore gas masks to calm the fears of their little viewers.[19] Minister of defense Moshe Arens and minister of housing Ariel Sharon both demanded an immediate retaliation. But Shamir did not retaliate. A grateful Bush remembered Shamir's restraint in the months following the war, with important ramifications for the Middle East peace process.

During the war, the American press stressed the impact of the new technology on both strategy and offensive capability. It was dubbed the "Nintendo War," after a popular video game of the time, and stories abounded of the technological marvels that gave the United States an overwhelming military superiority—the term "unbeatable" was omnipresent in press reports of the conflict. Certainly since World War II's mass-destruction bombings of Germany and Japan, the air force had developed technologies of precision guidance that by 1990 allowed it to pinpoint its targets with amazing accuracy. Few people who watched the drama unfold on television were not awed by pictures taken from within the cockpit of an F-15 fighter, showing a missile zoom down an airshaft and destroy a building.

The surgical nature of America's airpower might have given the impression to many observers that the war was bloodless. It often seemed to the American public that the key to the war was the skill of a military technician who sat behind a computer, punched in coordinates, and launched missiles that simply erased the enemy from memory. American bombardiers apparently never missed. Bush himself perpetuated this perception, calling the bombing "fantastically accurate"; Schwarzkopf's chief of staff, General Robert Johnson, declared, "I quite truthfully cannot tell you of any reports that I know of that would show inaccurate bombing."[20]

It is now clear, however, that the Americans were far less accurate with their precision bombing than was portrayed by either Washington or Riyadh. Rick Atkinson reports that of the 167 laser-guided bombs dropped by F-117s during the first five nights of combat, 76 missed their targets completely, a fact that was not acknowledged to the press by either the Pentagon or the White House.[21] One bizarre example of this inaccuracy was an F-15 attack on what was purported to be seven mobile missile launchers. When the cockpit tape was played back for CIA analysts, however, they immediately saw that the destroyed targets were not missile sites; some thought them to be oil tankers, and others believed them to be milk trucks (the error was not immediately revealed to the public).[22] There were other examples. On 22 January, coalition bombing destroyed what Central Command (CENTCOM) claimed was a factory that made biological weapons; Iraqi claims at the time, broadcast by CNN's Peter Arnett, suggest that the factory actually made baby formula.[23] In a 1997 interview, William Webster argued that it was his understanding "that it had been identified back in [William] Casey's [Reagan's first director of the CIA] time . . . that it might've been used for chemical weapons storage," and that Arnett had been "sold a bill of goods."[24]

Along with accusations of targeting errors came reports of problems with the Patriot missile. A postwar army investigation claimed that the greatest single loss of American life in the war—twenty-eight American soldiers killed—resulted from a Scud hit on an army barracks. The Scud had sneaked through coalition defenses due to a computer failure that shut down a Patriot missile's capacity to intercept it.[25] These complications were kept from media and public scrutiny, as was the astoundingly high number of coalition deaths resulting from errant bombardment by their own forces. Thirty-five coalition soldiers, a full 23 percent of the total, were killed by friendly fire—"fratricide," in military parlance. In comparison to past wars, this percentage was much higher, and it took the Pentagon some five months to inform the families of the killed soldiers of that fact.[26]

The "bloodlessness" of the war can also be challenged by the number of civilian deaths. The most publicized tragedy took place on 13 February. The coalition had been closely monitoring a building in the Al Firdos section of Baghdad that had been labeled Public Shelter Number 25. But the allies believed that the bunker had become, in the words of the attack plan that sealed its fate, an "activated, recently camouflaged command-and-control bunker." Available evidence suggests both that the coalition had evidence that showed this assessment to be true and that this evidence—a newly camouflaged roof, captured radio messages, and a new protective fence—was hardly irrefutable. Nevertheless, the bunker was destroyed, killing 204 civilians, many of them children, who had been sleeping in an air-raid shelter in the bunker. Administration and military planners remain convinced to the present day that somewhere in the bunker there had been a command-and-control center. But the tragedy, quite aside from the human loss, took on a political life of its own. To avoid any further public relations disasters, CENTCOM was ordered to choose its bombing targets in Kuwait rather than in Baghdad.

Some analysts argue that this decision lengthened the air war and gave Saddam badly needed time to regroup.[27]

In a postwar study, the group Human Rights Watch evaluated the civilian death toll during the war and largely exonerated the American military: "In many if not most respects the allies' conduct was consistent with their stated intent to take all feasible precautions to avoid civilian casualties."[28] The evidence suggests that this assessment was quite accurate. Nevertheless, one must also agree with Atkinson's assessment: "The sanitary conflict depicted by Bush and his commanders, though of a piece with similar exaggerations in previous wars, was a lie."[29]

This lie was perpetuated, although not altogether willingly, by the press. Unlike in Vietnam, where television shots of ravaged bodies became daily fare for the nightly news, in the Persian Gulf the military constricted the operations of the approximately 1,600 reporters to the point where they got little film footage other than what the central command wanted them to have. The U.S. Armed Forces Joint Information Bureau decided which reporters actually got to visit, and film, the front. The wire services and a few newsmagazines, television networks, and radio outlets were given priority in the field, and even those lucky enough to get into the pool were most often fed information by the armed services and taken only where the army wanted them to go. Other reporters were, in their jargon, "corralled" behind the lines, left to file their stories largely from watching CNN reports and from attending official military press conferences (a common joke at the time: "Q: How many Iraqis does it take to fire a Scud missile? A: Three. One to arm, one to fire, and the third to watch CNN to see where it landed").[30] As one reporter put it, "For most journalists, coverage of the war has been by invitation only."[31] As a result, Americans saw more video clips of successful bombing raids than they saw human beings in combat; they also saw virtually no casualties and heard few if any references to coalition errors.

Smitten with the impressive show of American technological might, the press did little to challenge the situation. The general tone of the coverage—particularly on television, and especially on CNN, the most watched network during the conflict—made it clear that reporters largely accepted CENTCOM's line at face value. Reports such as those from the *New York Times* on 21 January claiming that American Patriot missiles "intercepted most or all of [the Scuds] and knocked them from the sky before they could hit their targets" were the norm.[32]

Bush speaking to the Joint Session of Congress, 6 March 1991. (Courtesy of the George Bush Presidential Library and Museum)

With remarkably few exceptions, the Gulf War was sanitized for popular consumption.

On 6 March 1991, Bush went before a joint session of Congress, each member having been given a miniature American flag to wave. In the most dramatic moment of his presidency, Bush turned to face the Kuwaiti ambassador, sitting in the House gallery, and announced to a standing ovation: "Ambassador [Salem] Al-Sabah—Kuwait is free." Bush then recalled the CNN footage of an American soldier who was guarding several Iraqi prisoners, softly and carefully telling them, "You're all right." When Bush recalled that moment, to thunderous applause, he took out his handkerchief and dabbed his eyes. At the end of the talk, he gave Colin Powell a hug.

Certainly, one outcome of the war was a tremendous surge of patriotism, typified for many Americans by the near-constant radio airplay of Lee Greenwood's signature song, "God Bless the U.S.A." For others, it was the pageantry of the 8 June victory parade held in the streets of Washington. Schwarzkopf was immediately enshrined as the first American military hero since Eisenhower; Cheney and Powell were christened overnight as presidential contenders. Journalist Fred Barnes, one of Bush's most severe critics, declared in his column in the *New Republic*: "I can't think of another president who could have pulled this off."[33] For George Bush, these accolades were quite quantifiable; those people expressing faith in the Bush administration increased from 43 percent in September 1990 to 67 percent at war's end.[34]

The biggest controversy arising from the Gulf War revolved around Bush's judgment as to when it should end.

It is important to note that nowhere in his public statements—or anywhere in the available records of the administration or in the memories of any of the individuals present in the decision-making loop—did George Bush (or the UN, which specifically and carefully avoided any such reference in any of its resolutions on the crisis) ever call for pressing on into Baghdad, or for using the coalition military to force the overthrow of Saddam from his position of power in Iraq. Nor is there evidence of any internal debate on the issue. Powell remembers that when he got the news that the war was to end, Schwarzkopf responded, "I could live with that."[35] Atkinson reports that Schwarzkopf "seemed neither upset nor surprised" at Bush's decision (when one of his staffers asked why they were not being allowed to encircle the enemy completely before the cease-fire, Schwarzkopf replied, "Because that's what the commander-in-chief wants. The president says we've accomplished enough").[36] In his memoirs, Powell writes that "every member of [Schwarzkopf's] policy-making team agreed" with the decision.[37] Scowcroft later agreed: "There was no dissent."[38]

But on the issue of the war's end, Schwarzkopf seems to have wanted to rewrite history. In a later interview with David Frost, Schwarzkopf claimed that Bush had been too hasty: "Frankly, my recommendation had been, you know, continue the march"—an assertion that made Powell, in his words, "mad as hell."[39] Schwarzkopf's statement, made during the 1992 presidential campaign, gave fodder to Bill Clinton and Ross Perot, both of whom charged the administration with ignoring the supposed recommendation of its field general to end the war one day later, a recommendation that, as it turned out, was never made. The tempest prompted Powell to issue a statement on 27 August 1992, which read in part, "General Schwarzkopf and I both supported terminating Desert Storm combat operations at 12 p.m., 27 February 1991 (EST), as did all the president's advisers. There was no contrary recommendation.

There was no debate.... Those who claim that another twelve or twenty-four hours of fighting *without a cease-fire* would have fundamentally changed the residual capability of the Iraqi army are mistaken."[40]

Despite the well-produced public euphoria that followed the end of the Persian Gulf War, many Americans felt that Bush was too hasty in his desire to end the conflict and that his decision had denied the United States its rightful victory. Despite the success of the coalition at expelling Saddam Hussein from Kuwait, he was still very much alive and in control of Iraq's destiny. He had also escaped with a full one-third of his army intact. Even Brent Scowcroft seemed to hedge on the issue. When I asked him if the United States won the war with Iraq, he did not hesitate for a moment when he answered in the affirmative. Yet he later mused that "very few geopolitical problems are solved by any one action."[41] And the decision to leave Saddam Hussein in power left the geopolitical situation in flux; his presence was a problem that would be addressed by Bush's son, who would in 2003 once again send American troops to Iraq.

Thus it is important to ask why Bush ended the Persian Gulf War—both when he did and how he did. One must start by recognizing the revulsion that Bush felt at the carnage taking place in Iraq. As coalition forces bombed the fleeing Iraqis at will, Bush found himself appalled at the slaughter. After seeing the images along the "Highway of Death" on CNN, National Security Council deputy Robert Gates recalled that Bush used the word "unchivalrous" to describe the infliction of any further carnage on the Iraqis.[42] Bush had been clearly told by both Powell and Cheney that Saddam's capability to make war had been obliterated by the end of the first day of the ground war, and Powell also argued for ending the fighting as soon as possible. Powell summarized the situation: "You don't do unnecessary killing if you can avoid it."[43] Bush agreed with him. Put simply, when faced with the choice between any further bloodshed or ending the war ahead of schedule, Bush did not hesitate to end the war.

Also playing a role in the administration's calculations were three "syndromes." First came the "Panama Syndrome": How could an army that could not catch one Panamanian dictator dislodge Saddam Hussein, still in command of one of the world's largest armies? Second came the "Korea Syndrome." After the 1950 invasion of South Korea by its neighbors to the north led to a stalemate along the Pusan Perimeter in the south, General Douglas MacArthur broke that stalemate by landing behind enemy lines at Inchon. Although he received counsel to have

MacArthur stop at the thirty-eighth parallel, which divided the two Koreas, President Harry Truman gave the general the order to chase the North Korean forces back north, into their own country. MacArthur did not stop until his advancing soldiers were at the Yalu River and could literally see Chinese soldiers across the border. Most analysts believe that it was this unwillingness to stop at the border of North and South Korea—a "counterinvasion," if you will—that led to the table-turning entry of the People's Republic of China into the war. Bush and his advisers believed that chasing Saddam deep into his own country might well break the coalition apart—rumblings were that neither Iran, Syria, nor the Soviet Union would countenance such a "counterinvasion."[44]

Third, and most pressing, was the "Vietnam Syndrome." If the coalition decided to chase Saddam Hussein deep into Iraq, that decision would necessitate having marines fight in the streets of Baghdad, guaranteeing thousands of coalition casualties and ensuring a protracted military commitment, and possibly an army of occupation after the war. None of this was acceptable either to the Pentagon or to Bush, for whom any further escalation of the war—reminiscent of Vietnam—was abhorrent. As Baker would later note, the administration worried that "the resulting urban warfare would surely have resulted in more casualties to American GIs than the war itself";[45] Cheney, who in 2003 as vice president would argue vociferously for invading Iraq, even used the term "quagmire" in a 1994 interview to describe the morass that the administration was trying to avoid in 1991.[46]

There was a fourth, equally pressing issue: should the coalition be successful in taking Baghdad and/or overthrowing Saddam, a completely demolished Iraq would leave a gaping power vacuum in the Gulf area that either Iran or Syria could quickly exploit. Such a situation was clearly not in the best interests of the United States.[47] Along the same lines, both Saudi Arabia and Syria opposed the overthrow of Saddam Hussein because they were afraid that the Shiites would take control of the country, while Turkey and Iran were both concerned that the fall of Saddam would empower the Kurds in the north.[48]

As Scowcroft later put it, getting Saddam out of power was "never a goal—only a hopeful by-product."[49] Privately, Bush reportedly told his aides that he hoped "some kind of Ceausescu scenario" would befall the Iraqi dictator.[50] As Bush would write later, "I was convinced, as were all our Arab friends and allies, that Hussein would be overthrown once the war ended. . . . We were disappointed, but I still do not regret my decision to end the war when we did."[51] Thus, throughout the conflict, the president's goal, as clearly stated in press briefing notes dated 2 August 1990, was to "get Iraq out of Kuwait and Kuwait back to the status quo ante."[52] In a 2008 interview, Scowcroft agreed with the validity of each of these three points and then summarized his on-the-spot advice to Bush, advice the president heeded: once Saddam was out of Kuwait, "stop."[53]

But these arguments would be saved for a later day. The immediate result, however, of Schwarzkopf's miscalculations at Safwan and Bush's refusal to attempt to capture or kill Saddam Hussein was a continued genocide of ethnic minorities in Iraq. Sensing an instability in Saddam's regime, Shiite Muslims, a religious minority located in southern Iraq and longtime vocal critics of Saddam's claim that he headed the one, true branch of the Muslim faith, rose up in revolt in early March 1990. In response, Saddam's helicopters decimated Shiite strongholds. Noncombatants perished wholesale. The no-fly zone, established by UN Resolution 688 some six weeks after the war ended, meant nothing. Saddam and his helicopters were brutal in their response, and the Shiites suffered terrible losses. Bush had given the rebels hope when he said that "the Iraqi military and the Iraqi people should take matters into their own hands, to force Saddam Hussein, the dictator, to step aside."[54] Citing what they saw as Bush's promise of support, the Shiite rebels fully expected American help.

The same fate awaited the Kurds, an ethnic minority living in the north of Iraq who had been systematically denied a political homeland of their own for almost a century. Emboldened by the same statement from Bush that had encouraged the Shiite rebels, the Kurds proclaimed their own nation, Kurdistan. Saddam would have none of it. He once again used his helicopters to wreak havoc on the Kurds, who tried to flee to refugee camps in nearby Iran and Turkey. Like the Shiites, the Kurds faced horrendous casualties; they too pleaded for Western assistance.

According to one source, during one Oval Office meeting on the subject, Powell spelled out a "precise military case against" intervention in either conflict.[55] In his memoirs, Powell was clear: "Neither revolt had a chance. Nor, frankly, was their success a goal of our policy."[56] Plus, any American interference in the region that might smack of supporting the creation of Kurdistan would most certainly alienate the Turks. The thought of a long, brutal war to protect these minorities brought up visions of another conflict—as Robert Gates put it, "Therein lay Vietnam, as far as we were concerned."[57] Newspaper editorials were clear in their advice: "Iraq: The Limits of Sympathy"; "A Blood Bath beyond Our

Grasp"; "Caution on New War with Iraq"; "The Quicksand in Iraq."[58] As a result, for all intents and purposes, the Bush administration ignored the pleas of the Kurds and the Shiites. A year and a half after the crackdown—far too late to do any good—a second no-fly zone was established around southern Iraq. Baker paid a pro forma visit to a Kurdish refugee camp but spent only seven minutes there.[59]

On a more positive note, the Gulf War was directly responsible for rejuvenating the peace process in the Middle East. Tensions between the United States and Israel, coupled with the violent Palestinian intifada and the refusal of Israel to talk to the Palestine Liberation Organization (PLO), and vice versa, had kept the administration from attempting to move the peace process forward before 1991. But the outcome of the war offered a window of opportunity. Syria had supported the coalition, and as a result relations between that nation and the United States had improved. Gorbachev had been promised the conference at Helsinki, and he would welcome the chance to shine on the world stage. Most important, relations between Bush and Shamir had vastly improved as a result of Israel's refusal to retaliate against Iraqi scuds. Bush therefore committed his administration to a peace conference on the Middle East. No less a Bush critic than journalist Daniel Schorr stated in his 10 June 1991 radio commentary that Bush's push for such a conference was "as bold in its way as war with Iraq, and less likely to be celebrated with any early victory parade."[60]

The real drama to this story was in seeing who Bush could talk into attending his peace conference. Bush wanted a conference that included representatives of all Middle East nations, including representatives of the Palestinian people—but not the PLO. Once again, Bush and Baker had to put together a coalition. It took nine months of shuttle diplomacy on the part of Baker—a total of eight trips to the Middle East—and nine months of personal diplomacy on the part of Bush to put together assurances from these mutual enemies that they would accept the invitation of the Soviet Union (one of Bush's gifts to Gorbachev for his support of the Gulf War coalition was that the Soviets would nominally host the conference) to participate in a peace conference. Bush turned first to the Arab nations, and the key to their participation was Syria. Initially, Syrian president Hafez el-Assad tried to scuttle the conference by demanding that it be sponsored by the UN—he knew that Israel would never participate in a conference sponsored by a body that resolved, as the UN did in 1975, that "Zionism is racism."[61] In February 1991, Bush moved to outflank Assad by announcing his opposition to further loan guarantees for Israel, as long as Israel continued to build settlements in the occupied territories.[62] While this brought the wrath of the American Jewish lobby down upon Bush—no small factor in the upcoming presidential election—Bush stuck to his guns. He also kept the pressure on Assad. On 31 May, he wrote Assad, addressing his concerns about the role of the UN (promising that a UN observer would attend the conference, that the process would be based on UN Security Council Resolutions 242 and 248, that the parties would deposit any agreements with the UN and seek UN endorsement of the agreements, and that the UN and the USSR would agree to keep the secretary-general informed of the negotiations) and promising that any reconvening of the conference would be done by consensus. Bush also promised that the United States would not back down from its policy of nonrecognition for "Israel's purported 'annexation' of the Golan Heights" and that he was prepared to make an offer of a "United States security guarantee of the border that Israel and Syria mutually agreed upon." It may have been wishful thinking when Bush wrote that he was virtually certain that Israel would agree to those conditions, but he was firm with Assad: "It is difficult for me to see how your interest could be served by saying 'no' to this process."[63] On 14 July, Assad agreed to participate. His agreement led directly to the participation of Egypt and Saudi Arabia.

Shamir was, according to Baker, "shocked, almost thunderstruck," by Assad's acceptance.[64] Bush's task was to make clear to Israel that despite the fight over loan guarantees and settlements, it was in their own self-interest to attend the conference. Bush pressed as well. On 31 May—the same day he wrote Assad—Bush wrote Shamir. Bush promised the prime minister that the negotiations would be a staged process, "ensuring that you don't have to confront final status issues early in the process," and that "the conference we are talking about is not a forum for negotiations or for decision making. It is a forum for breaking the taboos about a face-to-face meeting and for promoting direct dialogue." As he had been with Assad, Bush was firm with Shamir: "I am personally counting on you, Mr. Prime Minister."[65] On 31 July, Shamir told Baker that Israel would attend the conference; a few days later, Baker informed Shamir that the USSR had decided to resume diplomatic relations with Israel.[66]

By the first week of August, Jordan had quietly agreed to participate—King Hussein's support of Iraq during the Gulf War was, for the moment, shelved (Bush had spoken to King Hussein: "We want to let bygones be bygones." Hussein responded: "If there is a process, we will be there").[67] But it was not until 18 October that the Palestinians agreed to participate, and they only did so when it became clear that they were about to be completely shut out of the process. As the Soviets prepared to send out the invitations, the Palestinians made one final, almost comic, request: they wanted it to be announced that they were the first delegation to agree to attend the conference.[68] By 26 October, all the nations invited had formally accepted; Bush wrote each leader, asking all of them to do their best to guarantee the peace before the conference convened.[69]

The rest was a letdown. Little of substance emerged from the conference, which convened in Madrid on 30 October 1991. Indeed, despite Baker's note to Gorbachev, in which he claimed that "the multilateral conference on the Middle East went well, but we ran out of time,"[70] Bush's letter to Shamir, quoted earlier, made it clear that little was expected of the conference.[71] Throughout the process of getting nations to attend, the undertaking had been referred to as a "launch" toward other, greater, as yet unspecified things.[72] For his part, Gorbachev was not a major factor at Madrid—he had just survived a coup attempt and was but a month away from resignation (discussed in chapter 10). But the symbolic effects of Madrid were nonetheless earth-shattering. For the first time in decades, age-old enemies had all sat together and talked in the same room.[73] Jim Baker spoke for many: Madrid's "enduring legacy is that it happened at all."[74]

9

PRESIDENT BUSH

Despite Americans' latent affection for Ronald Reagan, long before 1988 they had become troubled with his hands-off, detached approach to presidential leadership. In George Bush they found Reagan's polar opposite. Bush's style of executive leadership was characterized by indefatigable energy. Indeed, the words "energetic" and "hyperactive" damn Bush with faint praise; by any definition, he was a workaholic. Jim Baker later stated that Bush has "the finest manners of any man you'll ever meet. But somewhere along the way he never learned to sit still."[1] Bush's staff continually complained (or boasted, depending on whom they were talking to) about the long hours and the phone calls in the middle of the night from a boss who just wanted to talk. There was no question that Bush loved his work; biographer Herbert S. Parmet has observed that he "never did get over how special it was to be president of the United States."[2]

Frederic Malek, one of Bush's campaign managers in 1992, observed in a television interview that "this was a guy who above all else wanted to do *everything* well."[3] All forms of outdoor activity were treated not as restful recreation but as serious competition. In comparison to Reagan, who had been characterized in the press as a doddering grandfather type, there were pictures of Bush taking his daily jog, leaving the press corps in his wake (prompting cute headlines about how Bush was always "'running' for president"). As the White House Press Corps,

President and Mrs. Bush, President Mikhail Gorbachev, and the "Ringer," 2 June 1990. (Courtesy of the George Bush Presidential Library and Museum)

hardly athletic by nature, tried its best to keep up, it could not help but be impressed with the president's stamina (Maureen Dowd of the *New York Times*, a pronounced Bush critic, marveled, "This President relaxes by wearing the others out").[4] Whether fishing at Kennebunkport, playing golf, or playing tennis, Bush kept score, and his former aides make it clear that the boss was not so much a fool that opponents could "let him win" just to impress him. Horseshoes was the most serious business. Bush had new pits installed at the White House, and he was so eager to try them out that he took off their covers and pitched a round before the paint was dry. Every foreign dignitary of consequence was compelled to be taught the finer points of the game. This led to one of the most comic moments of the Bush presidency. During the May 1990 summit, Mikhail Gorbachev, who had never before played the game, pitched a ringer on his first—and only—try. Bush was astounded (some aides remember that he was angry) at being outshone by a rookie at his game. Nevertheless, in the spirit of good sportsmanship, Bush had the offending horseshoe framed and presented to Gorbachev as a gift.

A second factor to consider in looking at Bush's personality was that he was truly neither of Texas nor of Connecticut. He was, like many of his friends from the wildcatting days, what native Texans called (and still call) a "transplant." As such, Bush adopted those parts of the Texas lifestyle that he particularly enjoyed, such as pork rinds and country music. These were mixed with a homespun patriotism that was born of World War II but had by the time he entered public service taken on a rural flavor (he kept Oak Ridge Boys tapes in his briefcase to play on the cassette deck in his limousine, and in his diary, he wrote that country music "sticks with me. . . . It's a great mix of music, lyrics, barrooms, Mother, the flag, and good-looking large women. There is something earthy and strong about it all").[5] Yet despite spending the balance of his adult life in the Lone Star State, Bush never exorcised his New England prep school upbringing, nor did he seem to wish to do so. No less an expert on the modern presidency than Hugh Sidey has observed that there was, indeed, a "dimension" of George Bush that separated him from other people, but that "he didn't have the least idea about it."[6] In his 1964 congressional campaign, for example, his manager begged him to stop wearing button-down collars; Bush refused.[7] At one point on a presidential outing, he seemed confused when he went to buy a pair of socks for himself. Bush was that rare breed of individual who lived in two worlds—the world of the rich and famous and the world of a real Texas barbecue. This created a dichotomy in his personality that was effectively captured in the title of Parmet's biography, *Lone Star Yankee* (1997). The *New York Times* was a bit more direct, with a headline referring to Bush as "A Special Mix: Ivy League and Pork Rinds."[8]

Yet to come to the harsh, and indefensible, conclusion, as did David Mervin, that Bush was a "rather cold-blooded and uncaring patrician, out of touch with the needs of the people,"[9] completely ignores examples seen so far in this book of Bush's close connection with the people (in terms of policy, I would only mention once again the Americans with Disabilities Act). It also ignores three areas of Bush's personality that were both pronounced and sincere. The first was his humility, learned from his mother. For but one example, in one of his first meetings with his speechwriters, Bush made it clear that he did not want them to use the word "I" in his speeches.[10] It also ignores evidence of a softness and an emotionalism that Bush wore on his sleeve—not unlike his son and successor in the White House. Unlike Lyndon Johnson, whose manhood was never in question, Bush was no yahooing Texan in the White House. Bush cried, in private and in public, at the drop of a hat, particularly when it came to displays of patriotism—despite his attempts to control his emotions. On 19 April 1989, an explosion aboard the USS *Iowa*, then 300 miles off the coast of Puerto Rico, killed forty-seven sailors. As he prepared for the speech he would give at their memorial service, Bush knew that he was running the risk of breaking down in public. As he confided in his diary, "I did pray for strength, because I cry too easily. . . . I tried not to personalize it when I gave it. . . . but then I got to the end, I choked, and had to stop."[11] But if there is one personal characteristic that best defines George Bush, it is the place that loyalty plays in his life and career. It is absolutely clear that loyalty is what makes him tick. James Baker has written, "Friendships mean a lot to George Bush. Indeed, his loyalty to friends is one of his defining personal strengths."[12] It was also the key to his political choices. Craig Fuller lost his chance to be chief of staff for perceived disloyalty to the Bush family; Bush held on to John Tower, John Sununu, and Dan Quayle out of the same sense of loyalty.

There is no evidence to suggest that Bush's humility, loyalty, or emotionalism was at all contrived or phony. Indeed, these qualities contribute to something to which every person who came in contact with him, on either side of the political aisle, pays tribute—his genuine decency. There are very few authentically nice people in the political arena. Most have become so hardened by the process that they lack any authenticity, any real warmth—except, of course, that which has been created for them in their advertisements. This was never the case with George Bush. It is difficult to find fault with the assessment of Daniel Heimbach, then Bush's deputy assistant secretary of the Domestic Policy Council: "George Bush set a tone in terms of personal example . . . that was focused on doing the right thing for America and as an individual . . . whether the law required it or not."[13] Courtly, almost Victorian in his mannerisms, Bush showed a genteelness that was innately gracious; when he told me in 1998, "I'm not the kinda guy who likes to hurt feelings," it was both believable and provable through the testimony of those with whom he served.[14] Generous to a fault, he was willing to make available his personal time for virtually any aide who asked for it. In the spring of 1992, for example, Bush became the first president to allow his staff to use Camp David when he was not there.[15] And yet, as his eldest son has noted, his father was not the kind of man to say sentimental things in person—"the handwritten note was his style."[16] Bush's thank-you notes, written for what one might consider the most trivial of favors, were Washington legends. Republican strategist Ed Rollins, far from a Bush fan or supporter, remembered that he had to tell his wife, a member of the Bush White House, to stop sending Bush a thank-you note for his note, or the correspondence would continue forever.[17]

Bush was also quite funny. His sense of humor ranged from the droll style of the New Englander to the often uproarious guffawing of the Texan. As vice president, he visited West Germany as the guest of Chancellor Helmut Kohl. During dinner, the head of the anti-Kohl German Green Party, a young woman named Petra Kelly, burst in and began to berate Kohl. Bush turned to his host and deadpanned, "Is your attachment to Petra emotional, or is it a physical attraction?" The usually staid Kohl burst out laughing.[18] He also had no problem poking fun at himself. On Halloween 1988, Bush put on a rubber George Bush mask and strutted through his campaign plane chanting, "Read my lips! Read my lips!"[19] He loved the parody of his nasal speaking voice by comic Dana Carvey; following his defeat in 1992, Bush even invited Carvey to the White House, where, as we will see in chapter 12, the two men had reporters in stitches as they each tried to sound most like the real George Bush.

This Bush—the man who can be seen, if one will pardon the gratuitous reference, as "kinder and gentler"—was not well known to the American people. One reason for this came out of the experience of the 1988 campaign. George Bush the politician was never the full measure of George Bush the man. But as is the case with any political leader, his political style is on display for all to see, and thus is for the press easier to cover, and to generalize from. Clearly, Bush's 1988 campaign style was harsh, often shrill, consistently a take-no-prisoners approach. In many ways, Lee Atwater and John Sununu existed to counter Bush's kinder, gentler side, to give him an edge of toughness. Pragmatic to a fault, Bush not only openly courted these individuals to become a part of his campaign team but he also embraced them, placing little or no distance between himself and their rather vicious way of doing business. Once these prodigal sons were aboard, Bush allowed them to work their political magic, and he stayed loyal to them far beyond the point at which other presidents would have let them go.

The second reason was that Bush himself never allowed his White House communications staff to smooth out the image of Bush the campaigner. A private, humble person at heart, Bush hated image makers, and he resisted full-bore any attempt to have his staff create a "positive image" of him in public. His director of communications, David Demarest, explained it: "The president does not see himself as the center of national attention."[20] This may well have been a function, as many of his aides contend, of Bush's natural humility. Another reason seems to have been, in the words of one scholar, that Bush "worked hard to distance himself from the Reagan years, and that included public leadership."[21] One observer noted that in the meeting of Bush and his speechwriters described earlier, Bush cautioned them: "I am not President Reagan," saying that he was prone to looking at a speech draft and marking it up: "Too much like Reagan. Take it out."[22]

The third reason was simple: George Bush was, to put it charitably, an uninspiring speaker. One White House aide summed up his public pronouncements crudely but accurately: "[Bush] doesn't give speeches. He gives remarks."[23] But just as Bush refused to allow his communications staff to present a fuller image of his personality, so too did he never see his role as a second great communicator. Therefore, he did not worry much about improving himself as a public speaker. In his memoirs, he wrote, "Some wanted me to deliver fireside chats to explain things, as Franklin Roosevelt had done. I am not good at that."[24]

It is impossible to know if the 1992 election would have been different had Bush's communications staff been allowed to show a more personal side of Bush—especially when he was faced off against two such gregarious backslappers as Bill Clinton and Ross Perot—or if Bush had been able or willing to develop speeches that stirred the soul. But one cannot contest the result. By 1992, the prevailing public image of the president was that of a limousine preppy who somehow did not have the gravitas of his predecessor—a fact made all the more regrettable because it was Bush who would not allow his staff to show him otherwise.

Few observers have bothered to look at how George Bush viewed the presidency. Dismissing him as a passive, guardian president, they seem to work under the assumption that he had no overriding philosophy of executive power other than being reelected in 1992. This assumption is false, but Bush has not helped in this regard. Not given to sweeping, philosophical statements on any subjects, and with a businessman's distrust of abstractions, Bush was famous for his impatience with any discussion that tried to force him to be introspective, calling such academic exercises "yellow pad sessions."[25] Likewise, he was rarely willing to publicly discuss what he thought of the presidency. Bush came closest to a specific statement of his view of presidential power on 10 May 1991 in a speech at Princeton University. The speech was largely a criticism of Congress for trying to "micromanage" the executive branch and a reinstatement of his call for a line-item veto ("our founders never envisioned a Congress that would churn out hundreds of thousands of pages worth of reports and hearings and documents and laws every year....[They] waste the time and energy of the executive"). But Bush also spoke to the "real power of the presidency," not the constitutional powers but the power to lead "through example [and] through encouragement."

The Princeton speech suggests that Bush viewed the power of the presidency along the lines set out by Richard Neustadt in his master-piece on the executive mind-set, *Presidential Power* (1960). Neustadt emphasized that the real power of the American president was not constitutional in nature but personal—successful presidents were successful persuaders. Yet if one uses this as a barometer, Bush's grades are mixed. In his one-to-one dealings with people, Bush was a master of the persuasive art. He cultivated people not as allies—although they often were used for such—but as friends (according to Maureen Dowd, "There have been some unconfirmed reports that Mr. Bush sometimes spends time alone. But no one believes this").[26] Bush's ubiquitous use of the telephone and thank-you notes was representative of his preference for personal dealings rather than the use of backchannels or political aides. But in the area of the public presidency—that part of leadership that requires the president to connect with the citizenry at large—historians will find Bush wanting. As noted earlier, Bush was rarely able to connect with the American people from behind a podium. It was simply not his style; as noted by one aide, "Rhetoric for the sake of rhetoric did not fit [Bush's] vision of the office."[27]

Perhaps this explains why Bush clearly relished crisis situations and was better at managing them than he was at managing the day-to-day demands of being the nation's chief executive officer. In times of crisis, the president can, and most often does, withdraw from the people and then makes his decisions surrounded only by a small number of his closest aides. Here, Reagan was lacking—a born delegator, he would rather make a speech than make a tight decision. As in so many ways, Bush was the opposite of Reagan in this regard. A born crisis manager, Bush listened, quickly sifted through the advice of his staff, and then made immediate decisions. Christopher Buckley was quite correct when he observed, "George Bush is at his best when his dander is up."[28] The same can be said for Bush's ability to negotiate and to build a consensus in favor of his preferred action—as we have seen, the examples from foreign policy are legion, but the Gulf War coalition is the best known. Two close observers slyly note that when Bush "looked at the globe, he thought of the ultimate Rolodex."[29] Such skills were, as noted by political scientist Lori Cox Han, "not on public display";[30] neither were those parts of his character that the public might have found appealing.

These characteristics help to explain Bush's abysmal relationship with the press. It had never been very good to begin with. The "wimp factor," the mud-wrestling match with Dan Rather during the 1988 Iowa primary campaign, the mishandled choice of Dan Quayle, and the Willie Horton mess had combined to make the press wary of reporting Bush's human side and led them to treat him as a lightweight—a treatment that exasperated him.

Nevertheless, Bush made a genuine attempt as president-elect to repair his rocky relationship with the Fourth Estate. As noted in chapter 3, a key to Bush's "kinder, gentler" transition to the presidency was a genuine attempt to distance himself from his predecessor's rather imperious relationship with the press. Essential to that strategy was the rehiring of Marlin Fitzwater. Fitzwater had earned his bachelor's degree from Kansas State University (1965) and had worked as a reporter and as an advertising executive for several Kansas newspapers. After working for the Appalachian Regional Commission and the Department of the Treasury, he was made press secretary to Vice President George Bush, serving from 1 April 1985 to January 1987, after which he began his service as Ronald Reagan's press secretary. His successor on Bush's staff did not fare as well. Bush's press secretary during the 1988 campaign, Sheila Tate, was pilloried by the press for both a lack of availability and an imperious manner; thus, Bush did not keep her into the administration. Instead, he broke precedent and became the first president to retain his predecessor's press secretary.[31] The modest, affable Fitzwater was universally seen by the press as a strong press secretary: in the words of Hugh Sidey, he was "honest . . . straightforward . . . not grandstanding."[32] But he was no pushover. He often clashed with Sununu, whom he described in his memoirs as "an overweight Kermit the Frog walking head down with his hands in his pockets. . . . That's John Sununu, only shorter."[33] Fitzwater quickly became one of Bush's most trusted aides.

When I asked in a 1998 interview if he hated the press when he was in the White House, Bush responded diplomatically, with a smile, "Well, not the whole time." In his own defense, he remembered that in the early months of his presidency, he "bent over backwards" to provide "availability" to the press.[34] Indeed, early on, Bush raised accessibility to an art form, often dropping by the White House briefing room for unscheduled questions and answers. He made himself available for one-on-one interviews, continuing to hold them even when the result was an article that was critical of him or his policy.[35] In his first year as president, Bush held almost as many press conferences (thirty-two) as Reagan had held in eight years (forty-seven).[36] This was initially quite beneficial for Bush. During his first three months, the tone of his coverage improved markedly from the campaign, running two-to-one positive, compared with the three-to-one negative coverage during the campaign.[37]

But even Fitzwater's affability and Bush's accessibility could not keep the president's relationship with the press from eventually reverting to its campaign-time hostility. Bush and Fitzwater seem to have believed that increased access alone would lead to long-term better coverage. It did not. Bush did not partake in the good-natured banter with the press that Reagan had so enjoyed: none of the humor, none of the playful reminders of the power structure (Reagan would often cup his ears and pretend not to hear an offending question, much to the enjoyment of the press corps). Bush perhaps met with the press more often, but the press instinctively knew that Reagan liked them more.

The relationship seems to have soured after the failed October 1989 Giroldi coup in Panama, which, as was seen in chapter 6, resurrected the "wimp factor." An angry Bush, publicly castigating purported leakers from within his own administration, began to withdraw from the press. For example, on the way to a February 1990 drug summit in Colombia, a visibly angry Bush went back to the press seats on Air Force One. He condemned stories that had been written on his tendency for secrecy and announced that from that point forward, "we've got a whole new relationship."[38] That relationship worsened, and the tone of Bush's coverage became more negative,[39] as the press felt itself—rightfully, as the evidence shows—to have been closed out of the field of battle in the Panamanian and the Persian Gulf conflicts. By 1991 there was an open hostility between Bush and the press that had become difficult to contain. On 4 September 1990, the White House Press Corps was asking the president questions before he went into a cabinet meeting. Helen Thomas of United Press International (UPI) looked directly at Bush and asked, "Who's in charge here?" According to the pool report of the exchange, Bush stared straight ahead, and Baker flashed a glance at him. Bush responded, "Some people never learn."[40] By the administration's end, by all accounts, the relationship had gone past thrust and parry. Always, and in all things, a man of the old school, Bush never adjusted to the twenty-four-hour news cycle that was just beginning to dominate American journalism at the end of Reagan's presidency. The advent of cable television and the plethora of narrowcasted channels; the rise of CNN at the expense of both print and radio news sources; the rise of talk radio and philosophically pigeonholed radio and television talk shows—all this was foreign to Bush. By 1992, George Bush truly seemed to hate the press, and in many journalism quarters, the feeling was mutual. It became an important factor in his electoral travails in 1992.

Like her husband, Barbara Bush has been judged by historians as a passive player in the Bush administration. No less an expert on the First Lady than Gil Troy has concluded that Barbara Bush was, as First Lady, "low profile" and that the Bushes "embraced the traditionally separate spheres distinguishing the home and the office, the woman's domain and the man's."[41] Troy treats Barbara as a throwback to the age of Mamie Eisenhower, a traditionalist whose silver hair, faux pearls, and perpetually twinkling eye establish her as less a partner of the president than a submissive, grandmotherly presence. Virtually all studies of the Bush presidency ignore the role played by his wife, accepting her role, as does Troy, as "apolitical."[42]

The evidence simply does not support this assessment. When one consults the documentary evidence, an alternative, more convincing view appears. It is best told in Myra G. Gutin's solid and interesting biography of Barbara Bush, the first to utilize the sources of the George Bush Library in telling the story of the First Lady. Gutin makes it clear that she believes that despite the prevailing view of Barbara as "America's grandmother," she was indeed involved in her husband's administration. Gutin calls Barbara "her husband's political watchdog and . . . a capable politician."[43] Gutin's Barbara Bush is an activist First Lady who not only supports her husband's policies and politics but also advances her own political agenda. The area where even contemporary observers noted Barbara's influence was in the realm of the public First Ladyship. Put simply, as a speaker, she was the class of the family. One can start with sheer numbers—Barbara outdid her immediate predecessors by giving some 449 speeches as First Lady—at that time a number that was eclipsed only by Eleanor Roosevelt. But it was not just the number of speeches that set her apart—of the modern first ladies, Barbara Bush is challenged only by Betty Ford in her ability to connect with her audience; she clearly transcended her husband's abilities in this regard.

Barbara Bush reads "The Three Billy Goats Gruff" to Head Start students at the Library of Congress, 7 March 1989. (Courtesy of the George Bush Presidential Library and Museum)

The most famous example of this—a speech given under tremendous political stress—came on 1 June 1990 at Wellesley College, where she went to speak even after the student body protested that it did not want to hear from a woman whose own person was subservient to the needs and ambitions of her husband. Despite predictions of booing from her audience, Barbara refused to cancel her appearance. With Raisa Gorbachev by her side, Barbara caught the graduates off guard with her wit and self-depreciating humor: "I know that you wanted Alice Walker, known for the *Color Purple*—guess how I know? Instead you got me, known for the color of my hair." But the laughter turned to cheers when Barbara ended her talk, giving one of the most oft-quoted speech lines of the entire Bush presidency: "And who knows? Somewhere out in this audience may even be someone who will one day follow in my footsteps and preside over the White House as the President's spouse. And I wish him well!"[44] By August 1992, Barbara Bush's poll ratings were three times higher than her husband's.[45]

Most important, Barbara Bush was an active and successful lobbyist for a cause dear to the heart of both herself and her husband. Born of her challenges with her son Neil, who was dyslexic, Barbara was a tire-less advocate for the cause of literacy long before she became First Lady. She served on the board of Reading Is Fundamental and was a sponsor of Laubach Literacy Actions. In 1990 she wrote her second book, a biog-raphy of the First Dog. Called *Millie's Book,* the delightful story depicted the life of the vice president and president as seen through the eyes of a dog ("My name is Mildred Kerr Bush"). Full of color pictures of Millie with the rich and famous, *Millie's Book* was also full of information on the vice president's home at Observatory Circle. The book also made many less than subtle points about Millie's master—the pictures and text were clearly chosen to emphasize the influence of Bush's family on him. *Millie's Book* ultimately grossed almost $1 million for the Barbara Bush Foundation for Family Literacy.[46] The First Lady's direct lobbying of members of Congress, along with the help of Democratic senator Paul Simon (D-IL), was instrumental in securing the passage of the National Literacy Act (signed 25 July 1991).[47] It is impossible to agree with Troy's assessment of Barbara's advocacy for public literacy as a "stunt."[48]

George and Barbara Bush were also the proud scions of a massive family, and stories abound of the freewheeling vacations at the family home at Kennebunkport. Bush's faith in public service was reinforced as he watched two of his sons, Jeb and George W., gingerly take the first steps toward political life while he was still president. He reveled in each opportunity to roughhouse with his grandchildren. His devotion to his wife was completely sincere, open, and loving. Referring to the attempt by the Reagan conservatives to co-opt the issue of traditional values, one observer noted, "George Bush was a family man before be-ing a family man was cool."[49]

In many ways, both Bush the man and Bush the president are well ex-plained by the Points of Light movement. The concept of rewarding and advancing citizen volunteers, whom he saw as bright, shining stars, had long been in Bush's mind. Long before he won the White House, he was smitten with this imagery. While he was at the United Nations, Bush made a speech in Houston. Handwritten into his notes was a telling comment: "Ideals are like stars. You cannot touch them with your hands but like the seafaring man on desert waters if you use them as a guide they will lead U [sic] to your destiny."[50] He used the metaphor again in his 1988 acceptance speech at the Republican National Convention, in his 1989 inaugural address, and in virtually every domestic-oriented speech as president. This gave him the opportunity to express some of the most spirited rhetoric of his presidency, as in his 1991 State of the Union address, when he called on Americans to "join the community of conscience" and "do the hard work of freedom."

Once president, Bush moved quickly to set his idea into concrete form. His administration established several organizations dedicated to the principle of, as Bush later wrote, "put[ting] our principles of volunteer service into practice."[51] These included the Commission on National and Community Service, which helped local community service programs find financial and technical assistance, and the National Center for Community Risk Management and Insurance, which worked to reduce the legal liability for those starting a local volunteer effort.[52]

But the most famous was the Office of National Service (ONS), which was made a part of the Executive Office of the President. The ONS was run by C. Gregg Petersmeyer, a friend of the Bush family and chairman of Bush's campaign in Colorado. Despite the problems with the budget deficit, Bush was able to secure a $25 million allocation for the ONS, whose task was to identify and honor community and volunteer groups.[53] According to the reference guide written by the ONS, the criterion for choosing the honored groups was "hands on work" that was focused on "serious problems." The group or organization "had to be replicable," had to have been in operation for at least one year, and must be "working systematically" on a community problem.[54]

Six days a week, the ONS would recognize a Daily Point of Light. According to Bush, in his foreword to a book on the subject, during his presidency 1,020 Daily Point of Light Awards were given out.[55] Bush often found the time to attend that formal recognition. During his term, he met with representatives of 675 Points of Light, and Vice President Quayle met with another 103.[56] Petersmeyer, clearly an evangelist for the ONS, believed it to be "a movement rather than a program."[57] The zeal of both Petersmeyer and the president for a program that seemed to many observers at the time more symbolic than substantial led the press to treat the Points of Light largely as a joke. However, it had created an instrument for the volunteerism that Reagan had preached but had taken few concrete steps to accomplish.

Moreover, in a tribute to its resilience, the program outlived the Bush administration. The nonpartisan, nonprofit Points of Light Foundation, founded in May 1990, still serves to foster the spirit of American volunteerism. At present the foundation has 500 centers around the nation; as late as November 1998, it was sponsoring relief to Honduras, a nation completely devastated by Hurricane Mitch. On 15 July 2013, President

Barack Obama—joined by a beaming George H. W. Bush and his son Neil, now the chairman of the Points of Light Foundation—awarded the 5,000th Daily Point of Light Award. Obama, who began his public career as a community organizer, noted that he had been inspired by Bush's example: "I am one of millions of people who have been inspired by your passion and your commitment. You have helped so many Americans discover that they, too, have something to contribute—that they, too, have the power to make a difference."[58]

When asked by Peggy Noonan, in preparation for drafting his acceptance speech at the 1988 convention, to write a few words that described him, Bush replied: "Others may speak better, look better, be smoother, more creative but I must be myself." He provided for her a list of words that were important to him, including "family, kids, grandkids, love, decency, honor, pride, tolerance, hope, kindness, loyalty, freedom, caring, heart, faith, service to country, fair (fair play), strength, healing, excellence."[59] It can be said that George Bush knew himself well.

10

★ ★ ★ ★ ★

"THE SITUATION IS ABOUT
AS BAD AS IT CAN BE"

Whether it is put to scholar, generalist, or citizen, it is the most frequently asked question about the Bush presidency: How could he have
lost the presidency when he won the war? In February 1991, at the time
of the cease-fire, Bush enjoyed an astounding 84 percent approval rating. However, by the end of 1991, his administration was in free fall.
In mid-November the approval rating was at 51 percent; it dropped to
46 percent in December and to 42 percent in spring 1992. By summer
1992, Bush's ratings had hit their lowest point—a mere 29 percent.[1] In
fall 1988, 58 percent of the people polled thought that the country was
"headed in the right direction"; in fall 1992, that number had plum-
meted to a microscopic 16 percent.[2]

There are many reasons for this development. Between the time of
the cease-fire in the Persian Gulf and the start of the 1992 campaign,
Bush's administration faced serious difficulties—largely but not entirely
of its own making, and in rapid succession. These problems combined
to make the reelection of George Bush, a sure thing only a year earlier,
a long shot at best. Small wonder that David Bates, then Bush's cabinet secretary, and Bush's son George remembered that in summer 1991,
Bush told them that he was considering not running again.[3]

In retrospect, the beginning of the end of the Bush reelection campaign
came on 5 March 1990. Along with several other party leaders, chairman

of the Republican National Committee (RNC) Lee Atwater was making an appearance at a party fund-raiser for Senator Phil Gramm (R-TX) at Washington's Ramada Renaissance Hotel. The beginning of Atwater's speech was a hit; the guaranteed sound bite—that the 1988 tank ad made Michael Dukakis "look like Rocky the Flying Squirrel"—got a big laugh. Suddenly, Atwater's left foot started twitching uncontrollably. The spasm moved through the left side of his body, and Atwater collapsed, screaming in pain. Later that day he was diagnosed with a terminal brain tumor and given one year to live. Throughout that year, as Atwater suffered through a new kind of chemotherapy that, at best, bought him only a few extra weeks, the RNC disintegrated into factional feuding. In January 1991, Atwater resigned as its chair. Bush's first choice for the job was former drug czar William Bennett, who turned down the appointment to take a lucrative position in the private sector. Bush then chose Clayton Yeutter, previously his secretary of agriculture but a man with virtually no political experience.[4]

It mattered little; the damage had been done. Short on funds (while ill, Atwater had been unable to raise funds, and his chief of staff, Mary Matalin, who took over the reins during his illness, had not been very good at it), the RNC had to lay off 25 percent of its staff just before Yeutter arrived. Because of the political fallout from Bush's flip-flop on taxes, the RNC fund-raising machinery never fully recovered.[5] Moreover, without Atwater to sit on party conservatives, those conservatives were not appeased by the RNC's attempts at party building.[6] As a result, the RNC played a muted role in the 1992 election. There are individuals today who believe that had Atwater remained healthy and in control of the political machinery, the damage from Bush's decision in summer 1990 to embrace new taxes would have been less severe.[7]

The death of Atwater on 29 March 1991 cost Bush one of the few people who could devise and articulate a successful campaign strategy. But his death was not the last personnel jolt to the campaign. It was followed by the departure of advertising guru Roger Ailes, who refused to participate in the campaign (Rich Bond, who succeeded Yeutter at the RNC, described Ailes as "burnt out in his personal life, [and] alienated from the White House by intrigue." Bond later remembered that as the White House tried to gear itself up for the coming campaign, "the A-Team was missing").[8]

Two months after the death of Atwater, Bush's own health became an issue. On 4 May 1991, during a jog at Camp David, the sixty-six-year-old president was stopped by severe shortness of breath. Bush told his Secret Service agent that he needed a doctor. Rushed to Bethesda Naval Hospital, he was diagnosed with an atrial fibrillation—a tiny flutter in the small chamber at the top of the heart that controls its rhythm.[9] Later that week, however, the diagnosis was changed. Bush had Graves' disease, which had led to both the arrhythmia and an overactive thyroid.[10] Many members of his team began to privately wonder if Bush would have the strength to endure another grueling presidential campaign. But in the privacy of his diary, Bush tried to keep it light: "And my whole mind goes, 'Oh no, here we go—here comes a bunch of Democrats charging out of the woodwork to run.'"[11]

On 28 June 1991, after twenty-four years as the liberal voice of the Supreme Court, Thurgood Marshall retired. It was immediately clear that Bush would not be able to get away with another "stealth candidate" like David Souter. Marshall's retirement left only one member of the Court who had been appointed by a Democratic president (Byron White, appointed by Kennedy), and though no one believed that Bush would appoint a liberal, the Democratic Congress was ready to pounce if he appointed a cipher. Marshall's resignation also left the Court with no African American justices, and liberal groups immediately called for Bush to fill Marshall's seat with a person of color.

On 1 July 1991 at Kennebunkport, Bush announced that he would nominate Clarence Thomas of the Circuit Court of Appeals for the District of Columbia. The *New York Times* bemoaned Thomas as "a conservative Republican with a scanty judicial record on civil rights and abortion."[12] This was an understatement. In his seven and a half years as director of the Equal Employment Opportunity Commission (EEOC), Thomas had opposed both affirmative action and quota hiring, and in 1987 he had praised an article that criticized the Court's decision in *Roe v. Wade*. Thomas's record from the bench was thin, to say the least; when Bush tapped him for the Supreme Court, he had served only eight months on the Circuit bench. He had been considered for the Supreme Court when Justice William Brennan resigned, but it was decided he needed more experience.

In the years since the Thomas appointment, no criticism of the Bush administration has drawn the ire of administration alumni—and Bush himself—as has the charge that Bush appointed Thomas simply because he was black. Bush has responded to this claim in a number of venues. He was at his clearest when interviewed by Kenneth T. Walsh in 2000

President Bush announces Clarence Thomas as his nominee for Associate Supreme Court Justice at his home on Walker's Point in Kennebunkport, 1 July 1991. (Courtesy of the George Bush Presidential Library and Museum)

for his book *Family of Freedom*. Noting that "I was fortunate to grow up in a home where prejudice of any kind was not tolerated," Bush went on: "As for choosing people for key roles, race did not play a role at all. I did not choose Clarence Thomas because he was black. Or Colin Powell. Or Louis Sullivan. I thought they were the best person for the job at hand."[13] Alumni of the administration have defended their boss's motives. At Hofstra University in 1997, in response to an academic paper arguing that Bush had appointed Thomas simply because he was black, Boyden Gray indicated his disagreement with the paper when he sniffed that "only liberals can say that the appointment of a black is racist. Only liberals can appoint blacks, I guess."[14]

The Thomas appointment was, indeed, not only about race. For Bush, this was a golden opportunity to mend fences with the right wing of his party. He operated from the start on the premise that he would have to nominate a conservative African American. Indeed, the appointment of a moderate, no matter what his or her race, would never satisfy the right wing, particularly because Souter had proved to be a more moderate judge than expected. Sununu had privately promised conservatives that Bush's next appointment to the Court would be a true conservative: a solidly antiabortion, strict constructionist judge.[15]

In his speech introducing Thomas, Bush referred to the judge as a man with a poor rural past who had pulled himself up and labeled him as a "model for all Americans." When Thomas testified on his own behalf before the Senate Judiciary Committee on 10 September, he emphasized the same themes, outlining in his opening remarks the segregation and poverty that his parents had lived under and how he had come to value hard work as a young man. Like Souter, Thomas danced around the issue of abortion, refusing to comment directly on *Roe v. Wade* (arguing that as a potential Supreme Court justice he would be required to hear arguments on the case, and he did not want to prejudice himself by discussing the case before his confirmation), although he did endorse the constitutional right to privacy.

For the White House, it was to be the Souter strategy all over again, and it initially seemed that it would work.[16] There was more tension than had been experienced at the Souter hearings—civil rights organizations, for example, were solidly against Thomas. But conservative forces were wary of opposing the nomination, lest they be branded in the press as racists. On 27 September, the Judiciary Committee voted 7 in favor of the nominee and 7 against, but it voted 13 to 1 to send Thomas's name to the Senate floor for full debate and a vote on 8 October.

During the committee's investigations, however, employees of Thomas had been contacted by the Federal Bureau of Investigation (FBI) and asked for their response to rumors of sexual harassment at the EEOC. One of those employees, Anita Hill, then a law professor at the University of Oklahoma, gave the FBI a detailed statement that not only charged Thomas with harassment but also detailed his affection for pornographic movies and his penchant for discussing his sexual prowess with his female aides. That report was not made public until after the Judiciary Committee had voted to send Thomas's nomination to the Senate floor; it might not have been made public at all had not members of the press obtained copies of Hill's supposedly confidential report.

On 6 October, Hill's allegations broke on National Public Radio and in *Newsday*. Faced with the public airing of this report, the members of the Judiciary Committee fell over each other to get their spin before the press. Alan Simpson (R-WY) appeared on ABC's *Nightline* brandishing Hill's telephone records, showing that she had stayed in contact with

Thomas, even asking his advice on getting research grants, long after she had resigned from the EEOC.[17] Hill responded to this charge in her first volume of memoirs:

> [This suggests] that I was seeking something I had no right to expect, though I had worked for Clarence Thomas for two years and had performed my job conscientiously. . . . Never would I have considered these solicitations opportunism. I received no personal gain. Besides, I had not been the one to behave inappropriately. So why should I later allow his behavior to deprive me of a job I had rightfully earned?[18]

Arlen Specter (R-PA) and Orrin Hatch (R-UT) criticized the broad nature of the sexual harassment laws themselves, which, in their argument, made it possible for any accuser to smear an innocent party. On the floor of the Senate, John Danforth (R-MO) read a statement in which he claimed that Thomas had sworn in an affidavit that Hill's allegations were false and that he was "terribly saddened and deeply offended" by her charges. Congressional Republicans were in full attack, and Hill had few defenders. The one person on the Judiciary Committee who might have been expected to defend her, Edward Kennedy of Massachusetts, was himself so tainted from charges of womanizing that he could not speak too loudly, lest the press throw stones at his glass house.

After the release of Hill's statement, Thomas's confirmation was in serious jeopardy. Many conservatives, particularly those from the religious Right, were privately urging Bush to withdraw the nomination. But as Bush had done two years earlier with John Tower, he stood by his nominee. On 9 October, he told the press, "I've got strong feelings but they all end up in support for Clarence Thomas." Bush had approved a new tactic: reopening the Judiciary Committee hearings. On 11 October, Thomas again appeared before the committee and turned his wrath on both Anita Hill and the confirmation process. He called the procedure a "lynching" and "Kafka-esque," claiming, "I never asked to be nominated. It was an honor. Little did I know the price, but it is too high. . . . Confirm me if you want, don't confirm me if you are so led. But let this process end." Thomas was excused after reading his statement; then it was Hill's turn. In her statement, she outlined her recollection of Thomas's transgressions and asserted that "telling the world is the most difficult experience of my life, but it is very close to having to live through the experience that occasioned this meeting." For the rest of that day, Hill was grilled as to the validity of her charges. That evening and for part of the next day, Thomas returned to the committee room to deny them all, charging that they played "into the most bigoted racist stereotypes that any black man will face."[19]

The hearings were a media circus, and the senators played to the cameras. Hatch suggested that Hill had concocted her story and waved a copy of the novel *The Exorcist* before the cameras, claiming that it was where the story had come from. Specter accused her of perjury (though the result was inadmissible, the *New York Times* reported on 14 October that Hill had passed a polygraph test).[20] The incivility oozed from the committee room and onto the Senate floor. When Kennedy rose to challenge those who would "tolerate any unsubstantial attack on a woman in order to rationalize a vote for this nomination," Hatch snapped back, "Anybody who believes that, I know a bridge up in Massachusetts that I'll be happy to sell them," a reference to the 1969 incident where Kennedy had driven off the Dike Bridge at Chappaquiddick, drowning his passenger, Mary Jo Kopechne.[21] During a pause in the acrimony, on 16 October, the Senate voted to confirm Thomas by a vote of 52 to 48.

Clarence Thomas has described his reaction to the hearings in his memoir, *My Grandfather's Son* ("In the deep south you didn't need a strong case to send a black man to the gallows").[22] For his part, Bush told the press, "In my view Judge Thomas made a very, very powerful and convincing statement. This decent and honorable man has been smeared."[23] Personally hurt by the treatment of Thomas, Bush wrote a friend from Lubbock: "What is happening to Clarence Thomas is just plain horrible. . . . I know nothing of Ms. Hill who makes a nice appearance but I know a lot about Clarence Thomas."[24] In 2014, while doing media interviews in advance of the release of a documentary on her life, Anita Hill reflected on her experience for Sheryl Gay Stolberg of the *New York Times*: "I believe in my heart that he shouldn't have been confirmed. I believe that the information I provided was clear, it was verifiable, it was confirmed by contemporaneous witnesses that I had talked with. And I think what people don't understand is that it goes to his ability to be a fair and impartial judge."[25]

There can be no debate about the fact that the mangled process of choosing and confirming Clarence Thomas seriously wounded Bush's administration. Once again, Bush was charged with putting loyalty above either competence or political common sense, as many observers claimed that he should have jettisoned Thomas as soon as Hill's charges were made public. Bush had also done little to endear himself to conservatives, who ignored Thomas's opposition to affirmative action and excoriated the administration for nominating a man with a checkered moral past. Also, by opening up sexual harassment as a major political and social issue, during what had been proclaimed as the "Year of the Woman," any hope that Bush might have had of making gains in the women's vote were dashed.

Yet Bush has remained steadfast. In his 1999 collection of letters, Bush defended his choice of Clarence Thomas: "I have never regretted selecting and standing by him."[26]

The recent history and development of the position of White House chief of staff makes it clear that the primary role of the job was, in the words of Nixon staffer H. R. "Bob" Haldeman, to be "the president's son of a bitch." But few modern chiefs relished this role more than John Sununu. He had played the part of Bush's bad cop—a necessary task, given Bush's courtly manner—to perfection and had made few friends in the White House as a result. On the same day that Bush's heart flutter was reported, Sununu also made the *New York Times*, as he was quoted in a story about his tenure as chief of staff: "I don't care if people hate me, as long as they hate me for the right reasons."[27] The reasons were varied, but he was certainly hated. Yet though he was reviled by virtually everyone in Bush's inner circle, there can be no question that Sununu's power and influence were incredible. More so than any other member of the administration, Sununu was responsible for holding the right wing in line during the many episodes in 1989 and 1990 that strained the conservative alliance with Bush to the breaking point. Even this role became suspect after Sununu's brazen performance during the 1990 budget negotiations discussed in chapter 5, but once again the chief of staff made himself indispensable. During the Persian Gulf crisis, acting under the authority given him through National Security Directive 1, Sununu was a key player in the "Gang of Eight" that worked the president through the decision of wartime policy. Indeed, for a man with few friends in high places, Sununu's position in May 1991 could not have been stronger.

That month, stories that exposed Sununu's abuse of his White House position began to leak. It was reported that he had taken ninety-nine taxpayer-financed flights on air force jets for personal use; several were for family ski vacations, one for a dental appointment in Boston. It was also reported that the cost of those trips was nearly $500,000, as opposed to the approximately $45,000 they would have cost had he flown first class on a commercial flight.[28] It was also revealed that Sununu had traveled in his chauffeured government limousine to New York City to purchase $5,000 worth of rare stamps at a Christie's auction (he argued that he took the limo because his job required him to stay in constant touch with Washington). *New York Times* conservative columnist William Safire called for his resignation "because he lacks a presidential aide's most essential attribute: political judgment."[29]

Although none of the activities that the press dubbed the "Air Sununu" scandal were illegal, they were certainly indiscreet. It was also the type of story that the White House Press Corps could sink its teeth into. But Sununu dug in his heels, telling press secretary Marlin Fitzwater, "I'm not going to give them a damn thing. It's none of their business. Every trip I made was authorized on behalf of the president."[30] Bush could hardly ignore the issue; as noted in chapter 3, he himself had made ethical behavior in his administration a hot issue. Thus, Sununu was admonished. He was forbidden to take trips without prior consent from the White House. Then, to add insult to injury, Sununu had to preapprove all his flights with White House counsel Boyden Gray, who had himself been the subject of an ethics investigation early in 1989 and whose office was under Sununu's in the executive office chain of command.

Yet Bush could not bring himself to take the next logical step, particularly in view of the upcoming presidential campaign, and dismiss Sununu. Fitzwater remembers that the reasons were complex: "[Bush] liked him and his take-charge attitude. Furthermore, he had staked a great deal of his presidency on Sununu."[31] But Sununu repaid this loyalty by getting himself deeper into trouble. In November he accosted *Washington Post* reporter Ann Devroy at a White House ceremony, shouting, "You're a liar! Your stories are all lies!" The next day, he revealed on national television that Bush had "ad libbed" a line in a speech (on Sununu's initiative, Bush had inserted a line calling for a lowered interest rate on credit cards; the Senate passed the measure, and the stock market dropped 120 points). Rather than fall on his own knife, Sununu publicly blamed Bush for the gaffe, thus giving the impression that he was criticizing his boss's judgment.[32]

Sununu had now become the subject of ridicule, and a reluctant Bush decided he had to go. Who wielded the ax has been the subject of discussion for years. The story that it was George W. Bush who fired Sununu still has legs, most likely because, as reported by Robert Draper, "George W. had long bragged that he himself had dropped the hammer on his dad's behalf."[33] George W. Bush did try to get Sununu to resign, but Sununu would not budge.[34] To help push him out the door, a series of leaks to the press from Bush's supporters followed, predicting Sununu's impending demise, a sure sign that he had lost whatever support he might have had left in the administration.[35] Ultimately, it was Andrew Card, then Sununu's deputy chief of staff, who told Sununu that the president would accept his resignation.[36] On 3 December 1991, Sununu stepped down.

On the surface, at least, Bush's choice as Sununu's successor, announced the day of the latter's resignation, was a winner. Thanks to his role in dealing with the *Exxon Valdez* disaster and in coordinating the administration's response to the October 1989 San Francisco earthquake that killed more than 250 people, secretary of transportation Samuel Skinner had earned a deservedly high reputation as the Mr. Fix-It of the administration. The polar opposite of Sununu, Skinner was quiet and thoughtful (on himself to the *Washington Post*: "Not bad for a guy who went to night law school").[37] It also did not hurt that Skinner's wife was friends with George W. Bush's wife, Laura, and that Skinner reportedly lobbied the couple on his own behalf.[38] In further staff restructuring, Skinner was joined at the White House by the equally cerebral Clayton Yeutter, who left the RNC to serve as counselor to the president for domestic policy.

However, as secretary for veterans affairs Edward Derwinski observed, when Skinner came aboard, "the White House bureaucracy collapsed."[39] Virtually all present in the White House at the time remember Skinner as a poor chief of staff. One staff member remembered that at his first 7:30 a.m. staff meeting, Skinner announced that he now expected the staff to work Saturdays; the staff member remembered that "attendance at the 7:30 meetings began to fall swiftly."[40] Perhaps Card put it best: "Sununu relished the opportunity to make a decision. . . . Skinner wanted decisions made for him."[41] Skinner simply was not ready for turf battles with savage political operators such as Richard Darman, who, according to several members of the administration, regularly undercut him.[42] For his part, Yeutter had accepted his job only after being promised that he would receive control over the flailing domestic and economic council. He abolished those two cabinet councils and created the Policy Coordinating Group, but it failed to produce any more coherent a policy strategy than had the earlier councils.[43]

Foreign policy also offered Bush many challenges in 1991. When the flags had stopped waving and the parades were done, Bush faced what foreign policy adviser Richard Haass has called the "messy aftermath" to the Persian Gulf War,[44] particularly the pressure he faced to alleviate the suffering of the Shiites and Kurds, described in chapter 8. Moreover, the situation in the Soviet Union was equally messy, and Bush was forced, only months after he had engineered the end of the Cold War, to deal with the end of the Soviet Union.

In the middle of the Persian Gulf crisis, Mikhail Gorbachev had made a major miscalculation. In the spring of 1990, Gorbachev had eased up on his suppression of the protests in the Soviet Republics and had acceded to the two-plus-four talks on the unification of Germany, in order to get a trade agreement. Now, trade agreement in hand, and believing the Americans to be preoccupied, he once again cracked down on the secessionist outbreaks in the republics. On 11 January 1991 in Lithuania, Soviet troops seized several government buildings; two days later, Lithuania was placed under martial law. In the rioting that followed, 14 people were killed and about 170 wounded at a TV station in Vilnius. Boris Yeltsin blamed Gorbachev; Gorbachev blamed Lithuania. Former Soviet foreign minister Eduard Shevardnadze (who had resigned over Gorbachev's policies in December), could only sigh, "[Gorbachev] always thinks he is the master of events."[45]

For Bush's part, as he had been in spring 1990, he was once again caught in the middle of diplomatic and political imperatives. Both Democrats and Republican conservatives accused Bush of abandoning Lithuania. Senator Bill Bradley (D-NJ) remarked, "It would be a sad irony if the price of Soviet support for freeing Kuwait was American acquiescence in Soviet aggression against another illegally annexed country."[46] But the clampdown came in the middle of the coalition-led air war against Iraq, and Bush needed to keep Gorbachev in the Gulf War coalition more than he needed to placate his political opponents. Despite a series of sharp letters to Gorbachev, accompanied by threats of freezing the economic relationship between the two nations, Bush let Gorbachev's moves in Lithuania go largely unchallenged.[47]

After the Gulf War, Bush was pressured from both within his White House and without to abandon Gorbachev in favor of Yeltsin, who had been elected to Moscow's at-large seat in the legislature with 89 percent of the vote, and who by the summer of 1991 had been elected president of Russia.[48] But Gorbachev had, in Bush's mind, earned several chits by backing the United States in the Gulf Crisis. Indeed, Gorbachev's support of the coalition during the war was but another example of the improvement in relations between the two nations since the end of the *pauza*—an improvement that Bush did not want to jeopardize by coming down too hard on Gorbachev. This, as well as a belief that Yeltsin was the less stable choice of the two—a choice that Bush did not trust with the Soviet nuclear arsenal—led Bush to continue to support Gorbachev, despite the fact that the Soviet Union was imploding before their eyes.[49] As Bush confided to his diary, "My view is, you dance with who is on the dance floor."[50]

In July 1991, during a summit in Moscow, Bush and Gorbachev signed the Strategic Arms Reduction Treaty (START I) in which they agreed not to use some 6,000 nuclear warheads against each other; they also reduced overall nuclear batteries on both sides by 30 percent, and Soviet intercontinental ballistic missiles by 50 percent. It was a momentous agreement, one in which, in the words of historian Serhii Plokhy, "the conflict at the core of the Cold War was resolved."[51] They also made a private agreement—Gorbachev pledged that he would refrain from any further use of force in Ukraine, and Bush pledged that the United States would not give aid and comfort to the nationalist movements in the republics.[52]

Bush was true to his word, as he made clear during a visit to Ukraine following the summit. In Kiev, the capital city of that republic, on 1 August, Bush made it clear that he expected the republics to begin to work out their problems with the Soviet Center. And should they attempt to go their own way, Bush made it clear that his administration would stand with Gorbachev: "Americans will not support those who seek independence in order to replace a far off tyranny with a local despotism." Scowcroft would later attempt to spin the speech as being not about warning the Ukraine to stay within the Soviet Union but "about Ukraine not breaking up into its constituent parts, as Yugoslavia was trying to do."[53] But it is difficult to see it this way from the text of the speech. Taking Bush at his word that he was siding with Gorbachev over Ukraine, American conservatives were livid with rage; Safire dubbed it the "Chicken Kiev" speech.[54]

But it was precisely Bush's public support for Gorbachev, coupled with the belief on the part of his hard-line military advisers, that Gorbachev had not only given away the store in START I but had shown weakness in his dealings with the republics, that ultimately doomed him. On 18 August 1991, Gorbachev was placed under house arrest at his dacha on the Black Sea. Bush learned of the coup by flipping on the television;[55] in speaking to Bush by telephone, Prime Minister Brian Mulroney of Canada asked, "Any doubt in your mind that he was overthrown because he was too close to us?" Bush's response: "I don't think there is any doubt."[56] But the coup was poorly planned, and its leadership far from adept.[57] When the coup leaders appeared on Soviet television, they were nervous and inarticulate; their leader, Soviet vice president Gennady Yenayev, was clearly drunk (prompting the *Wall Street Journal* to call their effort the "Vodka Putsch").[58] For his part, Yeltsin—now seemingly on Gorbachev's side, but actually looking out for both his own interests and those of his Russia—denounced the plotters, jumping on top of a tank parked outside the Russian Federation Building and shouting, "Aggression will not go forward! Only democracy will win!"[59] Yeltsin's chief biographer claims that it was at this moment that Bush had a change of heart toward Yeltsin.[60] This would explain Bush's providing Yeltsin—in violation of American law—with intercepts of telephone communications between the coup leaders and the Soviet military leadership in Moscow.[61] It would also explain Bush's quiet reserve when he spoke with Yeltsin on the phone on 20 August, noting of the conversation in his diary that Yeltsin was "obviously committed to the restoration of Gorbachev."[62]

The poorly planned coup ultimately collapsed. Gorbachev returned to Moscow on 22 August and publicly thanked Yeltsin by name for his steadfastness. Ultimately, one member of the coup plotters would commit suicide, and the others were driven from power. From the American vantage point, Bush had not alienated Yeltsin, and Gorbachev was back in power.

But Gorbachev was correct when he turned to one of his aides on the flight back to Moscow and observed, "We are flying to a new country."[63] Gorbachev hoped that he would be able to guide the transition of the Soviet Union into a democratic federation, thus keeping his job. But it was not to be. Yeltsin, whose hand had been strengthened worldwide by his defense of Gorbachev and his denouncement of the plotters, moved swiftly to capitalize on his good fortune. Yeltsin's power grab amounted to what Serhii Plokhy calls a "countercoup" that virtually stripped Gorbachev of any of his remaining power.[64] On 24 August, the embattled Gorbachev disbanded the Central Committee and resigned as the general secretary of the Communist Party. That same day, Yeltsin ordered the Russian Council of Ministers to seize all property of the Communist Party of the Soviet Union and its Russian chapter. This led directly to the passage of resolutions of secession in eight of the republics, including Russia.[65] The next day, the Communist Party was voted out of existence by the Russian Parliament (the vote was 283 to 29, with

52 abstaining).[66] On Sunday, 8 September, Yeltsin called Bush to tell him, "Mr. President, the Soviet Union is no more."[67]

In an effort to save his quasi détente with Gorbachev, and in an effort to keep Gorbachev as an ally both for German reunification and in the Gulf War coalition, Bush had spent the better part of three years finding reasons not to push the USSR into the abyss of history. In so doing, he had alienated the right wing of his party—as well as members of his own administration like Gates and Cheney—who wanted to hasten along the fall of the Communist behemoth. He had also set Gorbachev up for disaster, as Bush's support was one of the main reasons the military had turned against him. Now, as Bush admitted to Scowcroft, "I'm afraid he may have had it."[68] Recognizing this, on 2 September 1991, Bush reversed his policy as stated in the "Chicken Kiev" speech and recognized the independence of the Baltic republics.[69] Gorbachev quietly complied with U.S. recognition of the breakaway republics, first because he still held out hope for U.S. aid for his floundering country, and second, because he had no other choice. While Gorbachev may have hoped that the Madrid Conference on the Middle East, held in October and discussed in chapter 8, might help him to regain his prestige both at home and abroad, it did not happen; in the words of one observer, Gorbachev in Madrid was "a shadow of his former self," and he did not play a serious role in the proceedings.[70] By the end of the year, any fear that Bush may have held of Yeltsin having the nuclear codes had been superseded by the fact that Gorbachev could hold on no longer.

On 21 December, the eleven former republics formed the Commonwealth of Independent States and accepted Gorbachev's resignation as president of the Soviet Union, even though it had yet to be submitted. Gorbachev resigned four days later, on Christmas Day—two years to the day after Nicolae Ceausescu of Romania had been executed. Bush spoke to Gorbachev that day. It was a brief but poignant conversation. Bush thanked Gorbachev for all he had done for world peace; Gorbachev replied that Bush had "said to me many important things and I appreciate it." Later, in his collection of letters, Bush would remember that that day, Gorbachev's was "the voice of a good friend."[71]

All these factors played into the hands of a Democratic Party that hoped to use the reversal of Bush's fortunes against him in the upcoming presidential election. It was, however, the severe economic downturn that Bill Clinton would use as his most potent weapon. Campaign manager James Carville put a large sign on the wall of the Arkansas campaign war room: "Change versus More of the Same. The Economy, Stupid. Don't Forget Health Care."[72] The sign stayed up for the entirety of the campaign.

By August 1990 the long-predicted recession had arrived with a vengeance. By the end of the year, the Big Three automakers (Chrysler, General Motors, and Ford) had lost a total of $1 billion—their first combined loss since the 1978–1982 recession—and they were predicting that they would lose money in the first quarter of 1991 as well. In that first quarter, the Big Three had temporarily shut down or slowed production in more than twenty American assembly plants, letting go of some 60,000 workers.[73] But this recession was not just a working-class phenomenon. Layoffs hit suburbia as well, as large corporations were forced to cut back on their middle management; the term "downsizing" became a grotesque part of the American vocabulary. In January 1991, as Operation Desert Storm began, unemployment was close to 6.1 percent; by June 1991, the national unemployment rate had risen to 7.8 percent, the highest in eight years.[74] Bush's advisers tried to keep any talk of an economic crisis on the back burner. Indeed, it was not until December 1991 that, despite all evidence to the contrary, the White House officially admitted that the nation was in a recession.[75] Bush's own economic advisers felt that the downturn would last ten months at most and that the recovery would begin in time for the fall election.[76]

Once the crisis was too large to ignore, Bush took only halting steps. In September 1991, he vetoed the Unemployment Insurance Reform Act because it would "destroy the bipartisan budget agreement" with excessive levels of benefits. The move, though fiscally prudent, played into the hands of Bush's critics, who claimed that he did not understand the depth of the anxiety that the recession was causing working-class Americans. To the chagrin of the administration, the Federal Reserve Board refused to take the only step that was open to a debtor economy in a recession—raising the interest rate so as to discourage borrowing. By fall 1991, the explanation of Treasury secretary Nicholas Brady sounded weak: "We're in a recovery that's slower than we want it to be."[77]

As Bush struggled with the recession, he was also faced with a policy dilemma that mixed economic, political, and national security factors. With the fall of the Berlin Wall and the implosion of the Soviet Union came a renewed cry for a reduction in American defense spending. Many people argued that it was the moral thing to do; others argued that it was the fiscally responsible thing to do. The monies that would be saved by defense cutbacks—the "peace dividend"—could help to balance the budget or, in some cases, be applied to expensive social programs. The issue came to a head when the budget agreement of 1990 mandated a $67 billion decrease in defense spending over five years. The Department of Defense soon announced that it was planning to decrease U.S. military personnel by approximately 25 percent over the next five years.[78] But defense secretary Dick Cheney saw the issue in a broader light. He believed that cutbacks would have to apply not only to defense technology and manpower, as many on Capitol Hill were arguing; he resolved that the nation's defense infrastructure would also have to be drastically reduced. Bush and Cheney looked specifically at the 479 open and functioning military bases in the country.[79]

The Bush administration was not the first to propose the closing of military bases. It had been discussed since 1960, only to be derailed by the Vietnam War and the post-Vietnam boom in defense spending. In the final year of the Reagan administration, which had become besieged with criticism about the deficit, secretary of defense Frank Carlucci created a commission that proposed that fifty-five bases be closed. Arguing that the bases were useless parts of an already bloated infrastructure, the commission targeted those that were small, recreational, or largely administrative. Ultimately, after lobbyist and congressional intervention, only sixteen bases were closed.[80] Nevertheless, there was a cry of outrage from congressional Democrats, already stung by Bush's victory, who believed that Carlucci had deliberately targeted bases in Democratic districts. Ultimately the bases were closed, but the ad hoc process needlessly raised the hackles of Congress, exacerbating an already acrimonious relationship as a result of the failed Tower nomination.

As the process was revisited in spring 1990, Cheney concluded that the approach to base closures had to be changed. He strove to make it fairer and at the same time to place some of the burden for the closures on Congress, just in time for the off-year elections. After collecting data on every base that had been marked for extinction over the past decade, Cheney announced that he intended the procedure to follow the guidelines of the National Environmental Protection Act, which included public hearings, environmental impact statements, and the like. Thus the process would last close to a year and involve congressional testimony both in Washington and in the affected districts. Congress, however, was not about to let the administration stick it with all the blame. In fall 1990, Congress proposed the Defense Base Closure and Realignment Act. The act established the Defense Base Closure and Realignment (BRAC)

Commission "to ensure a timely, independent, and fair process for closing and realigning U.S. military installations." The act ordered the secretary of defense to submit a list of proposed closures and realignments no
later than 15 April 1991. Using a rigid set of criteria that were defined in
the act, the BRAC Commission was authorized to add or subtract from
the list, and then Congress would vote on its recommendations. Out-
flanked, and recognizing the fiscal need for such cutbacks, Bush resisted
the temptation to use a veto threat to get a better deal; he signed the bill
into law on 5 November 1990—two months before the start of Operation
Desert Storm.[81]

The BRAC Commission's final report to the president recommended
that thirty-eight bases be closed, along with the closure of seven Naval
Research Development, Testing and Engineering, and Engineering and
Fleet Support activities. There would also be seventeen base realignments.[82] On 11 April 1991, Cheney announced his recommendations to
close thirty-one major military bases, a move that would eliminate some
70,000 jobs in twenty states by the end of the year.[83] Many observers
reacted angrily to the closings, as they had reacted to the cutbacks in
manpower, contending they would hurt the American defense position.
They argued that it had been the Reagan buildup that had created the
military machine that defeated Iraq, and if Bush's closures had come
before the Gulf War, the United States would not have won.[84] They also
argued that the people left unemployed by the closures would have a
difficult time finding a job in the recession economy. The lobbying was
intense; the Bush papers are full of pleas from both citizens and Congress members for Cheney to withdraw his recommendations.

Still, the administration was completely wedded to the plan; with
only a few exceptions, Cheney approved the BRAC Commission's list,
and Congress largely approved Cheney's recommendations. In the end
twenty-six bases were closed.[85] The political fallout was immense. Seven
bases were closed in California and three in Texas, both states Bush
needed to win if he hoped to be reelected. Many Republican politicians
who had been straddling the fence over other policies now abandoned
the administration in an effort to save their own political fate.[86]

Base closures were only the most recent policy initiative that angered
the right wing of Bush's party. Indeed, as we have seen, it is not an over-
statement to say that Bush had been alienating Republican conservatives in some way, shape, or form his entire career. Many of them would

strike back at Bush by supporting Newt Gingrich's revolt against Bush's tax hike. Now, in 1991, many more would strike back by supporting an insurgent candidacy for the Republican nomination.

A former journalist for the *St. Louis Post-Dispatch* and a speechwriter in the Nixon White House, Patrick J. Buchanan was best known for his appearances on several television talk shows, including a stint as cohost of CNN's *Crossfire*. One fellow journalist understated the case when he described Buchanan as "a lightning rod for an angry message."[87] From his prime-time pulpits, Buchanan had spent much of his time voicing views that at the time were known as "paleoconservative"—wanting to turn the clock back to a simpler, pre-1932 time.[88] Indeed, Buchanan was on the far-right wing of his party, a party he had come to feel was imploding from within. While Buchanan had long been a critic of the Bush administration, it was his attacks on the administration's policy during the Gulf War that thrust him into the national debate. Buchanan believed that Saddam Hussein had a legitimate grievance; as he said on the 24 August 1990 edition of the PBS program *The McLaughlin Group*, "There are only two groups that are beating the drums right now for war in the Middle East, and that is the Israeli Defense Ministry and its 'Amen' corner in the United States."[89] For the rest of 1991, Buchanan slammed Bush, whom he labeled "King George," on everything from the war to free trade, from the Madrid Conference to the civil rights bill of 1991 (calling it a "betrayal").[90] But it was Buchanan's message of fiscal conservatism that caught on in states like New Hampshire that had been hit hard by the recession under Reagan, and were about to be hit hard again. Sensing the moment, Buchanan began to think about challenging Bush for the Republican nomination, telling his sister, "We've got to show people what real conservatism is. . . . We've got to take [the party] back."[91]

Bush's problems were mounting, and many Americans were fed up— not just with Bush, although that moment of reckoning was coming; they were fed up with what they called "politics as usual." Some observers trace the genesis of this "revolt" of 1992 to the revelations of the Iran-Contra scandal within the Reagan administration. Others date its beginnings to the first months of the Bush administration, citing the public's disgust with the congressional morality play over ethics. That reaction grew when, during the height of the furor over the Tower nomination, the House of Representatives voted itself a 50 percent pay raise, only to withdraw the decision two weeks later due to intense public pressure. The administration added fuel to the fire with the flip-flop on taxes, and the Congress added to the fire when in November 1990 it voted to raise the salaries not only of its own members but also of top executive branch officials.[92]

But for many Americans, the last straw was the tempest that hit the front pages in October 1991 when several members of Congress were charged with bouncing checks. As a perk for its members, the House Credit Union provided a much greater amount of protection against overdrafts than any commercial bank could offer. According to a later audit by the Government Accountability Office, 325 House members "had written 8,331 bad checks in the 12 months after July 1, 1989."[93] A freshman Republican from Ohio, John Boehner, decried: "We have a crisis in the U.S. House of Representatives."[94] Whatever the origins of the discontent, by the end of 1991 a large segment of the population was decrying "politics as usual" with a vehemence that had not been seen since Watergate.[95]

This contempt for politicians played a key role in the off-year elections in fall 1991. The two most watched races were in Pennsylvania and Louisiana. Attorney General Richard Thornburgh had resigned from Bush's cabinet to run against Pennsylvania senator Harris Wofford, appointed to complete the term of John Heinz, who had been killed in a plane crash. With the help of his campaign manager, James Carville—who would soon be managing the presidential campaign of Bill Clinton—Wofford portrayed Thornburgh as the consummate political insider and won with 57 percent of the vote. Many Bush aides point to this defeat of a candidate that Bush had handpicked as being their first hint of what was to come. Others point to the gubernatorial race in Louisiana, where former Klansman David Duke excoriated the system, and his own Republican Party, in an attempt to defeat Democrat Edwin Edwards. Duke lost, partly because the Republican Party disowned his candidacy. But his strong showing in defeat, and the immediate announcement of his candidacy for the presidency, shocked many party observers into a realization of the depth of voter discontent.

The Bush administration attempted to spin this disenchantment as a natural reaction to the economic downturn. But others saw it as a more global problem. William Greider, former editor of the *Washington Post*, emphasized the feeling in *Who Will Tell the People? The Betrayal of American Democracy*, one of the most important books of the year—a National Book Award nominee and voted one of the ten most notable books of 1992 by the *New York Times Book Review*. Greider painted these developments as business as usual: "The most troubling proposition in this book is that the self-correcting mechanisms of politics are no longer working."[96] The *New York Times* called the discontented public "dealignment voters," who could no longer be counted upon to stick to the confines of the two-party system.[97]

Texas billionaire H. Ross Perot rode this voter discontent into one of the most unusual presidential campaigns in American history. Born in 1930 in Texarkana, Texas, the high-energy, high-achieving Perot earned his Eagle Scout badge after only thirteen months in the organization. He began his higher education at Texarkana Junior College in 1947, and after two years there entered the U.S. Naval Academy. At Annapolis, Perot ranked in the top 1 percent of his class in leadership and was elected class president each of his last two years. He saw active duty during the Korean War and received, at his request, an early discharge. In June 1957, Perot went to work for International Business Machines (IBM) in Dallas as a sales trainee; he would finish at the top of his sales class. In 1962 he left IBM to form his own computer services company, Electronic Data Systems (EDS), where he would make millions on providing the computer services necessary for Medicare and Medicaid contracts.

By 1968 Perot was parlaying his wealth into access, particularly in the Nixon administration, where he loaned his EDS workers to Nixon as advance men. He utilized that access to advance a cause dear to his heart—the plight of the prisoners of war still left in North Vietnam. In December 1969, Perot chartered a jet with thirty tons of food, gifts, and medicine for American prisoners of war being held in North Vietnam. The plane never made it to Hanoi, but it got Perot a ton of publicity, and the following year Perot personally visited Laos and Saigon. But the Nixon people began to get irritated at Perot's penchant for promising more than he could deliver, and they were well aware of his paranoiac behavior and his desire to dig up usable dirt on all his business contacts. Thus there was a falling-out between Perot and the Nixon administration. Perot stayed out of the headlines until 1978, when he assembled a cadre of military mercenaries and charged them with freeing two EDS executives who had been arrested while in Iran. The executives were actually freed when Qasr Prison was liberated by Iranian revolutionaries, but Perot embellished the story to make it look like a Perot-financed Rambo-like extraction. The 1980s found Perot as chairman of the Texas War on Drugs Committee (where he argued for more law enforcement and tougher sentencing); a leading critic of the plans for a Vietnam Memorial in Washington, DC (which he called a "tombstone" that forgot the POWs); and chair of the Texas Select Committee on Public Education (Perot blamed teacher tenure—teachers being the only people who get "paid extra for being alive").[98]

Where Bush had underestimated the depth of voter anger, Perot not only recognized but also channeled it as a vehicle for his own considerable presidential ambitions. He seemed to understand that the way to make political profit from this anger was to present himself as a national leader who did not really want the presidency but who could be cajoled into accepting it if drafted by the people. A master of the television media, particularly the political talk shows, Perot used such shows as *Larry King Live* to dangle the possibility of his candidacy before the American people, professing to be uninterested unless his band of volunteers got his name on the ballot in all fifty states. In a quixotic storm of grassroots political activism, supporters from all over the political and economic map professed their devotion to Perot and actively worked for his candidacy. His motives were suspect: George Bush and Jim Baker and others believed that Perot ran only to gain revenge against Bush, who as vice president had refused to sanction Perot's plan for freeing American POWs.[99] Others believed that Perot ran to gain revenge on Bush for refusing his offer as president of help to get Manuel Noriega dislodged from the residence of the papal nuncio in Panama in 1989.[100] Either way, the evidence suggests that what one Perot aide told a reporter is correct: "If [Perot] denies Bush the presidency, he'll be on top of the world. He hates George Bush."[101]

An aide of Bush pollster Bob Teeter summed up the matter in March 1992: "We face a twenty month recession, a 78 percent wrong track number, and (likely) a southern conservative Democrat [in Bill Clinton]. The situation is about as bad as it could be."[102]

11

★ ★ ★ ★ ★

"THE PRESIDENT SHOULD HAVE
FIRED US ALL"

Bush's eldest son, however, was not worried about facing a southern conservative Democrat—or any Democrat, for that matter. Flying on Air Force One late in 1991, George W. Bush was chatting with a reporter about his father's record in foreign policy over the first three years of his term. Bush's son pointed to the instability in the world, particularly in the Soviet Union, which he argued required a steady, experienced hand in order for the United States to avoid becoming embroiled in any further crises. Turning to the reporter, he exclaimed, "Do you think the American people are going to turn to a Democrat *now*?"[1]

This perspective largely mirrored the mood of those in the Bush camp as the nation spun into its 1992 presidential election cycle. They could not bring themselves to believe that the voters would turn to a Democrat to guide the nation through the next four years of economic and international insecurity. Bush biographer Herbert S. Parmet puts it quite succinctly: "Throughout, Bush remained convinced that the American people would, in the end, reward him for his patriotism, dedication, and spotless leadership. He had trouble imagining it otherwise."[2]

Nevertheless, Bush's problems were staggering. Bush had to convince an angry electorate that he deserved four more years—despite the defection of his party's conservatives, despite grassroots antipathy toward politicians in general, despite the recession, and despite his own natural difficulty with articulating his vision in a public forum. Such obstacles would have been a challenge for any campaign, but one must agree with the assessment of president-watcher Hugh Sidey: "In reelective politics, [Bush] was lousy."[3] Bush's 1992 campaign was as poorly run as his 1988 campaign had been brilliant. This failing left the door open for his opponents—one in a particularly divisive Republican primary campaign and two in the fall election—each of whom seemed to understand the temper of the times better than George Bush.

During the first weekend of August 1991, Bush met with his political advisers at Camp David. Despite his grumblings to staffers and family, Bush had decided to run for reelection. But to everyone's dismay, he made it clear that he would not begin campaigning until after the new year, telling them, "I want to postpone politics 1992."[4] When his staff voiced their concern about Ross Perot, Bush reportedly replied, "I'm not worried about him. You guys get paid to worry about him."[5] As late as fall 1991, Bush had formed no committee, nor had he begun any serious polling operation. He had also not raised any significant money.[6] He believed, as he told his staff, that "the longer we wait, the more money we'll have in the end," and he postponed the formal announcement of his candidacy until 12 February 1992.[7] Five days later, Bush complained to his diary: "Buchanan is attacking and he's mean and ugly."[8]

Many observers felt that Bush had deliberately adopted for his campaign the leisurely timetable of the Reagan juggernaut of 1984. This strategy, however, presupposed that the money and the support of the conservative wing of his party—the major source of funding for any Republican candidate—would still be there in 1992. This assumption was a major miscalculation. Conservatives were abandoning Bush in droves, and Bush found that he could not call attention to several major achievements—most notably the amendments to the Clean Air Act and the Americans with Disabilities Act—because they cost a lot of money— red meat to the conservatives. In December 1991, the *National Review*, a bellwether for conservative thought, formally broke with the president. By the end of 1991, Bush had raised only $10 million and was forced to fund-raise rather than make campaign appearances.[9]

New Hampshire in 1992 was ripe for a revolt. Its housing market had been hit hard between 1988 and 1992, the state's five biggest banks had closed, its unemployment rate had tripled, and it had lost 10 percent of its jobs to other states.[10] Pat Buchanan's anti-Bush message found willing ears in the Granite State. The reactionary *Manchester Union Leader* carried a front-page editorial ("Go, Pat, Go!") written by Buchanan himself, even before he announced.[11] Buchanan and his supporters, whom he dubbed "Buchanan Brigades," set up shop all over the state, and their candidate seemed to be everywhere at once. Buchanan's key issues were the flip-flop on taxes and what he saw as the "betrayal" on the Civil Rights Act of 1991.[12] Well experienced in front of a camera, Buchanan had a grasp of the sound bite that was a broadcast producer's dream. In his 10 December 1991 announcement of his candidacy in Concord, New Hampshire, Buchanan proclaimed that Bush was "yesterday, and we are tomorrow."[13] When the White House sent Dan Quayle to New Hampshire, Buchanan, when asked if he would attack the vice president, snorted, "No . . . I don't want to be accused of child abuse."[14] Buchanan was a hit; money poured into his campaign.

Buchanan's attacks were even more difficult for Bush to deflect because former New Hampshire governor John Sununu, who had been fired as Bush's chief of staff, had served as Bush's chief link with the conservative wing of the party. And Bush himself did not help his own cause by not visiting New Hampshire until 15 January, and not formally entering the primary until 12 February—one week before the primary election.[15] For his part, the day before the primary, Buchanan made a thirteen-city tour of the state.[16] On 18 February, Buchanan finished a startling second in New Hampshire, garnering 34 percent of the vote (the *Manchester Union Leader*, which had run daily anti-Bush editorials, ran a three-inch headline the day after the primary: "READ OUR LIPS").

In early 1989, the Democratic strategy was simple. As noted by one reporter, the party was "depending on Bush's screwing up and the economy going to hell in a handbasket."[17] Until late 1990, neither had happened, and Bush was riding high in the polls. As a result, the story of the race for the Democratic presidential nomination in 1992 was, initially at least, the same as it had been in 1988: the story of who would not run. A lengthy list of nationally known Democrats—the Reverend Jesse Jackson, New Jersey senator Bill Bradley, Georgia senator Sam Nunn, House majority leader Dick Gephardt—once again chose to sit out the race rather than face George Bush, who in early 1991 was at the height of his popularity. As he had done in 1988, New York's Mario Cuomo toyed with a candidacy, but once again he refused to run (indeed, Cuomo decided not to run at the very moment that an airplane was waiting on the tarmac to fly the governor to New Hampshire to announce his candidacy).[18] Exasperated Democrats even approached Colin Powell; he turned them down with a not-too-gentle rebuff.

Just as in 1988, with the party's best-known names out of the race, the Democrats were left with a list of lesser-known candidates. Douglas Wilder, the first African American governor of Virginia, was treated as a stand-in for Jesse Jackson; Wilder withdrew from the race before the first primary (Clinton would later see this as a seminal moment in his campaign, as it led to "reducing the competition for African-American voters, especially in the South").[19] Paul Tsongas, former senator from Massachusetts and author of *A Call to Economic Arms: Forging a New American Mandate*, was treated as a dull policy wonk with a one-issue message: "There is no reason why the United States should not be the preeminent economic power on earth. No reason whatsoever. . . . It's not just another issue. It is *the issue*."[20] Like Tsongas, Senator Tom Harkin of Iowa was earnest in his attempt to turn the national debate to the economy. But, also like Tsongas, his lack of charisma cost him any serious support, and he dropped out of the race three days before the Super Tuesday primaries. Senator Bob Kerrey of Nebraska ran a lackadaisical campaign, was dubbed "Cosmic Bob" by the press, and was never taken seriously. Former governor Jerry Brown of California won several upset victories in the primaries, but his past record as a liberal reformer, a reputation for the offbeat that earned him the nickname "Governor Moonbeam" (just before the New York primary, he announced that his running mate would be Jesse Jackson, thus eliminating any hope of winning that state's white, blue-collar vote),[21] and a lack of money doomed his campaign.

It is all too easy to explain away the victory of Arkansas governor William Jefferson Clinton by pointing to the rather weak field of candidates who opposed his drive for the nomination. Though this was a part of the story, it downplays the strengths of the Clinton juggernaut. Clinton, who at age forty-five was, in 1992, the nation's longest-serving governor, had been working hard for the nomination since the mid-1980s, when he became chairman of the National Governor's Association. From this post, and through his tireless fund-raising and his speaking efforts on behalf of his fellow Democrats, Clinton earned a reputation as a tough campaigner. He was also known for his serious approach to domestic issues (as noted in chapter 4, Bush had appreciated his role at the 1989 education summit), and Clinton's fund-raising team was the best in modern memory. Clinton understood, particularly through his time at the Democratic Leadership Council (DLC), that only a moderate Democrat had a chance to win. The further to the left he ran, the more he enraptured the old liberal wing of his party, but also the more he would alienate the much more populous moderate wing, as well as moderate Republicans who had become disenchanted with Reagan. Thus was born the philosophy of the "New Democrat."[22] It was articulated by Clinton at the May 1991 convention of the DLC:

> Too many of the people who used to vote for us, the very burdened middle class we are talking about, have not trusted us in national elections to defend our national interests abroad, to put their values into our social policy at home, or to take their tax money and spend it with discipline. We have got to turn those perceptions around or we cannot continue as a national party.[23]

Clinton had grasped the key to winning a Democratic victory in a conservative environment—move, gently, to the right.

Despite his message, Clinton faced serious questions about his character. A letter surfaced that he had written to the director of the Reserve Officers Training Corps (ROTC) program at the University of Arkansas to thank him for "saving me from the draft." Other problems included his admission that he had smoked marijuana as a youth (but claimed he had never inhaled), and charges of his being a womanizer of mammoth proportions. As little as four years earlier, such charges would have destroyed both Clinton's candidacy and his career. But things in the world of politics had changed since 1988, a point best articulated in W. Lance Bennett's book *The Governing Crisis: Media, Money and Marketing in American Elections* (1996). Bennett argued convincingly that in the new, twenty-four-hour media of the 1980s and 1990s, the politicians who would survive were those who could, when faced with the day's controversy, instantly reinvent themselves before the populace—to play to the public's short attention span and to give them something different on a daily basis. Clinton understood this, and because of his natural charisma and his comfort before the cameras was able to make it work. It was this constant reinvention of self, not his policy messages, that allowed Clinton to withstand revelations of marital infidelity, youthful indiscretions with marijuana, and draft dodging.[24] Thus, rather than avoiding a controversy, Clinton relished in jumping to the offensive. With his wife at his side, he came tantalizingly close to admitting to an extramarital affair on CBS's *60 Minutes* on 26 January (Mrs. Clinton: "We've gone further than any one we know of, and that's all we're going to say").

By striking out at his accusers, Clinton turned his second-place finish in the New Hampshire primary on 18 February—the same day as the Republican primary—into a triumph for an embittered candidate. Thus the "Comeback Kid" was born. As Clinton would tell an adoring crowd in Dover, New Hampshire: "I'll be there for you until the last dog dies."[25]

Where the gregarious Clinton was addicted to the crowd, Ross Perot had relied almost entirely on television appearances and commercials to attract voters—no candidate had ever tried such a strategy.[26] His folksy humor and blunt assessment of national issues made him somewhat of a cult hero to Americans who had tired of "politics as usual." On 60 Minutes, for example, he compared the federal deficit to "a crazy aunt you keep down in the basement. All the neighbors know she's there, but no one talks about her."[27] Two days after the New Hampshire primary, on the evening of 20 February, he appeared on CNN's Larry King Live. While he continued to protest that he was not a candidate, Perot told the viewers that if they wanted him to become a candidate, they should join a movement to get his name on the ballot in all fifty states. If they did that, Perot promised that he would pay for his entire campaign out of his own pocket ("If enough people want me, I'll be their hero").[28] The response to Perot's "nonannouncement" was overwhelming. His popularity even drew, at least for the time being, two political super-stars—Republican Ed Rollins and Democrat Hamilton Jordan—to his "campaign" as consultants.[29] At the end of March, Perot announced that he had picked his friend, Admiral James Stockdale, the highest-ranking naval prisoner of war of the Vietnam War period, as his running mate.[30]

The New Hampshire primary was Pat Buchanan's high-water mark. As the primaries moved south, he changed the focus of his message from a fiscal message to a social message. Most notably, Buchanan attacked the National Endowment for the Arts, and its chair John Frohnmeyer, for the funding of artists whose work Buchanan deemed to be pornographic. He also courted the state's rights vote, slamming the Civil Rights Act of 1991 in virtually every speech.[31] It did not work. Bush won the Georgia primary with 64 percent of the vote, and Buchanan won only one-third of the vote on Super Tuesday. Between 25 February (South Dakota) and 9 June (North Dakota), Bush won thirty-eight of thirty-eight primaries against Buchanan, with an average of 72.84 percent of the popular vote against Buchanan's 22.96 percent.[32]

However, Buchanan was openly defiant to those who suggested that he withdraw from the race in the name of party unity (Nixon met with Buchanan in New Jersey and asked him to drop out; Buchanan told his old boss no).[33] Buchanan made it clear that win, lose, or draw, he was staying in the race until the convention. This he did, becoming an ever-present force on Bush's right flank, nipping at Bush's heels in every primary and caucus all the way to the convention. Although there was never any possibility of Buchanan's winning the nomination, his candidacy forced Bush to spend a great deal more money on advertisements in the primaries than he had planned. When the fall campaign began, the Bush campaign was strapped for cash, having spent $27 million to keep Buchanan at bay, while Bush's other two opponents were in good shape. Moreover, Buchanan's campaign made it clear that after the arduous primary season, there was a sizable portion of Republicans who would find it difficult to support Bush in November. As Buchanan's biographer put it, Bush had the difficult task of defeating Buchanan without alienating his supporters.[34] Political analyst Kevin Phillips accurately quipped, "George Bush is winning and sounds like a loser. Pat Buchanan is losing and sounds like a winner."[35]

In April the Bush campaign mishandled a golden opportunity to make points in voter-rich California. On 29 April, not-guilty verdicts for three of the four policemen accused of beating robbery suspect Rodney King sparked a rampage in the streets of Los Angeles in which 52 people died, 2,500 were injured, and an estimated $446 million in property damage occurred.[36] Ironically, some six months earlier, Mayor Tom Bradley had come to the White House to discuss with Bush the possibility of such an outburst in his city. Thus, the administration had been planning for just such an eruption in Los Angeles for almost six months. The administration acted swiftly after the verdict: members of Bush's team were in Los Angeles within twenty-four hours of the start of the riots (one staffer remembered that when he arrived, "there was still smoke coming out of the buildings").[37] But while his staff was indeed in L.A., it was not until the second or third day that Bush told chief of staff Sam Skinner that he wanted to go on television to address the nation. The subsequent staffing out of the drafts of the speech, the dueling over speech drafts, and Skinner's inability to make up his mind lost precious time.[38] It took the president five days—during which Ross Perot had publicly scolded Bush for his inaction—to finally get to Los Angeles to view the destruction and to meet with local leaders, leaving him exposed to charges of being aloof to the crisis.

In early June, Bush further angered conservatives in an interview on ABC's *20/20*. When asked if he would "knowingly" appoint a homosexual to his cabinet, Bush replied that there should be no "litmus test" on gays in his administration.[39] This statement even drew the not-altogether-quiet protests of Quayle, who had made his opposition to gay rights clearly known in several speeches. On the domestic front, Bush's veto of the Family Leave Act handed the Democrats ammunition with which to call Bush an uncaring, rich patrician.[40] In foreign policy, Bush was in the midst of delicate post-Madrid discussions with both the Israelis and the Palestinians over the settlement of the West Bank. The Israelis, however, were being intransigent about their right to continue settling the region. To light a fire under the peace process, Bush delayed $10 billion in requested loan guarantees to the Israelis because he believed, as he later wrote, that "the money, either directly or indirectly, would support those settlements." Bush was correct when he noted in his memoir that "all hell broke out";[41] this move hurt Bush's already minuscule support in the Jewish community.

The issue of free trade played right into the hands of both Perot and Buchanan. In 1987 the United States had successfully concluded a free trade agreement with Canada. Reagan dreamed of expanding that deal into a comprehensive North American Free Trade Agreement (NAFTA), which would eradicate most tariffs within ten years of its passage. The next logical step was to negotiate a treaty with Mexico. However, it was not until the 1988 election of Carlos Salinas de Gortari to the presidency that the Mexican government was amenable to opening such a dialogue. Thanks to Bush's personal diplomacy and the aid of his close friend Brian Mulroney, then prime minister of Canada, Salinas threw his support behind NAFTA. Negotiations with the Mexicans began in summer 1990.

From Bush's vantage point, NAFTA could not happen fast enough. Both Bush and secretary of state James Baker wanted to complete the treaty negotiations before 1992, not only because they were philosophically in favor of free trade but also because they wanted to close the deal before the presidential election season. Thus, on 5 February 1991, Bush requested that Congress extend the "fast track" status that had been granted to the 1988 negotiations with Canada. Fast track gave authority to the president to negotiate a treaty in three months; once it was presented to Congress, that body was given ninety days to vote on its approval, without being able to amend the treaty from the floor.

The debate on Bush's fast-track request began the next day. A Mexican observer of the process was quite correct when he concluded, "Arguments against the fast-track were really against the concept of a free trade agreement with Mexico."[42] House majority leader Richard Gephardt, at that time mentioned as a possible presidential candidate, led the opposition to the proposal. However, the lobbying blitz, particularly by the American Hispanic community, carried the day. On 24 May the request to extend fast-track status was approved by the House, 231 to 192. It then passed the Senate, 59 to 36.

The debate over fast-track and the subsequent negotiations for NAFTA were carried out during the heart of the presidential primary season. The proposed treaty was cautiously supported by Democratic front-runner Bill Clinton but vehemently opposed by Buchanan and Perot, who argued that it would result in the relocation of American industry and the loss of American jobs. In the midst of a recession, their arguments struck home to a large number of voters, and opposition to NAFTA became an anti-Bush rallying cry. The treaty, one of Bush's most notable diplomatic successes, was finally signed on 17 December 1992—but not soon enough to keep the issue from exacting a political cost.[43]

Many of Bush's closest advisers felt that they had the solution to the president's political problems. On 19 May 1992, Vice President Dan Quayle, who had been carving out a name for himself as the administration's most vocal adherent to the conservative line, gave a speech in San Francisco; in it, he attacked a fictional television character. Quayle blamed the Los Angeles riots on a "poverty of values" and noted, "It doesn't help matters when prime time TV has Murphy Brown—a character who supposedly epitomizes today's intelligent, highly paid, professional woman, mocking the importance of fathers by bearing a child alone, and calling it just another 'lifestyle choice.'" The slap at the television character Murphy Brown, a journalist and single mother played by Candice Bergen, was a throwaway line that pleased many movement conservatives. But from virtually every other corner, the remark was met with ridicule and derision. In his memoirs, Quayle writes that Bush called him to express his support. Publicly, however, the White House did its best to distance itself from the vice president's opinions.[44]

Many White House insiders began to lobby privately for dropping Quayle from the fall ticket. James Baker said plainly in his memoirs that

Quayle "had become a liability" for Bush's reelection chances, and that pollster Robert Teeter told Baker that Powell, Cheney, or even Baker, polled better than Quayle.[45] All agreed that the only way that Quayle could be replaced was if he could be convinced to take himself off the ticket. The "Dump Quayle" movement was not a deep secret: reporters Rowland Evans and Robert Novak reported—errantly—that Governor Carroll Campbell of South Carolina was the front-runner to replace the vice president on the ticket.[46] While one reporter claims that there was a "cabal," which included campaign aide Spencer and Baker, and that "a strategy memo prepared by one of Baker's closest aides in the summer of 1992 had in fact recommended the veep be replaced by Colin Powell,"[47] there is no record of Baker speaking directly with Bush on this matter.

But others did. In an interview with Thomas DeFrank, former president Gerald Ford remembered that he, too, had become convinced that thanks to the economy, Bush could not win with Quayle still on the ticket. Ford telephoned one of Bush's aides, who told him that he should speak directly with Bush. Ford called Bush while the president was traveling on Air Force One. He made his pitch, but he knew that Bush was not in favor of it. As Ford interpreted it, Bush had been burned with "read my lips" and did not want to be hammered with another flip-flop.[48] George W. Bush also claimed that he had spoken to his father and suggested that he replace Quayle with Dick Cheney, but "Dad said no."[49] For his part, in a footnote in his collection of memoirs, Bush once again defended his decision: "He kept his head and was loyal to me, and I never regretted my choice."[50]

In his memoirs, Baker is clearly angry with Quayle for not stepping down: "The biggest favor he could have done for the president—and the country, in my opinion—would have been to graciously take himself off the ticket."[51] This misses the point. Quayle mattered not in the 1992 election; there is no evidence that his presence either on or off the ticket made any difference whatsoever to the final result. The fact of the matter was that the public was blaming the president, whose polls continued to drop.

Clinton had resurrected his political career in New Hampshire. By April, with a victory in New York's primary paving the way, he had wrapped up the Democratic nomination. But the "Comeback Kid" was not strong enough to win the general election. For that, Clinton needed to adopt a statesmanlike approach. Enter *The Man from Hope*, a particularly effective documentary on Clinton's life, played at the convention, which emphasized his rise from poverty and his message of hope (also conveniently the name of his hometown in Arkansas). If measured by the Gallup poll, the Democratic convention was a triumph. At its end, Clinton and his new running mate, Senator Al Gore Jr. of Tennessee, were the recipients of the highest postconvention bounce in the poll's history; their base of support grew from 40 percent just before the convention to 56 percent immediately after it. This surge turned Clinton's eight-point deficit against Bush into a twenty-two-point lead—a spectacular thirty-point swing in the race.

On 15 July, in the middle of the Democratic convention, after a disagreement over whether or not to mount a $150 million publicity offensive, Perot fired Ed Rollins and, declaring that the Democratic Party had "revitalized itself," announced that he would not be a candidate in the 1992 election.[52]

Unlike Buchanan, who reveled in the primary campaign, Bush often seemed listless, as if he were just going through the motions. There was none of the spark, none of the crackle that had accompanied his campaign three years earlier. Bush did not even provide for himself a convention spectacle that would increase his standing in the polls once he had been renominated. In a series of tactical blunders, the Bush team lost control of its own convention. Instead of its being a carefully scripted showcase for the renomination of the president, the Republican convention, held in Houston, became a bully pulpit for Buchanan and his conservative supporters.[53]

The administration virtually ceded the platform hearings to Buchanan, who turned them into a rancorous debate over the issue of abortion.[54] More important than the platform (which Bush would simply ignore in the fall election, as would his two opponents ignore their parties' platforms) was the decision—later characterized by Richard Bond (who had succeeded Clayton Yeutter as the chairman of the Republican National Committee in January 1992) as a "flat-out mistake"[55]—to allow Buchanan to speak during the first night of the convention in prime time. Buchanan's 17 August speech was a screed designed not to promote party unity but to energize his brigades to declare a holy war on all things liberal. He charged that "there is a religious war going on in our country for the soul of America" and then pilloried homosexuals to make his point. Buchanan called the Democratic ticket "the most

225

pro-gay and pro-lesbian ticket in history" and decried the Democrats' convention ads as "the greatest single exhibition of cross-dressing in American political history." He claimed that the Democratic agenda— which included, according to Buchanan, homosexual rights, gays in the military, and abortion on demand—offered "change all right, but not the kind of change America needs."[56] Buchanan's was but the opening speech in an evening of right-wing polemic, ironically billed as "Family Night" at the convention. Even Second Lady Marilyn Quayle joined in, as she maintained to her audience that liberals were "disappointed because most women do not wish to be liberated from their essential natures as women."[57] All of these speeches could be taken as attacks both on Clinton and on the moderate programs of the Bush administration; conservative columnist George Will observed the convention and concluded, "The crazies are in charge."[58]

Bush's 20 August acceptance speech did nothing to help his own situation. Indeed, in delivery and style of writing, it paled in comparison to Buchanan's. Gone was the defiant tone of his 1988 speech, when he demanded that the nation read his lips. Bush had wanted to use this opportunity to focus on his fall opponent and to call attention to his foreign policy successes. But the feeling that many listeners got from the speech was that Bush had become embittered about the criticism he was getting ("When the Berlin Wall fell, I half expected to see a headline: 'Wall Falls, Three Border Guards Lose Jobs,' and underneath it probably says, 'Clinton Blames Bush'"). Bush's call to arms—"Here is my question for the American people—who do you trust in this election?"—fell flat. For many Americans, long since soured on the political system, the Republican convention, aptly described by columnist Molly Ivins as "a feast of hate and fear . . . sour, mean, and dull," was the last straw.[59] Many observers viewed both Bush and his party as out of touch with mainstream, moderate Americans.

Despite the fact that Perot had said that he was formally out of the race, his volunteers refused to end their efforts to get his name on the ballot. By mid-September, Perot's name was finally on the ballot in all fifty states. On 28 September, delegations from the Bush and Clinton campaigns met with Perot, in an effort to try to keep him out of the race and to secure his endorsement. Both suitors were spurned. On 1 October, Perot announced that he was back in the race. He would do well in each of the debates, scoring points against both Bush and Clinton with his folksy banter. But on Sunday, 25 October, on *60 Minutes*, Perot explained why he had originally withdrawn—he had, he claimed, received reports of a Republican Party plot to disrupt the August wedding of his daughter.[60] The resulting fallout from this bizarre announcement stopped any momentum that Perot might have had.

It was the first time in American history that three southerners had vied for the presidency in the fall election. But at virtually every opportunity, Clinton beat both Bush and Perot to the punch. By presenting the nation with a new Clinton whenever adversity hit, the Democratic candidate showed that he could weather an attack. In another election year, it might have been seen as crass opportunism. But in 1992 Clinton's makeovers played well with disenchanted voters who believed him to be under attack from the very institutions that they had come to hate. Perhaps it was as simple as Ed Rollins claimed: "The country [wasn't] as mad at [Clinton] like they were at the president, and he was three times the campaigner Bush was."[61] Indeed, borrowing from the words of the candidate, many Americans had come to believe that Clinton "felt their pain."

One of the most telling examples of this came during the Bush administration's response to Hurricane Andrew, which struck southeastern Florida on 24 August. A category four hurricane with winds of 140 miles per hour when it hit land, to that point Andrew was the costliest hurricane in American history—some 1.4 million families were without electricity, 107,800 homes were damaged, and 49,000 homes were left uninhabitable.[62] Bush flew to the site within twelve hours of the hurricane hitting. He landed at Opa Locka Airport, proceeded by motorcade to Cutler Ridge Mall, made a speech in front of a record store that had been looted, posed in front of an uprooted tree, and left—the entire trip took only a few hours.[63]

It did not take long for Bush to be pilloried in the press for making a photo op stop in Florida that meant little. Clinton pounced, traveling to Florida to criticize the government relief effort. Aid was promised, but it was not immediately forthcoming. According to two students of the crisis, the immediate response of the Federal Emergency Management Agency, established in 1979 by President Carter, "proved totally inadequate."[64] On 27 August, Kate Hale, the Dade County emergency relief director, was seen on the national news; through tears, she demanded: "Where is the cavalry? . . . I'd like Bush to follow up on the commitments he made." He did. Later that day, the administration sent 35,000 troops to the South Dade area and sent a task force, including secretary of transportation Andrew Card, to the stricken area; the task force stayed some seven weeks.[65] Further visits followed: Bush traveled to the South Dade area for the second time on 1 September; later that day he spoke to the nation about the storm and asked for assistance from the American Red Cross, as well as a new group called "We Will Rebuild."[66] Jack Kemp and Louis Sullivan went down on 2 September; Quayle and his wife visited the stricken area on 12 September.[67] Bush visited again on 3 October, accompanied by Card and his son Jeb; in Homestead, Bush visited a shopping plaza, several temporary housing units, and a tent city.[68]

The response of the Bush administration eventually grew to record levels of spending and action (a later eleven-page report, listing the administration's response minute by minute is impressive).[69] But lives had been shattered, and no administration would ever have been able to respond fast enough to satisfy a family whose house had blown away. Clinton, however, was not above making political hay out of the situation, and Bush was once again—this time unfairly—painted as aloof. It was a lesson that would, to the detriment of the city of New Orleans in 2005, not be learned by Bush's son.

That November, Bill Clinton won 43 percent of the popular vote to George Bush's 38 percent and Ross Perot's astonishing 19 percent. The popular vote was indicative of the three-way race, where analyses showed that Perot drew voters away from both candidates. In every significant area of support, Clinton outpolled Bush—except for the Christian Right (a fact that surprised Bush).[70] But in the Electoral College, Clinton's victory was complete; he won 370 electoral votes to Bush's 168. Clinton made inroads in every area of the country; of the states that Bush had won in 1988, Clinton recaptured California, Pennsylvania, Ohio, and Illinois—four states with a combined total of 122 electoral votes. Perot's impact was largely on voter turnout; 1992 was the first time in thirty years that there had not been a decline. Clinton's victory was a personal one, with very short coattails. The Democrats lost nine seats in the House but retained their majority, and the party composition in the Senate did not change. Nevertheless, Bush's loss was complete. It was the worst rejection of a sitting president since 1912; 27 percent of Republicans and 68 percent of Independents voted for Bill Clinton.

In a loss that big, there is simply no credible way to isolate one factor to explain the defeat. But that has not stopped people from trying. In the many accounts of the election of 1992 written by the alumni of the Bush administration, virtually none give Clinton much credit for winning the race. Many of them blame the press. Granted, the press not only was virulently anti-Bush but openly flaunted that fact. One of the most frequently quoted statistics that I heard in my interviews with the Bush people was that, following the election, 89 percent of the correspondents on the election trail said that they had voted for Clinton. Certainly neither Bush nor the press had softened on each other. On 11 August 1992, during a press conference at Kennebunkport with Yitzhak Rabin, Mary Tillotson of CNN asked Bush point-blank if he had had an affair with Jennifer Fitzgerald, a former secretary, as a "recently published book" had claimed. Bush was livid; his granddaughter Noelle started to cry. Then Bush snapped: "I'm not going to take any sleazy questions like that from CNN. No, it's a lie."[71] Barbara Bush eventually addressed the stories: "George Bush sleeps with two girls: Millie and me."[72] Despite his hatred of the press, Bush nevertheless hoped that the journalists would eventually wise up to Clinton and report his trysts. Marlin Fitzwater remembered that Bush "had a curious code of media discipline that said: 'If I am doing the right thing, I can take any punishment.'"[73]

Other observers blame Bush's health, seeing him as more listless and disengaged during the campaign than ever before.[74] As early as July 1991, Bush was complaining in his diary: "My medicine is making me tired."[75] In January 1992, while on a state visit to Japan, Bush contracted a severe case of intestinal influenza and vomited on Prime Minister Kiichi Miyazawa, a scene that was inadvertently taped by Japanese television and soon replayed all over the world (Bush in his diary: "That was the damndest experience").[76] Even Bush's personal physician, Dr. Burton Lee, would tell biographer Herbert Parmet: "We paid a penalty for that thyroid disease. . . . That was for sure."[77] In his memoirs, Marlin Fitzwater observed: "The old competitive juices that might have gotten the president into the 1992 campaign in the spring and summer seemed to have lost their edge. He desperately wanted to wait until after Labor Day to start the campaign. I think his body was a reluctant warrior."[78]

In a 1998 interview, Bush offered a response to those who blamed his health for the fate of the campaign. It deserves to be quoted at length:

> You know, Marlin Fitzwater wrote that, and of course I take violent exception to it, because I don't think that's true. I campaigned my heart out. . . . We just couldn't have done any more. . . . But the fact that Marlin felt that way makes me question my own view that it's all

wrong, because he was right there by my side. I think that it's used ex post facto as an explanation.[79]

The fall campaign was clearly a grueling affair for Bush. He was exhausted, and his health often seemed on the verge of giving out. In the last weekend of the campaign, Bush made an appearance on *Larry King Live*, despite a serious case of the flu. But he campaigned hard. There is absolutely no evidence that he gave up.

Others blame the campaign itself. John Sununu's condemnation—"It was the worst-run presidential campaign in history"[80]—is undoubtedly part sour grapes from a fired aide, but there is still more than a grain of truth to the assessment. From the start, the campaign lacked any focus, discipline, or conceptual strategy. There were several reasons for these shortcomings, not the least of which was that Lee Atwater was dead and a disgusted Roger Ailes had decided to sit out the campaign. In their stead was a group of Bush loyalists, several of whom were working in positions that were new to them. Secretary of commerce and chief fund-raiser Robert Mosbacher was named general chairman of the campaign; he named pollster Robert Teeter as chief strategist; Marriott executive Fred Malek, who had managed the 1988 Republican National Convention, as campaign manager; and Charles Black of the RNC as campaign adviser. None of them had any experience with running a national campaign, and the internecine fighting among them was bitter. Marlin Fitzwater recalls in his memoirs that when he was called upon to announce the campaign team to the press, the three men were arguing over whose name should go first in the press release; Mosbacher demanded that the phrase "standing at the president's side in campaigns for the last twenty years" be included. According to Fitzwater, Bush simply remarked, "Gee, if it's this bad on the first day, what are we in for?"[81] No less a political expert than Gerald Ford commented in 1993 on the bona fides of one of his former advisers: "Bob [Teeter] is a good pollster, but he isn't necessarily a good political strategist."[82] For his part, Fitzwater took an unannounced vacation in the middle of the primary season; press reports concluded that he was disgusted with the campaign.[83] One operative spoke for many: "No one ran 1992. No one was running the campaign in 1992. [It was] a campaign adrift."[84]

Quite aside from the backbiting, there was never any real strategy for victory. On 12 June, Teeter was asked to meet with David Demarest's speechwriters and explain the message of the campaign. As was his wont, Teeter brought along complicated flowcharts. The first box on the chart was entitled "The Bush Record," which flowed to one marked "Theme"; from that box flowed several policy boxes—domestic, foreign, social—but all the boxes were as yet unfilled. David Demarest remembered Teeter looking at the speechwriters, pointing to the "Theme" box, and proclaiming, "Now, *that's* where we need your help." Thus, in Demarest's view, "The campaign manager had just admitted to us that the campaign had no theme or vision." For his part, Teeter reportedly told a colleague, "That was a bunch of dead weight I met with on Friday," and he hired a former public relations man for Kentucky Fried Chicken with no experience in a national campaign as the new campaign speechwriter.[85]

In April, George W. Bush moved into his father's campaign in an attempt to right the rudder. It was not enough. All concerned knew that if the president was to have any chance of catching Clinton, Jim Baker had to leave the State Department and take over the campaign. But consumed by the Middle East peace process, Baker did not want to come on board.[86] By the time Bush prevailed upon him to come back to the White House (on 13 August, ostensibly replacing Clayton Yeutter as chief of staff and senior counselor to the president, but in reality to run the sagging campaign),[87] it was too late (Yeutter caustically remembered, "It was too late when *I* came over").[88]

Without effective guidance from the top, the Bush campaign floundered. Most notably, it seemed to want to ignore an offensive push altogether.[89] Fearing that negative advertisements that criticized Clinton's character and focused on Perot's instability would backfire, the Bush campaign delayed the airing of those ads until it was too late. Even then, it ran considerably watered-down versions of the ads, rewritten, in the words of one analyst, with a "touch of humor to soften their effect."[90] A sophomoric pseudo-Watergate attempt to gather dirt on Clinton by searching for incriminating information in his passport file boomeranged immediately and caused the Bush campaign embarrassment.[91] Bush would remember that toward the end of the campaign, the usually taciturn Scowcroft was "getting a little militant, thinking I ought to attack the press more."[92] When he finally began to return fire, Bush gave the appearance of a fighter who was flailing to get in a punch. His attacks against Clinton were shrill (at one point, he publicly castigated Clinton and his running mate, Tennessee senator Al Gore, by observing that "my dog Millie knows more about foreign policy than those two bozos");[93] thus they were easily deflected by the opposition, who ignored them as "cheap shots."

Bush, Ross Perot, and Bill Clinton in the second presidential debate, Richmond, Virginia, 15 October 1992. (Courtesy of the George Bush Presidential Library and Museum)

Further, there would be no Bush-led offensive in the televised debates; one reason was that he was overprepared on the issue of the tax-cut pledge by Richard Darman, who was in charge of debate preparation (indeed, Bush did better in the last debate, when, in the words of one White House staffer, he said "nuts to everybody" and went to Camp David rather than practice).[94] For many observers the defining media moment of the campaign came during the second presidential debate held in Richmond, Virginia, when an obviously preoccupied Bush, quite unaware that he was on camera, took a look at his watch, as if he were bored with the entire proceedings. Perhaps more telling at that debate was when an African American woman asked a question about the national debt. Bush stumbled through an answer. In contrast, Clinton took three steps toward the woman and asked her, "Tell me how it affected you again?"[95] It is difficult to disagree with Clinton biographer Joe Klein's assessment of the Richmond debate: "The presidential campaign was, in effect, over."[96]

Bush should have counterattacked when Clinton painted both Bush and his administration as uncaring in the days after Hurricane

Andrew. He did not. For Bush, the 1992 election was the complete inverse of the 1988 election. In his postelection analysis in 1988, Michael Dukakis had noted that one of the lessons he learned was to "respond quickly" to attack; in 1992, it was the Bush campaign's turn to forget that lesson of modern, media-driven elections. For most of the campaign, Bush sat back and waited for Perot and Clinton to self-destruct. Perot did so; Clinton did not. Those few times when Bush went on the attack, he faced a Clinton campaign that was masterful at instant reaction and spin. Clinton stuck largely to one issue—the economy—throughout the campaign, and Bush had no effective answer to his criticisms. Several staffers begged Bush to announce a new set of domestic and economic policy initiatives, perhaps a capital gains tax cut, to blunt Clinton's thrusts on the economy. But for a host of reasons, what some have later called an "Operation Domestic Storm" did not happen.[97] Unlike 1988, when Atwater and Ailes were able to focus their advertisements on several effective symbols, the Bush media campaign in 1992 offered only a litany of past accomplishments to offset Clinton's attacks on an economy gone awry and Perot's symbol of government gridlock. The Bush campaign never served its candidate by offering a cogent plan for how to beat either Pat Buchanan or Bill Clinton. Indeed, if there was a part of the Bush administration that showed no vision, it was the presidential campaign of 1992. Perhaps Fitzwater had the answer: "The president should have fired us all."[98]

For those in the right wing of his party, the reason Bush lost was simple—he had alienated them. Immediately after the election, Grover G. Norquist wrote a searing postmortem of the Bush campaign for *Policy Review*. In it, he concluded that despite Bush's "masterful" foreign policy, "Bush lost because he had reversed Reagan's economic policies, and because he abused the successful political coalition Reagan had built." Like most conservatives, Norquist believed that "the most dramatic departure from Reaganomics" was the 1990 budget deal ("It is hard to overestimate the damage the tax hike did to the Republican Party and George Bush"), and he offered that Bush should have allowed the Gramm-Rudman-Hollings sequester to happen and then blamed the Democrats. He also castigated Bush for returning to an age of "over-regulation" with the amendments to the Clean Air Act and the ADA, a "misuse of the veto," the firing of Reaganites when he came into office, the "mistreatment of Reagan" (particularly "Bush's failure to give credit to Reagan for playing such an important role in winning the Cold War"), and his alienation of the religious Right.[99] Norquist was an embittered movement conservative, but his instant analysis has merit. It is impossible to dismiss the conclusion, eloquently articulated by Donald T. Critchlow in his history of modern American conservatism, that in 1988 Bush won because he paid attention to his conservative base, and he lost in 1992 because he ignored it.[100]

All these reasons have merit; all these reasons are debatable. But not for George Bush. Devastated by his loss, Bush would not blame abstractions or theories. He would blame people. In later writing and conversation, Bush would blame three people for costing him his victory in 1992.

On 31 March 1992, Bush had lunch with Howard Baker and legislative aide Fred McClure. The two men shared their concern with the president about the oncoming train that was Ross Perot. It was a concern that Bush did not share. In his diary, Bush remembered: "I told them that in three months, he will not be a worry anymore, Perot will be defined, seen as a weirdo, and we shouldn't be concerned with him." Some seven years later, Bush would write of this entry: "They were right and I was wrong. In the final analysis, Perot cost me the election."[101] The anger never died. In September 1993, Bush traveled back to the White House, where he, Ford, and Carter stood with Clinton and announced their support for NAFTA. In the breakfast that followed, all the presidents took turns bashing Ross Perot—but Bush was the most bitter.[102] Despite analysis that shows that Perot cost Clinton just about as many votes as he did Bush, Bush has not forgiven. In 2012, for a HBO documentary on his life, Bush was asked by an off-camera interviewer: "Can you talk about Ross Perot?" Bush then unloaded: "No. Can't talk about him. I think he cost me the election, and I don't like him. Other than that, I have nothing to say."[103]

The second person Bush blamed for his defeat had kept Iran-Contra alive throughout the campaign and, to Bush, committed the cardinal sin of playing politics with a federal investigation. In an election cycle that concentrated on the flagging economy, it was tough to make the public pay attention to a scandal. A lengthy investigation by Representative Henry Gonzalez (D-TX) into the Bush administration's pre–Gulf War courting of Saddam Hussein—most notably the commodity credit loans discussed in chapter 7, as well as $5 billion in unauthorized loans from an Atlanta-based bank to Iraq (and administration intervention to keep the offending bank from being indicted during the Persian Gulf War)—got little traction. The Clinton campaign tried to make hay over what some in the press had lamely dubbed "Iraqgate" (in an October

Clinton press release: "If George Bush thought he was doing the right thing by trying to bring Saddam Hussein into the 'family of nations,' why won't he come clean?"),[104] but these and other protests largely fell on deaf ears.[105]

Also toiling in the background was Lawrence Walsh. A former judge on the U.S. District Court in New York, and then deputy attorney general under Eisenhower, in 1986 Walsh had been named independent prosecutor for Iran-Contra by a three-judge panel. His investigations had led to the convictions of both former Reagan national security adviser John Poindexter, and National Security Council staffer Colonel Oliver North. Walsh had kept his investigation of Iran-Contra going throughout the Bush administration, a fact that the Clinton campaign tried to use to deflect attention from his own credibility issues.[106] But the public paid them as little attention as they did Iraqgate. On 16 June 1992, Walsh had his grand jury indict Caspar Weinberger on five felonies, including obstruction of justice, making false statements, and perjury.[107] On 29 September, the judge in the Weinberger case dismissed a crucial obstruction charge and demanded proper reindictment "within the next month."[108] Walsh did so, and the timing was disastrous for the Bush campaign. On 30 October, Walsh issued a second indictment for Weinberger, dealing specifically with Weinberger's making false statements to a congressional investigation. In this new indictment, Walsh specifically referenced Weinberger's notes on the 7 January 1986 meeting where Reagan approved the sale of arms to Iran in return for the release of the hostages (see chapter 1), which included the observation "VP favored."[109]

Suddenly, five days before the election, whether or not Bush had been "in the loop" during Iran-Contra was back on the front page with a vengeance. The headline in the *New York Times* read: "'86 Weinberger Notes Contradict Bush Account on Iran Arms Deal."[110] One can note that Walsh was merely following the dictum of the court—indeed, his second indictment was, by that court's order, late (it is important to note that much of the secondary literature on the campaign refers to this incident as the "Weinberger indictment," when it was, in actuality, the "Weinberger *re*indictment). For those who argue that Clinton was involved, I can only offer Clinton's own weak explanation: "Whether it would hurt him or not, I didn't know; I was too busy to think about it."[111] Bush and his supporters, however, knew exactly who to blame. Walsh's reindictment of Weinberger was, to them, a deliberate act of political sabotage designed to cost Bush the election. Jim Baker: "What was wrong with the indictment? Let me count the ways. . . . [It was] clearly timed to try and destroy President Bush."[112] Mosbacher: the reindictment was "one of the sleaziest acts in modern politics."[113] And finally, Bush, who would write in 1999: "There is no doubt in my mind that this indictment—written by Walsh's deputy, who was a large contributor to Democratic campaigns—stopped our forward momentum."[114] Of this, there can be no doubt. At that point, the race, by one reporter's memory, was too close to call, with Clinton leading Bush 41 to 30; Bush's tracking polls showed that he lost 7 points overnight.[115]

And then there was the final culprit. George Bush did not spare himself. He came to believe that one reason he had lost was because he was an engaged leader. As he wrote in 1999: "Many of my friends and supporters felt my campaign was in disarray. Part of the problem was I was too darn busy trying to be President. . . . I will always feel [that the fault] was mine because I was unable to communicate to the American people that the economy was improving."[116]

At the Houstonian Hotel on 3 November 1992, after Bush got the news that he had been beaten, it was left to Barbara to say the obvious: "Well now, that's behind us. It's time to move on."[117]

12

★ ★ ★ ★ ★

THE "F.L.F.W."

Winston Churchill jokingly called it "the Order of the Boot." But for George Bush, there was little that was funny about his defeat at the hands of Bill Clinton. Immediately following the election, Gerald Ford called Bush. In the course of their conversation, Bush told Ford that he was fine, but Ford did not believe him.[1] Ford was right—George and Barbara were devastated by the loss. In his diary the day after the election: "But it's hurt, hurt, hurt and I guess it's the pride, too. . . . On a competitive basis, I don't like to see the pollsters right at the end."[2] Yet on that same day, Bush would see an example of the respect with which he was held from within his administration. After flying back from Houston, Bush found that he had to drive from Andrews Air Force Base to the White House; the Bushes found that there was no room on the South Lawn to land the president's helicopter, Marine One, because the entire White House staff had gathered there to welcome them home.[3]

Bush appointed his secretary of transportation, Andrew Card, to run the transition.[4] On 18 November, Bush met with Clinton at the White House. In a conversation that was always proper, and often pleasant, Bush told his successor that he felt that the Balkans, an area where earlier that year he had decided not to intervene, would be the "prime trouble spot."[5] After their business had been completed, Bush made it absolutely clear to Clinton that "when I leave here, you're going to have no trouble from me. . . . I will do nothing to complicate your work."[6] All that Bush asked of Clinton was to preserve his Points of Light program.[7]

In the months before Clinton took office, Bush paused for both reflection and laughter. Perhaps the most reflective moment came only days after the election. On 10 November 1992, the Vietnam War Memorial was celebrating its tenth anniversary. Bush wanted to go there, and he wanted to go without entourage or media. A car took him to the site, adjacent to the Lincoln Memorial, flashing no sirens and stopping at all red lights. When he arrived, Bush found family members reading the names of those honored dead engraved on the long black wall. The crowd was stunned when they saw the president of the United States and the First Lady walk down the long traverse toward the wall. They each read ten names, and when they were done, the crowd exploded in applause.[8]

The funniest moment came in early December. *Saturday Night Live* comic Dana Carvey had long been a hilarious scourge of Bush's. His impersonation of Bush's nasal twang—a cross between frigid Maine and Deep South Texas—and his stiff, pointing gestures was dead-on. But key to his caricature was his repetition of oft-used Bushisms, such as "Not gonna do it. Wouldn't be prudent." Always one to take a joke, Bush invited his alter ego to the White House to perform at a Christmas party on 7 December. The night before his performance, Carvey and his wife were guests of the Bushes at the Kennedy Center; they then spent the night in the Lincoln Bedroom. The next day the comedian was clearly nervous when he faced his audience—which included, to his apparent surprise, the president and First Lady, who were standing in the back of the East Room. But Carvey quickly hit his stride. He told the appreciative crowd how he did Bush's voice: "You start out with Mr. Rogers—'It's a beautiful day in the neighborhood'—add a little John Wayne—'Here we go over the ridge'—put 'em together and you have George Herbert Walker Bush." Then he pleaded with Bush to join him at the podium. When Bush went on stage with Carvey, the crowd roared with delight when it was left to them to decide which performer—Bush or Carvey—sounded most like the president of the United States.[9]

During the transition period, Bush faced two foreign policy issues of enormous import. Since the downfall of the Soviet Union, Bush had been negotiating with Russian president Boris Yeltsin to extend START I, which had been negotiated with Gorbachev in mid-1991 and which limited both the use of and expansion of nuclear weaponry (see chapter

10). The negotiations quickened after the election, and by mid-December, an agreement had been reached. START II now placed the maximum capacity in nuclear warheads for each side at between 3,000 and 3,500 warheads.[10] An excited Bush informed his successor of the deal on 29 December. Bush noted in his diary that Clinton seemed "very pleased, and also pleased that I'm going to Somalia."[11]

The crisis in the East African nation of Somalia, which had fallen into brutal clan warfare, had been dogging the administration since the summer of 1992. The war had laid waste to much of that nation's population, as well as decimated their food supply. In April, the United Nations instituted an emergency plan of assistance to Somalia; under the auspices of the World Food Programme, food began to be shipped to that war-ravaged nation. It only made a dent in the problem.[12] By the summer of 1992, it was estimated that two-thirds of the Somali population was in immediate danger of dying from malnutrition.[13] In July, the British Red Cross reported that more than 5,000 people—including almost 2,000 in the capital city of Mogadishu alone—were dying from starvation in Somalia every day. The long-term prognosis was frightening: the Red Cross report predicted that 1.5 million Somalis—a full one-third of that nation's population—was in "acute danger of disappearing."[14]

In July 1992, Bush received a cable from the U.S. ambassador to Kenya, describing the situation in Somalia. In the margins of the cable, Bush wrote: "This is a terribly moving situation. Let's do everything we can to help."[15] As the recession deepened, however, that help would have to be limited, as Bush left the problem squarely on the UN's doorstep. On 27 July 1992, the White House issued a statement on Somalia, reminding the world that the United States had already committed $63 million over the past two years to humanitarian efforts; "additional resources" were promised, but only after more was done "to create conditions where this vital assistance can reach the people who desperately need it." For this, the White House urged the UN "to move as quickly as possible to deploy an effective number of security guards to permit relief supplies to move into and within Somalia."[16]

But starvation was not the only concern. In early July, the UN sent a team of observers to Somalia. The team's report, released on 24 August, was jarring. It concluded not only that the amount of food that had been shipped to Somalia was "in no way adequate to meet the needs of the Somali people," but that what food had been shipped was often hijacked by "heavily armed gangs" who "overrun delivery and distribution points and loot supplies directly from docked ships as well as from airports and airstrips." While admitting that "current security conditions do not permit the assured delivery" of the foodstuffs, the secretary-general nevertheless was loathe to call for an armed commitment. Instead, he called for an "urgent airlift," one that would be supported by the entire international community.[17] It took almost two months to organize the airlift. Under UN auspices, relief supplies that had been donated by the international community were airlifted to Kenya, and to four locations inside Somalia. The approximate cost to the United States was $10 million.[18]

By October, it was clear that none of this was enough. Most of the capital city of Mogadishu was armed, and gangs ambushed UN aid workers and hijacked the airlifted supplies. Donor agencies and organizations were routinely shaken down, having to pay for "protection." The UN sent peacekeeping forces to Somalia to control the situation. Arguing that the UN had invaded his land, on 28 October, Somalian strongman General Mohammed Aidid declared that the Pakistani battalion that had been carrying out peacekeeping patrols was no longer welcome in Mogadishu, and the coordinator for UNOSOM (UN operation in Somalia) was expelled. On 10 November, a battalion of Pakistanis took control of the airport at Mogadishu; Aidid demanded that they leave, and the UN refused. The next day, the airport came under heavy rifle and mortar fire, but the Pakistanis kept it under their control.[19]

An American public that for centuries had largely ignored the problems of Africa did not change its stripes in 1992. But in the last months of the Bush administration, what to do next in Somalia became a pressing foreign policy issue. On 24 November, Bush met with his national security team to discuss U.S. options in Somalia. To prep him, Scowcroft wrote a memo: "Death and starvation in Somalia are at an unacceptable level and getting worse. Current strategies are not working and have no prospect of success unless the security situation is changed." The airlift "can only meet a small fraction of the need." For Scowcroft, "providing adequate security is the key. . . . Food, the only thing of value in the country, is simply stolen at gunpoint at every opportunity." Scowcroft recommended an "aggressive peacekeeping effort followed by traditional peacekeeping once stable, secure conditions have been established." To those in the administration who were seeing parallels between Somalia and the growing ethnic tension in Yugoslavia, Scowcroft told Bush that there were "significant differences. The level of suffering is incomparably greater in Somalia, the odds of military success are higher and the risks of casualties lower, and the political circumstances are much different."[20] Clearly, unlike the situation in Yugoslavia, Scowcroft saw Somalia as a limited engagement, one that was quite winnable.[21]

Because he was already predisposed to help, it did not take much to convince Bush. All involved believed, in the words of Kenneth Juster, a senior adviser at the Department of State, that "when you have it in your power to prevent the deaths of several million people, you do it."[22] There was a legal issue: Did the president have the constitutional authority to send U.S. troops into a foreign country on a humanitarian mission when combat was possible? On this point, Bush's advisers were torn. However, in much the same manner as he had done in the Persian Gulf, Bush wanted a UN authorization for his actions. On 25 November, in what became known at the White House as "the Thanksgiving Decision," he directed secretary of state Lawrence Eagleburger to take a plan to the UN.[23] On 3 December the Security Council passed Resolution 794, authorizing "humanitarian relief efforts."[24] The next day, Bush announced that the United States would "lead a coalition to relieve starvation in war-torn Somalia." That same day, Bush wrote to UN Secretary-general Boutros Boutros-Ghali, telling him that the United States, would, "in accordance with the resolution, . . . discharge the responsibilities which fall to it in a full and comprehensive manner." Bush also made it clear that the mission of the coalition would be "limited and specific: to create security conditions which will permit the feeding of the starving Somali people and allow the transfer of this security function to the UN peace-keeping force. . . . As soon as they are [fed and secure], the coalition force will depart from Somalia."[25]

Operation Restore Hope would be Bush's last coalition. He made several phone calls to get membership in the peacekeeping coalition; Pakistan would take a leading role.[26] In December 1992, the United Task Force (UNITAF) deployed to Mogadishu with 31,000 UN troops;[27] 24,000 of them were American.[28] On 9 December, the first contingent of U.S. Marines arrived in Mogadishu. On 31 December, Bush visited the troops at Mogadishu.[29] But those troops, and the problems they would face, would become Clinton's problem.

There was also one political matter that was left to address. On Wednesday, 4 November, Bush met with Attorney General William Barr in the Oval Office. The president directed his bile against special prosecutor Lawrence Walsh, who, in Bush's mind, "cost me the election" with the reindictment of Caspar Weinberger discussed in the previous chapter—an assessment with which Barr agreed. But anger quickly turned to strategy. Walsh's continuing investigation presented an immediate problem for Bush, particularly because Weinberger's diary flatly contradicted Bush's public recollection of events as they pertained to his role in Iran-Contra. The two men danced around the idea of firing Walsh, but the idea was soon dismissed.[30] There was another way to deal with the issue.

In December, Bush met with both Barr and White House counsel C. Boyden Gray and told them that he was going to pardon Caspar Weinberger, thus effectively ending Walsh's investigation. Barr and Gray did not disagree, but they counseled Bush that if he was going to do that, it made sense to pardon, in Gray's words, "everybody who has been convicted or indicted in connection with this matter, and everyone who might be prosecuted in the future, with the exception of President Reagan and yourself."[31] Bush knew the downside: he confided in his diary that "the pardon of Weinberger will put a tarnish, a kind of a downer, on our legacy."[32] Nevertheless, on Christmas Eve, calling him a "true American patriot," Bush pardoned the former secretary of defense and five others—Elliott Abrams, a former assistant secretary of state for inter-American affairs; Duane Clarridge, Alan Fiers, and Clair George—all of the CIA; and former national security adviser Robert "Bud" McFarlane.[33]

Walsh was furious, releasing a statement that claimed that the pardon "undermines the principle that no man is above the law" and "demonstrates that powerful people with powerful allies can commit serious crimes in high office deliberately abusing the public trust without consequence."[34] He considered bringing Bush before the grand jury anyway, but his staff talked him out of it.[35] Walsh then tried to get Bush to turn over recordings and pages from his diary—found in a White House safe by Bush's personal secretary in September 1992 and kept from Walsh until December 1992. But the act of not turning over the notes was not in and of itself a crime. More important, Walsh no longer had control of the investigation. On 15 January 1993, five days before Clinton's inauguration, the White House released a fourteen-page report that, not surprisingly, exonerated Bush for any wrongdoing with respect to the handling of his diary. Walsh seethed but could do nothing.[36]

Barbara Bush's diary entry for Inauguration Day 1993 showed no nostalgia for the job: "Well, this is the day. Both of us are ready. . . . We need to get out of here."[37] For his part, Bush was a bit more sanguine, when he penned the traditional note to leave in the top drawer of his successor's desk in the Oval Office:

Dear Bill:
When I walked into this office just now I felt the same sense of wonder and respect that I felt four years ago. I know that you will feel that, too.

I wish you great happiness here. I never felt the loneliness that some Presidents have described.

There will be very tough times, made even more difficult by criticism you may not think is fair. I'm not a very good one to give advice; but just don't let the critics discourage you or push you off course.

You will be our president when you read this note. I wish you well. I wish your family well.

Your success is now our country's success. I am rooting hard for you.

Good Luck—George.[38]

George Bush was no longer interested in politics—at least as it pertained to himself—when he left office. There was never any serious talk about him running again for the presidency, in 1996 for a rematch against Clinton, or any other year. There was, in the Bush post-presidency, a decided air of relaxation. Glad to be rid of the pomp and circumstance of the presidency, Bush liked to joke that he was "de-imperializing" the post-presidency.[39] Not taking his new role particularly seriously, Bush took to calling himself the "grandfather in chief,"[40] and he chose "F.L.F.W."—"Former Leader of the Free World"—for his web domain.[41] Bush initially gravitated to a quiet retirement, bolstered by his participation on many boards, particularly those related to the medical field. He served on the board of the Mayo Clinic (where Barbara, who also served on the board there, would go for two toe amputations).[42] He also did fund-raising work for, and would eventually become chairman of the board of, the M. D. Anderson Cancer Center in Houston,[43] and he continued to attend to his Points of Light Foundation.

Bush also moved to make himself some money. One author has estimated that when he left office, Bush's net worth was $3.2 million, along with his yearly $150,000 presidential pension.[44] But a former president can command a great price. Both Bushes were in great demand on the speaking circuit. George charged about $100,000 per speech, Barbara between $40,000 and $60,000.[45] About half the speeches they made were for pay; the rest went to their charitable foundations.[46] Bush also lent his name to the Carlyle Group, formed in 1987 as a private equity group that specialized in leveraged buyouts of aerospace and defense companies. At Carlyle, he was among friends. Frederic Malek joined the firm in September 1988, as did former secretary of defense Frank Carlucci in the winter of 1989. In 1993, Richard Darman and James Baker both joined, and in 1997 Bush became Carlyle's paid senior adviser to the Carlyle Asia Advisory Board. By the late 1990s, Carlyle had become an international political and economic dynamo, and Bush was traveling all over the world in its name. This would eventually cause Bush some embarrassment; in March 2001, the *New York Times* published a story that claimed that Bush was making money from private interests that had business before his son's administration. It would also become known that former British prime minister John Major, who had joined the advisory board in 2001, and Bush had, in their role as advisers for Carlyle, met with members of the bin Laden family (not Osama, who had broken with these family members).[47] After having his role exposed in Michael Moore's documentary *Fahrenheit 9/11*, Bush left Carlyle in October 2003.

But Bush did not spend his entire retirement in the corporate world. He was far too active a man for that. On 11 February 1997, Bush wrote his children: "Okay, so you might think I've lost it. I plan to make a parachute jump. So there!"[48] Since 1997, Bush has made seven parachute jumps with the U.S. Army's Golden Knights. His first jump was on 25 March 1997 near Yuma, Arizona. When he was back on the ground, Bush would confide to his diary, "I had lived a dream."[49] But he wanted more. He would jump six more times, all of them part of his birthday celebration. The second jump, code-named Operation Spring Colt and held on 9 June 1999 over the grounds of his presidential library at his beloved Texas A&M University, celebrated his seventy-fifth birthday. However, this one was almost a fatal disaster, as he got tangled up and spun out of control, only to be saved by two Golden Knights.[50] In 2004, again at his library, Bush celebrated his eightieth birthday by jumping not once but twice in the same day (his total of five lifetime jumps now qualified him for his skydiver pin); in 2007, he jumped to celebrate the reopening of the library. In 2009 he jumped on his eighty-fifth birthday; and in

2014 for his ninetieth birthday, Bush jumped near his summer home at Kennebunkport, Maine. Bush's comeback to those who felt this either incredibly undignified or unduly dangerous: "Old guys can do stuff."[51]

Bush the parachutist also became Bush the author. It is interesting that in 1998, when reporter Bob Woodward asked Bush to cooperate with interviews for the book that would become *Shadow: Five Presidents and the Legacy of Watergate,* Bush refused, claiming that one of his reasons for saying no was that "I do not want to try to direct history."[52] But Bush had every intention of writing a memoir that would allow him the chance to "direct history." It is surprising the number of writers who have claimed that, in the words of one, "Bush opted not to write a memoir,"[53] when in reality he wrote two of the most useful and revelatory presidential memoirs of the modern period. Perhaps these historians have come to this conclusion because Bush shared authorship of *A World Transformed* (1998) with his former national security adviser, Brent Scowcroft. The book took almost seven years to write; Bush would confide to Ronald Reagan that it was "one slow piece of work," and that "a basic problem may be that neither Brent nor I is too hot a writer."[54] He need not have worried. Concentrating almost exclusively on foreign policy and national security issues, the book is written in an engaging point-counterpoint style, with Bush giving his point of view on a subject, followed by Scowcroft—or vice versa. The two writers are not afraid to show where they disagreed over policy development, and each distinctive voice comes through. One year after the publication of *A World Transformed,* Bush published a collection of letters. As it had in his previous book, Bush's voice shouts through his *All the Best, George Bush: My Life in Letters and Other Writings.* The book is based on excerpts from letters and diary entries chosen by Bush with the help of his chief of staff, Jean Becker. But it is much more; indeed, it serves as a second presidential memoir. Fully half of the book covers Bush's prepresidential years, much of what is included in the book was not previously published, and Bush's extensive editorial comments give more insight into the author than most presidential memoirs that tip the scales at more than 500 pages.

Bush originally wanted his presidential library built on the campus of his alma mater, Yale University. However, the prospect of student and faculty protests of his policies soured him on that idea.[55] Then came a proposed joint deal between Rice University and the University of Houston, which eventually fell through.[56] Donald M. Wilson, then the Archivist of the United States, described to a conference on the Bush presidency why the president then turned to Texas A&M University: "They tend to be a somewhat conservative student body. . . . The traditions prevail, and those traditions are very much George Bush: duty, honor, patriotism. . . . He knew—and I could reassure him—that there certainly would never be a protest against George Bush at Texas A&M University. If there was, it wouldn't last very long because the Corps would likely stop it quickly."[57]

Texas A&M also offered Bush ninety acres of land on the westernmost side of its campus, offered to help raise funds, and offered to incorporate the library into the George Bush School of Government and Public Policy.[58] All this was important, as the Bush Library was the first presidential library that was constructed under the Presidential Libraries Act of 1986, which required the private foundation charged with fund-raising for the library's construction to raise an endowment equal to 20 percent of the final cost of the library structures in order to support their upkeep.[59] In the end, the library and museum cost $40 million, the Bush School $43 million, and more than $4.5 million was raised as an endowment.[60]

In October 1989, Wilson met with members of A&M's board of regents, the chancellor, and architects, where both potential plans for the library (Wilson was assured that it would be a "living entity" with "maximum public access") and those for a link between the library and the proposed Bush school were discussed (Wilson: "I believe this a unique and needed program").[61] On 3 May 1991, it was announced that the George Bush Presidential Library and Museum would be built on the A&M campus; ground was broken on 30 November 1994. In January 1993, 36 million pages of records and 40,000 museum objects from the Bush administration were brought to College Station, Texas, and temporarily stored in a converted bowling alley—it took two military transport aircraft making two trips each from Washington, and the efforts of soldiers from Fort Hood, to move and unload all the material.[62] Processing of the records began immediately, in accordance with the Presidential Records Act of 1978, and the George Bush Presidential Library and Museum was dedicated on 6 November 1997.[63]

When journalist Bob Greene asked Bush in a 2004 interview if he had ever believed that the job was done, and thought that his family should

Dedication, George Bush Presidential Library and Museum, 6 November 1997. *Left to right*: Lady Bird Johnson, Jimmy and Rosalyn Carter, George and Barbara Bush, Bill and Hillary Clinton, Gerald and Betty Ford, Nancy Reagan. (Courtesy of the George Bush Presidential Library and Museum)

walk away from politics, Bush was emphatic. "No," Bush said. "Never. Not once."[64]

There were two Bush sons who gravitated toward their father's business. George W. Bush, the eldest child, started the soonest. In 1978, while his father was planning his first run for the presidency, George W. ran for the House seat from Texas's Nineteenth Congressional District. He lost by some 6,000 votes. Only lightly involved in his father's campaigns for the vice presidency, George W. would work in his father's 1988 campaign, and, as noted in chapter 2, he helped with the transition. George W.'s brother John Ellis, or "Jeb," was at the same time entering politics from the same direction as had his father—through the party organization. After serving as the chairman of Florida's Dade County Republican Party, Jeb served as Florida's secretary of commerce from 1987 to 1988. He resigned that position to work with his brother in his father's 1988 campaign. From 1989 to 1994, Jeb worked on a congressional campaign and planned for a gubernatorial campaign; his brother was the managing general partner of the Texas Rangers Major League

Baseball franchise and worked as an adviser on their father's 1992 campaign. In 1994, both Bush brothers ran for the governorship of their respective states. While George W. was elected, defeating incumbent Ann Richards with 53.5 percent of the vote, Jeb lost to incumbent Lawton Chiles. It would not be until 1998 that Jeb Bush joined his brother as a governor, defeating Lieutenant Governor Buddy McKay with 55.3 percent of the vote. George W. was reelected in 1998; in 2002, Jeb became the first Republican to be reelected to a second term as Florida's governor.

George and Barbara Bush did not universally embrace their son's moves into politics. Bush struggled to find an appropriate distance from his sons' efforts—close enough to be useful, far enough away for propriety.[65] He raised funds for both sons; Jeb had less of an issue with his father's public show of support than did his brother, who preferred to go it alone (George W. quipped: "I can take care of myself. But I hope he raises me a whole bunch of cash").[66] But both parents had trouble seeing their sons get criticized during their campaigns. Old scores continued to interfere—for example, in 1994, Ross Perot publicly supported Richards against George W.[67] But their victories were personally satisfying: Barbara Bush never tired of telling friends that one in eight Americans lived in a state whose governor was a Bush.[68]

It was George W. who took the first steps toward the White House. There is no evidence that his father saw the 2000 election, as many in the press as well as historians have assumed, as some sort of "revenge" for 1992. It would be completely out of character for Bush to ever say so, and there is no evidence that he ever wrote it. But Bush had come to find the Clinton administration to be wanting, both morally and in its policies, and he was spoiling for a fight. In 2000, he moved toward a greater insider's role in his son's campaign, as he worked the phones and called in his due bills. For example, in the fall of 1997 he called his close friend Prince Bandar bin Sultan, the Saudi ambassador to the United States, and asked him to go and talk to George W. about the decision he was making whether or not to run for the presidency.[69] He also prevailed upon Condoleezza Rice, who had served on his National Security Council staff, and Al Hubbard, a former deputy chief of staff to Dan Quayle, to meet with George W.[70] Bush also called his party contacts, asking them to keep from endorsing a candidate until George W. had announced his intentions.[71]

After George W. announced his candidacy, Bush did indeed campaign for his son, but his efforts were circumscribed after he endured a less than charitable welcome in New Hampshire, where the presence of a Bush was a reminder of the damage done to that state by the 1991–1992 recession.[72] Bush also let go with a slip of the tongue while introducing his son to a Granite State crowd: "This boy, this son of ours, is not going to let you down"—the Clinton White House began to call the candidate "Boy George."[73] Yet Bush was useful in other ways. When Dan Quayle, making what would be a short-lived run for the nomination, called the elder Bush to ask if the Bush and Quayle camps could take it easy on each other, Bush's response—no doubt remembering Quayle's criticism of him in the last year of the administration—was "We'll do what we have to do."[74]

After George W. won the nomination, he called his father to ask his opinion on the choice of former secretary of defense Richard Cheney as a running mate. According to George W., his father was effusive with his praise: "Dick would be a great choice. He would give you candid and solid advice. And you'd never have to worry about him going behind your back."[75] After questions emerged regarding the state of Cheney's health, George W. announced that a doctor would perform an independent examination. Bush's father suggested a doctor—Denton A. Cooley of the Texas Heart Institute, who not surprisingly pronounced Cheney fit.[76]

Immediately following George W.'s acceptance address, Bush wrote his friend Brian Mulroney. Sighing that "I felt that finally my political days were over—the record sealed and finished, with the historians left to decide," Bush told the Canadian prime minister, "For us, the mission is now to stay offstage and pray for our 'boy.'"[77] This turned out to be only partially the case. The campaign against Democrat Al Gore Jr. was a very close affair from the start; Jeb Bush remembered that "my dad was a living wreck. It was horrible."[78] In terms of public appearances, Bush did, indeed, largely fly under the radar, making few campaign speeches.[79] However, when the election ran aground in Florida and the recount began, Bush entered the fray with gusto. He wrote *Time* magazine's Hugh Sidey, "I have had more phone conversations over the last month with George than one could imagine."[80] James Baker was asked by the campaign to go to Florida and oversee the recount efforts there.[81] When it was all over, it took the Supreme Court in *Bush v. Gore* to rule 5 to 4 to end the recount and make George W. Bush president-elect of the United States.[82] Of his father's two appointments to the court, Clarence Thomas voted in favor of ending the recount; David Souter—a surprise and a disappointment to Bush loyalists on so many matters—voted against it.

On a frigid 20 January 2001, the day his son was inaugurated the forty-third president of the United States, Bush attended the swearing-in ceremonies as well as the inaugural parade that followed. Returning to the White House, he went to take a hot shower to thaw out a bit. Suddenly, the valet knocked on the bathroom door. Bush was told that the president of the United States wanted to see him immediately. Quickly drying off, Bush entered the Oval Office from the Rose Garden. He met his son in the middle of the office, where Clinton's blue rug had already been replaced with the old Reagan/Bush carpet. "Mr. President," said the father. "Mr. President," said the son. The new president would later write: "Neither of us said much. We didn't need to. The moment was more moving than either of us could have expressed."[83]

On many occasions and to many interviewers, both George W. and Jeb have described their father as "the beacon." Familial love, however, did not translate to political loyalty. In much the same way that his father had attempted to separate himself from Ronald Reagan, George W. Bush attempted to tie himself to Reagan and separate himself from his father. Examples of this abound. On the micro level, advisers to his father clearly understood that they were not going to have a privileged place in the son's administration—one complained, "We had to be the back-of-the-bus group."[84] When asked or forced to make a comparison between himself and his father, George W. would often use the same line as he did to House Minority Leader Dick Armey (R-TX): "You know Dick, I'm more like Ronald Reagan than my Dad. The difference is, my dad was raised in the East, and I was raised in Texas."[85] At a dinner party in the fall of 2005, Senator John McCain (R-AZ) told Brent Scowcroft that George W. had said to him, "I don't want to be like my father. I want to be like Ronald Reagan."[86] This seems to be equal parts philosophy—Bush 43 would, by any yardstick, turn out to be a much more conservative leader than was Bush 41—and political survival, as George W. had come to believe that the retreat of the conservatives had been a major part of his father's electoral defeat in 1992.

On the morning of 11 September 2001, Bush, who had been visiting Washington, dropped into his son's senior staff meeting at the White House, just to say hello.[87] He and Barbara then boarded a private plane and left for Houston via St. Paul, Minnesota, where they were both scheduled to speak. Over Wisconsin, their pilot informed them that two commercial planes had flown into the World Trade Center in New York City, a third into the Pentagon, and a fourth had crashed in southwestern Pennsylvania. When it became clear that the nation was under terrorist attack and all commercial planes had been grounded, Bush's plane was diverted to Milwaukee, where he and Barbara were taken away by their Secret Service detail to a motel near that city.[88] In a letter to his friend Hugh Sidey, Bush recalled that he had talked to his son, who was visiting Florida at the time of the attack, advising him that "the sooner he got back to Washington the better. He totally agreed with that."[89] The president's first words to the nation were: "Terrorism against our nation will not stand." This evoked memories of his father using essentially the same phrase on 5 August 1991 when faced with Saddam Hussein's invasion of Kuwait.[90] On 14 September, Bush, Barbara, and the other former presidents and First Ladies attended a prayer service at the National Cathedral in Washington. Following George W.'s comments to the congregation, his father reached over and touched his son on the arm.

Almost immediately, indeed, the day after the tragedy, the former president began to speculate obliquely about how the nation might retaliate, noting for Sidey that "having headed a terrorism task force for President Reagan back in the '80s I am somewhat familiar with what can and can't be done."[91] He became even more familiar with the options: director of central intelligence George Tenet remembered that on 24 December 2002, when he attended a meeting at Camp David to evaluate the odds of weapons of mass destruction being in Iraq, the first President Bush was there and participated in the discussion.[92]

The retaliation—both in Afghanistan and in Iraq—would last for the next decade and a half, affecting the course of world geopolitics to the present day. There has been much written, and even more speculated, about whether or not there was a break between father and son over policy after 9/11. George W. Bush is clear: "That was ridiculous. Of all people, dad understood the stakes. If he thought I was handling Iraq wrong, he damn sure would have told me himself."[93] Perhaps he did. Journalist James Risen reports that in 2003, "several highly placed sources" told him that there was a rift between first and second Bush; 41 was upset that his son was ignoring moderates like his secretary of state, Colin Powell, and listened instead to the neoconservatives like his vice president, Dick Cheney, as well as his secretary of defense, Donald Rumsfeld—with whom the father had long since had a strained relationship. According to Risen, one angry conversation led to the son angrily hanging up on the father (with the son later calling to apologize).[94] Journalist Bob Woodward reported several instances where the senior

Bush began to send messages that he was less than satisfied with his son and his advisers. For example, Bush said to former senator from Oklahoma David Boren: "Do you ever see our mutual friend, Colin? . . . Be sure to tell him I sure think he is doing a good job."[95] In January 2003, Bush confided to Scowcroft: "Condi is a disappointment, isn't she? She's not up to the job."[96]

In this regard, many observers have attempted to interpret a 15 August 2002 op-ed piece by Brent Scowcroft in the *Wall Street Journal*, entitled "Don't Attack Saddam," as a message from the first Bush to the second Bush. Scowcroft argued that "any campaign against Iraq, whatever the strategy, costs, and risks, is certain to divert us for some indefinite period from our war on terrorism. Worse, there is a virtual consensus in the world against an attack against Iraq at this time."[97] The president was reported to have been "livid," and he took it out on Scowcroft's friend in the administration, Condi Rice, who in return called Scowcroft and pointedly shared her displeasure with him.[98] For his part, George W. was so upset that he called his father, who carefully replied, "Son, Brent is a friend."[99] Speculation soon arose that Bush had either approved of, or even requested the writing of, the article. Woodward argues to the positive, writing in his *Plan of Attack* that Scowcroft had sent Bush an advance copy of the article; according to Woodward, "he received no reaction. That meant it was okay."[100] Interviewing George W. Bush for that same book, Woodward asked the president about his relationship with his father. George W. sounded evasive in his answer, claiming to have no specific recollection of any time that he had asked his father's advice on the Iraq War:

> I'm confident—sure we did. I'm trying to remember . . . I'm not trying to be evasive. I don't remember. I could ask and see if he remembers something. But how do you ask a person, what does it feel like to send somebody in and then lose life? . . . You know, he is the wrong father to appeal to in terms of strength. There is a higher father that I appeal to.[101]

If his son's presidency challenged the relationship between father and son, that same presidency led to the improvement of the relationship between George Bush and Bill Clinton. It did not begin with promise. Part of this stemmed from the 1992 defeat; part of it stemmed from how the Clinton administration dealt with the attempted assassination of

Bush. On 14 April 1993, Bush, Barbara, James Baker, Nicholas Brady, and John Sununu visited Kuwait to celebrate the second anniversary of the coalition's liberation of that country. A few weeks later, the Kuwaiti government informed the Clinton administration that it had seized a Toyota Land Cruiser carrying 180 to 200 pounds of explosives. Seventeen men were arrested, and after interrogating the suspects, the CIA concluded that the conspirators had planned a suicide bombing of the Bush party. The CIA also learned that the plot had been ordered by Saddam Hussein. In retaliation, Clinton ordered a cruise missile hit on Baghdad; on 26 June, the U.S. Navy launched twenty-three Tomahawk missiles bound for Iraqi intelligence services in Baghdad. The majority of the missiles hit their target, but three landed in a residential neighborhood, killing eight and wounding twelve.[102] It would be Saddam's last act of terrorism, and Clinton's first act of military retaliation. Yet many in Bush's family and on his team felt that not enough was done, an opinion that was shared by R. James Woolsey Jr., the director of the CIA.[103] Bush did not speak publicly of the assassination plot or Clinton's response. But he was highly disappointed in Clinton over his sexual peccadilloes, and in terms of policy began to break with the administration over Haiti. In November 1995, Bush accompanied Clinton to the funeral of assassinated Israeli prime minister Yitzhak Rabin, but he does not seem to have written anything about it.

It seems that the relationship began to thaw in February 1999, when Bush accompanied Clinton, Carter, and Ford to the funeral of Jordan's King Hussein. In his diary, Bush wrote about his conversations with Clinton on board Air Force One: "The man is good—a great grasp of facts, apparently an in-depth knowledge on the issues. . . . I felt more at ease than I thought I would."[104] Five years later, at the dedication of the Clinton Library in November 2004, observers were astounded to see Bush and Clinton sneaking away on their own. While alone, they talked about personal matters, such as where each man was to be buried. Frustrated that the two former presidents were taking so long with their chat, President Bush sent an irritated message to his father: "Tell 41 and 42 that 43 is hungry."[105]

Perhaps 43 remembered this incident one month later. On 26 December 2004, an earthquake thirty miles off the coast of Sumatra sent successions of enormous tsunamis to the shores of Southeast Asia. More than 230,000 died; the property damage was incalculable. President Bush asked his father and Clinton to spearhead private fund-raising for relief efforts. At first glance, the thought of the eighty-one-year-old Bush and the fifty-nine-year-old Clinton working together on any project left heads shaking. But it proved to be a perfect match—the Bush-Clinton Tsunami Relief Fund raised more than $1 billion.[106] Traveling to the affected areas, Bush professed to see another side of Clinton, one that was "very considerate of me" and "enjoys interacting people," and "went out of his way not to criticize the president." While Clinton "did have an opinion on everything" and tended to follow his own schedule—which usually meant his being late ("Clinton Standard Time")—Bush seemed to surprise himself: "You cannot get mad at the guy."[107]

On 29 August 2005, the worst natural disaster in American history struck the Gulf Coast. Hurricane Katrina ultimately killed about a thousand people and caused approximately $108 billion in property damage. The plodding response of the Federal Emergency Management Agency (FEMA) led George W. Bush to receive even more criticism than his father had faced in 1992 over his reaction to Hurricane Andrew (see chapter 11). As part of a public relations recovery, the president once more called his two immediate predecessors into service. They formed the Bush-Clinton Katrina Fund and raised $130 million in aid.[108]

George W. was grateful, writing later that he "appreciated that Bill treated dad with deference and respect, and I grew to like him."[109] For his part, Clinton attributed his new and improved relationship with Bush to the fact that Bush had "offload[ed] electoral politics to ideologues and professionals."[110] At its heart, it was fun to watch. Their relationship—between the oldest and the youngest living ex-presidents—was closer than that between any two former American presidents. Barbara Bush told her son, "I see you've reunited your father and your stepbrother,"[111] and it was she who dubbed 41 and 42 the "Odd Couple."[112] Neil Bush called Clinton his "brother of another mother";[113] the friendship between the two former presidents has, by all accounts, lasted to the present day.

During his last plane ride on Air Force One in December 1992, traveling to his beloved Kennebunkport for the holidays, George Bush wrote a brief note to himself: "I hope history will show I did some things right."[114] Six years later, on 29 May 1998, George Bush did a favor for an old friend. On his way to his fifty-year reunion at Yale University, Bush stopped to deliver a talk at Harvard University, where former senator Alan Simpson was a visiting professor at the John F. Kennedy School of Government. It was a singular experience; here was a comfortable, animated George Bush such as most of the country had never seen. His humor, delivered in a practiced deadpan, delighted the audience. Bush quipped that he refused to lecture them, taking his cue from Socrates, who had gone around giving advice, "and then they poisoned him." He remarked that he had been criticizing the national press all around the country, until a friend told him that such trash talk was beneath him. Now he claimed that he had "joined Press Bashers Anonymous. It's been ten days since I joined, and I'm going through withdrawal symptoms." Bush then observed that he had invited Prime Minister Kiichi Miyazawa ("He was the guy I threw up on in Tokyo. Remember him?") to speak at the Bush Library. "He came, and I told him this time, the dinner's on me."

In a more serious mode, Bush took the opportunity to highlight what he believed were the major accomplishments of his presidency. On the world scene, he listed the fall of communism, the dismantling of the Berlin Wall, and a victory in the Persian Gulf War that "raised respect for America around the world [and] mysteriously and wondrously healed the wounds inflicted upon many who served in Vietnam." On the domestic front, Bush observed:

> We cleaned up the S&L crisis...[a] huge expenditure, but looking back, it was the right thing to do.... [We] cleaned up the environment with the Clean Air Act...[and] expanded opportunities for 37 million people with disabilities in a very bipartisan way [when] Congress passed the ADA and I was privileged to be the president who signed it.... We forewent the "reading of lips" by passing a budget agreement that put firm controls really for the first time on discretionary spending.[115]

George H. W. Bush accomplished each of the things on his list, and more. Thus, it is difficult to understand how some historians and political scientists continue to characterize him as a passive president.

In his book *The Postmodern Presidency: George Bush Meets the World* (1991), Richard Rose labels Bush a "guardian . . . [doing] a limited number of things that are obligations of the Oval Office and refraining from actions that expand the role of government." Rose concedes that "internationally, a guardian will be active," but he concludes that overall, a guardian president—Bush—is "a player, but not in charge."[116] Many scholars, taking their cue from Rose, have labeled Bush a guardian president and have characterized his executive style as passive. British scholar David Mervin went even further than Rose, arguing in *George*

Bush and the Guardianship Presidency (1996) that Bush was hands-off with both domestic and foreign policy. Mervin argued that, like Dwight D. Eisenhower, Bush was a conservative "in the traditional sense of being largely content with things as they were. Such presidents are moreover, skeptical about what can be achieved by passing laws." To Mervin, Bush "was to become a guardian president. He was a conservator rather than an advocate of change. . . . inclined to be cautious, anxious not to arouse hopes that could not be fulfilled while holding himself in readiness to deal with crises as they arose."[117] Other scholars followed suit. Speaking at the 1997 conference on the Bush presidency at Hofstra University, David Cohen argued that Bush "consciously delegate[d] much of the domestic responsibility" to Sununu and Darman, leaving the two men "directing domestic policy."[118] More recently, political scientists Ryan J. Barilleaux and Mark J. Rozell, in their *Power and Prudence: The Presidency of George H. W. Bush* (2004), label Bush an "incrementalist."[119] Going for the quip, Gil Troy, in his *Morning in America: How Ronald Reagan Invented the 1980s* (2005), claimed that "unlike his bold predecessor, George Bush felt duty-bound by the political argument of the Hippocratic Oath: 'First, do no harm.'"[120] Journalists Michael Duffy and Dan Goodgame summarized these scholarly observations: "When faced with a decision, Bush often concluded that the best course was to do as little as possible."[121]

There is no question but that Bush resisted the temptation to make hasty decisions. He used the words "patient" and "prudent" on many occasions to describe his thought processes as well as his goals. And one must also accept that Bush had no long-range vision for his presidency because, as we saw in chapter 9, he consistently said—both as president and in interviews following his presidency—that he had none. But this does not necessarily mean, as many have claimed, that Bush was a passive president, allowing others to formulate, articulate, and defend policy or, in extreme cases, having no policy at all. Assessing him as such may be the fault of a narrow, celebrity-charged view of the activist presidency. It is often assumed that if a president's stage presence is anything but masterful, both scholars and the citizenry tend to see the president as passive.[122] By this measure, either when compared with his garrulous predecessor, or when seen through his description of himself as "prudent," or when seen in light of his own lack of desire to proclaim a broad vision to the American people, George Bush seems to play the part of a passive president. However, a broader view of presidential activism—one not restricted to charisma, performance, haste, and volume—places Bush in a different light. In *The Keys to Power: Managing the Presidency* (2005), political scientist Shirley Anne Warshaw defines presidential activism as the ability of the president to "dominate the policy process."[123] She is joined in this view by John F. Freie, who sees activism as the ability of the president to "activate the system."[124] If an activist president is seen as an initiator of action, then one need not limit their view of activism to public displays of advocacy. Indeed, there is room to consider a president as activist who unobtrusively works the system to his advantage, well away from the spotlight.

When one accepts presidential activism as the ability to activate the system—regardless of personal style—George H. W. Bush was clearly an activist president. This is most pronounced when one analyzes his foreign policies. While he was deliberate and private ("prudent") in his international dealings, he personally advanced his policies through a number of methods. With China after Tiananmen, Bush utilized private threats, public praise, executive vetoes, and secret diplomacy, all with the goal of keeping the post-détente relationship between the United States and the People's Republic of China intact after the bloodshed. With respect to Eastern Europe, Bush carefully shepherded the chaos following the opening of the Berlin Wall, all with the goal of keeping Mikhail Gorbachev from retaliating and causing another bloody Tiananmen in the streets of Berlin. After the invasion of Kuwait, Bush singlehandedly pushed the United Nations into action and put together an international coalition against Saddam Hussein, all with the goal of extracting Iraq from Kuwait. With the Soviet Union, Bush used private negotiation and promises of giving—then threats of retracting—economic aid, and he utilized the bully pulpit in the "Chicken Kiev" speech, all with the goal of keeping the Soviet Union alive, both for the sake of world stability and to keep Gorbachev in the anti-Iraq coalition. In the post–Gulf War Middle East, Bush used personal diplomacy to craft out of whole cloth a peace conference at Madrid, with the goal in mind of it being a first step, where age-old combatants would, initially, talk. And in the greatest success of his presidency—perhaps the greatest diplomatic feat of the post-war period, Bush affected the reunification of Germany with the goal in mind of a stable post–Cold War Europe. His foreign policy was not completely successful—despite his efforts, the Soviet Union crumbled and Gorbachev was overthrown. But with that notable exception, Bush succeeded in achieving each of the objectives stated here. Moreover, it was hardly, using the words of one scholar of the period, a "cautious and risk-averse" foreign policy, one that simply guided the world to a soft landing after Reagan had done all the heavy lifting, pushing communism to the precipice.[125] The Bush administration took tremendous chances; it is not hyperbolic to argue that the foreign policy of George Bush changed the world.

Some scholars, including myself in the first edition of this book, have been willing to give Bush relatively high marks in terms of having control of his foreign policy, but then have found him passive and wanting as he presented a domestic policy that I, for one, pronounced as limited.[126] This assessment seems to have been formulated by my concentration on outcomes—clearly the outcomes of Bush's domestic policy were more of a mixed bag than were those of his foreign policy—as opposed to taking into account Bush's executive style. But more recent scholarly studies, as well as documents recently opened at the Bush Library, make it clear that Bush was equally activist in his domestic and foreign policy. The key to Bush's activism was both the veto threat and his use of the veto, which as seen in chapter 4 affected legislation in many areas. Speaker of the House Thomas Foley (D-WA), all too often on the receiving end of Bush's veto threats, believed that due to the fact that vetoes are commonly seen as a *negative* decision rather than a *positive* one (a strategy to affect legislation), Bush's vetoes contributed to the erroneous view that he was less engaged in domestic policy than in foreign policy.[127] That may well be, but Bush's veto policy clearly shows an engaged president who affected the legislative process in an effective manner. But there was more. While it is true that Bush did not use the bully pulpit a great deal in domestic policy, he did, indeed, use it—his speeches to the nation on education reform and drug policy, as well as his speech on the 1990 budget deal that he tied to the patriotic fervor of Operation Desert Shield, are several examples. Bush also used staff intervention, private consensus building (with Rostenkowski on the budget bill), and a tack that, given its complexity and the high chances for failure, few presidents dare to use—he placed two constitutional amendments before the Congress in an attempt to affect the course of legislation (two on flag desecration; one, on abortion, was considered by Bush, but ultimately dismissed). The results, as we saw in chapters 4 and 5, were decidedly mixed: Bush failed to get the civil rights package that he wanted and failed to get a constitutional amendment on flag desecration; the budget negotiations of 1990 were riddled with errors; and he did not get the education bill for which he hoped. But the threat of the veto kept more liberal abortion laws at bay; the bailout of the savings and loans, while a budget-buster, ultimately strengthened the nation's banking system; the budget bill of 1990 helped stabilize the economy through to the millennium; and Bush advanced the cause of environmentalism and disability advocacy more than any president of the postwar period. But regardless of outcomes, these initiatives did not come from a guardian president or a passive presidency. The record shows the assessment of John Sununu, speaking at a conference on the Bush presidency in 1997, to be correct: "This was a president who, contrary to perception, got himself involved on a daily basis in serious domestic issues. The perception of George Bush as only caring about foreign policy, I think, is the most erroneous perception that exists in terms of examining what this president did."[128]

Americans, particularly scholars of the American presidency, want their presidents to move fast. This, George Bush refused to do. Moreover, he refused to inflate his rhetoric to compensate for his caution by proclaiming a vast vision for the future. But Bush's was not a Whig presidency; it was indeed an activist one, one where the president personally drove both domestic and foreign policy. The result was a foreign policy that set the parameters for the post–Cold War world and would define his successor's foreign policy agenda, and a domestic policy with fewer successes than he had in his diplomacy, but successes of note nonetheless. Further, Bush's basic honesty and sense of government service brought no discredit to the office of the presidency, and his careful stewardship bequeathed to his successor a nation more stable than the one he had inherited from his predecessor. If that is not the stuff of presidential vision, it is, nevertheless, a more than adequate legacy.

NOTES

All public statements made by either Ronald Reagan or George H. W. Bush while president can be found in Ronald W. Reagan, *Public Papers of the Presidents: Ronald Reagan, 1981–1989*, 15 vols. (Washington, DC: U.S. Government Printing Office, 1982–1991), and George H. W. Bush, *Public Papers of the Presidents: George Bush, 1981–1989*, 8 vols. (Washington, DC: U.S. Government Printing Office, 1990–1993). They are also available online at http://www.presidency.ucsb.edu /ws/. Thus, speeches and proclamations by these two presidents are not cited in this book unless a videotape or script of a specific speech was consulted.

ACRONYMS AND SHORT TITLES

Baker Papers	James A. Baker III Papers, Princeton University, Public Policy Papers, Seeley G. Mudd Manuscript Library
Bush PR	George Bush Presidential Records, GBL
GBL	George Bush Presidential Library, College Station, Texas
GBM	George Bush Presidential Museum, College Station, Texas
GFL	Gerald R. Ford Presidential Library, Ann Arbor, Michigan
Hofstra	Remarks to the Hofstra University Conference on the Bush Presidency, 17–19 April 1997
NJ	*National Journal*
NYT	*New York Times*

Bush *PP*	George H. W. Bush, *Public Papers of the Presidents: George H. W.*
	Bush, 1981–1989, 8 vols. (Washington, DC: U.S. Government
	Printing Office, 1990–1993)
PBS	Public Broadcasting System
USN&WR	*U.S. News & World Report*
WHORM	White House Office of Records Management
WHPO	White House Press Office
WP	*Washington Post*
WPNWE	*Washington Post National Weekly Edition*

CHAPTER 1: "ONE SHOULD SERVE HIS COUNTRY"

1. *41* (HBO Documentary Films, 2012).

2. Fitzhugh Green, *George Bush: An Intimate Portrait* (New York: Hippocrene Books, 1989), p. 2.

3. Quoted in Herbert S. Parmet, *George Bush: The Life of a Lone Star Yankee* (New York: Scribner, 1997), p. 28.

4. Quoted in *American Experience*: "George H. W. Bush" (PBS Home Video, WGBH Educational Foundation, 2008).

5. Tom Wicker, *George Herbert Walker Bush: A Penguin Life* (New York: Penguin, 2004), p. 5.

6. Elizabeth Mitchell, *W: Revenge of the Bush Dynasty* (New York: Berkley Books, 2003), p. 42.

7. Green, *Bush: An Intimate Portrait*, p. 19.

8. Ibid., p. 12.

9. Ibid., p. 23.

10. Parmet, *Lone Star Yankee*, p. 44.

11. Myra G. Gutin, *Barbara Bush: Presidential Matriarch* (Lawrence: University Press of Kansas, 2008), p. 2.

12. "George Bush: A Sense of Duty," for Arts and Entertainment Network's *Biography* series (first broadcast November 1996).

13. Parmet, *Lone Star Yankee*, p. 42.

14. "George Bush: A Sense of Duty."

15. Parmet, *Lone Star Yankee*, p. 46.

16. Quoted in *American Experience*: "George H. W. Bush."

17. Exhibit, GBM; Joe Hyams, *Flight of the Avenger: George Bush at War* (New York: Harcourt Brace Jovanovich, 1991), p. 47.

18. Letter on exhibit, GBM.

19. Hyams, *Flight of the Avenger*, pp. 83–84.

20. Quoted in "George Bush: A Sense of Duty."

21. Letter on exhibit, GBM.

22. Parmet, *Lone Star Yankee*, p. 59.

23. Wicker, *Bush*, p. 6.

24. Bush comment in exhibit, GBM.

25. Quoted in "George Bush: A Sense of Duty."

26. Parmet, *Lone Star Yankee*, p. 59. Bush was also awarded the navy Air Medal with two stars, the Asiatic Campaign Medal with three battle stars, and the Victory and American Campaign Medals (exhibit, GBM).

27. Bush comment in exhibit, GBM.

28. Parmet, *Lone Star Yankee*, pp. 63–64.

29. Green, *Bush: An Intimate Portrait*, p. 47. Readers can judge Bush's baseball talent for themselves: in fifty-one college games, Bush hit .251 with two home runs and twenty-three runs batted in. Out of 451 fielding attempts at first base, Bush made only nine errors (exhibit, GBM).

30. Bush to FitzGerald Bemiss, June 1948, in George Bush, *All the Best, George Bush: My Life in Letters and Other Writings*, 2nd ed. (New York: Scribner, 2013), p. 62.

31. Exhibit, GBM.

32. Exhibit, GBM; Green, *Bush: An Intimate Portrait*, p. 57.

33. Mitchell, *W.*, p. 24.

34. Bush to FitzGerald Bemiss, 21 October 1949, in Bush, *All the Best*, p. 68.

35. Bill Minutaglio, *First Son: George W. Bush and the Bush Family Dynasty* (New York: Times Books, 1999), pp. 28–30.

36. Burton I. Kaufman, *The Post-presidency from Washington to Clinton* (Lawrence: University Press of Kansas, 2012), p. 488.

37. Timothy Naftali, *George H. W. Bush* (New York: Times Books, 2007), p. 10; Wicker, *Bush*, p. 9.

38. Minutaglio, *First Son*, p. 35. See also Bush to Bemiss, 30 June 1951, in Bush, *All the Best*, p. 71.

39. Minutaglio, *First Son*, p. 44; Wicker, *Bush*, p. 11.

40. Kaufman, *Post-presidency*, p. 489.

41. Minutaglio, *First Son*, p. 44.

42. Wicker, *Bush*, pp. 12–13.

43. Bush, *All the Best*, p. 82.

44. See interviews in *American Experience*: "George H. W. Bush"; also Bush, *All the Best*, p. 77; Gutin, *Barbara Bush*, pp. 14–15.

45. Exhibit, GBM. Robin was originally buried in Greenwich, Connecticut, at the family plot. In 2000, she was moved to the presidential grave site at the George Bush Presidential Library in College Station, Texas, where she was reinterred (see GBL, Jan Burmeister Files, Misc. List Family/Friends [Family Tree—Bush Ancestral Table]).

46. "George Bush: A Sense of Duty."

47. Quoted in Naftali, *Bush*, p. 11.

48. *American Experience*: "George H. W. Bush."

49. Bush to T. Ludlow Ashley, 18 March 1963, in Bush, *All the Best*, p. 85.

50. *American Experience*: "George H. W. Bush."

51. Robert A. Mosbacher Sr., *Going to Windward: A Mosbacher Family Memoir* (College Station: Texas A&M University Press, 2010), pp. 143–146.

52. Ibid., p. 117.

53. Exhibit, GBM; Mosbacher, *Windward*, p. 117.

54. Wicker, *Bush*, p. 15.

55. *American Experience*: "George H. W. Bush."

56. Bush's later explanation of his opposition to the Civil Rights Act deserves a hearing: "I opposed discrimination of any kind . . . but I agreed with Barry Goldwater and others who supported the concept of civil rights but felt strongly this bill was unconstitutional and threatened more rights than it protected. I decided I could not support the bill and said so in my campaign. . . . My reasons for not supporting the bill were very different from those who hated the bill for racist reasons" (in Bush, *All the Best*, p. 88).

57. For 1964, see Mosbacher, *Windward*, p. 118.

58. Mitchell, *W.*, p. 87.

59. Minutaglio, *First Son*, p. 82.

60. Parmet, *Lone Star Yankee*, p. 113.

61. Bush to Richard M. Nixon, 10 November 1964, in Bush, *All the Best*, pp. 89–90. In that letter, Bush unconvincingly explained to Nixon that African Americans had voted against him not because of his stance against the 1964 Civil Rights Act but because they simply voted a straight Democratic ticket.

62. *American Experience*: "George H. W. Bush." For a strong summary of the election, see Parmet, *Lone Star Yankee*, pp. 98–114.

63. 369 U.S. 186 (1962).

64. Minutaglio, *First Son*, p. 94; Wicker, *Bush*, p. 19.

65. Two years later, Treleaven would join the Nixon campaign for the presidency, pioneering a new methodology for presenting the candidate to the public through canned "questions and answers" at rallies. This story is well told in Joe McGinniss, *The Selling of the President, 1968* (New York: Trident Press, 1969).

66. Parmet, *Lone Star Yankee*, pp. 115–122.

67. Naftali, *Bush*, p. 16.

68. Quoted in Geoffrey M. Kabaservice, *Rule and Ruin: The Downfall of Moderation and the Destruction of the Republican Party, from Eisenhower to the Tea Party* (New York: Oxford University Press, 2012), p. 307.

69. Bush explains this work in *All the Best*, p. 124. See also Gutin, *Barbara Bush*, p. 18.

70. Bush, *All the Best*, p. 107.

71. Ibid.

72. Mosbacher, *Windward*, p. 122.

73. The speech is reprinted in its entirety in Bush, *All the Best*, pp. 107–111. Commentary can be found in Green, *Bush: An Intimate Portrait*, p. 106; Mitchell, *W.*, pp. 110–111; Mosbacher, *Windward*, pp. 122–123; Parmet, *Lone Star Yankee*,

pp. 131–133; and Kenneth T. Walsh, *Family of Freedom: Presidents and African Americans in the White House* (Boulder, CO: Paradigm Publishers, 2011), p. 151.

74. Bush, *All the Best*, pp. 117–118. Reporters Nancy Gibbs and Michael Duffy claim that the offer was made to Bush at the instigation of Billy Graham (who held Bible study classes for Bush's parents), Nancy Gibbs, and Michael Duffy (*The President's Club: Inside the World's Most Exclusive Fraternity* [New York: Simon & Schuster, 2012], p. 375). Timothy Naftali writes that it was the letter-writing campaign of Neil Mallon, Bill Liedke (then serving as Nixon's finance chairman in Texas), and others that led to the offer (*Bush*, p. 20).

75. Quoted in Lewis L. Gould, *The Modern American Presidency* (Lawrence: University Press of Kansas, 2003), p. 205.

76. Arthur M. Schlesinger Jr., *Journals: 1952–2000* (New York: Penguin, 2007), p. 530.

77. Chapin to Haldeman, 17 September 1969, in Bruce Oudes, ed., *From the President: Richard Nixon's Secret Files* (New York: Harper & Row, 1988), p. 43.

78. Walter Pincus and Bob Woodward, "Bush and the Politics of Who You Know," *WPNWE*, 22 August–28 August 1988, p. 15.

79. Doro Bush Koch, *My Father, My President: A Personal Account of the Life of George H. W. Bush* (New York: Warner Books, 2006), p. 67. Other summaries of the 1970 campaign can be found in Gibbs and Duffy, *The President's Club*, pp. 375–377; Minutaglio, *First Son*, pp. 127–128; Mitchell, W., p. 137; Mosbacher, *Windward*, p. 125; Wicker, *Bush*, p. 23. At about the same time, Connally surprised no one by switching parties and becoming a Republican, and Nixon surprised no one by naming Connally his secretary of the Treasury.

80. Bush, *All the Best*, p. 121.

81. Bush Diary, 11 December 1970, in Bush, *All the Best*, pp. 131–133.

82. Quoted in Minutaglio, *First Son*, p. 133. Bush was replacing the affable Charles Yost, who had never been a Nixon favorite.

83. Colson to Pat O'Donnell, 24 July 1971, in Oudes, ed., *From the President*, p. 302.

84. The very best summary of Bush's tenure at the United Nations is Jeffrey A. Engel and George H. W. Bush, *The China Diary of George H. W. Bush* (Princeton, NJ: Princeton University Press, 2008), pp. 410–432. See also Bush, *All the Best*, pp. 140–143; Edward Derwinski, telephone interview with author, 6 October 1998; Green, *Bush: An Intimate Portrait*, pp. 120–122; John Robert Greene, *The Limits of Power: The Nixon and Ford Administrations* (Bloomington: Indiana University Press, 1992), pp. 110–112; Walter Isaacson, *Kissinger: A Biography* (New York: Simon & Schuster, 1992), p. 352; Kaufman, *Post-presidency*, p. 490.

85. Bush to Nixon, 21 November 1972, in Bush, *All the Best*, pp. 162–163. See also Daniel Schorr, *Come to Think of It: Notes on the Turn of the Millennium* (New York: Viking, 2007), pp. 25–26. In an interesting sidebar to this story, Nixon found himself quite unable to tell Dole the bad news. Instead, the president

called Dole and asked him to prevail upon Bush to take over at the RNC—a job that Bush had already told the president he would take. Saying nothing to Dole about his commitment to Nixon, Bush allowed Dole to "talk him into" taking the position. When Dole later learned of Bush and Nixon's duplicity, he grumbled that he had been "Bushwhacked."

86. *American Experience*: "George H. W. Bush."

87. Ibid.

88. Bush, *All the Best*, p. 171; Bush to Tex McCrary, 24 May 1974, in Bush, *All the Best*, p. 177.

89. Bush's memory of the cabinet meeting is found in his diary entry for 6 August 1974 in Bush, *All the Best*, pp. 190–192. The letter to Nixon can be found in exhibit, GBM. See also Greene, *Limits of Power*, p. 178; Parmet, *Lone Star Yankee*, p. 166; and Wicker, *Bush*, pp. 34–35.

90. Bush Diary, 6 August 1974, in Bush, *All the Best*, p. 190.

91. Gerald R. Ford, *A Time to Heal: The Autobiography of Gerald R. Ford* (New York: Harper & Row, 1979), pp. 142–146; Green, *Bush: An Intimate Portrait*, pp. 139–140; John Robert Greene, *The Presidency of Gerald R. Ford* (Lawrence: University Press of Kansas, 1995), p. 30; Robert Hartmann, *Palace Politics: An Inside Account of the Ford Years* (New York: McGraw-Hill, 1980), pp. 222–239. There were a lot of lists going to Ford during these days of decision. In a 1990 interview, Ford aide Robert Hartmann showed me a slip of paper in Ford's handwriting. On it was a list of names, in this order—Bush, (Donald) Rumsfeld, (Elliot) Richardson, (Nelson) Rockefeller, and (Ronald) Reagan (Reagan's name had been badly misspelled by Ford). Ford wanted to have these men investigated prior to choosing a vice president. Before he passed the list on to his investigatory contact, Hartmann recopied the list, spelling Reagan's name correctly. The order was now Richardson, Rockefeller, Reagan, Bush, and Rumsfeld. Hartmann also asked Ford to tell him which ones he was really interested in. Hartmann checked three names—Rockefeller, Bush, and Rumsfeld (Robert T. Hartmann, interview with author, 22 March 1990). Journalist Tom DeFrank, who related that Ford adviser Bryce Harlow made a chart of the preferences of his congressional contacts and presented that chart to Ford—the chart showed that Bush was the clear first choice; Rockefeller came in fifth out of five (Thomas DeFrank, *Write It When I'm Gone: Remarkable Off-the-Record Conversations with Gerald R. Ford* [New York: Putnam, 2007], p. 150). In his memoirs, then Ford adviser Donald Rumsfeld writes that Ford asked him, too, for a list of vice presidential possibilities. Rumsfeld suggested George Shultz, Melvin Laird, John Connally, Howard Baker, William Brock, George Bush, James Buckley, and William Scranton. Rumsfeld's memoirs do not reveal whether or not this list was ranked in any fashion (Donald Rumsfeld, *Known and Unknown: A Memoir* [New York: Sentinel, 2012], p. 234n).

92. Bush to Baker, 21 August 1974, in Bush, *All the Best*, p. 195.

93. Naftali, *Bush*, p. 30.

94. Wicker, *Bush*, p. 37.

95. Henry Kissinger, *Years of Renewal* (New York: Simon & Schuster, 1999), p. 555; Greene, *Ford*, p. 150.

96. Engel and Bush, *China Diary*, pp. 399–400, 405.

97. Rumsfeld to Ford, 10 July 1975, in Richard B. Cheney Files, GFL, box 5, Intelligence: Appointment of CIA Director.

98. Kathryn S. Olmsted, *Inside the Secret Government: The Post-Watergate Investigations of the CIA and the FBI* (Chapel Hill: University of North Carolina Press, 1996), p. 222n91.

99. Ford, *A Time to Heal*, p. 325.

100. Kissinger to Bush, 1 November 1975 (declassified cable); Bush to Kissinger, 2 November 1975 (declassified cable); Kissinger to Bush, 2 November 1975 (declassified cable); Henry Kissinger and Brent Scowcroft Files, GFL, box A1, Backchannel re: George Bush's CIA Appointment folder. Portions of this correspondence are found in Bush, *All the Best*, p. 233.

101. Memo, Connor to Friedersdorf, 22 November 1975, Gerald R. Ford Presidential Papers, GFL, Handwriting File, box 9, CIA folder no. 2.

102. See *Christian Science Monitor*, 2 June 1976, p. 26; DeFrank, *Write It When I'm Gone*, pp. 150–151.

103. Bush to Tom Lias, 6 November 1975, in Bush, *All the Best*, p. 238; Tim Weimer, *Legacy of Ashes: The History of the CIA* (New York: Doubleday, 2007), p. 347.

104. Quoted in Weimer, *Legacy of Ashes*, p. 347.

105. Ibid., p. 364.

106. The report, Bush to Ford (declassified), 3 August 1976, can be found in Gerald R. Ford Presidential Papers, GFL, Handwriting File, box 9, CIA folder no. 2; and in Bush, *All the Best*, pp. 257–259.

107. Bush to Champion, 24 January 1977, in Bush, *All the Best*, p. 269.

108. Quoted in Wicker, *Bush*, p. 49.

109. Green, *Bush: An Intimate Portrait*, p. 166.

110. Exhibit, GBM; Minutaglio, *First Son*, p. 195.

111. Bush, *All the Best*, p. 272.

112. The Fund for Limited Government was nominally chaired by Jim Baker, but in 1978 Baker was running for the Texas attorney general, so the day-to-day operation of the PAC was passed to political newcomer Karl Rove.

113. Parmet, *Lone Star Yankee*, p. 209.

114. Mosbacher, *Windward*, pp. 160–161.

115. Bush to Nixon, 31 January 1979, in Bush, *All the Best*, p. 279.

116. Mosbacher, *Windward*, p. 161.

117. Parmet, *Lone Star Yankee*, p. 224.

118. Mosbacher, *Windward*, p. 165.

119. Robert Shogan, *The Riddle of Power: Presidential Leadership from Truman to Bush* (New York: Dutton, 1991), p. 257.

120. Parmet, *Lone Star Yankee*, p. 226.

121. Ibid., pp. 227–229.

122. Wicker, *Bush*, pp. 54–56.

123. The moderator's name was actually Jon Breen.

124. Green, *Bush: An Intimate Portrait*, pp. 176–177.

125. Laura Kalman, *Right Star Rising: A New Politics, 1974–1980* (New York: Norton, 2010), p. 347.

126. Robert Scheer, *Playing President: My Close Encounters with Nixon, Carter, Bush I, Reagan and Clinton—And How They Did Not Prepare Me for George W. Bush* (New York: Akashic Books, 2006), p. 180.

127. Chase Untermeyer, comments at Hoover Library Conference on the Vice Presidency, Ames, Iowa, 27 October 1995.

128. Bush to Knoche, 30 May 1980, in Bush, *All the Best*, p. 298.

129. Gibbs and Duffy, *Billy Graham*, p. 287.

130. Kalman, *Right Star*, p. 357.

131. Mosbacher, *Windward*, p. 170.

132. Ed Rollins, *Bare Knuckles and Back Rooms: My Life in American Politics* (New York: Broadway Books, 1994), p. 170.

133. Mitchell, *W.*, pp. 189–191.

134. Reagan's diary makes clear the number of luncheons, horseback rides, dinners, and private briefings he had with his vice president over eight years. There are too many to list here; see Ronald Reagan, *The Reagan Diaries* (New York: HarperCollins, 2007).

135. Note in exhibit, GBM.

136. George Bush, *Looking Forward: An Autobiography* (New York: Bantam Books, 1987), p. 222; Chase Untermeyer, "Looking Forward: George Bush as Vice President," in Timothy Walch, ed., *At the President's Side: The Vice Presidency in the Twentieth Century* (Columbia: University of Missouri Press, 1997), p. 161.

137. Untermeyer, "Looking Forward," p. 162.

138. C. Boyden Gray, interview with author, 18 April 1997.

139. Ibid.

140. Untermeyer, "Looking Forward," p. 164.

141. Chase Untermeyer, interview with author, 18 June 1996.

142. C. Boyden Gray, interview with author, 18 April 1997; Lou Cannon, *President Reagan: The Role of a Lifetime* (New York: Simon & Schuster, 1991), pp. 127, 441, 821.

143. Gil Troy, *Morning in America: How Ronald Reagan Invented the 1980s* (Princeton, NJ: Princeton University Press, 2005), p. 133.

144. *WP*, 6 August 1987.

145. George P. Shultz, *Turmoil and Triumph: My Years as Secretary of State* (New York: Scribner, 1993), p. 809.

146. Wicker, *Bush*, p. 79.

147. Shultz, *Turmoil and Triumph*, pp. 803–804.

148. Quoted in Wicker, *Bush*, p. 79.

149. Quoted in ibid., p. 83.

150. Bush to Nixon, 12 January 1982, in Bush, *All the Best*, p. 316.

151. Seymour Hersh, "Our Man in Panama: The Creation of a Thug," *Life*, March 1990, p. 90.

152. *NYT*, 19 January 1991, p. 2; Colin Powell, *My American Journey* (New York: Random House, 1995), p. 515; John Dinges, *Our Man in Panama: How General Noriega Used the U.S.—And Made Millions in Drugs and Arms* (New York: Random House, 1990); Frederick Kempe, *Divorcing the Dictator: America's Bungled Affair with Noriega* (New York: Putnam, 1990); Parmet, *Lone Star Yankee*, pp. 202–205; Wicker, *Bush*, pp. 70–71.

153. Bush Diary, 18 May 1988, in Bush, *All the Best*, pp. 386–387.

154. Reagan Diary, 21 May 1988, in Reagan, *Diaries*, pp. 610–611.

155. Ibid., p. 611.

156. Bush Diary, 12 October 1987, in Bush, *All the Best*, p. 368.

CHAPTER 2: "JUGULAR POLITICS"

1. Bush Diary, 4 November 1986, in George Bush, *All the Best, George Bush: My Life in Letters and Other Writings*, 2nd ed. (New York: Scribner, 2013), p. 352.

2. Quoted in Leonard Benardo and Jennifer Weiss, *Citizens-in-Chief: The Second Lives of the American Presidents* (New York: Morrow, 2009), p. 220.

3. *NYT*, 18 May 1986, p. 50.

4. *WPNWE*, 9–15 June 1986, p. 12; *NBC Nightly News*, 4 May 1986.

5. *WPNWE*, 16–22 June 1986, pp. 12–13.

6. John Brady, *Bad Boy: The Life and Politics of Lee Atwater* (Reading, MA: Addison-Wesley, 1997), p. 36.

7. *Boogie Man: The Lee Atwater Story* (Roco Films, 2009).

8. Brady, *Bad Boy*, p. 109.

9. *Boogie Man*.

10. Brady, *Bad Boy*, p. 130.

11. Fitzhugh Green, *George Bush: An Intimate Portrait* (New York: Hippocrene Books, 1989), p. 82.

12. See, for but one example, Gil Troy, *Morning in America: How Ronald Reagan Invented the 1980s* (Princeton, NJ: Princeton University Press, 2005), p. 305.

13. *American Experience*: "George H. W. Bush" (PBS Home Video, WGBH Educational Foundation, 2008).

14. George W. Bush relates this story in both of his memoirs: *A Charge to Keep: My Journey to the White House* (New York: Morrow, 1999), pp. 178–179, and *Decision Points* (New York: Crown, 2010), p. 43. See also Elizabeth Mitchell, *W: Revenge of the Bush Dynasty* (New York: Berkley Books, 2003), p. 214.

15. Bush, *A Charge to Keep*, p. 180.

16. Richard Ben Cramer, *What It Takes: The Way to the White House* (New York: Random House, 1992), p. 17.

17. Peter Baker, *Days of Fire: Bush and Cheney in the White House* (New York: Doubleday, 2013), p. 37; Mitchell, W., pp. 4, 206 (Mitchell tells this story twice in her book).

18. Nancy Gibbs and Michael Duffy, *The Presidents Club: Inside the World's Most Exclusive Fraternity* (New York: Simon & Schuster, 2012), p. 478.

19. Ground zero for these rumors was an article by Richard Ryan, "The Mistress Question," *L.A. Weekly*, 14–20 October 1988, pp. 21, 39, 48: "George Bush has the reputation of being the Republican Gary Hart. . . . Bush is said to have had a number of affairs over the years; indeed, in some Washington circles, it is common gossip." It is important to note that Ryan interviewed Walter Pincus of the *Washington Post*, who, with Bob Woodward, had investigated these allegations and concluded: "We spent a great deal of time checking out these rumors and we were never able to confirm anything."

20. Quoted in Baker, *Bush and Cheney*, p. 38. See also Mitchell, W., p. 220–222.

21. *WP*, 30 January 1986, p. A25.

22. Bush, *Decision Points*, pp. 43–44.

23. Baker, *Bush and Cheney*, p. 38; Mitchell, W., p. 224. Writing about the confrontation, George W. does not mention the name of the reporter, nor does he mention that it was a woman. He just writes that he was "livid, and I let a lot of people know exactly how I felt" (Bush, *A Charge to Keep*, p. 181).

24. *WP*, 29 October 1987, p. A1.

25. Bush Diary, 25 January 1988, in Bush, *All the Best*, p. 376.

26. Quoted in Bob Schieffer and Gary Paul Gates, *The Acting President* (New York: Dutton, 1989), p. 349.

27. Tom Wicker, *George Herbert Walker Bush: A Penguin Life* (New York: Penguin, 2004), p. 87n.

28. Brady, *Bad Boy*, p. 162.

29. Herbert S. Parmet, *George Bush: The Life of a Lone Star Yankee* (New York: Scribner, 1997), p. 327.

30. Wicker, *Bush*, p. 85.

31. *Boogie Man*.

32. John H. Sununu, interview with author, 8 July 1987.

33. Sig Rogich, telephone interview with author, 6 October 1998; *WPNWE*, 27 June–3 July 1988, p. 13.

34. Wicker, *Bush*, p. 88.

35. Timothy Naftali, *George H. W. Bush* (New York: Times Books, 2007), p. 54.

36. Michael Duffy and Dan Goodgame, *Marching in Place: The Status Quo Presidency of George Bush* (New York: Simon & Schuster, 1992), p. 23.

37. Sig Rogich, telephone interview with author, 6 October 1998.

38. Geoffrey M. Kabaservice, *Rule and Ruin: The Downfall of Moderation and*

the Destruction of the Republican Party, from Eisenhower to the Tea Party (New York: Oxford University Press, 2012), p. 370.

39. *WP*, 15 November 1985. Kennedy announced that he would not be a candidate during a 19 December 1985 interview on the Cable News Network (CNN).

40. *WPNWE*, 2–8 February 1987, p. 4.

41. Bill Clinton, *My Life* (New York: Knopf, 2004), p. 331–335.

42. Andrew A. Card, interview with author, 18 April 1987.

43. *WPNWE*, 27 June–3 July 1988; Andrew A. Card, interview with author, 18 April 1997.

44. Sig Rogich, telephone interview with author, 6 October 1998.

45. James A. Baker III, *"Work Hard, Study . . . Keep Out of Politics": Adventures and Lessons from an Unexpected Public Life* (New York: Putnam, 2006), p. 246.

46. Bob Woodward, *The Commanders* (New York: Simon & Schuster, 1991), p. 57.

47. Jack Germond and Jules Witcover, *Whose Broad Stripes and Bright Stars? The Trivial Pursuit of the Presidency, 1988* (New York: Warner Books, 1989); Dan Quayle, *Standing Firm* (New York: Harper, 1994), p. 5; Schieffer and Gates, *Acting President*, p. 365.

48. David S. Broder and Bob Woodward, *The Man Who Would Be President: Dan Quayle* (New York: Simon & Schuster, 1992), pp. 35–38; Richard F. Fenno, *The Making of a Senator: Dan Quayle* (Washington, DC: Congressional Quarterly Books, 1989), p. 3.

49. Broder and Woodward, *The Man Who Would Be President*, pp. 15, 23.

50. Germond and Witcover, *Whose Broad Stripes and Bright Stars?* p. 378.

51. Daniel Heimbach, interview with author, 19 April 1997.

52. Fenno, *Making of a Senator*, p. 20.

53. Ibid., p. 8.

54. Broder and Woodward, *The Man Who Would Be President*, p. 27.

55. Parmet, *Lone Star Yankee*, p. 349.

56. Bush Diary, 21 August 1988, in Bush, *All the Best*, pp. 394–395.

57. Baker, *"Work Hard,"* pp. 247–248. Baker: "For the record, I don't believe any of us knew about the National Guard issue" (p. 247).

58. Broder and Woodward, *The Man Who Would Be President*, p. 62; Parmet, *Lone Star Yankee*, p. 346.

59. Peggy Noonan *What I Saw at the Revolution: A Political Life in the Reagan Era* (New York: Ivy Books, 1990), p. 324.

60. Ibid., pp. 315–329; Bob Woodward, "The Anatomy of a Decision," *WPNWE*, 12–18 October 1992, p. 6. See also Baker, *"Work Hard,"* pp. 257–258.

61. *American Experience*: "George H. W. Bush."

62. John Gray Geer, *In Defense of Negativity: Attack Ads in Presidential Campaigns* (Chicago: University of Chicago Press, 2006), pp. 110–111.

63. Bush to Giamatti, 29 July 1982, in Bush, *All the Best*, p. 320.

64. Robert Justin Goldstein, *Flag Burning and Free Speech: The Case of* Texas v. Johnson (Lawrence: University Press of Kansas, 2000), p. 82.

65. Schieffer and Gates, *Acting President*, p. 367.

66. George Will, "The Rubber Ducky Campaign," *Newsweek*, 26 September 1988, p. 84.

67. *Boogie Man*.

68. Parmet, *Lone Star Yankee*, p. 336.

69. Wicker, *Bush*, p. 101.

70. Andrew A. Card, interview with author, 18 April 1997.

71. Chase Untermeyer, interview with author, 18 June 1996.

72. Card remembered that "we didn't even want them to run it," and Baker remembered that "as far as I know . . . we had nothing to do with that ad" (Andrew A. Card, interview with author, 18 April 1997; James A. Baker, *"Work Hard, Study, and Keep Out of Politics": Adventures and Lessons from an Unexpected Public Life* [New York: Putnam, 2006], p. 270).

73. Michael Gilette, ed., *Snapshots of the 1988 Presidential Campaign*, vol. 1, *The Bush Campaign* (Austin: LBJ School of Public Affairs, University of Texas, 1992), pp. 70–72.

74. Quoted in Brady, *Bad Boy*, p. 191.

75. Quoted in Troy, *Morning in America*, p. 305.

76. *WP*, 3 September 1988, p. A8.

77. Geer, *In Defense of Negativity*, p. 121.

78. Baker, *"Work Hard,"* p. 266. We do not yet know how Bush felt about the quality of his campaign—in his collection of letters and autobiographical comments *All the Best*, there is no mention of the flag issue—or of Willie Horton.

79. *Boogie Man*.

80. Brady, *Bad Boy*, p. 172.

81. For a good survey of the entire ad campaign, see David Mark, *Going Dirty: The Art of Negative Campaigning* (Lanham, MD: Rowman and Littlefield, 2009), pp. 200–203.

82. Quoted in Schieffer and Gates, *Acting President*, p. 372.

83. Baker, *"Work Hard,"* p. 269.

84. Germond and Witcover, *Whose Broad Stripes and Bright Stars?* p. 406.

85. Sig Rogich, telephone interview with author, 6 October 1988; C-SPAN video, "Presidential Campaign Commercials," broadcast on 2 October 1988 (ID no. 8705).

86. John G. Tower, *Consequences: A Personal and Political Memoir* (Boston: Little, Brown, 1991), p. 11.

87. James T. Patterson, *Restless Giant: The United States from Watergate to Bush v. Gore* (New York: Oxford University Press, 2005), p. 224.

88. When the Electoral College finally met in January 1989, the final vote was 426 for Bush, 111 for Dukakis, with 1 vote cast for Lloyd Bentsen by

Margarette Leach, an elector from West Virginia, as a protest against the outdated Electoral College system. As president of the Senate, George Bush proclaimed his own electoral victory (*NYT*, 4 January 1989, p. B6).

89. "Quest for the Presidency: The Candidates Debate," *Reader's Digest*, October 1988, p. 73.

90. Steven Wayne in Leslie D. Feldman and Rosanna Perotti, eds., *Honor and Loyalty: Inside the Politics of the George H. W. Bush White House* (Westport, CT: Greenwood Press, 2002), p. 50.

91. *NYT*, 10 November 1988, p. B5.

92. William Boot, "Campaign '88: TV Overdoses on Inside Dope," *Columbia Journalism Review* 2 (January/February 1989): 27.

93. Clinton, *My Life*, p. 344.

94. *NYT*, 12 November 1988, p. 8.

95. D. Sunshine Hillygus and Todd G. Shields, *The Persuadable Voter: Wedge Issues in Presidential Campaigns* (Princeton, NJ: Princeton University Press, 2009), p. 24n16.

96. For end-of-election statistics, see *NYT*, 10 November 1988, pp. B6–B7; *NJ*, 29 April 1989, pp. 1050–1054.

97. Will, "Rubber Ducky," p. 84.

98. W. Lance Bennett, *The Governing Crisis: Media, Money, and Marketing in American Elections* (New York: St. Martin's Press, 1996), pp. 28–29.

CHAPTER 3: "THE UNTOUCHABLES"

1. George Bush and Brent Scowcroft, *A World Transformed* (New York: Knopf, 1998), p. 18.

2. James A. Baker III, *The Politics of Diplomacy: Revolution, War, and Peace* (New York: Putnam, 1995), pp. 19–20.

3. Roman Popadiuk, *The Leadership of George Bush: An Insider's View of the Forty-First President* (College Station: Texas A&M University Press, 2009), p. 3.

4. Chase Untermeyer, interview with author, 18 June 1996; *WPNWE*, 6–11 December 1988, p. 12; Bill Minutaglio, *First Son: George W. Bush and the Bush Family Dynasty* (New York: Times Books, 1999), pp. 232–233. In their *The President's Club: Inside the World's Most Exclusive Fraternity* (New York: Simon & Schuster, 2012), Nancy Gibbs and Michael Duffy call this group the "Silent Committee" (p. 478).

5. Andrew A. Card, interview with author, 18 April 1997.

6. Charles Peters, *How Washington Really Works* (Reading, MA: Addison-Wesley, 1992), p. 14.

7. Chase Untermeyer, interview with author, 18 June 1996.

8. *WPNWE*, 28 November–4 December 1988, p. 13.

9. Michael Beschloss and Strobe Talbott, *At the Highest Levels: The Inside Story of the End of the Cold War* (Boston: Little, Brown, 1993), p. 8.

10. Shirley Anne Warshaw, *The Domestic Presidency: Policy Making in the White House* (Boston: Allyn and Bacon, 1997), p. 158.

11. *WPNWE*, 28 November–4 December 1988, p. 13.

12. Andrew A. Card, interview with author, 18 April 1997.

13. John H. Sununu, interview with author, 8 July 1997; *NYT*, 20 November 1988, p. 1.

14. Michael Duffy and Dan Goodgame, *Marching in Place: The Status Quo Presidency of George Bush* (New York: Simon & Schuster, 1991), p. 38.

15. *NYT*, 1 December 1988, p. B17.

16. *WPNWE*, 5–11 December 1988, p. 12.

17. Bob Woodward, *The Commanders* (New York: Simon & Schuster, 1991), p. 68.

18. Herbert S. Parmet, *George Bush: The Life of a Lone Star Yankee* (New York: Scribner, 1997), p. 360.

19. *NYT*, 25 November 1988, p. 1.

20. James P. Pfiffner, *The Bush Transition: A Friendly Takeover* (Richmond, VA: Institute of Public Policy, George Mason University, 1995). Indeed, James Baker was quoted as telling his staff, "Remember, this is *not* a friendly takeover" (quoted in Beschloss and Talbott, *At the Highest Levels*, p. 26). At the 1997 Hofstra University Conference on the Bush Presidency, Roscoe B. Starek III, who served as deputy director of personnel, voiced a view that he seems to hold on his own: "The perception that you got from the press at the beginning of the administration was that 'they fired all the Reaganites and all the desks are empty.' Well, that's baloney! We didn't fire the Reaganites. The Reagan appointees, many of whom we knew, stayed on in most cases well into the summer until the confirmation process played out" (in Leslie D. Feldman and Rosanna Perotti, eds., *Honor and Loyalty: Inside the Politics of the George H. W. Bush White House* [Westport, CT: Greenwood Press, 2002], pp. 146–147).

21. See, for example, the observations in *NYT*, 17 January 1989, p. A1.

22. Philip D. Brady, interview with author, 17 April 1997; Edward Derwinski, telephone interview with author, 6 October 1998.

23. Richard Darman, *Who's in Control? Polar Politics and the Sensible Center* (New York: Simon & Schuster, 1996), p. 206.

24. Quoted in Maynard, *Out of the Shadows: George H. W. Bush and the End of the Cold War* (College Station: Texas A&M University Press, 2008), p. 7. Also on Scowcroft's background, see *NYT*, 24 November 1988, p. B13; *NYT*, 28 November 1988, p. 1; Bush and Scowcroft, *A World Transformed*, pp. 11–12; Ivo H. Daalder and I. M. Destler, *In the Shadow of the Oval Office: Profiles of the National Security Advisers and the Presidents They Served—From JFK to George W. Bush* (New York: Simon & Schuster, 2009), pp. 170–172; Woodward, *The Commanders*, p. 51.

25. Quoted in Leslie Stahl, *Reporting Live* (New York: Simon & Schuster, 1999), pp. 328–329.

26. Beschloss and Talbott, *At the Highest Levels*, p. 12.

27. *NJ*, 3 December 1988, p. 3087 (the title of the article: "Scowcroft's Views Often at Odds with Those Held by Reagan's Team").

28. Bush and Scowcroft, *A World Transformed*, p. 19.

29. John P. Burke, *Honest Broker? The National Security Advisor and Presidential Decision Making* (College Station: Texas A&M University Press, 2009), p. 169.

30. Ibid., pp. 169–171; Daalder and Destler, *In the Shadow of the Oval Office*, p. 181; John Hart, *The Presidential Branch: The Executive Office of the President from Washington to Clinton* (Chatham, NJ: Chatham House, 1995), pp. 76–77.

31. Burke, *Honest Broker?* pp. 162, 167.

32. Ibid., p. 165.

33. Daalder and Destler, *In the Shadow of the Oval Office*, p. 183.

34. Fitzhugh Green, *George Bush: An Intimate Portrait* (New York: Hippocrene Books, 1989), p. 112.

35. John G. Tower, *Consequences: A Personal and Political Memoir* (Boston: Little, Brown, 1991), p. 280.

36. *Atlanta Constitution*, undated (quoted in Tower, *Consequences*, pp. 30–31).

37. Chase Untermeyer, interview with author, 18 June 1996.

38. Interview with author, not for attribution.

39. Quoted in Parmet, *Lone Star Yankee*, p. 373.

40. "Summary of Work Performed for Consulting Clients," undated, Bush PR, Counsel's Office: C. Dean McGrath Jr. Files, Sherrie Marshall File—Working File for Hearing.

41. William Webster, interview with author, 8 July 1997.

42. Bush and Scowcroft, *A World Transformed*, p. 21.

43. *NYT*, 21 January 1989, p. 7.

44. *NYT*, 15 February 1989.

45. *NYT*, 11 March 1989, p. 7.

46. Duffy and Goodgame, *Marching in Place*, p. 37.

47. *NYT*, 5 February 1989, p. 1; *NYT*, 6 February 1989, p. A15; *NYT*, 7 February 1989, p. A1.

48. *NYT*, 15 February 1989, p. A1.

49. *NYT*, 19 February 1989, p. E4.

50. *NYT*, 26 January 1989, p. D23; *NYT*, 29 January 1989, p. A1.

51. *NYT*, 12 February 1989, p. 30.

52. *WP*, 27 February 1989, p. A4. See also memo, "Conflict of Interest Allegations" (undated), Bush PR, White House Counsel's Office, C. Dean McGrath Files, John Tower Files, Sherrie Marshall's File (1 of 2), OA/ID CF00481-016.

53. *NYT*, 2 February 1989, p. D20.

54. Memo, Sam Nunn and John Warner to Judge William S. Sessions, 10 February 1989, Bush PR, White House Counsel's Office, C. Dean McGrath Files, John Tower Files, Miscellaneous Allegations, Letters, etc. folder, OA/ID CF00482-013.

55. "Infidelity Led to Tower's Exit from Geneva, Investigator Says," 16 February 1989, Knight-Ridder Newspapers.

56. Woodward, *The Commanders*, pp. 58–59.

57. Press Pool Report, 8 February 1989, Bush PR, WHPO, Lower Press Office Pool Reports, box 13, dated folder.

58. Bush to Charles L. Bartlett, 21 February 1989, Bush PR, WHORM Subject Files: General, FG-37.

59. *NYT*, 10 February 1989, p. A1; *NYT*, 11 February 1989, p. 10.

60. *NYT*, 24 February 1989, pp. A1, D19.

61. "Report Together with Minority Views," 28 February 1989, Bush PR, Counsel's Office, C. Dean McGrath Jr. Files, Tower Files: SASC—Report with Minority folder; *Consideration of the Honorable John G. Tower to Be Secretary of Defense: Report Together with Minority, Supplemental, and Additional Views* (Washington, DC: Government Printing Office, 1989). On the day of the committee vote, Bush was in Japan, attending the funeral of Emperor Hirohito (Bush on meeting Hirohito: "I couldn't believe that this little guy . . . the kind of guy you might see running around with a butterfly net . . . a dainty little fellow . . . [had been] the epitome of all evil" [*41* (HBO Documentary Films, 2012); see also Bush Diary, 24 February 1989, in George Bush, *All the Best, George Bush: My Life in Letters and Other Writings* (New York: Scribner, 1999), p. 415]).

62. Schedule, 28 February 1989, Bush PR, White House Office of Legislative Affairs, Rebecca Anderson: Trip Files and Miscellaneous Files, Tower Nomination: 1989 folder.

63. *NYT*, 27 February 1989, p. A1.

64. *NYT*, 24 February 1989, p. A1.

65. George H. W. Bush, interview with author, 9 November 1998.

66. On 5 April 1991, Tower, who had been named by Bush to the President's Foreign Intelligence Advisory Board (PFIAB), was killed along with twenty-two others, including one of his three daughters, in the crash of a commuter airplane off the Georgia coast.

67. Woodward, *The Commanders*, p. 71.

68. Colin Powell, *My American Journey* (New York: Random House, 1995), p. 405.

69. Richard B. Cheney, telephone interview with author, 7 March 1997; Richard Cheney, *In My Time: A Personal and Political Memoir* (New York: Threshold Editions, 2011), pp. 153–155.

70. Bush to Tower (Xerox of photo with inscription), 15 March 1989, Bush PR, WHORM Subject File: General, PR005.

71. *NJ*, 1 July 1989, pp. 1678–1683.

72. Gloria Borger, "Dennis the Menace Comes In from the Cold," *USN&WR*, 27 March 1989, p. 27.

73. *WPNWE*, 13–19 March 1989, p. 12.

74. John M. Barry, *The Ambition and the Power: The Fall of Jim Wright—A True Story of Washington* (New York: Viking, 1989), p. 762.

75. John Brady, *Bad Boy: The Life and Politics of Lee Atwater* (Reading, MA: Addison-Wesley, 1997), pp. 241–247.

76. *NYT*, 26 August 1989, p. A1.

77. *NYT*, 10 June 1990, p. 22; *NYT*, 26 July 1990, p. A1.

78. Indicative of this view is Lewis L. Gould, *The Most Exclusive Club: A History of the Modern United States Senate* (New York: Basic Books, 2005), pp. 291–293, and Joe Klein, *The Natural: The Misunderstood Presidency of Bill Clinton* (New York: Broadway Books, 2002), pp. 103–104.

79. *WPNWE*, 13–19 March 1989, pp. 6–7.

CHAPTER 4: DOMESTIC POLICIES

1. Julie Kosterlitz and W. John Moore, "Saving the Welfare State," *NJ* 14 May 1988, p. 1278.

2. Sean Wilentz, *The Age of Reagan: 1974–2008* (New York: Harper Perennial, 2008), p. 154.

3. *NJ*, 14 May 1988, p. 1257; Richard E. Cohen, *Rostenkowski: The Pursuit of Power and the End of the Old Politics* (Chicago: Ivan R. Dee, 1999), 195.

4. One alumni of the Bush administration remembers that in several speeches, Bush called his domestic vision the "Good Society." If so, it didn't happen too many times, and it didn't stick. (Roman Popadiuk, *The Leadership of George Bush: An Insider's View of the Forty-First President* (College Station: Texas A&M University Press, 2009), p. 51.

5. Maureen Dowd and Thomas Friedman, "The Bush and Baker Boys," *New York Times Magazine*, 6 May 1990, p. 64.

6. George H. W. Bush, interview with author, 9 November 1988.

7. For excellent summaries of the Bush veto strategy, see Robert J. Spitzer, "The Veto King: The 'Dr. No' Presidency of George Bush" (pp. 233–253), and Nancy Kassop, "The Bush Administration's Approach to Separation of Powers: An Invitation to Struggle" (pp. 215–231), in Leslie D. Feldman and Rosanna Perotti, eds., *Honor and Loyalty: Inside the Politics of the George H. W. Bush White House* (Westport, CT: Greenwood Press, 2002).

8. See Richard S. Conley, "George Bush and the 102nd Congress: The Impact of Public and Private Veto Threats on Policy Outcomes," *Presidential Studies Quarterly* 33 (2003): 734.

9. Rob Portman, interview with author, 13 June 1997; Kenneth E. Collier, *Between the Branches: The White House Office of Legislative Affairs* (Pittsburgh: University of Pittsburgh Press, 1997), p. 242.

10. For a discussion of Ford's veto strategy, see John Robert Greene, *The Presidency of Gerald R. Ford* (Lawrence: University Press of Kansas, 1995), pp. 76–77.

11. The only time that a Bush veto was overridden was on the Cable Television Protection and Competition Act of 1992.

12. *NYT*, 9 March 1989, p. A20.

13. Interview Transcript, Bush with *WP*, 23 March 1989, Bush PR, WHPO, Press Office Internal Transcripts, box 133, dated folder.

14. *NYT*, 24 March 1989, p. A13.

15. *NYT*, 15 June 1989, p. A21.

16. "President Bush's Position on the Minimum Wage," undated, Bush PR, Council of Economic Advisors, Michael Boskin Files, Minimum Wage folder, OA/ID 080737; *NYT*, 9 November 1989, p. 2.

17. Exhibit, GBM.

18. Robert Justin Goldstein, *Flag Burning and Free Speech: The Case of* Texas v. Johnson (Lawrence: University Press of Kansas, 2000), pp. 44–49.

19. *Texas v. Johnson*, 491 U.S. 397 (1989). See also Goldstein, *Flag Burning*, pp. 102–107.

20. *NYT*, 7 July 1989, p. B4.

21. Goldstein, *Flag Burning*, p. 119.

22. *NYT*, 25 July 1989, p. A17.

23. Goldstein, *Flag Burning*, p. 125.

24. *NYT*, 23 February 1990, p. 2.

25. *U.S. v. Eichman*, 496 U.S. 310 (1990).

26. 410 U.S. 113 (1973).

27. *NYT*, 26 January 1989, p. A23.

28. Bush to J. Bayard Boyle Jr., 15 February 1990, Bush PR, WHORM Subject File, box 36, WE003-119410 [underlining in original].

29. Bush to Mrs. Becky Orr, 10 April 1990, Bush PR, WHORM Subject File: General, box 36, WE003-141529.

30. Bush to Thomas W. Ford, 8 May 1990, Bush PR, WHORM Subject File: General, box 30, WE003-143-084.

31. Bush to Lofton, 24 April 1986, Bush PR, Marlin Fitzwater Files, Subject File: Alpha File, box 1, Abortion folder.

32. Bush to Henry Hyde, 5 May 1989, Bush PR, WHORM Subject File: General, WE003, box 34, no. 029331.

33. 492 U.S. 490 (1989).

34. Ted Gest, "The Abortion Furor," *USN&WR*, 17 July 1989, p. 19.

35. Statement by the President, 3 July 1989, Bush PR, Marlin Fitzwater Files, OA 6784, Subject File: Alpha File, box 1, Abortion folder.

36. Morton Kondracke, "The New Abortion Wars," *New Republic*, 28 August 1989, pp. 18–19.

37. Bush to Dole, 4 June 1991, Bush PR, WHPO, General Office Files, Press Office Subject File, box 83, Abortion folder. Bush used essentially this same boilerplate when writing other members of Congress regarding his stance on abortion (see, for example, Bush to Robert Byrd, 17 October 1989, Bush PR, Marlin Fitzwater Files, box 1 Abortion folder).

38. *NYT*, 13 April 1990, p. 2.

39. John Berlau, "The Quota Paradox," *Policy Review*, no. 68 (Spring 1994): 7.

40. *WPNWE*, 13–19 March 1989, p. 4.

41. 491 U.S. 164 (1989).

42. 490 U.S. 642 (1989).

43. Kenneth O'Reilly, *Nixon's Piano: Presidents and Racial Politics from Washington to Clinton* (New York: Free Press, 1995), pp. 392–393.

44. Charles M. Cameron, *Veto Bargaining: Presidents and the Politics of Negative Power* (Cambridge: Cambridge University Press, 2000), p. 243.

45. Atwater to Bush, 18 October 1990, Baker Papers, box 99, folder 7 (Atwater, Lee).

46. W. Gary Fowler, Donald W. Jackson, and James Riddlesperger Jr. "Symbolic Politics Revisited: The Bush Administration and the Civil Rights Act of 1991," in Richard Himelfarb and Rosanna Perotti, eds., *Principle over Politics? The Domestic Policy of the George H. W. Bush Presidency* (Westport, CT: Praeger, 2004), pp. 197–198; Kenneth T. Walsh, *Family of Freedom: Presidents and African-Americans in the White House* (Boulder, CO: Paradigm, 2011), p. 154.

47. Brennan to Bush, 20 July 1990, Bush PR, Legislative Affairs, Rebecca Anderson Files, Souter Nomination folder.

48. Jan Crawford Greenburg, *Supreme Conflict: The Inside Story of the Struggle for Control of the United States Supreme Court* (New York: Penguin, 2007), p. 89.

49. Ibid., pp. 89–91; Bob Woodward, *Shadow: Five Presidents and the Legacy of Watergate* (New York: Simon & Schuster, 1999), p. 180.

50. Greenburg, *Supreme Conflict*, p. 93.

51. C. Boyden Gray, interview with author, 18 April 1997; see also John H. Sununu, interview with author, 8 July 1997.

52. Greenburg, *Supreme Conflict*, p. 96; Tinsley E. Yarborough, *David Hackett Souter: Traditional Republican in the Rehnquist Court* (New York: Oxford University Press, 2005), p. 104.

53. C. Boyden Gray, interview with author, 18 April 1997; Yarborough, *Souter*, p. 95.

54. Rob Portman, interview with author, 13 June 1997.

55. Quoted in Yarborough, *Souter*, p. 100. This did not stop the press from trying to find skeletons. Bob Woodward would later write that just before the congressional hearings were to start, Rudman learned that a "New York gay newspaper" was going to out Souter as gay. According to Woodward, Souter was

beside himself and wanted to drop out—he even went to the phone in his apartment to call the president. Rudman, who was with Souter at the time, physically restrained his friend until he changed his mind (Woodward, *Shadow*, p. 181).

56. Untermeyer to Souter, 3 February 1990, Bush PR, Personnel, Chase Untermeyer Files, Souter folder.

57. Greenberg, *Supreme Conflict*, p. 99.

58. *Boston Globe*, 24 July 1990.

59. *Washington Times*, 24 July 1990, p. 10.

60. Greenberg, *Supreme Conflict*, p. 103.

61. George W. Bush, *Decision Points* (New York: Crown, 2010), p. 96. See also George W. Bush, *41: A Portrait of My Father* (New York: Crown, 2014), p. 220.

62. Patrick J. McGuinn, *No Child Left Behind and the Transformation of Federal Education Policy, 1965–2005* (Lawrence: University Press of Kansas, 2006), pp. 43–47.

63. *Chronicle of Higher Education*, 6 September 1989, p. 5; Edith Rasell and Lawrence Mishel, "The Truth about Education Spending," *Roll Call*, 21 May 1990, p. 23.

64. White House Press Release, 5 April 1989, Bush PR, Marlin Fitzwater File, Subject File, box 10, education folder, OA6784.

65. George H. W. Bush, interview with author, 9 November 1998.

66. *NYT*, 26 April 1989, p. B8.

67. Theodore Roosevelt had met with the governors to discuss the issue of the conservation of natural resources, and Franklin D. Roosevelt had met with them to discuss possible solutions to the Great Depression.

68. Bush to Clinton, 29 September 1989, Bush PR, WHORM General File, Subject File, MC083600. An excellent survey of the conference can be found in McGuinn, *No Child Left Behind*, pp. 60–63. See also D. Alan Bromley, *The President's Scientists: Reminiscences of a White House Science Advisor* (New Haven, CT: Yale University Press, 2004), pp. 107–108.

69. *NYT*, 26 April 1989, p. B8.

70. "America 2000: The President's Education Strategy, Fact Sheet," 18 April 1991, Bush *PP*, 1991, vol. 1, p. 389; McGuinn, *No Child Left Behind*, p. 65.

71. *Wall Street Journal*, 6 February 1991, p. A14.

72. *WP*, 28 April 1991, p. C7.

73. Susan Chira, "Lamar Alexander's Self-Help Course," *New York Times Magazine*, 23 November 1991, p. 52.

74. Charles F. Levinthal, "Beyond Saying No: Domestic Drug Policy and Its Effects during the Bush Administration, 1989–1992," in Himelfarb and Perotti, eds., *Principle over Politics?* p. 203.

75. Hugh Sidey, "Back in the Bully Pulpit," *Time*, 23 January 1989, p. 19.

76. Robert Schlesinger, *White House Ghosts: Presidents and Their Speechwriters* (New York: Simon & Schuster, 2008), pp. 372–374.

77. Quoted in ibid., p. 374.

78. Fact Sheet, National Drug Control Strategy, 5 September 1989, Bush PR, WHPO, General Office Files, Press Office Subject File, box 84, Drug folder no. 3.

79. *NYT*, 31 March 1989, p. A11.

80. *NYT*, 24 August 1989, p. B6.

81. *NYT*, 21 January 1990, p. 2.

82. The bill, the Andean Trade Preference Act of 1990, was signed into law on 5 October 1990. See Bush PR, WHPO, General Office Files, Press Office Subject File, box 83, Andean–Caribbean Basin Initiative folder.

83. *NYT*, 5 April 1990, p. 2; *NYT*, 14 April 1990, p. 2.

84. White House, "National Drug Control Strategy, February 1991," Bush PR, WHPO, General Office Files, Press Office Subject File, box 84, Drug folder no. 3. See also *NYT*, 1 February 1991, p. 2; *San Diego Union*, 16 June 1991, p. C2.

85. Rodman D. Griffin, "The Disabilities Act: Protecting the Rights of the Disabled Will Have Far-Reaching Effects," *CQ Researcher* 1, no. 32 (1991): 999.

86. Major R. Owens, *Americans with Disabilities Act: Initial Accessibility Good but Important Barriers Remain* (Washington, DC: U.S. General Accounting Office, 1993), p. 1.

87. Susan Gluck Mezey, *Disabling Interpretations: The Americans with Disabilities Act in Federal Court* (Pittsburgh: University of Pittsburgh Press, 2005), p. 11.

88. Fred Pelka, ed., *What We Have Done: An Oral History of the Disability Rights Movement* (Amherst: University of Massachusetts Press, 2012), p. 44. Kemp died in 1997 (obituary, *NYT*, 14 August 1997).

89. Mezey, *Disabling Interpretations*, p. 23.

90. Bush *PP*, 1990, vol. 2, p. 1068; Griffin, "The Disabilities Act," p. 996.

91. Mezey, *Disabling Interpretations*, pp. 25–26.

92. Ibid., pp. 26–31.

93. Pelka, *What We Have Done*, pp. 468, 536.

94. David Mervin, *George Bush and the Guardianship Presidency* (New York: St. Martin's Press, 1996), p. 98.

95. Quoted in Mezey, *Disabling Interpretations*, pp. 31–32.

96. C. Boyden Gray, interview with author, 18 April 1997; Gray, in Himelfarb and Perotti, eds., *Prestige over Politics?*, p. 159; Gray in Pelka, ed., *What We Have Done*, p. 506.

97. Letter in exhibit, GBM.

98. *NYT*, 1 December 1988, p. B15.

99. *NYT*, 1 February 1989, p. 1.

100. Patrick Barry, "A Master Plan from Bush's Unlikely Star," *USN&WR*, 24 July 1989, p. 24.

101. Skinner to Bush, 22 March 1990, Bush PR, WHORM Subject File: General, DI001. For a good narrative presentation of the disaster, see Steve Coll, *Private Empire: Exxon Mobil and American Power* (New York: Penguin, 2012), pp. 1–16.

102. Rogich to Bush, 30 March 1989, Bush PR, WHORM Subject File, General, DI001.

103. Richard E. Cohen, *Washington at Work: Back Rooms and Clean Air* (New York: Macmillan, 1982), p. 85.

104. Louis Jacobsen, "The Green Hornet," *NJ*, 27 January 1996, p. 167; Margaret Kris, "Politics in the Air," *NJ*, 6 May 1989, pp. 1098–1102.

105. Cohen, *Washington at Work*, p. 89.

106. "Fact Sheet: The Clean Air Act Amendments of 1990," 15 November 1990, Bush PR, Marlin Fitzwater Files, OA 6784, Subject File: Alpha File, box 6, Clean Air Act folder no. 3; Bromley, *The President's Scientists*, p. 157; Johnathan M. Davidson and Joseph M. Norbeck, *An Interactive History of the Clean Air Act: Scientific and Policy Perspectives* (Waltham, MA: Elsevier, 2012), p. 15.

107. Al Gore, *The Future: Six Drivers of Global Change* (New York: Random House, 2013), p. 345.

CHAPTER 5: PAYING FOR REAGANOMICS

1. Herbert S. Parmet, *George Bush: The Life of a Lone Star Yankee* (New York: Scribner, 1997), p. 367.

2. *NYT*, 19 January 1989, p. B9.

3. Richard Darman, *Who's in Control? Polar Politics and the Sensible Center* (New York: Simon & Schuster, 1996), p. 200.

4. *NYT*, 9 January 1989, p. B6.

5. Press Pool Report, 13 February 1989, Bush PR, WHPO, Lower Press Office Pool Reports, box 13, dated folder.

6. George Bush, interview with author, 9 November 1998.

7. Press Pool Report, 24 April 1989, Bush PR, WHPO, Lower Press Office Pool Reports, box 13, dated folder.

8. Richard E. Cohen, *Rostenkowski: The Pursuit of Power and the End of the Old Politics* (Chicago: Ivan R. Dee, 1999), p. 197; Darman, *Who's in Control?*, pp. 205–209.

9. Interview transcript, Bush and Don Feder, 18 May 1989, Bush PR, WHPO, Press Office Internal Transcripts, box 133, folder OA6237.

10. Darman, *Who's in Control?*, pp. 236–237.

11. An accessible short explanation of the S&L crisis can be found in Naftali, *George H. W. Bush* (New York: Times Books, 2007), pp. 73–76.

12. L. William Seidman, *Full Faith and Credit: The Great S&L Debacle and Other Washington Sagas* (New York: Times Books, 1993), p. 178.

13. Seidman, *Full Faith and Credit*, p. 176; WPNWE, 26 June–2 July 1989, pp. 6–8.

14. *NYT*, 11 January 1989, p. A1; *NYT*, 31 January 1989, p. 1.

15. "Fact Sheet: The President's Reform Plan for the Savings and Loan Industry," 6 February 1989, Bush PR, Marvin Fitzwater Files, Subject File: Alpha File, OA 6546, box 26, S&L folder; *NYT*, 7 February 1989, p. D9; Catherine Wang, "Bush's S&L Plan: Full of Good Intentions—and Holes," *Business Week*, 20 February 1989, p. 32.

16. Parmet, *Lone Star Yankee*, p. 395; Seidman, *Full Faith and Credit*, p. 209.

17. Alan Greenspan, *The Age of Turbulence: Adventures in a New World* (New York: Penguin, 2007), p. 116. Greenspan reported that when it disbanded in 1995, the RTC had liquidated 744 S&Ls, "more than a quarter of the industry" (p. 117).

18. *WPNWE*, 15–21 May 1989, p. 14. See also Greenspan, *Age of Turbulence*, p. 116.

19. "Neil Bush Statement to the Press on Charges Brought by Office of Thrift Supervision," 19 January 1990, Bush PR, Marvin Fitzwater Files, Subject File: Alpha File, OA6546, box 26, S&L folder; Bush, *All the Best*, pp. 448–449; Joshua Micah Marshall, "Presidential Brother Watch," *Salon.com*, 12 April 2002, accessed 3 July 2014, http://www.salon.com/2002/04/12/neil/; Naftali, *Bush*, pp. 74–75; Parmet, *Lone Star Yankee*, pp. 396, 428. For a mother's view of Silverado, see Myra G. Gutin, *Barbara Bush: Presidential Matriarch* (Lawrence: University Press of Kansas, 2008), pp. 67–68.

20. Karen Penmar, "Inflation Stages a Comeback," *Business Week*, 3 April 1989, p. 32.

21. Greenspan, *Age of Turbulence*, p. 119. And yet, in the summer of 1991, Bush reappointed Greenspan. Some speculated that the administration thought that they could better control him, and the Fed, if he was their appointee.

22. *NYT*, 13 October 1989, p. 2; *NYT*, 16 October 1989, p. 2; *NYT*, 17 October 1989, p. 2.

23. Press Release, 29 January 1990, Bush PR, WHPO, General Office Files, Press Office Subject Files, box 83, Bush—1991 folder.

24. Darman, *Who's in Control?* p. 245.

25. Bush Diary, 4 May 1990, in George Bush, *All the Best, George Bush: My Life in Letters and Other Writings* (New York: Scribner, 1999), p. 471.

26. Cohen, *Rostenkowski*, p. 204.

27. George H. W. Bush, interview with author, 9 November 1998.

28. Darman, *Who's in Control?*, p. 264. Bush could not have been more wrong about Gingrich; in his diary on the day that Gingrich was elected Whip, Bush mused: "Will he be difficult for me to work with? I don't think so. . . . He's going to have to get along to some degree, and moderate his flamboyance" (Bush Diary, 22 March 1989, in Bush, *All the Best*, p. 418).

29. Darman, *Who's in Control?* p. 251; Parmet, *Lone Star Yankee*, p. 433.

30. Michael Duffy and Dan Goodgame, *Marching in Place: The Status Quo Presidency of George Bush* (New York: Simon & Schuster, 1991), p. 119.

31. Porter in Richard Himelfarb and Rosanna Perotti, eds., *Principle over Politics? The Domestic Policy of the George H. W. Bush Presidency* (Westport, CT: Praeger, 2004), p. 69.

32. Darman, *Who's in Control?* p. 265.

33. Cicconi in Himelfarb and Perotti, eds., *Principle over Politics?* p. 49.

34. Richard N. Haass, *War of Necessity, War of Choice: A Memoir of Two Iraq Wars* (New York: Simon & Schuster, 2009), p. 92.

35. Bush Diary, 6 August 1990, in Bush, *All the Best*, p. 477.

36. George Bush and Brent Scowcroft, *A World Transformed* (New York: Knopf, 1998), p. 363.

37. White House Press Release, 25 September 1990, Bush PR, WHPO, General Office Files, Press Office Subject Files, box 83, Bush—1991 folder.

38. Bush, *All the Best*, p. 481.

39. Darman, *Who's in Control?* p. 272.

40. *American Experience*: "George H. W. Bush" (PBS Home Video, WGBH Educational Foundation, 2008); Darman, *Who's in Control?* p. 273.

41. Bush and Scowcroft, *A World Transformed*, p. 380. Bill Clinton told one of his biographers that after he left the White House, Bush had refused Gingrich's request for a personal loan to help him pay a $300,000 ethics fine levied on him by the House of Representatives (Taylor Branch, *The Clinton Tapes: Wrestling History with the President* [New York: Simon & Schuster, 2009], p. 446).

42. Cohen, *Rostenkowski*, p. 206.

43. Parmet, *Lone Star Yankee*, p. 470.

44. See, for example, Cohen, *Rostenkowski*, p. 201; David Wessel, *Red Ink: Inside the High-Stakes Politics of the Federal Budget* (New York: Crown, 2012), pp. 55–56.

45. Ed Rollins, *Bare Knuckles and Back Rooms: My Life in American Politics* (New York: Broadway Books, 1996), pp. 199–208. See also Wicker, *Bush*, p. 114.

46. Parmet, *Lone Star Yankee*, p. 434.

47. Duffy and Goodgame, *Marching in Place*, p. 85.

CHAPTER 6: "ENLIGHTENED REALISM" AND
THE END OF THE COLD WAR

1. See *NYT*, 8 December 1988, p. A17.

2. George Bush and Brent Scowcroft, *A World Transformed* (New York: Knopf, 1998), p. 7.

3. Mikhail Gorbachev, *Memoirs* (New York: Doubleday, 1995), p. 463; Michael Beschloss and Strobe Talbott, *At the Highest Levels: The Inside Story of the End of the Cold War* (Boston: Little, Brown, 1993), pp. 10–11.

4. Notes on a Meeting between Kissinger and Gorbachev, 17 January 1989, Baker Papers, box 108, folder 1 (1989 January folder).

5. Richard A. Clarke, *Against All Enemies: Inside America's War on Terror* (New York: Free Press, 2004), p. 243.

6. See, for example, Robert G. Kaufman, *In Defense of the Bush Doctrine* (Lexington: University Press of Kentucky, 2007), pp. 60–61; Christopher Maynard, *Out of the Shadows: George H. W. Bush and the End of the Cold War* (College Station: Texas A&M University Press, 2008), pp. x–xi; Timothy Naftali, *George H. W. Bush* (New York: Times Books, 2007), pp. 66–67; and Sean Wilentz, *The Age of Reagan: 1974–2008* (New York: Harper Perennial, 2008), p. 290.

7. Jeffrey A. Engel, "When George Bush Believed the Cold War Ended," in Michael Nelson and Barbara Perry, eds., *41: Inside the Presidency of George H. W. Bush* (Ithaca, NY: Cornell University Press, 2014), p. 103.

8. Stephen Skowronek, *Presidential Leadership in Political Time: Reprise and Reappraisal* (Lawrence: University Press of Kansas, 2011), p. 99.

9. Quoted in Michael F. Cairo, *The Gulf: The Bush Presidencies and the Middle East* (Lexington: University Press of Kentucky, 2012), p. 4.

10. Cairo's was one of the first works to identify this duality. Cairo also adopts Scowcroft's term "enlightened realism" to describe Bush's foreign policy approach.

11. Bush and Scowcroft, *A World Transformed*, p. 8.

12. Beschloss and Talbott, *At the Highest Levels*, p. 11.

13. Bush to Gorbachev, 13 January 1989, Baker Papers, box 108, folder 1 (1989 January).

14. Beschloss and Talbott, *At the Highest Levels*, p. 34.

15. James A. Baker III, interview with author, 17 April 1997.

16. James A. Baker III, *The Politics of Diplomacy: Revolution, War and Peace* (New York: Putnam, 1997), p. xii; David Mervin, *George Bush and the Guardianship Presidency* (New York: St. Martin's Press, 1996), p. 161.

17. Beschloss and Talbott, *At the Highest Levels*, p. 27.

18. General Brent Scowcroft, interview with author, 11 June 1997.

19. Bush and Scowcroft, *A World Transformed*, p. 15.

20. Gates's hawkishness troubled Baker; in October 1989, Baker barred a speech proposed for delivery by Gates because he viewed it as too pessimistic regarding Gorbachev's chances for success (*NYT*, 27 October 1989, p. 1).

21. James A. Baker III, interview with author, 17 April 1997.

22. Mikhail Gorbachev, Hofstra, 19 April 1997.

23. Beschloss and Talbott, *At the Highest Levels*, p. 39.

24. *NYT*, 21 May 1989.

25. Ibid.

26. Maynard, *Shadow*, p. 16.

27. Draft, Texas A&M Speech—Bush markup, Bush PR, Office of Speechwriters, Speech File: Drafts, dated folder.

28. Bush and Scowcroft, *A World Transformed*, p. 54; Maynard, *Shadow*, pp. 20–21.

29. Press Release, 29 May 1989, Bush PR, Marlin Fitzwater Files, Subject Files: Alpha File, box 1, Arms Control folder; Bush and Scowcroft, *A World Transformed*, pp. 43–45, 79–85; Ivo H. Daalder and I. M. Destler, *In the Shadow of the Oval Office: Profiles of the National Security Advisers and the Presidents They Served—From JFK to George W. Bush* (New York: Simon & Schuster, 2009), p. 194; Maynard, *Shadow*, pp. 30–32.

30. Bush Diary, undated, in George Bush, *All the Best, George Bush: My Life in Letters and Other Writings* (New York: Scribner, 1999), p. 426.

31. James A. Lilley, interview with author, 19 April 1997.

32. Jean Garrison, *Making China Policy: From Nixon to George W. Bush* (Boulder, CO: Lynne Rienner, 2005), pp. 107–108; George C. Herring, *From Colony to Superpower: U.S. Foreign Relations since 1776* (New York: Oxford University Press, 2008), p. 901.

33. James A. Lilley, interview with author, 19 April 1997; Bush and Scowcroft, *A World Transformed*, pp. 91–94.

34. Herbert S. Parmet, *George Bush: The Life of a Lone Star Yankee* (New York: Scribner, 1997), p. 392. Bush had to make a decision on the extension of China's MFN status by 3 June.

35. Garrison, *Making China Policy*, p. 111; Roman Popadiuk, *The Leadership of George Bush: An Insider's View of the Forty-First President* (College Station: Texas A&M University Press, 2009), p. 41.

36. See Dusko Doder, "Reinventing China," *New York Times Magazine*, 17 May 1989, pp. 30–36.

37. Cables to White House Situation Room, Bush PR, NSC, White House Situation Room Files, Tiananmen Square Crisis, China—Part 1 of 5 Tiananmen Square Crisis (May–June 1989), OA/ID CF 01722-010.

38. Quoted in Dusko Doder and Louise Branson, *Gorbachev* (New York: Penguin, 1990), pp. 363–364.

39. John Lewis Gaddis, *The Cold War: A New History* (New York: Penguin, 2005), p. 241.

40. Cables to White House Situation Room, Bush PR, NSC, White House Situation Room Files, Tiananmen Square Crisis, China—Part 1 of 5 Tiananmen Square Crisis (May–June 1989), folder 1, OA/ID CF 01722-010.

41. Cables to White House Situation Room sent as the massacre unfolded offer a minute-by-minute account of events. See Bush PR, NSC, White House Situation Room Files, Tiananmen Square Crisis, China—Part 1 of 5 Tiananmen Square Crisis (May–June 1989), folder 1, OA/ID CF 01722-011.

42. Baker, *Politics of Diplomacy*, p. 104.

43. James A. Lilley, interview with author, 19 April 1997.

44. Notes of Baker Meeting with Han Xu, 7 June 1989, Baker Papers, box 108, folder 6 (June 1989).

45. General Brent Scowcroft, interview with author, 11 June 1997.

46. Undated Meeting Notes (Fitzwater's handwriting), Bush PR, Subject File: Alpha File, box 3, China folder.

47. See Jeffrey Bader (Acting Director, Office of Chinese and Mongolian Affairs, Department of State) to William Hua, 19 June 1989, Bush PR, WHORM, Subject File–General, CO034, China, 040873.

48. Bush to Deng Xiaoping, 20 June 1989, in Bush, *All the Best*, pp. 428–431.

49. Bush to Deng Xiaoping, 21 June 1989, in Bush, *All the Best*, pp. 435–437.

50. Bush and Scowcroft, *A World Transformed*, p. 89.

51. Baker, *Politics of Diplomacy*, p. 109.

52. Ibid., p. 110.

53. General Brent Scowcroft, interview with author, 11 June 1997; Michael Duffy and Dan Goodgame, *Marching in Place: The Status Quo Presidency of George Bush* (New York: Simon & Schuster, 1991), p. 183; Parmet, *Lone Star Yankee*, p. 399.

54. Bush and Scowcroft, *A World Transformed*, p. 174.

55. Quoted in *USN&WR*, 5 June 1989, p. 27.

56. Sakharov to Bush, 23 June 1989, Bush PR, WHORM, Subject File-General, CO034, China 047605.

57. Snowe to Bush, 27 June 1989; Frederic McClure to Snowe, 3 August 1989; Lorne W. Craner (State) to Snowe, 25 August 1989, Bush PR, WHORM, Subject File-General, CO034, China 048632.

58. Bush and Scowcroft, *A World Transformed*, p. 98.

59. Garrison, *Making China Policy*, pp. 119–120; Herring, *Colony to Super-power*, p. 903.

60. James A. Lilley, interview with author, 19 April 1997.

61. Quoted in Tom Wicker, *George Herbert Walker Bush: A Penguin Life* (New York: Penguin, 2004), p. 122.

62. An outstanding and accessible survey of the implosion of the Soviet economy can be found in Wicker, *Bush*, pp. 120–122.

63. See Maynard, *Shadow*, pp. 2–3.

64. This came six days after the CIA had reported that "the basic elements of Soviet defense policy and practice thus far have not been changed by Gorbachev's reform campaign." In the words of a close student of U.S. intelligence history, "The agency had somehow missed the fact that its main enemy was dying" (Tim Weiner, *Legacy of Ashes: The History of the CIA* [New York: Doubleday, 2007], p. 429).

65. *NYT*, 8 December 1988; Gorbachev, *Memoirs*, pp. 459–462.

66. Beschloss and Talbott, *At the Highest Levels*, p. 53.

67. Minton F. Goldman, "President Bush and the Collapse of Communist Rule in Poland: The Search for Policy in 1989–1990," in William F. Levantrosser and Rosanna Perotti, eds., *A Noble Calling: Character and the George H. W. Bush Presidency* (Westport, CT: Praeger, 2004), p. 276.

68. James A. Baker III, *"Work Hard, Study . . . and Keep Out of Politics!"*: *Adventures and Lessons from an Unexpected Public Life* (New York: Putnam, 2006), p. 288.

69. Goldman, "President Bush and the Collapse of Communist Rule in Poland," p. 277; Gaddis, *Cold War*, p. 241; Maynard, *Shadow*, p. 36.

70. Gaddis, *Cold War*, pp. 240–241.

71. General Brent Scowcroft, Hofstra, 17 April 1997.

72. Goldman, "President Bush and the Collapse of Communist Rule in Poland," p. 281.

73. Bush and Scowcroft, *A World Transformed*, p. 117.

74. Beschloss and Talbott, *At the Highest Levels*, pp. 88–89.

75. Goldman, "President Bush and the Collapse of Communist Rule in Poland," p. 284.

76. Bush and Scowcroft, *A World Transformed*, pp. 123–126.

77. Vladislav M. Zubok, *A Failed Empire: The Soviet Union in the Cold War from Stalin to Gorbachev* (Chapel Hill: University of North Carolina Press, 2007), p. 319.

78. Parmet, *Lone Star Yankee*, p. 407; Serhii Plokhy, *The Last Empire: The Final Days of the Soviet Union* (New York: Basic Books, 2014), p. 34.

79. Bush and Scowcroft, *A World Transformed*, pp. 141–143; Leon Aron, *Yeltsin: A Revolutionary Life* (New York: St. Martin's Press, 2000), pp. 333–336; Beschloss and Talbott, *At the Highest Levels*, pp. 102–105; Timothy J. Colton, *Yeltsin: A Life* (New York: Basic Books, 2008), pp. 171–172; Duffy and Goodgame, *Marching in Place*, p. 188; Plokhy, *Last Empire*, pp. 27–37.

80. Maynard, *Shadow*, p. 39.

81. Bush to Gorbachev, 21 July 1989, in Bush, *All the Best*, p. 433.

82. Mikhail Gorbachev, Hofstra, 19 April 1997.

83. Baker, *Politics of Diplomacy*, p. 161.

84. *NYT*, 26 October 1989, p. 2.

85. Ibid.; *NYT*, 10 November 1989, p. 1.

86. Maynard, *Shadow*, pp. 41–46; Elizabeth Pond, *Beyond the Wall: Germany's Road to Unification* (Washington, DC: Brookings Institution, 1993), pp. 1–6.

87. Zubok, *Failed Empire*, pp. 318–319, 322.

88. Bush Diary, 10 November 1989, in Bush, *All the Best*, p. 442.

89. Baker, *"Work Hard,"* pp. 289–290.

90. Gorbachev, *Memoirs*, pp. 485–486.

91. Baker Handwritten Notes taken on 11 November 1989, Baker Papers, box 108, folder 11 (November 1989).

92. Bush Diary, 8 November 1989, in Bush, *All the Best*, p. 442.

93. Lesley Stahl, *Reporting Live* (New York: Simon & Schuster, 1999), pp. 355–356. Stahl's conclusion from this incident: "Bush was missing a characteristic essential for a president, an emotional ignition key" (p. 356). See also Maynard, *Shadow*, pp. 43–44.

94. Bush and Scowcroft, *A World Transformed*, pp. 148–149; Beschloss and

Talbott, *At the Highest Levels*, p. 135; Duffy and Goodgame, *Marching in Place*, p. 135.

95. George H. W. Bush, interview with author, 9 November 1998. In another interview, Bush observed that "the stupidest, dumbest idea I've heard [was] to stick a finger in Gorbachev's eye when things were moving peacefully" (quoted in Popadiuk, *Leadership of George Bush*, p. 119).

96. See http://bushlibrary.tamu.edu/research/pdfs/memcons_telcons /1989-11-10--Kohl.pdf, accessed September 2014.

97. Maynard, *Shadow*, pp. 54–56.

98. Kohl Speech, 28 November 1989, Bush PR, WHORM Subject File, CO054, ID#094952.

99. Mikhail Gorbachev, *Gorbachev: On My Country and the World* (New York: Columbia University Press, 2000), p. 202; Margaret Thatcher, *The Downing Street Years* (New York: HarperCollins, 1993), pp. 795–796.

100. Bush Diary, 2 December 1989, in Bush, *All the Best*, p. 448.

101. A transcript of Bush's discussion with Gorbachev can be found in Bush PR, Staff and Office, Presidential Memcon Files, OA/ID CF01729. See also Baker, *Politics of Diplomacy*, pp. 168–171; Bush and Scowcroft, *A World Transformed*, pp. 162–174; Beschloss and Talbott, *At the Highest Levels*, p. 163.

102. Bush and Scowcroft, *A World Transformed*, p. 167.

103. Tim Weiner, *Legacy of Ashes: The History of the CIA* (New York: Doubleday, 2007), p. 424.

104. Talking Points, Baker Meeting with Bush (on Panama), 5 May 1989, Baker Papers, box 108, folder 5 (May 1989 folder).

105. Nancy Gibbs and Michael Duffy, *The Presidents Club: Inside the World's Most Exclusive Fraternity* (New York: Simon & Schuster, 2012), p. 401; Joseph L. Galloway, "Standoff in Panama," *USN&WR*, 22 May 1989, pp. 28–29; *NYT*, 12 May 1989, pp. A1, 8. As Carter watched the beatings, he jumped onto a platform and shouted, "*Son ustedes honestos, o ladrones?* (Are you honest people, or thieves?; quoted in Leonard Benardo and Jennifer Weiss, *Citizen-in-Chief: The Second Lives of the American Presidents* [New York: Morrow, 2009], p. 160).

106. Colin Powell, *My American Journey* (New York: Random House, 1995), pp. 420–421; Bob Woodward, *The Commanders* (New York: Simon & Schuster, 1991), pp. 85–93.

107. See, for example, Baker, *The Politics of Diplomacy*, p. 179; Dick Cheney, *In My Time: A Personal and Political Memoir* (New York: Threshold Editions, 2011), p. 168.

108. Apparently Noriega returned Bush's antipathy. The museum at the Bush Presidential Library has on exhibit a target from Noriega's pistol range. Several holes are shot through it, and the target—human in form—is labeled "Bush."

109. Interview Transcript, Bush and Arnaud De Borchgrave, 15 May 1989, Bush PR, WHPO, Press Office Internal Transcripts, box 133, folder OA6237.

110. Richard B. Cheney, telephone interview with author, 7 March 1997; Cheney, *In My Time*, pp. 163–164. In actuality, Welch had not freelanced; he had cleared his comments with the White House before Cheney's confirmation. Cheney later told the University of Virginia's Miller Center in an oral history interview that Welch had "got a bit of a bum rap," but "it was a target of opportunity if you wanted to sort of reassert civilian control" (quoted in Peter Baker, *Days of Fire: Bush and Cheney in the White House* [New York: Doubleday, 2013], p. 39).

111. Cheney's view of this incident can be found in Cheney, *In My Time*, p. 167.

112. *NYT*, 2 February 1989, p. A1.

113. Baker, *Politics of Diplomacy*, p. 22.

114. Cheney, *In My Time*, p. 161.

115. Powell, *An American Journey*, pp. 388–389.

116. Bush and Scowcroft, *A World Transformed*, p. 23.

117. Cheney, *In My Time*, pp. 161, 170.

118. Maynard, *Shadow*, p. 10.

119. *NYT*, 15 November 1988, p. B10.

120. William Webster, interview with author, 8 July 1997.

121. Ibid.

122. Thurman had replaced Fred Woerner as CINC for the Southern Command after Cheney relieved Woerner, who refused to accept 3,000 additional troops to Panama as reinforcements (Cheney, *In My Time*, pp. 168–169).

123. Woodward, *The Commanders*, p. 122.

124. Parmet, *Lone Star Yankee*, p. 413.

125. Ibid.

126. William Webster, interview with author, 8 July 1997.

127. Baker, *Politics of Diplomacy*, pp. 185–186.

128. Woodward, *The Commanders*, p. 128.

129. Parmet, *Lone Star Yankee*, p. 414.

130. Quoted in Wicker, *Bush*, p. 140.

131. *NYT*, 15 October 1989, p. A1.

132. Woodward, *The Commanders*, p. 128.

133. General Brent Scowcroft, interview with author, 11 June 1997; Daalder and Destler, *In the Shadow of the Oval Office*, pp. 184–186. Gates was the first national security adviser to be designated an assistant to the president; in so doing, Gates was given direct access to Bush (Daalder and Destler, *In the Shadow of the Oval Office*, p. 186).

134. Bush and Scowcroft, *A World Transformed*, p. 161.

135. Powell, *My American Journey*, pp. 440–445; Dan Quayle, *Standing Firm* (New York: Harper, 1994), chap. 16, passim.

136. For surveys of the crisis, see Cheney, *In My Time*, pp. 173–174; Barton Gellman, *Angler: The Cheney Vice Presidency* (New York: Penguin, 2008), pp. 58–59; Maynard, *Shadow*, p. 47; and Woodward, *The Commanders*, p. 149.

137. Bush Diary, 17 December 1989, in Bush, *All the Best*, pp. 449–450; Release, Assistant Secretary for Defense (undated), Bush PR, Fitzwater Files, Alpha Files: Subject File, OA 6546, box 21, Panama folder no. 2.

138. Meeting Notes, 17 December 1989, Baker Papers, box 108, folder 12 (December 1989 folder); Baker, *Politics of Diplomacy*, p. 189.

139. General Brent Scowcroft, interview with author, 11 June 1997.

140. Powell, *My American Story*, pp. 423–425; Woodward, *The Commanders*, pp. 160–171.

141. Various memcons in Baker Papers, box 108, folder 12 (December 1989 folder); Baker, *Politics of Diplomacy*, pp. 190–191.

142. Scott Slinger, "New Weapons, Old Problems," *Washington Monthly*, October 1990, p. 43.

143. Baker, *The Politics of Diplomacy*, chap. 11, passim; Cheney, *In My Time*, pp. 174–178; Woodward, *The Commanders*, pp. 182–195.

144. *NYT*, 21 December 1989, p. 1.

145. Kennedy, 79 percent; Eisenhower and Johnson, 70 percent; Nixon, 61 percent; Carter, 51 percent; Reagan, 49 percent; and Ford, 45 percent (*NYT*/CBS News poll; see *NYT*, 19 January 1991, p. A20).

146. Bush and Scowcroft, *A World Transformed*, p. 238.

147. Baker to Walters, February 1990, Bush PR, Staff and Office Files, National Security Council Files, Arnold Kanter Files, Subject Files, OA/ID CFO00775-019.

148. Bush and Scowcroft, *A World Transformed*, p. 239.

149. Maynard, *Shadow*, pp. 61–65.

150. *NYT*, 5 February 1990, p. 2.

151. *NYT*, 18 April 1990, p. 2.

152. *NYT*, 17 January 1990, p. A8.

153. Bush to Gorbachev, 29 April 1990, in Bush, *All the Best*, p. 467.

154. Gorbachev to Bush, 2 May 1990, Bush PR, Staff and Office Files, NSC, Condoleezza Rice Files, 1989–1990 Subject Files, OA/D CF 7213.

155. Beschloss and Talbott, *At the Highest Levels*, p. 223.

156. Baker's notes of the meeting can be found in Baker Papers, box 109, folder 1 (May 1990). Bush's memory of the meetings can be found in Bush Diary, 31 May and 1 June 1990, in Bush, *All the Best*, pp. 471–473, and Bush and Scowcroft, *A World Transformed*, pp. 279–289; Gorbachev's memory can be found in Gorbachev, *Memoirs*, pp. 532–534. See also *NYT*, 13 June 1990, p. 2; *NYT*, 17 July 1990, p. A1, A8; Beschloss and Talbott, *At the Highest Levels*, p. 220; Jeffrey A. Engel, *The Fall of the Berlin Wall: The Revolutionary Legacy of 1989* (New York: Oxford University Press, 2009), p. 141; Maynard, *Shadow*, pp. 68–70.

157. Maynard, *Shadow*, p. 72.

158. "Treaty on the Final Settlement with Respect to Germany," Bush PR, WHORM Subject File, CO054, ID#178066.

159. Bush and Scowcroft, *A World Transformed*, p. 283.

160. Kennan Diary, 8 October 1990, in Frank Costigliola, ed., *The Kennan Diaries* (New York: Norton, 2014), p. 612. Agreeing with Kennan's assessment is diplomatic historian George Herring, who also gives the credit to the German people, noting that "Wir Sind Ein Volk" (We are one people) was their "battle cry" (Herring, *Colony to Superpower*, p. 906).

161. Levantrosser and Perotti, eds., *A Noble Calling*, p. 152.

162. Bush and Scowcroft, *A World Transformed*, p. 231.

163. Baker, *"Work Hard,"* p. 291.

CHAPTER 7: DESERT SHIELD

1. "Saddam Hussein," in Charles Moritz, ed., *Current Biography Yearbook 1981* (New York: H. W. Wilson, 1982); John Robert Greene, ed., *Presidential Profiles: The George W. Bush Years* (New York: Facts on File, 2011), pp. 79–80. In a 1997 interview, William Webster revealed that the CIA had movies of Saddam sending twenty-three people out to be executed because he knew that one of them was a traitor (William Webster, interview with author, 8 July 1997).

2. Richard N. Haass, *War of Necessity, War of Choice: A Memoir of Two Iraq Wars* (New York: Simon & Schuster, 2009), p. 26; Lawrence Freedman and Efraim Karsh, *The Gulf Conflict, 1990–1991: Diplomacy and War in the New World Order* (Princeton, NJ: Princeton University Press, 1993), p. 39.

3. Freedman and Karsh, *The Gulf Conflict*, p. 39.

4. General Brent Scowcroft, interview with author, 11 June 1997.

5. Haass, *War of Necessity*, p. 26.

6. George Bush and Brent Scowcroft, *A World Transformed* (New York: Knopf, 1998), p. 306; Michael Cairo, *The Gulf: The Bush Presidencies and the Middle East* (Lexington: University Press of Kentucky, 2012), pp. 45–46; Freedman and Karsh, *The Gulf Conflict*, p. 25. See also Michael Klare, "Fueling the Fire: How We Armed the Middle East," *Bulletin of Atomic Scientists* 47, no. 1 (1990): 19–25; Don Oberdorfer, "The War No One Saw Coming," *WPNWE*, 18–24 March 1991, pp. 6–10.

7. Haass, *War of Necessity*, pp. 29–30; Rick Atkinson, *Crusade: The Untold Story of the Persian Gulf War* (Boston: Houghton Mifflin, 1993), p. 51.

8. James T. Patterson, *Restless Giant: The United States from Watergate to Bush v. Gore* (New York: Oxford University Press, 2005), p. 230.

9. Freedman and Karsh, *The Gulf Conflict*, p. 27; "The Ties That Bind," *WPNWE*, 24–30 September 1990, pp. 11–12.

10. Haass, *War of Necessity*, p. 48.

11. The domestic fallout from this policy, which would become an issue in the presidential election of 1992, will be discussed in chapter 11.

12. Freedman and Karsh, *The Gulf Conflict*, p. 35.

13. *WPNWE*, 18–24 March 1991, p. 8.

14. Bob Woodward, *The Commanders* (New York: Simon & Schuster, 1991), p. 201.

15. Ibid.

16. James A. Baker III, *The Politics of Diplomacy: Revolution, War, and Peace* (New York: Putnam, 1997), p. 268.

17. Woodward, *The Commanders*, pp. 199–204.

18. Freedman and Karsh, *The Gulf Conflict*, p. 44; Woodward, *The Commanders*, p. 206.

19. Atkinson, *Crusade*, p. 28.

20. Freedman and Karsh, *The Gulf Conflict*, p. 46.

21. Atkinson, *Crusade*, p. 1.

22. Ibid., p. 8.

23. Ibid., p. 3; Colin Powell, *My American Journey* (New York: Random House, 1991), p. 493.

24. Powell, *My American Journey*, p. 460.

25. Atkinson, *Crusade*, p. 107; Woodward, *The Commanders*, pp. 228, 247–255.

26. Powell, *My American Journey*, pp. 461–462; Woodward, *The Commanders*, pp. 205–210.

27. Baker to Bush, 29 August 1990, Baker Papers, box 288, Bush, George Personal Notes folder; Baker, *"Work Hard, Study . . . and Keep Out of Politics!": Adventures and Lessons from an Unexpected Public Life* (New York: Putnam, 2006), p. 293.

28. *NYT*, 23 September 1990; Bush and Scowcroft, *A World Transformed*, pp. 310–311; Haass, *War of Necessity*, p. 26; Cairo, *Gulf*, pp. 46–47; Michael Duffy and Dan Goodgame, *Marching in Place: The Status Quo Presidency of George Bush* (New York: Simon & Schuster, 1991), p. 132; Herbert S. Parmet, *George Bush: The Life of a Lone Star Yankee* (New York: Scribner, 1997), p. 446. A copy of the transcript of Glaspie's 25 July 1990 conversation with Saddam—the authenticity of which the State Department would neither confirm nor deny—is reprinted in Micha L. Sifry and Christopher Cerf, eds., *The Gulf War Reader: History, Documents, and Opinions* (New York: Times Books, 1991), pp. 122–133; William Webster, interview with author, 8 July 1997.

29. Bush and Scowcroft, *A World Transformed*, p. 309; Woodward, *The Commanders*, pp. 215–216.

30. Bush and Scowcroft, *A World Transformed*, p. 313.

31. Bush Diary, 2 August 1990, in George Bush, *All the Best, George Bush: My Life in Letters and Other Writings* (New York: Scribner, 1999), p. 476; Bush and Scowcroft, *A World Transformed*, p. 314.

32. Bush and Scowcroft, *A World Transformed*, p. 317.

33. Ibid., pp. 319–320; Haass, *War of Necessity*, p. 62.

34. Furious that Jordan had decided to support Iraq, Bush wrote King Hussein: "Had a cabinet member in my government attacked Jordan the way your Prime Minister attacked us, he would have been dismissed"; in return

for Mubarak's support, Bush forgave some $7 million of Egyptian debt to the United States (Bush to King Hussein, 20 October 1990, in Bush, *All the Best*, pp. 483–485; Haass, *War of Necessity*, p. 87). Eventually, there was no room left; when assistant secretary of state of political-military affairs Richard A. Clarke told Cheney that the Australians were ready to send F-111 aircraft to the fray, an exasperated Cheney said, "Dick, we do not have room for any more allies. Stop asking them" (Richard A. Clarke, *Against All Enemies: Inside America's War on Terror* [New York: Free Press, 2004], p. 61).

35. Charles-Philippe David, "Not Doing Too Badly for Guys Who Have No Vision Whatsoever and Operate Only on Instinct: Foreign Policy Decision Making under the Bush Administration," in William F. Levantrosser and Rosanna Perotti, eds., *A Noble Calling: Character and the George H. W. Bush Presidency* (Westport, CT: Praeger, 2004), p. 174. This was delivered as a conference paper at Hofstra University in 1997; upon hearing the paper, Scowcroft, who was called upon to respond, broke away from his usual gentlemanly reserve: "I don't recognize the man [David] describes, and I'll just leave it there" (ibid., p. 225).

36. Bush and Scowcroft, *A World Transformed*, p. 319; Margaret Thatcher, *Downing Street Years* (New York: HarperCollins, 1993), pp. 817–820.

37. Quoted in Bush and Scowcroft, *A World Transformed*, p. 320.

38. Quoted in Haass, *War of Necessity*, p. 63. See also Dick Cheney, *In My Time: A Personal and Political Memoir* (New York: Threshold Editions, 2011), p. 186.

39. Quoted in Bush and Scowcroft, *A World Transformed*, p. 324.

40. Cheney, *In My Time*, p. 187.

41. Bush and Scowcroft, *A World Transformed*, pp. 325–326; Powell, *My American Journey*, pp. 464–465; Duffy and Goodgame, *Marching in Place*, p. 145; Woodward, *The Commanders*, pp. 239–242.

42. Baker, *Politics of Diplomacy*, pp. 1–16; Baker, "Work Hard," p. 294; Bush and Scowcroft, *A World Transformed*, pp. 325–326; Michael Beschloss and Strobe Talbott, *At the Highest Levels: The Inside Story of the End of the Cold War* (Boston: Little, Brown, 1993), p. 248.

43. Bush and Scowcroft, *A World Transformed*, pp. 328–329. See also Cairo, *Gulf*, p. 48.

44. Woodward, *The Commanders*, pp. 258–259.

45. Bush and Scowcroft, *A World Transformed*, p. 329.

46. Powell, *My American Journey*, p. 467.

47. Ibid., pp. 466–467. Haass had been standing next to the president when he delivered this line; Haass remembered that Powell believed he was pushing the president to intervene to expel Saddam; nowhere in his memoir does Haass deny this (*War of Necessity*, pp. 69–70).

48. Cheney, *In My Time*, pp. 189–191; Clarke, *Against All Enemies*, pp. 57–60; Woodward, *The Commanders*, pp. 263–273.

49. Bush and Scowcroft, *A World Transformed*, p. 416.

50. Ibid., p. 340.

51. *NYT*, 22 August 1990, p. A1; *NYT*, 20 November 1990, p. A1.

52. Cheney, *In My Time*, p. 194.

53. *WPNWE*, 20–26 August 1990, p. 7.

54. Freedman and Karsh, *The Gulf Conflict*, p. 98.

55. Cairo, *Gulf*, pp. 113–118.

56. Freedman and Karsh, *The Gulf Conflict*, p. 216. One might ask how the nation, already mired in deficit, paid for the war. Douglas A. Brook, then the acting secretary of the army for financial management, was blunt: "We didn't." The Feed and Forage Act of 1861, an act that permitted the Northern cavalry to buy feed while they were marching through Georgia during the last days of the Civil War, allows for the deficit operation of the army in certain cases. This law was invoked in 1991 to allow the Congress to appropriate funds, despite a federal deficit and without congressional permission for it, in order to help a military mission. Brook remembered that most of the $19 billion ultimately spent by the army was appropriated in this fashion; in his words, "Spend it as if you have it" (Douglas A. Brook, interview with author, 17 April 1997).

57. Freedman and Karsh, *The Gulf Conflict*, pp. 110–127.

58. Haass, *War of Necessity*, p. 87.

59. Fact Sheet, 13 February 1991, Bush PR, Marlin Fitzwater Files, OA 6784, Subject File: Alpha File, box 17, Iraq folder 1991 no. 2.

60. Press Release, 22 February 1991, Bush PR, Marlin Fitzwater Files, OA 6784, Subject File: Alpha File, box 17, Iraq folder 1991 no. 2.

61. Freedman and Karsh, *The Gulf Conflict*, p. 221.

62. Notes of Telephone Conversation, Baker and Shevardnadze, 22 August 1990, Baker Papers, box 109, folder 4 (August 1990).

63. James A. Baker III, interview with author, 17 April 1997; Bush and Scowcroft, *A World Transformed*, pp. 352–353; Beschloss and Talbott, *At the Highest Levels*, p. 252.

64. Cairo, *Gulf*, p. 61.

65. Beschloss and Talbott, *At the Highest Levels*, pp. 261–262.

66. *NYT*, 11 September 1990, p. A1.

67. Alex R. Hybel and Justin Matthew Kaufman, *The Bush Administrations and Saddam Hussein: Deciding on Conflict* (New York: Palgrave Macmillan, 2013), pp. 5–6.

68. Powell, *My American Journey*, pp. 478–480; Woodward, *The Commanders*, pp. 297–301. Baker later claimed that it was unfair to say, as did others at the time, that he acted as a "brake" on the administration as it moved toward military intervention: "What I wanted to do was to make sure we knew the consequences of force. . . . I never argued internally not to use force" (James A. Baker III, interview with author, 17 April 1997).

69. Powell, *My American Journey*, pp. 464–466.

70. Bush and Scowcroft, *A World Transformed*, p. 382.

71. See, for example, Tom Wicker, *George Herbert Walker Bush: A Penguin Life* (New York: Penguin, 2004), p. 155. Cheney remembered in his memoir that it was not until 24 October that Bush "told me he was leaning toward action to remove Saddam from Kuwait" (*In My Time*, p. 203).

72. See Cairo, *Bush*, p. 50.

73. Baker, *Politics of Diplomacy*, pp. 276–277.

74. Powell, *My American Journey*, pp. 470–471.

75. Quoted in Bob Woodward, *Shadow: Five Presidents and the Legacy of Watergate* (New York: Simon & Schuster, 1999), p. 185.

76. Bush and Scowcroft, *A World Transformed*, p. 353.

77. *NYT*, 12 September 1990, p. 2.

78. Bush and Scowcroft, *A World Transformed*, p. 374.

79. Atkinson, *Crusade*, pp. 58–61.

80. Quoted in Thomas E. Ricks, *The Generals: American Military Command from World War II to Today* (New York: Penguin, 2012), p. 374.

81. Cheney, *In My Time*, pp. 198–200; Atkinson, *Crusade*, pp. 483–485.

82. Powell, *My American Journey*, pp. 487–489; Atkinson, *Crusade*, p. 113.

83. Atkinson, *Crusade*, p. 113. See also Cheney, *In My Time*, pp. 204–206.

84. Freedman and Karsh, *The Gulf Conflict*, p. 155.

85. *NYT*, 22 September 1990, p. 2.

86. As noted, Mubarak was the first world leader to compare Saddam to Hitler; the first American leader to do so was Senator Claiborne Pell (D-RI), who, on the day of the invasion, called the Iraqi leader the "Hitler of the Middle East" (*NYT*, 2 August 1990, p. A1).

87. Robert Schlesinger, *White House Ghosts: Presidents and Their Speechwriters* (New York: Simon & Schuster, 2008), p. 381.

88. David Frost interview with George Bush, Public Broadcasting System (PBS; first broadcast on 2 January 1991).

89. Baker, *Politics of Diplomacy*, p. 336.

90. See http://bushlibrary.tamu.edu/research/pdfs/nsd/nsd26.pdf, accessed September 2014.

91. Baker, *Politics of Diplomacy*, p. 336.

92. Ibid.

93. *NYT*, 21 October 1990, p. 14.

94. "Out Now," advertisement in *Nation*, 26 November 1990, p. 645.

95. Nancy Gibbs and Michael Duffy, *The Presidents Club: Inside the World's Most Exclusive Fraternity* (New York: Simon & Schuster, 2012), pp. 404–405.

96. Pat Buchanan, "How the Gulf Crisis Is Rupturing the Right," in Sifry and Cerf, eds., *Gulf War Reader*, pp. 213–215.

97. The papers from the Cato conference were published in Ted Galen Carpenter, ed., *America Entangled: The Persian Gulf War and Its Consequences* (San Francisco: Cato Institute Books, 1991).

98. Freedman and Karsh, *The Gulf Conflict*, p. 211.

99. Ibid., p. 218.

100. James A. Baker III, interview with author, 17 April 1997.

101. Letter on exhibit, GBM, and Bush to Saddam Hussein, 5 January 1991, in Bush, *All the Best*, pp. 499–500. Excerpted in Bush and Scowcroft, *A World Transformed*, pp. 441–442.

102. *NYT*, 10 January 1991, p. A1; Baker, *Politics of Diplomacy*, p. 362; Bush and Scowcroft, *A World Transformed*, pp. 441–443. See also Ricks, *The Generals*, p. 373.

103. The possibility that the administration did not "regret" the outcome of Baker's mission is strongly suggested by the reaction of those in the cabinet room, including Bush, immediately following Baker's press conference. John Gravois of the *Houston Post*, acting as that day's pool reporter for the White House Press Corps, observed, "There was much whooping and loud noises . . . suggesting something positive was afoot, but it turned out to be a somber-looking bunch when the writers and photogs entered." Bush told the reporters that he was not encouraged by Baker's report, but that he was "not giving up on peace at all" (Pool Report, 9 January 1991, Bush *PP*, WHPO, Lower Press Office Pool Reports, box 14, dated folder).

104. Bush, *All the Best*, p. 491.

105. General Brent Scowcroft, interview with author, 11 June 1997.

106. Cheney, *In My Time*, pp. 207–208.

107. George H. W. Bush, interview with author, 9 November 1998.

108. C. Boyden Gray, interview with author, 18 April 1997; interview with author, not for attribution.

109. *NYT*, 11 January 1991, p. A18.

110. Cheney, *In My Time*, p. 208.

111. Baker, *"Work Hard,"* p. 295; Bush and Scowcroft, *A World Transformed*, p. 446.

112. George H. W. Bush, interview with author, 9 November 1998.

113. See http://bushlibrary.tamu.edu/research/pdfs/nsd/nsd54.pdf, accessed September 2014.

CHAPTER 8: DESERT STORM

1. Letter on exhibit, GBM. Also in Bush to Children, 31 December 1990, in George Bush, *All the Best, George Bush: My Life in Letters and Other Writings* (New York: Scribner, 1999), pp. 496–498.

2. *WP*, 18 January 1991, p. A24; Lawrence Freedman and Efraim Karsh, *The Gulf Conflict, 1990–1991: Diplomacy and War in the New World Order* (Princeton, NJ: Princeton University Press, 1993), p. 300.

3. Thomas E. Ricks, *The Generals: American Military Command from World War II to Today* (New York: Penguin, 2012), p. 379.

4. *WPNWE*, 25–31 March 1991, p. 9.

5. Press Briefing (Background), 27 February 1991, Bush PR, Marlin Fitzwater Files, Subject File, Alpha File, OA 6546, box 17, Iraq 1991, folder 2.

6. A useful short summary of the Safwan meeting was done by Michael Gordon, "A 'Good War' with Iraq in '91 Had Its Flaws," *NYT*, 31 December 2012, p. A1.

7. Ricks, *The Generals*, p. 383.

8. Rick Atkinson, *Crusade: The Untold Story of the Persian Gulf War* (Boston: Houghton Mifflin, 1993), p. 9; Michael Gunther, "After the War: President Bush and the Kurdish Uprising," Hofstra, 18 April 1997; Scowcroft interview, "The Gulf War," *Frontline*, PBS (episode no. 2, first broadcast 10 January 1996).

9. Freedman and Karsh, *The Gulf Conflict*, p. 409.

10. Michael F. Cairo, *The Gulf: The Bush Presidencies and the Middle East* (Lexington: University Press of Kentucky, 2012), pp. 98–101.

11. Dick Cheney, *In My Time: A Personal and Political Memoir* (New York: Threshold Editions, 2011), p. 219; Atkinson, *Crusade*, p. 264.

12. *WPNWE*, 25–31 March 1991, p. 8.

13. Fitzwater, Demarest, and Rogich to Sununu, 14 January 1991, Bush PR, Marlin Fitzwater Files, Subject File: Alpha File, box 17, Iraq folder 1991 no. 1.

14. Colin Powell, *My American Journey* (New York: Random House, 1995), p. 511; Abe Dane, "Origins of the Scud Threat," *Popular Mechanics*, April 1991, p. 27.

15. Cheney, *In My Time*, pp. 214–216; Richard A. Clarke, *Against All Enemies: Inside America's War on Terror* (New York: Free Press, 2004), pp. 63–64; Ricks, *The Generals*, pp. 375–376.

16. Atkinson, *Crusade*, p. 175.

17. Richard N. Haass, *War of Necessity, War of Choice: A Memoir of Two Iraq Wars* (New York: Simon & Schuster, 2009), p. 119.

18. Freedman and Karsh, *The Gulf Conflict*, pp. 307, 336.

19. Atkinson, *Crusade*, p. 130.

20. Ibid., p. 226.

21. Ibid., p. 160.

22. Ibid., p. 232.

23. Freedman and Karsh, *The Gulf Conflict*, p. 319.

24. William Webster, interview with author, 8 July 1997. Regarding Arnett, Bush would later grumble, "I felt CNN should have done a better job of warning its viewers that everything that came out of Iraq was censored" (Bush Diary, 19 January 1991, in Bush, *All the Best*, p. 505).

25. *NYT*, 15 May 1991, p. A6; *NYT*, 6 June 1991, p. A9.

26. *WPNWE*, 18–24 November 1991, p. 32; Atkinson, *Crusade*, p. 315.

27. George Bush and Brent Scowcroft, *A World Transformed* (New York: Knopf, 1998), pp. 469–470; Atkinson, *Crusade*, pp. 272–288; Freedman and Karsh, *The Gulf Conflict*, pp. 327–329.

28. Human Rights Watch, *Needless Deaths in the Gulf War: Civilian Casualties during the Air Campaign and Violations of the Laws of War* (New York: Human Rights Watch, 1991), p. 4.

29. Atkinson, *Crusade*, p. 227.

30. James T. Patterson, *Restless Giant: The United States from Watergate to Bush v. Gore* (New York: Oxford University Press, 2005), p. 234.

31. Malcolm Browne, "The Military vs. the Press," *New York Times Magazine*, 3 March 1991, pp. 27–30. See also Stanley Cloud, "Volleys on the Information Front," *Time*, 2 February 1991, pp. 44–45; John Elson, "And on This Map We See . . . ," *Time*, 27 August 1990, p. 37; Andrew Sullivan, "The Big Schmooze," *Esquire*, October 1990, pp. 105–106; *WP*, 9 August 1990, p. D1.

32. *NYT*, 21 January 1991, p. A1.

33. Fred Barnes, "Hour of Power," *New Republic*, 3 September 1990, p. 13.

34. *WPNWE*, 18–24 March 1991, p. 38.

35. "The Gulf War," *Frontline*.

36. Atkinson, *Crusade*, p. 474.

37. Powell, *My American Journey*, p. 524.

38. Bush and Scowcroft, *A World Transformed*, p. 486.

39. Powell, *My American Journey*, p. 525.

40. Powell, Memorandum for Correspondents, Bush PR, Fitzwater Files, Subject File: box 7, Desert Storm folder; Powell, *My American Journey*, p. 524–525.

41. General Brent Scowcroft, interview with author, 11 June 1997.

42. "The Gulf War," *Frontline*.

43. Ibid. Cheney agreed with this assessment in *In My Time*, p. 223.

44. A useful discussion of what I have termed the "Korea Syndrome" can be found in Haass, *War of Necessity*, p. 117.

45. James A. Baker III, *"Work Hard, Study, and Keep Out of Politics": Adventures and Lessons from an Unexpected Public Life* (New York: Putnam, 2006), p. 299.

46. Barton Gellman, *Angler: The Cheney Vice Presidency* (New York: Penguin, 2008), p. 251.

47. Colin Powell spoke to this on the "American Experience: George H. W. Bush" (WGBH Educational Foundation, PBS Home Video, 2008): "We did not want to completely destroy the Iraqi army, and you can guess why—Iran." See also Baker, *"Work Hard,"* p. 299.

48. Cairo, *Gulf*, p. 98.

49. General Brent Scowcroft, interview with author, 11 June 1997.

50. Michael Beschloss and Strobe Talbott, *At the Highest Levels: The Inside Story of the End of the Cold War* (Boston: Little, Brown, 1993), p. 338.

51. Bush, *All the Best*, p. 514.

52. Glen to Fitzwater, inserts dated 2 August 1990, Bush PR, Fitzwater Files, Subject File: Alpha File, box 17, Iraq folder 1990.

53. Zbigniew Brzezinski and Brent Scowcroft, *America and the World:*

Conversations on the Future of American Foreign Policy (New York: Basic Books, 2008), p. 13.

54. Atkinson, *Crusade*, p. 488.

55. *WPNWE*, 22–28 April 1991, p. 6.

56. Powell, *My American Journey*, p. 531.

57. "The Gulf War," *Frontline*.

58. *Cleveland Plain Dealer*, 2 April 1991; *Los Angeles Times*, 2 April 1991; *San Francisco Examiner*, 15 March 1991; *NYT*, 20 March 1991.

59. "The Gulf War," *Frontline*.

60. Daniel Schorr, *Come to Think of It: Notes on the Turn of the Millennium* (New York: Viking, 2007), p. 7.

61. Baker, *"Work Hard,"* p. 303.

62. Cairo, *Gulf*, p. 128.

63. Bush to Assad, 31 May 1991, Bush PR, NSC, Haass Files, Middle East Peace Conference Files, May 1991 folder, OA/ID CF 01503-005.

64. Baker, *Politics of Diplomacy*, p. 493.

65. Bush to Shamir, 31 May 1991, Bush PR, NSC, Haass Files, Middle East Peace Conference Files, May 1991 folder, OA/ID CF01503-005.

66. Baker, *Politics of Diplomacy*, p. 495.

67. Memorandum of Conversation, Bush-Hussein, 15 May 1991, Bush PR, NSC, Haass Files, Middle East Peace Conference Files, May 1991 folder, OA/ID CF01503-005.

68. Baker, *Politics of Diplomacy*, p. 509.

69. Letters in Bush PR, NSC, Haass Files, Middle East Peace Conference Files, July 1991 folder, OA/ID CF01503-007.

70. Baker to Gorbachev, 30 January 1992, Baker Papers, box 100, folder 18 (Gorbachev).

71. In his memoir, Baker ultimately agreed with this assessment: Baker, *The Politics of Diplomacy*, p. 512.

72. See, for example, Cable, from U.S. Delegation Secretary to Secretary of State, 17 May 1991, Bush PR, NSC, Richard N. Haass Files, Middle East Peace Process Files, OA/ID CF01503-005.

73. James A. Baker III, interview with author, 17 April 1997; Bush and Scowcroft, *A World Transformed*, pp. 547–550.

74. Baker, *"Work Hard,"* p. 304.

CHAPTER 9: PRESIDENT BUSH

1. James A. Baker III, Hofstra, 17 April 1997.

2. Herbert S. Parmet, *George Bush: Life of a Lone Star Yankee* (New York: Scribner, 1997), p. 366.

3. "George Bush: A Sense of Duty," for the Arts and Entertainment Network's *Biography* series (first broadcast November 1996).

4. *NYT*, 4 July 1989, p. 34.

5. Bush Diary, 16 March 1983, in George Bush, *All the Best, George Bush: My Life in Letters and Other Writings* (New York: Scribner, 1999), pp. 329–330. For a more caustic look at this, see Maureen Dowd, "For Bush, Culture Can Be a Sometime Thing," *NYT*, 27 October 19, 1988.

6. Hugh Sidey, interview with author, 17 April 1997.

7. Michael Duffy and Dan Goodgame, *Marching in Place: The Status Quo Presidency of George Bush* (New York: Simon & Schuster, 1991), p. 204.

8. *NYT*, 20 January 1989, p. 1.

9. David Mervin, *George Bush and the Guardianship Presidency* (New York: St. Martin's Press, 1996), p. 19.

10. Robert Schlesinger, *White House Ghosts: Presidents and Their Speechwriters* (New York: Simon & Schuster, 2008), p. 363.

11. Bush Diary, 26 April 1989, in Bush, *All the Best*, p. 423. See also Schlesinger, *White House Ghosts*, p. 368–369.

12. James A. Baker III, *The Politics of Diplomacy: Revolution, War, and Peace* (New York: Putnam, 1995), p. 21.

13. Daniel Heimbach, interview with author, 9 November 1998.

14. George Bush, interview with author, 9 November 1998.

15. D. Alan Bromley, *The President's Scientists: Reminiscences of a White House Science Advisor* (New Haven, CT: Yale University Press, 2004), p. 24.

16. George W. Bush, *Decision Points* (New York: Crown, 2010), p. 58.

17. Ed Rollins, *Bare Knuckles and Back Rooms: My Life in American Politics* (New York: Broadway Books, 1996), p. 170.

18. George Bush and Brent Scowcroft, *A World Transformed* (New York: Knopf, 1998), p. 65.

19. Duffy and Goodgame, *Marching in Place*, p. 41.

20. Quoted in ibid., p. 46.

21. Lori Cox Han, *A Presidency Upstaged: The Public Leadership of George H. W. Bush* (College Station: Texas A&M University Press, 2011), p. 12.

22. Schlesinger, *White House Ghosts*, pp. 363–364.

23. *WPNWE*, 5–11 February 1990, p. 16.

24. Bush and Scowcroft, *A World Transformed*, p. 358.

25. Roman Popadiuk, *The Leadership of George Bush: An Insider's View of the Forty-First President* (College Station: Texas A&M University Press, 2009), p. 47.

26. *NYT*, 28 August 1989, p. A12.

27. Popadiuk, *Leadership of George Bush*, p. 47.

28. *NYT*, 24 December 1989, p. 9.

29. Michael Beschloss and Strobe Talbott, *At the Highest Levels: The Inside Story of the End of the Cold War* (Boston: Little, Brown, 1993), p. 18.

30. Han, *A Presidency Upstaged*, p. 3.

31. Maureen Dowd, "In Bush's White House, the Press Secretary Is the One in the White Hat," *NYT*, 18 January 1990, p. A20; Marlin Fitzwater, *Call the Briefing! Bush and Reagan, Sam and Helen: A Decade with Presidents and the Press* (New York: Times Books, 1995), pp. 172–173; Bill McAllister and Lou Cannon, "Fitzwater: Another Face," *WPNWE*, 5–11 December 1988, p. 15. In 1963, following the assassination of John Kennedy, Pierre Salinger stayed on for a brief period as Lyndon Johnson's press secretary; however, all concerned knew that that was a temporary arrangement.

32. Hugh Sidey, interview with author, 17 April 1997.

33. Fitzwater, *Call the Briefing!* p. 176.

34. George Bush, interview with author, 9 November 1988. See also Maureen Dowd, "Journalists Debate the Risks as President Woos the Press," *NYT*, 2 April 1989, p. A1.

35. Mark Rozell, *The Press and the Bush Presidency* (Westport, CT: Praeger, 1996), p. 149.

36. *NYT*, 31 December 1989, p. 1.

37. "President Is a Winner on Media Coverage," *Insight*, 3 April 1989, p. 6.

38. *NYT*, 16 February 1990, p. A12.

39. Jeffrey Cohen, *Presidency in the Era of 24-Hour News* (Princeton, NJ: Princeton University Press, 2008), p. 90.

40. Pool Report, 4 September 1990, Bush PR, WHPO, Press Office Pool reports, box 14, dated folder.

41. Gil Troy, *Hillary Rodham Clinton: Polarizing First Lady* (Lawrence: University Press of Kansas, 2006), p. 63.

42. Ibid.

43. Myra G. Gutin, *Barbara Bush: Presidential Matriarch* (Lawrence: University Press of Kansas, 2008), pp. xi, xii.

44. For a complete transcript of the speech, see http://www.wellesley.edu/events/commencement/archives/1990commencement/commencement address, accessed September 2014.

45. Gutin, *Barbara Bush*, p. 125.

46. Barbara Bush, *Millie's Book: As Dictated to Barbara Bush* (New York: Morrow, 1990). Her first book, *C. Fred's Story* (Garden City, NY: Doubleday, 1984), was a collection of anecdotes about Bush's late cocker spaniel. Proceeds of approximately $100,000 were donated to the Laubach Literacy Action and Literacy Volunteers of America.

47. Gutin, *Barbara Bush*, p. 85.

48. Troy, *Clinton*, p. 64. Ignoring Barbara's other two volumes of memoirs, Troy observes that "for Mrs. Bush, ghostwriting for a dog was easier than exposing her writing directly" (*Hillary*, p. 64).

49. Interview with author, not for attribution.

50. Speech notes on exhibit, GBM.

51. Robert Goodwin and Thomas Kinkade, *Points of Light: A Celebration of the American Spirit of Giving* (New York: Center Street, 2006), p. xiv.

52. Ibid.

53. Mervin, *Guardianship Presidency*, p. 108.

54. "Reference Guide, Points of Light Movement," on display at Hofstra.

55. Goodwin and Kinkade, *Points of Light*, p. xiv.

56. Mervin, *Guardianship Presidency*, p. 107.

57. Gregg Petersmeyer, Hofstra, 17 April 1997.

58. *NYT*, 15 July 2013. The 5,000th Daily Point of Light Award was given to Floyd Hammer and Kathy Hamilton, who founded a nonprofit organization that delivers free meals to children in fifteen countries.

59. Bush to Noonan, 15 July 1988, in Bush, *All the Best*, pp. 391–392. See also Peggy Noonan, *What I Saw at the Revolution: A Political Life in the Reagan Era* (New York: Ivy Books, 1990), p. 311.

CHAPTER 10: "THE SITUATION IS ABOUT AS BAD AS IT CAN BE"

1. "Trend to Approval of President Bush's Overall Job Performance," Bush PR, Marlin Fitzwater Files, Subject Files, Alpha File, box 22, Political folder no. 1; Herbert S. Parmet, *George Bush: The Life of a Lone Star Yankee* (New York: Scribner, 1997), p. 497; *NYT*, 26 November 1991, p. A18.

2. Rich Bond, Hofstra, 19 April 1997.

3. David Bates, telephone interview with author, 8 July 1997; George W. Bush, *Decision Points* (New York: Crown, 2010), p. 48. To his son, Bush said that he was considering not running because "I feel responsible for what happened to Neil" with the scandal regarding Silverado Savings and Loan (see chapter 5).

4. Daniel Galvin, *Presidential Party Building: Dwight D. Eisenhower to George W. Bush* (Princeton, NJ: Princeton University Press, 2010), p. 153.

5. Clayton Yeutter, interview with author, 8 July 1997.

6. Galvin, *Presidential Party Building*, p. 153.

7. For the story of Atwater's last days, see John Brady, *Bad Boy: The Life and Politics of Lee Atwater* (Reading, MA: Addison Wesley, 1997), pp. 267–269, chap. 11, passim.

8. Rich Bond, Hofstra, 19 April 1997.

9. *NYT*, 5 May 1991, p. 1. See also Marlin Fitzwater, *Call the Briefing! Bush and Reagan, Sam and Helen: A Decade with Presidents and the Press* (New York: Times Books, 1995), pp. 274–293.

10. Both George and Barbara Bush contracted Graves' disease within a year of moving into the White House. In fact, their dog Millie came down with lupus, which is in the same autoimmune category as Graves. This set off much speculation as to whether the White House environment posed a serious health hazard, a debate that was never satisfactorily concluded. See Burton J. Lee, MD

(physician to Bush), in Kenneth E. Thompson, ed., *Portraits of American Presidents*, vol. 10, *The Bush Presidency* (Lanham, MD: University Press of America, 1997); Myra R. Gutin, *Barbara Bush: Presidential Matriarch* (Lawrence: University Press of Kansas, 2008), p. 68.

11. Bush Diary, 4 May 1991, in George Bush, *All the Best, George Bush: My Life in Letters and Other Writings* (New York: Scribner, 1999), p. 517.

12. *NYT*, 2 July 1991, p. A1.

13. Quoted in Kenneth T. Walsh, *Family of Freedom: Presidents and African-Americans in the White House* (Boulder, CO: Paradigm, 2011), pp. 151, 153.

14. Gray in Leslie D. Feldman and Rosanna Perotti, eds., *Honor and Loyalty: Inside the Politics of the George H. W. Bush White House* (Westport, CT: Greenwood Press, 2002), p. 305. The paper arguing that Bush appointed Thomas simply because he was black was presented by John Massaro ("Pyrrhic Politics? President Bush and the Nomination of Clarence Thomas," pp. 275–302).

15. Jane Mayer and Jill Abramson, *Strange Justice: The Selling of Clarence Thomas* (Boston: Houghton Mifflin, 1994), p. 13.

16. For an excellent short survey of the hearings, see Lewis L. Gould, *The Most Exclusive Club: A History of the Modern United States Senate* (New York: Basic Books, 2005), pp. 296–298.

17. Copy of the phone logs in Anita Miller, ed., *The Complete Transcripts of the Clarence Thomas–Anita Hill Hearings, October 11, 12, 13, 1991* (Chicago: Academy Chicago Publishers, 1994), pp. 130–134.

18. Anita Hill, *Speaking Truth to Power* (New York: Doubleday, 1997), p. 138.

19. Miller, ed., *Thomas–Anita Hill Hearings*, pp. 13–144.

20. *NYT*, 14 October 1991, p. A1.

21. Mayer and Abramson, *Strange Justice*, pp. 347–348.

22. Clarence Thomas, *My Grandfather's Son: A Memoir* (New York: HarperCollins, 2007), p. 268.

23. Pool Report, dated (in error) 11 September 1991 (corrected to 11 October 1991), Bush PR, WHPO, Lower Press Office Pool Reports, box 14, dated folder.

24. Bush to Robert Blake, 10 October 1991, in Bush, *All the Best*, p. 538.

25. Quoted in Sheryl Gay Stolberg, "Standing by Her Story," *NYT*, 12 March 2014.

26. Bush, *All the Best*, p. 538. This is echoed by George W. Bush, who in his memoir noted how proud his father was of Thomas (Bush, *Decision Points*, p. 96).

27. *NYT*, 5 May 1991, p. 34.

28. *WP*, 21 April 1991, p. 1; Michael Duffy and Dan Goodgame, *Marching in Place: The Status Quo Presidency of George Bush* (New York: Simon & Schuster, 1991), pp. 124–130; Herbert S. Parmet, *George Bush: The Life of a Lone Star Yankee* (New York: Scribner, 1997), p. 492.

29. Fitzwater, *Call the Briefing!* p. 178.

30. Ibid., p. 177.

31. Ibid., p. 181.

32. Duffy and Goodgame, *Marching in Place*, pp. 126–127.

33. Robert Draper, *Dead Certain: The Presidency of George W. Bush* (New York: Free Press, 2007), p. 22.

34. George W. Bush biographer Bill Minutaglio has George W. telling Sununu: "I'm not speaking for my father. I'm not a messenger. But the way things are going, it might be in everybody's best interest if you would step aside." Then George W. suggested Sununu see his father (Bill Minutaglio, *First Son: George W. Bush and the Bush Family Dynasty* [New York: Times Books, 1999], p. 253). In his 2014 biography of his father, George W. Bush claims that his father asked him to talk to Sununu, George W. did, and after that conversation "I don't know what transpired after that" (George W. Bush, *41: A Portrait of My Father* [New York: Crown, 2014], p. 226). See also Bush, *Decision Points*, pp. 81–82; Peter Baker, *Days of Fire: Bush and Cheney in the White House* (New York: Doubleday, 2013), p. 42; Nancy Gibbs and Michael Duffy, *The Presidents Club: Inside the World's Most Exclusive Fraternity* (New York: Simon & Schuster, 2012), p. 479; and Elizabeth Mitchell, *W: Revenge of the Bush Dynasty* (New York: Berkley Books, 2003), p. 274.

35. *WPNWE*, 9–15 December 1991, p. 12; Duffy and Goodgame, *Marching in Place*, p. 128.

36. Andrew A. Card, interview with author, 18 April 1997; Fitzwater, *Call the Briefing!* p. 188; Draper, *Dead Certain*, p. 22; Mitchell, *W.*, p. 275.

37. *WPNWE*, 15–21 June 1992.

38. Andrew A. Card, interview with author, 18 April 1997; several interviews with author, not for attribution; Fitzwater, *Call the Briefing!* p. 192.

39. Kenneth E. Thompson, ed., *Portraits of American Presidents*, vol. 10, *The Bush Presidency* (Lanham, MD: University Press of America, 1997), p. 23.

40. D. Alan Bromley, *The President's Scientists: Reminiscences of a White House Science Advisor* (New Haven, CT: Yale University Press, 2004), p. 56.

41. Andrew A. Card, interview with author, 18 April 1997.

42. Several interviews with author, not for attribution.

43. Shirley Anne Warshaw, *Powersharing: White House–Cabinet Relations in the Modern Presidency* (Albany: State University of New York Press, 1996), pp. 193–195.

44. Richard N. Haass, *War of Necessity, War of Choice: A Memoir of Two Iraq Wars* (New York: Simon & Schuster, 2009), p. 154.

45. *NYT*, 12 January 1991, p. 2; *NYT*, 14 January 1991, p. 2; Michael Beschloss and Strobe Talbott, *At the Highest Levels: The Inside Story of the End of the Cold War* (Boston: Little, Brown, 1993), pp. 287–305; Douglas Stanglin, "Making His Move," *USN&WR*, 21 January 1991, pp. 30–31.

46. Quoted in Beschloss and Talbott, *At the Highest Levels*, p. 305.

47. Bush to Gorbachev, 23 January 1991, in Bush, *All the Best*, p. 508.

48. Beschloss and Talbott, *At the Highest Levels*, p. 47. Former president Richard Nixon was particularly vocal in his support of Yeltsin (Monica Crowley,

Nixon in Winter [New York: Random House, 1998], p. 43; Gibbs and Duffy, *The Presidents Club*, pp. 384–385).

49. Serhii Plokhy, *The Last Empire: The Final Days of the Soviet Union* (New York: Basic Books, 2014), p. 41.

50. George Bush and Brent Scowcroft, *A World Transformed* (New York: Knopf, 1998), p. 500.

51. Plokhy, *Last Empire*, pp. 4–5.

52. Vladislav M. Zubok, *A Failed Empire: The Soviet Union in the Cold War from Stalin to Gorbachev* (Chapel Hill: University of North Carolina Press, 2007), p. 320.

53. Zbigniew Brzezinski and Brent Scowcroft, *America and the World: Conversations on the Future of American Foreign Policy* (New York: Basic Books, 2008), pp. 163–164.

54. Bush and Scowcroft, *A World Transformed*, p. 500; Plokhy, *Last Empire*, pp. 55–65.

55. Bush Diary, 19 August 1991, in Bush, *All the Best*, p. 533.

56. Telcon, Bush and Mulroney, 19 August 1991, accessed September 2014, http://bushlibrary.tamu.edu/research/pdfs/memcons_telcons/1991-08-19—Mulroney.pdf.

57. The best available survey of the coup is found in Plokhy, *Last Empire*, chaps. 4–6. Also useful is Christopher Maynard, *Out of the Shadows: George H. W. Bush and the End of the Cold War* (College Station: Texas A&M University Press, 2008), pp. 93–115.

58. *Wall Street Journal*, 29 August 1991, p. A1.

59. *NYT*, 21 August 1991, p. A1.

60. Timothy J. Colton, *Yeltsin: A Life* (New York: Basic Books, 2008), p. 201.

61. Ibid.; Plokhy, *Last Empire*, pp. 123–124.

62. Bush Diary, 21 August 1991, in Bush, *All the Best*, p. 535.

63. Quoted in Plokhy, *Last Empire*, p. 134.

64. Ibid., p. 137.

65. Colton, *Yeltsin*, p. 203.

66. *NYT*, 30 August 1991, p. A1.

67. Quoted in Colton, *Yeltsin*, p. 206.

68. Quoted in Beschloss and Talbott, *At the Highest Levels*, p. 438; also in Colton, *Yeltsin*, p. 203; Plokhy, *Last Empire*, p. 145.

69. The story of Bush coming to this decision is told in Plokhy, *Last Empire*, chap. 10.

70. Beschloss and Talbott, *At the Highest Levels*, p. 447. See also Mikhail Gorbachev, *Gorbachev: On My Country and the World* (New York: Columbia University Press, 2000), p. 141.

71. Bush, *In My Life*, p. 543.

72. Bill Clinton, *My Life* (New York: Knopf, 2004), p. 425.

73. Briefing Memo, 20 March 1991, Bush PR, WHPO, General Office Files, Press Office Subject Files, box 35, Justice folder.

74. *WPNWE*, 13–19 July 1992, p. 5; Tom Wicker, *George Herbert Walker Bush: A Penguin Life* (New York: Penguin, 2004), p. 167.

75. *NYT*, 18 December 1991, p. A1.

76. Duffy and Goodgame, *Marching in Place*, p. 245.

77. *NYT*, 18 November 1991, p. A10.

78. Defense Base Closure and Realignment Commission, *Report to the President, 1991* (Washington, DC, 1991), p. 11.

79. Dina G. Levy et al., *Base Realignment and Closure (BRAC) and Organizational Restructuring in the Department of Defense* (Santa Monica, CA: RAND, National Defense Research Institute, 2004), pp. 3–5.

80. Ibid., pp. 3–5.

81. Defense Base Closure and Realignment Commission, *Report to the President, 1991*, p. 11.

82. Ibid.

83. *NYT*, 12 April 1991, p. 2.

84. Interestingly, in a 1997 interview, Cheney echoed those thoughts, remembering that it was "very fortunate that we had the Reagan buildup" (Richard B. Cheney, telephone interview with author, 7 March 1997).

85. Levy et al., *BRAC and Organizational Restructuring*, pp. 3–5.

86. Sean O'Keefe, interview with author, 7 January 1999; Defense Base Closure and Realignment Commission, *Report to the President, 1991*, p. 12; David S. Sorensen, *Shutting Down the Cold War: The Politics of Military Base Closure* (New York: St. Martin's Press, 1998), pp. 31, 47, 95–97. Aside from California and Texas, no other state had more than two bases affected (New York had none).

87. Michael Duffy, "How Bush Will Battle Buchanan," *Time*, 2 March 1992, p. 21.

88. Timothy Stanley, *The Crusader: The Life and Tumultuous Times of Pat Buchanan* (New York: Thomas Dunne, 2012), p. 141.

89. Quoted in ibid., p. 136.

90. Quoted in Wicker, *Bush*, p. 173.

91. Stanley, *Buchanan*, pp. 148–149.

92. *NYT*, 7 February 1989; *NYT*, 17 November 1989.

93. Richard E. Cohen, *Rostenkowski: The Pursuit of Power and the End of the Old Politics* (Chicago: Ivan R. Dee, 1999), pp. 210–211.

94. *NYT*, 4 July 1009; Cohen, *Rostenkowski*, p. 211.

95. I visited Capitol Hill on the day that the check overdraft story hit the press. One Republican congressman was carrying in his pocket a letter that claimed he had not bounced any checks. He was showing it to everyone he met, whether they brought up the subject or not.

96. William Greider, *Who Will Tell the People? The Betrayal of American Democracy* (New York: Simon & Schuster, 1992), p. 15.

97. *NYT*, 2 June 1992, p. A10.

98. The best biography of Perot continues to be Gerald Posner, *Citizen Perot: His Life and Times* (New York: Random House, 1994).

99. Bush Diary, 7 May 1987, and editorial comments in Bush, *All the Best*, p. 361; James A. Baker III, *"Work Hard, Study, and Keep Out of Politics": Adventures and Lessons from an Unexpected Public Life* (New York: Putnam, 2006), p. 312; Bush, *All the Best*, p. 126n.

100. Bush to Perot, 4 January 1990, Bush PR, Marlin Fitzwater Files, Subject File: Alpha File, OA 6546, Box 21, Perot folder.

101. Doug Halbrecht, "Is Perot After the Presidency, or the President?," *Business Week*, 6 April 1992, p. 41; *WPNWE*, 27 April–3 May 1992, p. 14; Posner, *Citizen Perot*, pp. 198–201. A third story should be included, although it comes to us with no other verification than the author's word. In his memoir, Robert Mosbacher claims that late in 1980, Perot approached him, telling him that he wanted to get into the oil business with Mosbacher. Mosbacher reluctantly said yes, but after Perot's meddling and micromanaging, Mosbacher ended the deal. According to Mosbacher, *this* is why Perot entered the 1992 race—to exact revenge on *Mosbacher* (Robert Mosbacher Sr., *Going to Windward: A Mosbacher Family Memoir* [College Station: Texas A&M University Press, 2010], pp. 172–173).

102. Fred Steeper to Bob Teeter, 16 March 1992, Bush PR, Fitzwater Files, Subject, box 21, Political File, folder no. 1.

CHAPTER 11: "THE PRESIDENT SHOULD HAVE FIRED US ALL"

1. Michael Beschloss and Strobe Talbott, *At the Highest Levels: The Inside Story of the End of the Cold War* (Boston: Little, Brown, 1993), p. 434.

2. Herbert S. Parmet, *George Bush: The Life of a Lone Star Yankee* (New York: Scribner, 1997), p. 504.

3. Hugh Sidey, interview with author, 17 April 1997.

4. Parmet, *Lone Star Yankee*, p. 493.

5. James Carville and Mary Matalin, *All's Fair: Love, War and Running for President* (New York: Random House, 1994), p. 148.

6. Bond, in Leslie D. Feldman and Rosanna Perotti, eds., *Honor and Loyalty: Inside the Politics of the George H. W. Bush White House* (Westport, CT: Greenwood Press, 2002), p. 35.

7. Parmet, *Lone Star Yankee*, p. 493.

8. Bush Diary, 16 February 1992, in George Bush, *All the Best, George Bush: My Life in Letters and Other Writings* (New York: Scribner, 1999), p. 548.

9. James Barnes, "Along the Campaign Trail," *NJ*, 14 October 1992, p. 21.

10. Timothy Stanley, *The Crusader: The Life and Tumultuous Times of Pat Buchanan* (New York: Dunne Books, 2012), p. 153.

11. Ibid., p. 155.

12. Tom Wicker, *George Herbert Walker Bush: A Penguin Life* (New York: Penguin, 2004), p. 173.

13. Quoted in Stanley, *Buchanan*, p. 157.

14. Quoted in ibid., p. 163.

15. Wicker, *Bush*, p. 174.

16. Stanley, *Buchanan*, p. 170.

17. Bill Whalen, "A Party's Time for Solving Riddles," *Insight*, 27 March 1989, p. 8.

18. Sean Wilentz, *The Age of Reagan: 1974–2008* (New York: Harper Perennial, 2008), p. 317.

19. Bill Clinton, *My Life* (New York: Knopf, 2004), p. 384.

20. Paul Tsongas, *A Call to Economic Arms: Forging a New American Mandate* (Boston: Tsongas Committee, 1992), p. 5 (italics in original).

21. *NYT*, 13 April 1992, p. A17.

22. The story of the shifting focus of the Democratic Party is told in Kenneth S. Baer, *Reinventing Democrats: The Politics of Liberalism from Reagan to Clinton* (Lawrence: University Press of Kansas, 2000); for Clinton's chairmanship of the DLC, see pp. 163–165. For an excellent survey of the development of Clinton's ideas, see David Bennett, *Bill Clinton: Building a Bridge to the New Millennium* (New York: Routledge, 2014). See also Clinton, *My Life*, p. 326.

23. Quoted in Wilentz, *Age of Reagan*, p. 318.

24. David Bennett, *Bill Clinton*, pp. 51–53; W. Lance Bennett, *The Governing Crisis: Media, Money and Marketing in American Elections* (New York: St. Martin's Press, 1996), p. 217. For Clinton on these points, see Clinton, *My Life*, pp. 384–390.

25. Clinton, *My Life*, p. 391.

26. Kenneth D. Nordin, "The Television Candidate: H. Ross Perot's 1992 and 1996 Presidential Races," in Ted G. Jelen, ed. *Ross for Boss: The Perot Phenomenon and Beyond* (Albany: State University of New York Press, 2001), p. 15.

27. Quoted in Nordin, "The Television Candidate," p. 17.

28. Quoted in ibid., p. 15.

29. Wicker, *Bush*, p. 184.

30. Background information on Stockdale, as well as an interview with the admiral regarding his time as a POW, can be found at http://www.pow network.org/bios/s/s118.htm, accessed September 2014.

31. Stanley, *Buchanan*, pp. 174–179.

32. See http://www.ourcampaigns.com/RaceDetail.html?RaceID=55213, accessed 6 July 2014.

33. Stanley, *Buchanan*, pp. 196–197.

34. Ibid., p. 173.

35. Quoted on NBC's "Super Tuesday" television coverage, 10 March 1992.

36. King's account of the beatings can be found in Rodney King, *The Riot Within: My Journey from Rebellion to Redemption* (New York: HarperCollins, 2012), pp. 41–49.

37. James J. Snyder, telephone interview with author, 14 October 1998.

38. David Demarest, interview with author, 18 April 1997.

39. Richard D. Land to Bush, 1 July 1992, Bush PR, White House Counsel's Office, Lee S. Lieberman Files, Subject Files, Gay Rights folder.

40. Charles M. Cameron, *Veto Bargaining: Presidents and the Politics of Negative Power* (Cambridge: Cambridge University Press, 2000), p. 8.

41. Bush, *All the Best*, p. 552.

42. Hermann Von Bertrab, *Negotiating NAFTA: A Mexican Envoy's Account* (Westport, CT: Praeger, 1997), p. 8.

43. See James A. Baker III, *The Politics of Diplomacy: Revolution, War and Peace* (New York: Putnam, 1995), pp. 606–609; David Mervin, *George Bush and the Guardianship Presidency* (New York: St. Martin's Press, 1996), p. 204; "InfoPacks: Mexico-U.S. Free Trade Agreement and Trade Issues: Background, Statistics, and Legislation," IP 445M (Congressional Research Service, Library of Congress).

44. Dan Quayle, *Standing Firm* (New York: Harper, 1994), chap. 32, passim; Wicker, *Bush*, p. 171; Wilentz, *Age of Reagan*, p. 320.

45. James A. Baker III, *"Work Hard, Study, and Keep Out of Politics": Adventures and Lessons from an Unexpected Public Life* (New York: Putnam, 2006), p. 317.

46. Elizabeth Mitchell, *W: Revenge of the Bush Dynasty* (New York: Berkley Books, 2003), p. 283.

47. Thomas DeFrank, *Write It When I'm Gone: Remarkable Off-the-Record Conversations with Gerald R. Ford* (New York: Putnam, 2007), p. 158.

48. Ibid., pp. 155–158.

49. George W. Bush, *Decision Points* (New York: Crown, 2010), p. 49. In an aside, George W. then noted, "I never completely gave up on my idea of a Bush-Cheney ticket" (p. 49). In *41: A Portrait of My Father* (New York: Crown, 2014), George W. is much vaguer about his own attitude toward Quayle in 1992, not mentioning that he had spoken to his father about dumping Quayle (p. 236). See also Peter Baker, *Days of Fire: Bush and Cheney in the White House* (New York: Doubleday, 2013), p. 42.

50. Bush, *All the Best*, p. 395n.

51. Baker, *"Work Hard,"* p. 318.

52. Nordin, "The Television Candidate," p. 19; Gerald Posner, *Citizen Perot: His Life and Times* (New York: Random House, 1996), pp. 284–285; Wicker, *Bush*, p. 186.

53. Richard Nixon was invited to the Houston convention, but he chose instead to vacation in Montauk, New York. He called the race "the dullest of them all, with the most vapid candidates" (quoted in Leonard Benardo and Jennifer

Weiss, *Citizen-in-Chief: The Second Lives of the American Presidents* [New York: Morrow, 2009], p. 222).

54. The story of the platform debates are well told in Wicker, *Bush*, p. 190.

55. Rich Bond, Hofstra, 19 April 1997.

56. See http://buchanan.org/blog/1992-republican-national-convention-speech-148, accessed September 2014.

57. *NYT*, 20 August 1992.

58. Quoted in Stanley, *Buchanan*, p. 211.

59. Molly Ivins, "A Feast of Hate and Fear," *Newsweek*, 31 August 1992, p. 32.

60. Nordin, "The Television Candidate," pp. 21–25; Wicker, *Bush*, pp. 198–199, 206.

61. Ed Rollins, *Bare Knuckles and Back Rooms: My Life in American Politics* (New York: Broadway Books, 1996), p. 217.

62. Eugene F. Provenzo Jr. and Asterie Baker, *In the Eye of Hurricane Andrew* (Gainesville: University Press of Florida, 2002), p. 1.

63. Ibid., p. 62.

64. Ibid., p. 65.

65. Andrew A. Card, interview with author, 18 April 1997; James Snyder, telephone interview with author, 8 October 1998.

66. David K. Twigg, *The Politics of Disaster: Tracking the Impact of Hurricane Andrew* (Gainesville: University Press of Florida, 2012), pp. 78–79.

67. Itinerary, 11 September 1992, Bush PR, Staff and Office Files, Cabinet Affairs, Jay Lefkowitz Files, OA/ID 07863.

68. Itineraries, 3 October 1992, Bush PR, Staff and Office Files, Cabinet Affairs, Michael P. Jackson Files, OA/ID 06384.

69. "Federal Response to Victims of Hurricane Andrew," Bush PR, Staff and Office Files, Cabinet Affairs, Jay Lefkowitz Files, CF07863. See also Twigg, *Politics of Disaster*, p. 100.

70. Chase Untermeyer, interview with author, 18 June 1996.

71. Kenneth T. Walsh, *From Mount Vernon to Crawford: A History of the Presidents and Their Retreats* (New York: Hyperion, 2005), p. 234.

72. Quoted in Myra G. Gutin, *Barbara Bush: Presidential Matriarch* (Lawrence: University Press of Kansas, 2008), p. 132.

73. Marlin Fitzwater, *Call the Briefing! Bush and Reagan, Sam and Helen: A Decade with Presidents and the Press* (New York: Times Books, 1995), p. 264.

74. Parmet, *Lone Star Yankee*, p. 502.

75. Bush Diary, 25 July 1991, in Bush, *All the Best*, p. 529.

76. Bush Diary, 9 January 1992, in Bush, *All the Best*, pp. 545–546 (in this entry, Bush misspells Miyazawa's name).

77. Lee quoted in Parmet, *Lone Star Yankee*, p. 491.

78. Fitzwater, *Call the Briefing!* p. 195.

79. George Bush, interview with author, 8 July 1997.

80. John H. Sununu, interview with author, 8 July 1997.

81. Fitzwater, *Call the Briefing!* p. 195.

82. Quoted in DeFrank, *Write It When I'm Gone*, p. 178.

83. *WP*, 4 April 1992.

84. Interview with author, not for attribution.

85. David Demarest, interview with author, 17 April 1997.

86. In the margins of a letter sent from a Houston correspondent, in which the writer outlines what is wrong with the Bush campaign and helpfully predicts that unless he has the opportunity to talk personally with Baker about these problems, "Ross Perot will be the next president," Baker writes, "A good example of why I should avoid 'getting back into it' like the plague" (Grover to Baker, 14 May 1992, Baker Papers, box 100, folder 20 (G: Misc.).

87. Baker later noted that he *had* to stay in government—if he had not become Bush's chief of staff and senior counselor to the president, ethics laws "would have prohibited my even talking to those with whom I had served in the cabinet" (Baker, *"Work Hard,"* p. 239n).

88. Notes for Press Secretary, undated, Bush PR, Marlin Fitzwater Files, Subject File: Alpha File, box 1, Baker folder; Clayton Yeutter, interview with author, 8 July 1997. See also D. Alan Bromley, *The President's Scientists: Reminiscences of a White House Science Advisor* (New Haven, CT: Yale University Press, 2004), p. 57.

89. There may have been sputtering attempts to put the opposition on the defensive. Bill Clinton tells a story of a July 1991 call from domestic policy adviser Roger Porter at the White House. Originally the call was to sound out Clinton to see if he was running for president, but Clinton pitches the rest of the call as a "fair warning." Clinton remembered that Porter said that "I actually had a chance to win. So if I ran, they would have to destroy me personally." Clinton then recalled, "I told Roger that what he said made me more likely to run. . . . Ever since I was a little boy I have hated to be threatened" (Clinton, *My Life*, pp. 368–369).

90. Stephen J. Wayne, *The Road to the White House, 1996: The Politics of Presidential Elections* (New York: St. Martin's Press, 1997), p. 219.

91. Baker, *"Work Hard,"* p. 329; Sidney Blumenthal, *The Clinton Wars* (New York: Farrar, Straus and Giroux, 2003), pp. 41–44; Clinton, *My Life*, 432; Wicker, *Bush*, p. 205. After the election, news broke that Elizabeth M. Tamposi—an assistant secretary of state—had run the point on the search of Clinton's files. She had contacted Janet Mullins, a top aide to Bush, and Baker. According to Bob Woodward, in his book *Shadow: Five Presidents and the Legacy of Watergate* (New York: Simon & Schuster, 1999), Baker was despondent; not wanting to end his career on the note of a scandal, he offered to resign. Even though the Special Prosecutor Act was due to expire on 12 December 1992, Attorney General William Barr did not want the appearance of a cover-up, so he filed a secret request

for an independent counsel to look into what the press had now dubbed "Passportgate." The three-judge panel appointed Joseph DiGenova, a Republican and former federal prosecutor. DiGenova spent three years on this investigation at a cost of $2.2 million. His report was released in December 1995—he had decided to bring no charges (Woodward, *Shadow*, p. 207–212, 220).

92. Bush Diary, 2 November 1992, in Bush, *All the Best*, p. 571.

93. *NYT*, 30 October 1992, p. A1.

94. Interview with author, not for attribution.

95. Joe Klein, *The Natural: The Misunderstood Presidency of Bill Clinton* (New York: Broadway Books, 2002), pp. 42–43.

96. Ibid., p. 43.

97. Baker, *"Work Hard,"* p. 321; Robert Mosbacher Sr., *Going to Windward: A Mosbacher Family Memoir* (College Station: Texas A&M University Press, 2010), pp. 257–258.

98. Fitzwater, *Call the Briefing!* p. 322.

99. Grover G. Norquist, "The Unmaking of the President," *Policy Review* 63 (1993): 10–17.

100. Donald T. Critchlow, *The Conservative Ascendancy: How the Republican Right Rose to Power in Modern America*, 2nd ed. (Lawrence: University Press of Kansas, 2011), pp. 220–227.

101. Bush Diary, 31 March 1992, in Bush, *All the Best*, p. 555, 555n.

102. Taylor Branch, *The Clinton Tapes: Wrestling History with the President* (New York: Simon & Schuster, 2009), p. 51.

103. *41* (HBO Documentary Films, 2012).

104. Clinton Campaign Press Release, 14 October 1002, in Bush PR, Counsel's Office, Lee S. Lieberman Files, Iraq Subject Files, OA/ID 45296-004. See also Clinton, *My Life*, p. 440.

105. For a summary of Gonzalez's investigations, see *WP*, 22 March 1992, p. A1. For his original criticism of Bush, see *Congressional Record*, 21 July 1992, H6339. In October 1992, Attorney General William P. Barr appointed Judge Frederick B. Lacey to investigate what had now been dubbed the "Iraqgate" scandal. Seven weeks later, Lacey reported that the allegations of a Justice Department cover-up in its probe of Atlanta's Banca Nazionale del Lavoro branch were without merit, and that "there are no reasonable grounds to believe that further investigation is warranted" ("Report of the Independent Counsel," 8 December 1992, p. 190, in Bush PR, White House Counsel's Files, William Otis Files, Iraq Subject Files, BNL Report of the Independent Counsel, OA/ID 45479-001). Both the *New York Times* and the *Washington Post* criticized the Lacey appointment, and Clinton attorney general Janet Reno reopened the investigation. Reno eventually decided that the original investigation had been properly handled, and the matter died (Benjamin Wittes, *Starr: A Reassessment* [New Haven, CT: Yale University Press, 2002], p. 196; see also Baker, *"Work Hard,"* pp. 326–328).

106. *Los Angeles Times*, 11 September 1992.

107. A copy of the reindictment, as well as the press release on the reindictment from the Special Prosecutor's Office, can be found in Bush PR, White House Counsel's Office, Janet Rehnquist's Files, Iran Contra Subject Files, Iran/Contra: Weinberger, Caspar folder, OA/ID CF01231-006.

108. Woodward, *Shadow*, pp. 156, 200.

109. Wicker, Bush, pp. 79–80, 207; Woodward, *Shadow*, p. 200.

110. *NYT*, 31 October 1992, p. A1.

111. Clinton, *My Life*, p. 441.

112. Baker, *"Work Hard,"* p. 330.

113. Mosbacher, *Windward*, p. 273.

114. Bush, *All the Best*, p. 571n.

115. Woodward, *Shadow*, pp. 202, 204.

116. Bush, *All the Best*, pp. 561n, 581.

117. Quoted in George W. Bush, *A Charge to Keep: My Journey to the White House* (New York: Morrow, 1999), p. 4.

CHAPTER 12: "THE F. L. F. W."

1. Thomas DeFrank, *Write It When I'm Gone: Remarkable Off-the-Record Conversations with Gerald R. Ford* (New York: Putnam, 2007), p. 149.

2. Bush Diary, November 4, 1992, in George Bush, *All the Best, George Bush: My Life in Letters and Other Writings* (New York: Scribner, 1999), p. 572.

3. Doro Bush Koch, *My Father, My President: A Personal Account of the Life of George H. W. Bush* (New York: Warner Books, 2006), p. 416.

4. Ibid., p. 418.

5. Bush Diary, 18 November 1992, in Bush, *All the Best*, p. 575.

6. Ibid., p. 576; Nancy Gibbs and Michael Duffy, *The Presidents Club: Inside the World's Most Exclusive Fraternity* (New York: Simon & Schuster, 2012), p. 412.

7. Ibid., p. 464.

8. Bush Koch, *My Father, My President*, pp. 422–423.

9. The performance can be found at https://www.youtube.com/watch?v=D815eVH6Kwg, accessed April 2013. See also Bush Koch, *My Father, My President*, pp. 424–425.

10. Herbert J. Ellison, *Boris Yeltsin and Russia's Democratic Transformation* (Seattle: University of Washington Press, 2006), p. 201; James T. Patterson, *Restless Giant: The United States from Watergate to Bush v. Gore* (New York: Oxford University Press, 2005), p. 229. START II would be replaced by a 2002 agreement concluded between George W. Bush and Vladimir Putin.

11. Bush Diary, 29 December 1992, in Bush, *All the Best*, p. 581.

12. Report from the Secretary-General of the United Nations, 24 August 1992, Bush PR, Staff and Office, National Security Council, Nancy Bearg Dyke, Subject File, OA/ID CF01437-015.

13. James Dobbins, Michele A. Poole, Austin Long, and Benjamin Runkle, *After the War: Nation-Building from FDR to George W. Bush* (Santa Monica, CA: RAND National Security Research Division, 2008), pp. 43–44.

14. Report, 21 July 1992, Bush PR, Staff and Office, National Security Council, Nancy Bearg Dyke, Subject File, OA/ID CF01437-016.

15. Dobbins et al., *After the War*, p. 44.

16. Press Release, Bush *PP*, 27 July 1992.

17. Report from the Secretary-General of the United Nations, 24 August 1992, Bush PR, Staff and Office, National Security Council, Nancy Bearg Dyke, Subject File, OA/ID CF01437-015.

18. Memo, "Emergency Humanitarian Relief for Somalia," 19 August 1992, Bush PR, Staff and Office Files, National Security Council, Nancy Bearg Dyke Files, Subject File, OA/ID CF01437-016.

19. Boutros Boutros-Ghali to Bush, 24 November 1992, Bush PR, Staff and Office Files, National Security Council, Nancy Bearg Dyke Files, Subject File, OA/ID CF 01435-015.

20. Scowcroft to Bush, undated, Bush PR, Staff and Office Files, National Security Council, Nancy Bearg Dyke Files, Subject File, OA/ID CF01437-015.

21. At Hofstra University, discussant Roy Gutman, a former diplomatic correspondent for *Newsweek* and author of a book on Bosnia, *A Witness to Genocide* (1993), was adamant on this point, noting that the commitment of American resources to Somalia was "an inadvertent go-ahead to the Serbs," who, believing the Americans to be otherwise disposed, stepped up their bombing of Sarajevo. Gutman was blunt: "The sending of troops [in Operation Restore Hope] undoubtedly saved lives in Somalia. But make no mistake: it cost lives in Bosnia." Quoted in Meena Bose and Rosanna Perotti, eds., *From Cold War to New World Order: The Foreign Policy of George Bush* (Westport, CT: Greenwood Press, 2002), pp. 293–294.

22. Kenneth Juster, discussant, in Rose and Perotti, eds., *From Cold War to New World Order*, p. 295.

23. Eagleburger was named acting secretary of state after Baker resigned to take over Bush's fall campaign. In November, Bush gave Eagleburger a recess appointment, and he served as secretary of state until the end of the administration.

24. Dobbins et al., *After the War*, pp. 45–46.

25. Bush to Boutros Boutros-Ghali, 4 December 1992, Bush PR, Staff and Office Files, National Security Council, Nancy Bearg Dyke Files, Subject File, OA/ID CF01437-015. Also in Bush, *All the Best*, p. 579.

26. Memcons, 3 December 1992; Cable, American Embassy Cairo to Secretary of State, 7 December 1992, Bush PR, Staff and Office Files, National Security Council, Richard N. Haass, Subject File, OA/ID CF01726-004.

27. Dobbins et al., *After the War*, p. 46.

28. Stephen F. Burgess, "Operation Restore Hope: Somalia and the Frontiers

of the New World Order," in Bose and Perotti, *From Cold War to New World Order*, p. 260.

29. Bush Diary, 3 January 1993, in Bush, *All the Best*, p. 582.

30. Bob Woodward, *Shadow: Five Presidents and the Legacy of Watergate* (New York: Simon & Schuster, 1999), p. 205.

31. Gray to Bush, 17 December 1992, Bush PR, White House Counsel's Office, Mark Paoletta Files, Pardon Files, Caspar Weinberger—Letter from Skadden Apps Requesting a Pardon and Materials Folder, OA/ID 45555-019.

32. 22 December diary entry, quoted in Woodward, *Shadow*, p. 213.

33. Of the five men, Abrams, McFarlane, and Fiers had pleaded guilty to charges; George had been convicted, and Clarridge had yet to be tried.

34. Associated Press story, 24 December 1992.

35. Benjamin Wittes, *Starr: A Reassessment* (New Haven, CT: Yale University Press, 2002), pp. 50–51.

36. David G. Savage, "Bush Refusal on Notes Not Crime, Experts Say," *Los Angeles Times*, 28 December 1992; Woodward, *Shadow*, pp. 197–198, 208–209, 215.

37. Quoted in Barbara Bush, *Reflections: Life after the White House* (New York: Scribner, 2003), p. 6.

38. Exhibit, GBM.

39. Burton I. Kaufman, *The Post-presidency from Washington to Clinton* (Lawrence: University Press of Kansas, 2012), p. 492; Mark K. Updegrove, *Second Acts: Presidential Lives and Legacies after the White House* (Guilford, CT: Lyons Press, 2006), p. 218.

40. Kaufman, *Post-presidency*, p. 494.

41. Updegrove, *Second Acts*, p. 218. The former First Lady came back to earth with her usual sense of humor. When asked by a woman in a grocery store, "Aren't you Barbara Bush?," she responded, "No, she's much older than I am" (Updegrove, *Second Acts*, p. 210).

42. Kaufman, *Post-presidency*, pp. 494–495.

43. Updegrove, *Second Acts*, p. 210.

44. Ibid., p. 218.

45. Kaufman, *Post-presidency*, p. 492.

46. Ibid., p. 494.

47. Leonard Benardo and Jennifer Weiss, *Citizen-in-Chief: The Second Lives of the American Presidents* (New York: Morrow, 2009), p. 70; Dan Briody, *The Iron Triangle: Inside the Secret World of the Carlyle Group* (Hoboken, NJ: Wiley, 2003), pp. 111–112.

48. Bush to "Dear Kids," 11 February 1997, in Bush, *All the Best*, p. 598.

49. Bush Diary, 25 March 1997, in Bush, *All the Best*, p. 602. See also Barbara Bush, *Reflections*, pp. 166–167.

50. Barbara Bush, *Reflections*, p. 285.

51. Kaufman, *Post-presidency*, p. 498.

52. Bush to Woodward, 12 February 1998, in Bush, *All the Best*, p. 610.

53. Updegrove, *Second Acts*, p. 214. Coming to the same conclusion are Bernardo and Weiss, *Citizen-in-Chief*, p. 69; Kaufman, *Post-presidency*, p. 486.

54. Bush to Reagan, 28 December 1993, in Kiron K. Skinner, Annelise Anderson, Martin Anderson, eds., *Reagan: A Life in Letters* (New York: Free Press, 2003), p. 828.

55. Wilson in William F. Levantrosser and Rosanna Perotti, eds., *A Noble Calling: Character and the George H. W. Bush Presidency* (Westport, CT: Praeger, 2004), p. 326; Kaufman, *Post-presidency*, p. 498.

56. Benardo and Weiss, *Citizen-in-Chief*, p. 108.

57. Wilson in Levantrosser and Perotti, eds., *A Noble Calling*, p. 327.

58. Kaufman, *Post-presidency*, p. 498.

59. Benardo and Weiss, *Citizen-in-Chief*, p. 81; Kaufman, *Post-presidency*, p. 499.

60. Kaufman, *Post-presidency*, p. 500.

61. Wilson to James W. Cicconi, 1 November 1989, Bush Library, Vertical File.

62. David E. Alsobrook, "The Birth of the Tenth Presidential Library: The Bush Presidential Materials Project, 1993–1994," *Government Information Quarterly* 12, no. 1 (1995): 36–38; Wilson in Levantrosser and Perotti, eds., *A Noble Calling*, p. 327.

63. For a blow-by-blow description of the day's events, see Barbara Bush, *Reflections*, pp. 193–197.

64. Bob Greene, *Fraternity: A Journey in Search of Five Presidents* (New York: Crown, 2004), p. 146.

65. For insights on how the family dealt with George W.'s and Jeb's 1994 campaigns, see Barbara Bush, *Reflections*, pp. 61–63.

66. Quoted in Updegrove, *Second Acts*, pp. 214–215.

67. George W. Bush, *A Charge to Keep: My Journey to the White House* (New York: Morrow, 1999), p. 40.

68. Timothy Naftali, *George H. W. Bush* (New York: Times Books, 2007), p. 165.

69. Bob Woodward, *State of Denial: Bush at War, Part III* (New York: Simon & Schuster, 2006), pp. 1–2.

70. Woodward, *State of Denial*, pp. 5, 7.

71. Updegrove, *Second Acts*, p. 224.

72. Bill Clinton would tell historian Taylor Branch that George W. had made a mistake in sending his parents to New Hampshire (Taylor Branch, *The Clinton Tapes: Wrestling History with the President* [New York: Simon & Schuster, 2009], p. 584).

73. DeFrank, *Write It When I'm Gone*, pp. 152–153.

74. Quoted in Updegrove, *Second Acts*, p. 224.

75. Quoted in George W. Bush, *Decision Points* (New York: Crown, 2010), p. 68; and George W. Bush, *41: A Portrait of My Father* (New York: Crown), p. 267.

76. Barton Gellman, *Angler: The Cheney Vice Presidency* (New York: Penguin, 2008), pp. 24–25.

77. Bush to Mulroney, 5 August 2000, in Bush, *All the Best*, p. 634.

78. Quoted in Updegrove, *Second Acts*, p. 229.

79. See Barbara Bush, *Reflections*, pp. 311, 343–348, 349–354, 358–365.

80. Bush to Sidey, 16 December 2000, in Bush, *All the Best*, p. 636.

81. Baker's story of the 2000 Florida recount is in his *"Work Hard, Study, and Keep Out of Politics": Adventures and Lessons from an Unexpected Public Life* (New York: Putnam, 2006), chap. 16.

82. 531 U.S. 98 (2000).

83. Bush, *Decision Points*, p. 109. See also Bush to Sidey, 21 January 2001, in Bush, *All the Best*, pp. 639–644; Peter Baker, *Days of Fire: Bush and Cheney in the White House* (New York: Doubleday, 2013), p. 84; Naftali, *Bush*, pp. 167–168.

84. Quoted in Baker, *Bush and Cheney*, p. 49.

85. Quoted in Robert Draper, *Dead Certain: The Presidency of George W. Bush* (New York: Free Press, 2007), p. 110.

86. Woodward, *State of Denial*, p. 419.

87. Draper, *Dead Certain*, p. 135.

88. Barbara Bush, *Reflections*, pp. 386–389.

89. Bush to Sidey, 12 September 2001, in Bush, *All the Best*, p. 646.

90. George W. to Bob Woodward: "Why I came up with those specific words, maybe it was an echo of the past, I don't know why. . . . I'll tell you this, we didn't sit around massaging the words. I got up there and just spoke" (quoted in Woodward, *Bush at War*, p. 16). Later, in his second memoir, George W. remembered that in his notes, he had written, "'Terrorism against America will not succeed.' Dad's words must have been buried in my subconscious, waiting to surface during another moment of crisis" (Bush, *Decision Points*, p. 128).

91. Bush to Sidey, 12 September 2001, in Bush, *All the Best*, p. 646.

92. George Tenet, *At the Center of the Storm: My Years at the CIA* (New York: HarperCollins, 2007), p. 364.

93. Bush, *Decision Points*, p. 238.

94. James Risen, *State of War: The Secret History of the CIA and the Bush Administration* (New York: Free Press, 2006), pp. 1–2. See also Donald Rumsfeld, *Known and Unknown: A Memoir* (New York: Sentinel, 2012), p. 275; and Woodward, *Bush at War*, pp. 20, 22.

95. Quoted in Woodward, *State of Denial*, pp. 114–115.

96. Quoted in ibid., p. 420.

97. Brent Scowcroft, "Don't Attack Saddam," *Wall Street Journal*, 15 August 2002.

98. Condoleezza Rice, *No Higher Honor: A Memoir of My Years in Washington* (New York: Broadway Paperbacks, 2011), p. 179 (Rice: "We've worked over the years to repair the damage and we remain very close friends" [p. 179]).

99. Quoted in Bush, *Decision Points*, p. 238; Baker, *Bush and Cheney*, p. 209; Gibbs and Duffy, *The Presidents Club*, p. 483.

100. Bob Woodward, *Plan of Attack* (New York: Simon & Schuster, 2004), p. 160.

101. Quoted in ibid., p. 421.

102. Madeleine Albright, *Madame Secretary* (New York: Miramax Books, 2003), p. 273; Barbara Bush, *Reflections*, p. 15; Richard Clarke, *Against All Enemies: Inside America's War on Terror* (New York: Free Press, 2004), pp. 80–84; Clinton, *My Life*, pp. 526–527; Gibbs and Duffy, *The Presidents Club*, pp. 421–424; Risen, *State of War*, p. 93; Updegrove, *Second Acts*, p. 213; Tim Weimer, *Legacy of Ashes: The History of the CIA* (New York: Doubleday, 2007), p. 444.

103. Clarke, *Against All Enemies*, p. 84; Weimer, *Legacy of Ashes*, p. 444.

104. Bush Diary, 12 February 1999, in Bush, *All the Best*, p. 628.

105. Gibbs and Duffy, *The Presidents Club*, p. 492.

106. Kaufman, *Post-presidency*, p. 496.

107. Bush to Sidey, 22 February 2005, in Bush, *All the Best*, pp. 673–678.

108. Gibbs and Duffy, *The Presidents Club*, pp. 497–498; Kaufman, *Post-presidency*, p. 496.

109. Bush, *Decision Points*, pp. 324–325.

110. Quoted in Branch, *Clinton Tapes*, p. 30.

111. Quoted in Bush, *Decision Points*, p. 325.

112. Quoted in Kaufman, *Post-presidency*, p. 496.

113. Gibbs and Duffy, *The Presidents Club*, p. 503.

114. Note on exhibit, GBL.

115. Speech at John F. Kennedy School of Government, Harvard University, 29 May 1998.

116. Richard Rose, *The Postmodern Presidency: George Bush Meets the World* (Chatham, NJ: Chatham House, 1991), pp. 48–49, 53, 307–308.

117. David Mervin, *George Bush and the Guardianship Presidency* (New York: St. Martin's Press, 1996), p. 8.

118. David B. Cohen, "The Domestic Policy Vicar: John Sununu as White House Chief of Staff," in Leslie D. Feldman and Rosanna Perotti, eds. *Honor and Loyalty: Inside the Politics of the George H. W. Bush White House* (Westport, CT: Greenwood Press, 2002), pp. 84–85.

119. Ryan J. Barilleaux and Mark J. Rozell, *Power and Prudence: The Presidency of George H. W. Bush* (College Station: Texas A&M University Press, 2004), p. 7.

120. Gil Troy, *Morning in America: How Ronald Reagan Invented the 1980s* (Princeton, NJ: Princeton University Press, 2005), p. 315.

121. Michael Duffy and Dan Goodgame, *Marching in Place: The Status Quo Presidency of George Bush* (New York: Simon & Schuster, 1992), p. 12. Others who share this view of Bush include David Broder, "The Reactor President," *WPNWE*, 27 August–2 September 1990, p. 4, and Charles Tiefer, *The*

Semi-Sovereign Presidency: The Bush Administration's Strategy for Governing without Congress (Boulder, CO: Westview Press, 1994).

122. For an excellent discussion of the rise of the president as performing persuader, see Lewis Gould, *The Modern American Presidency*, 2nd ed., revised and updated (Lawrence: University Press of Kansas, 2009).

123. Shirley Anne Warshaw, *The Keys to Power*, 2nd ed. (New York: Pearson, 2005), p. 220.

124. John F. Freie, *The Making of the Postmodern Presidency from Ronald Reagan to Barack Obama* (Boulder, CO: Paradigm, 2011), p. 9.

125. Michael F. Cairo, *The Gulf: The Bush Presidencies and the Middle East* (Lexington: University Press of Kentucky, 2012), p. 84.

126. John Robert Greene, *The Presidency of George Bush* (Lawrence: University Press of Kansas, 2000).

127. Foley, in Feldman and Perotti, eds., *Honor and Loyalty*, p. 256.

128. Sununu, in Feldman and Perotti, eds., *Honor and Loyalty*, p. 160.

BIBLIOGRAPHICAL ESSAY

The archival record of presidencies after 1980 is governed by the Presidential Records Act of 1978 (PRA).* Under that act, documents prepared by employees of the executive office in the performance of their daily duties remain the property of federal government, under the supervision of the Archivist of the United States. Those records are turned over to the National Archives for processing at a presidential library. However, in the processing of that material, the archivists are required under the PRA to keep closed certain documents for a period of twelve years following the end of the administration. And even after that twelfth year, material no longer covered by the PRA may continue to be closed from public scrutiny under the terms of the Freedom of Information Act (FOIA; 1966),† which closes material for the reasons listed under the PRA as well as for other reasons. An attempt was made by executive order during the presidency of George W. Bush to give the incumbent president, former presidents, former vice presidents, or their designees the authority to deny access to presidential documents even after the twelve-year period, but that order was rescinded on the first day of the presidency of Barack Obama.‡

* 44 U.S.C. §§2201–2207.

† 5 U.S.C. §552.

‡ See E.O. 13233 (1 November 2001) and E.O. 13489 (21 January 2009). For an excellent summary of this issue, see Wendy Ginsberg, "The Presidential Records Act: Background and Recent Issues for Congress," Congressional Research Service (7-5700, R0238, 30 May 2014); and David J. Mengel, "Access to United States Government Records at the U.S. National Archives and Records Administration" (paper presented at the Japan-U.S. Archives Seminar, May 2007), https://www.archivists.org/publications/proceedings/accesstoarchives/07_David_MENGEL.pdf, accessed August 2014.

The overall result of this legislation is that much more material on the presidents since 1980 is closed to the researcher than was ever closed for any of the previous presidents, whose papers (with the exception of a large portion of Richard Nixon's) remain the personal property of that president. Particularly troublesome for the researcher is the closure of material in one area listed under the PRA: material that if released would disclose confidential advice between the president and his advisers, or among such advisers. The lack of access to such material severely limits any archival study of decision making in a presidential administration.

Thus it is with the material on deposit at the George Bush Presidential Library (GBL; College Station, Texas). The researcher is consistently frustrated at the amount of material that is closed under the statutes of the PRA or the FOIA; at the time of the publication of this book, the author was told that 40 percent of the holdings of the GBL are presently available to scholars. But the available material is often rich. The Subject File of the White House Office of Records Management (WHORM), the filing successor to the old White House Central File, is the system into which general correspondence is filed. Although the bulk of it is constituent correspondence, many letters from Bush are included here. Thus, the WHORM file provides the best available archival evidence of Bush's decision making. This source should be followed by use of the files of the White House Press Office (WHPO). Of particular interest here is a small file of Internal Interview Transcripts—whenever Bush, Mrs. Bush, or a senior member of the administration was interviewed by a member of the press, the WHPO recorded that interview and provided all parties with a transcript. The frankness found in those transcripts, spanning the entire life of the administration, is quite useful. So are the Press Pool Reports, a small series of short reports on the president's daily activities written by a designated reporter (of the pool) to the entire White House Press Corps. The candor—and often raw humor—of these reports makes them not only insightful but also quite quotable (my personal favorite of many was the one that began, "President Harrison . . . no, President Bush, walked into the press conference"). Also available in the WHPO files are 147 boxes of records from the files of press secretary Marlin Fitzwater. The researcher can also consult a file containing the President's Daily Diary and a detailed Speechwriting File, which often contains Bush's annotations on drafts submitted to him by his speechwriters. Also quite useful for a study of Bush's background is the George H. W. Bush Papers: World War II Correspondence, showing all the honesty, depth, and pathos of a young man writing home from the front.

There have also been several useful sets of material at the GBL processed under the terms of the FOIA. For this book, the most helpful of these was the material pertaining to the fall of the Berlin Wall and the Reunification of Germany, John Tower, Somalia, Hurricane Andrew, Lawrence Walsh, Caspar Weinberger, the Madrid Conference, Tiananmen Square, the Scowcroft-Eagleburger trip to China, and David Souter. It must be noted that even though all material is subject to document-level closures under the terms of the PRA and the FOIA, newly processed collections are appearing every day, particularly those released under the FOIA. For a complete update, consult the Bush Library website at http://www.csdl.tamu.edu/bushlib/.

There is also Bush-related material in the papers of the presidents under whom he served. Sporadic entries are found in the files of the Lyndon B. Johnson Library (Austin, University of Texas); the Richard M. Nixon Presidential Materials Project (National Archives, College Park, Maryland); and the Gerald R. Ford Library (Ann Arbor, University of Michigan). Not surprisingly, the Ronald W. Reagan Library (Simi Valley, California) holds the most material—approximately 13,000 pages of Vice President Bush–related material—but the vast majority of it is presently closed under the terms of the PRA and the FOIA. Though much of the Bush material in the Reagan WHORM was transferred to the Bush Library, there remains Bush-related material in twenty different WHORM Subject Files at the Reagan Library, as well as a large amount of material in the files of other Reagan White House aides. A small, eclectic, and uncited collection of material, much of which is available elsewhere, can be found in the George H. Bush Presidential Papers [sic], BACM Research/Paperless Archives (CD format).

The vast majority of the papers of Bush's lieutenants are in private possession or else have been donated to an archive and are either restricted or not yet open to researchers. The exceptions at this writing are the Richard B. Cheney Files and Brent Scowcroft Files, Ford Library (consisting largely of material relating to Bush's tenure as director of central intelligence), and the incredibly rich James A. Baker III Papers, Princeton University, Department of Rare Books and Special Collections, Seeley G. Mudd Manuscript Library (MC#197).

The Miller Center at the University of Virginia has interviewed forty-four members of the Bush administration and made those interviews available online as the George H. W. Bush Oral History Project (http://millercenter.org /president/bush/oralhistory, accessed August 2014). Singular in their scope, these interviews are indispensable for a study of the first Bush.

For the public record of the Bush presidency, consult George H. W. Bush, *Public Papers of the Presidents: George Bush, 1989–1993*, 8 vols. (Washington, DC: U.S. Government Printing Office, 1990–1993), which includes all speeches, press releases, and public statements emanating from the White House or the 1992 presidential campaign. For background information, see also the *Public Papers of Richard M. Nixon* (6 vols., 1975), *Gerald R. Ford* (6 vols., 1975–1979), and *Ronald W. Reagan* (15 vols., 1982–1991). The Miller Center at the University of Virginia has made a key contribution to modern presidential historiography by publishing transcripts of presentations given by the alumni of the past ten presidencies. However, these volumes are marred by poor editing and proofreading and the lack of an index; Kenneth E. Thompson, ed., *Portraits of American Presidents*, vol. 10, *The Bush Presidency* (Lanham, MD: University Press of America, 1997) is no exception.

British journalist David Frost has done a series of interviews with Bush that is quite helpful. Frost's first set of interviews (including an interview with Mrs. Bush), originally broadcast on the Public Broadcasting System (PBS) on 2 and 3 January 1991, was of particular interest because at the moment he interviewed Bush, Desert Storm was about to commence. The second, broadcast on the Arts and Entertainment Network in June 1998, shows a more contemplative Bush, thinking beyond the immediacy of his presidency and toward its legacy; particularly poignant is a portion of the interview shot at the Berlin Wall.

It is impossible to research the modern presidency without using press reports—both in the popular newsmagazines of the period and in the more elite newspapers and political journals. For a depth of political reporting available in no other source, scholars must begin their study of the modern presidency in the pages of the *National Journal* (*NJ*). Despite the anti-Bush tone of its editorial page, the *New York Times* (*NYT*) continues to offer the best basis for a factual and chronological foundation for modern historical events. The *Washington Post* (*WP*) offers a greater depth of political reporting and analysis than does the *NYT*; it also offers an even deeper anti-Bush bias (for this book, readers will find that I followed the reporting of the *WP* in its weekly version, the *Washington Post National Weekly Edition* [*WPNWE*]). I consulted many popular newsmagazines in the course of my research; for depth of reporting, I found myself most often referring to the pages of *U.S. News & World Report* (*USN&WR*).

Bush's first memoir, *Looking Forward: An Autobiography* (New York: Bantam Books, 1987), written with his friend journalist Vic Gold, is a classic campaign biography—little depth of analysis, coupled with a hasty storytelling by the authors. But his second and third volumes of memoirs show a literary voice that sets him apart from his post–World War II predecessors—he is chatty, anecdotal, informal, brief and to the point, and only occasionally analytical. Bush's second memoir, written with Brent Scowcroft, is quite singular. *A World Transformed* (New York: Knopf, 1998) is a joint memoir by Bush and his director of national security, each of whom contributes to the volume in his own voice, with their contributions labeled by name. These recollections are fleshed out by lengthy inserts from Scowcroft's Memoranda of Conversations (Memcons). The result is a fascinating literary conversation between these two leaders about Bush's foreign policy (domestic policy is ignored). It is prone to a moment-by-moment account; nevertheless, it is highly readable and offers a fresh approach to the genre of the presidential memoir. It can be argued that *All the Best, George Bush: My Life in Letters and Other Writings*, 2nd ed. (New York: Scribner, 2013) is the third volume of George Bush's memoirs. Included with the collection of diary entries and letters, both official and personal, are Bush's reflective and chatty—and often revealing—annotations. While there are gaps (nothing, for example, on the Willie Horton controversy, and nothing that particularly illuminates the relationship between Bush and the presidency of his son), the depth of what is included qualifies this as the best published primary source on the Bush presidency. A full two-thirds of the book offers material dated before his presidency; there are four chapters on the presidency—one per year—and a chapter on the post-presidency ("Anchor to Windward") that features a particularly illuminating correspondence with Hugh Sidey and Bill Clinton.

Jeffrey A. Engel and George H. W. Bush, *The China Diary of George H. W. Bush* (Princeton, NJ: Princeton University Press, 2008), offers indispensable observations on that period in Bush's career. Aside from those included in the *Public Papers*, selected Bush speeches are included in George H. W. Bush, *Speaking of Freedom: The Collected Speeches* (New York: Scribner, 2009). Bush also contributed to David Valdez, *George Herbert Walker Bush: A Photographic Profile* (College Station: Texas A&M University Press, 1997)—the author was Bush's official White House photographer, and the book's captions are written by Bush.

The Bush administration has been well covered in the two most influential historical surveys of the period. James T. Patterson's entry into the iconic Oxford History of the United States series, *Restless Giant: The United States from Watergate to* Bush v. Gore (New York: Oxford University Press, 2005), includes a worthy chapter ("Bush 41") that is sourced by a wide swath of the available literature. Sean Wilentz, *The Age of Reagan: 1974–2008* (New York: Harper Perennial, 2008), is as well sourced as Patterson, but his chapter on Bush ("Reaganism and Realism") is more interpretative.

Bush has yet to find his perfect biographer, but there are four worthy entries. The most detailed, making wide use of the then-available primary sources, is Herbert S. Parmet, *George Bush: The Life of a Lone Star Yankee* (New York: Scribner, 1997); this strongly written and interesting read makes good use of a wide number of interviews and of an exclusive access to many of Bush's then-restricted papers and diaries. Parmet is particularly strong in analyzing the interplay of Bush's northeastern and Texas roots, on both his personality and his politics. However, he chooses to spend most of his time on the prepresidential years, and the whole of 1992 is covered in less than twenty pages. Iconic political reporter Tom Wicker, *George Herbert Walker Bush: A Penguin Life* (New York: Penguin, 2004), places Bush in a strong contextual background, despite a paucity of secondary sources ("one of my best sources was my own memory" [p. 228]); Wicker's chapter on the fall of the Soviet Union is particularly strong. Timothy Naftali's entry into the American Presidents Series, *George H. W. Bush* (New York: Times Books, 2007), is in reality a large interpretive essay that settles on being largely critical of its subject. Both thoughtful and written with grace and ease, the book is strongest on foreign policy. On a more limited scale, Joe Hyams, *Flight of the Avenger: George Bush at War* (New York: Harcourt Brace Jovanovich, 1991), offers a generally positive view of Bush's World War II service, written with the assistance of the Bush White House. The style is graceful, and it remains the best treatment of the young Bush.

Literally in a class by themselves are two biographies-cum-memoirs, written by Bush's children. Doro Bush Koch, *My Father, My President: A Personal*

Account of the Life of George H. W. Bush (New York: Warner Books, 2006), is a chatty entry and is based primarily on a large number of useful interviews. However, there is little new or revelatory here—most of the material has been discussed elsewhere. The same can be said for George W. Bush, *41: A Portrait of My Father* (New York: Crown, 2014), as it is largely a collection of previously published vignettes, with little new interpretation of the subject by his son.

The other biographies of Bush leave much to be desired. The most hagiographic is Fitzhugh Green, *George Bush: An Intimate Portrait* (New York: Hippocrene Books, 1989). Completely uncritical of his subject and providing little in the way of citation, the author irritates the reader by constantly dropping into the first person to tell the reader what *he* was doing at any point. Two biographies treat Bush as a common criminal. Webster Griffin Tarpley and Anton Chaitkin's *George Bush: The Unauthorized Biography*, rev. ed. (Washington, DC: Executive Intelligence Review, 2004) is an anti-Bush screed written by two supporters of Lyndon LaRouche who offer little substantive evidence for their message. Bill Weinberg, *George Bush: The Super-Spy Drug-Smuggling President* (New York: Shadow Press, 1992), labels Bush a "world-class drug trafficker. Sinister spymaster with tentacles spanning the planet—the most corrupt president in United States History" (p. 1). It too has no real evidentiary support; both Tarpley and Chaitkin's and Weinberg's books can be safely ignored by the serious researcher. Instant historical analyses, shallow in their scope, include Mark Sufrin, *The Story of George Bush: The Forty-First President of the United States* (Milwaukee: Gareth Stevens Publishers, 1989), and Doug Wead, *Man of Integrity* (Eugene, OR: Harvest House Publishers, 1988). Robert B. Stinnett, *George Bush: His World War II Years* (Washington, DC: Brassey's, 1992), deals less with Bush than with World War II in general. Richard Ben Cramer's *Being Poppy: A Portrait of George Herbert Walker Bush* (New York: Simon & Schuster, 2013) is adapted from his book on the 1992 election, *What It Takes* (below). It is also brief and unfinished, as Cramer died midproject.

Reference works with entries on Bush include Richard S. Conley, *Historical Dictionary of the Reagan-Bush Era* (Lanham, MD: Scarecrow Press, 2007); Gaddis Smith, "George Bush," in Henry F. Graff, ed., *The Presidents: A Reference History*, 2nd ed. (New York: Scribner, 1996); John Robert Greene, *Presidential Profiles: The George H. W. Bush Years* (New York: Facts on File, 2006); Peter B. Levy, *Encyclopedia of the Reagan-Bush Years* (Westport, CT: Greenwood Press, 1996); and Gary Boyd Roberts, *Ancestors of American Presidents* (Boston: New England Historic Genealogical Society, 1989). Particularly useful are the four volumes of the proceedings of the 1997 conference on the Bush presidency, held at Hofstra University (New York). These are Meena Bose and Rosanna Perotti, eds., *From Cold War to the New World Order: The Foreign Policy of George Bush* (Westport, CT: Greenwood Press, 2002); Leslie D. Feldman and Rosanna Perotti, eds., *Honor and Loyalty: Inside the Politics of the George H. W. Bush White House* (Westport, CT: Greenwood Press, 2002); Richard Himelfarb and Rosanna Perotti, eds., *Principle over Politics? The Domestic Policy of the George H. W. Bush Presidency* (Westport, CT: Praeger, 2004); and William F. Levantrosser and Rosanna Perotti, eds., *A Noble Calling: Character and the George H. W. Bush Presidency* (Westport, CT: Praeger, 2004).

"George Bush: A Sense of Duty," an hour-long production for the Arts and Entertainment Network's *Biography* series (first broadcast November 1996), concentrates almost exclusively on Bush's prepresidential years. That background, based largely on interviews with Bush family members, is strong. However, the treatment of Bush's political career is perfunctory, and the fleeting treatment of his presidency is platitudinal. A much fuller documentary treatment, with a wide array of interviews from alumni of the Bush administration, is *American Experience:* "George H. W. Bush" (PBS Home Video, WGBH Educational Foundation, 2008), for which this author served as a script consultant. The counterpoint to the *American Experience* piece is *41* (HBO Documentary Films, 2012). In this film, all the commentary is by Bush himself; perhaps as a result the film is a hagiographic gloss-over of its subject, with massive gaps in the narrative.

The reporting of Walter Pincus and Bob Woodward is an excellent starting point for a study of Bush's prepresidential career. Their six-part investigative series, which ran in the *WP* on 10–16 August 1988, forms an excellent short biography of Bush in the years before he reached the White House. Richard Nixon, *Memoirs of Richard Nixon* (New York: Grosset and Dunlap, 1978), is surprisingly silent on Bush's role in the Nixon administration. A bit more useful is Walter Issacson, *Kissinger: A Biography* (New York: Simon & Schuster, 1992), which is good on the relationship between UN ambassador Bush and the Nixon White House—particularly on the issue of the expulsion of Taiwan. Both Gerald R. Ford, *A Time to Heal: The Autobiography of Gerald R. Ford* (New York: Harper & Row, 1979), and Robert T. Hartmann, *Palace Politics: An Inside Account of the Ford Years* (New York: McGraw-Hill, 1980), offer useful accounts on Ford's passing over of Bush for the vice presidency in both 1974 and 1976, as well as on Ford's choice of Bush as the American envoy to the People's Republic of China and as his director of central intelligence. Tim Weiner, *Legacy of Ashes: The History of the CIA* (New York: Doubleday, 2007), is good on Bush's tenure as director of central intelligence. Laura Kalman, *Right Star Rising: A New Politics, 1974–1980* (New York: Norton, 2010), offers an excellent outline of the 1980 Republican primaries. See also Richard Ben Cramer, "How He Got Here," *Esquire*, June 1991, pp. 74–82+; John Robert Greene, *The Presidency of Gerald R. Ford* (Lawrence: University Press of Kansas, 1995); and Howard Kohn and Vicki Monks, "The Dirty Secrets of George Bush," *Rolling Stone*, 3 November 1988, pp. 41–44+.

Bush's vice presidency is examined by L. Edward Purcell, "George Herbert Walker Bush," in *The Vice Presidents: A Biographical Dictionary*, ed. L. Edward Purcell (New York: Facts on File, 1998), and in Chase Untermeyer, "Looking Forward: George Bush as Vice President," in Timothy Walch, ed., *At the President's Side: The Vice Presidency in the Twentieth Century* (Columbia: University of

Missouri Press, 1997). It was also scrutinized in *Running Mate* (Public Broadcasting System, first aired October 1996). Ronald Reagan, *The Reagan Diaries* (New York: HarperCollins, 2007), is quite useful, offering a broad documentation of the Bush-Reagan relationship—even to the point of being a seminal source for Bush's role in Iran-Contra. Less helpful are Kiron K. Skinner, Annelise Anderson, and Martin Anderson, eds., *Reagan: A Life in Letters* (New York: Free Press, 2003), and Ronald Reagan, *An American Life: The Autobiography* (New York: Simon & Schuster, 1990), in which the author all but ignores Bush. Nancy Reagan, however, pays particular attention to Bush in her memoir, *My Turn* (New York: Dell, 1989), where she makes it clear that, at best, she tolerated her husband's vice president. However, a more balanced analysis of Bush's tenure as vice president can be found in the growing literature on the Reagan presidency. The most telling observations on Bush are in Lou Cannon, *President Reagan: The Role of a Lifetime* (New York: Simon & Schuster, 1991), which establishes the personal affinity between Reagan and his vice president. Herbert Abrams, *The President's Been Shot: Confusion, Disability and the 25th Amendment in the Aftermath of the Attempted Assassination of Ronald Reagan* (New York: Norton, 1992), concludes that Bush "took pains to keep his conduct loyal, dutiful and unassuming," but that during the crisis Edwin Meese, James Baker, and Michael Deaver "were the President of the United States" (pp. 187–188). Books that offer the most telling details on Bush and Iran-Contra are Theodore Draper, *A Very Thin Line: The Iran-Contra Affairs* (New York: Hill & Wang, 1991), and Jane Mayer and Doyle McManus, *Landslide: The Unmaking of the President, 1984–1988* (Boston: Houghton Mifflin, 1988), George P. Shultz, *Turmoil and Triumph: My Years as Secretary of State* (New York: Scribner, 1993), and Bob Woodward, *Shadow: Five Presidents and the Legacy of Watergate* (New York: Simon & Schuster, 1999).

The best brief survey of the 1988 presidential election is found in the final three chapters of Bob Schieffer and Gary Paul Gates, *The Acting President* (New York: Dutton, 1989). Also useful for an overview of the election is Donald Morrison, ed., *The Winning of the White House, 1988* (New York: Time Incorporated Books, 1988). The best scholarly analysis of the election—indeed, one of the most thoughtful works on presidential politics written in recent years—is W. Lance Bennett, *The Governing Crisis: Media, Money, and Marketing in American Elections* (New York: St. Martin's Press, 1996). Using admirable detail and excellent anecdotal examples, Bennett argues that the 1988 election began a political age "in which electoral choices are of little consequence" (p. 28). He suggests that successful presidential campaigns in the modern period are those that emphasize symbolism as opposed to issues—a fact that Bush's 1988 campaign understood and Michael Dukakis's did not. Much thinner in substance, but entertaining nonetheless, is Jack W. Germond and Jules Witcover, *Whose Broad Stripes and Bright Stars? The Trivial Pursuit of the Presidency, 1988* (New York: Warner Books, 1989). A great deal of press coverage resulted from the release of Richard Ben Cramer's *What It Takes: The Way to the White House* (New York: Random House,

1992). Most observers noted the informality of Cramer's "inside the campaign" writing style. However, that technique often becomes shrilly hyperbolic (particularly irritating is his use of capital letters and multiple exclamation points to get the reader's attention). Just as important to note is the fact that 125 of the 130 chapters of this massive work deal with the primaries as opposed to the general election.

The design of the Bush campaign is best explored in an excellent biography of its primary strategist, John Brady's *Bad Boy: The Life and Politics of Lee Atwater* (Reading, MA: Addison-Wesley, 1997). Brady's book should be joined with *Boogie Man: The Lee Atwater Story* (2009), an award-winning documentary with a balanced script and excellent interviews. Peggy Noonan served as a speechwriter for both Reagan and Bush; her breezy *What I Saw at the Revolution: A Political Life in the Reagan Era* (New York: Ivy Books, 1990) is particularly interesting on the crafting of Bush's acceptance speech to the Republican convention ("a thousand points of light" and "read my lips"). For more information on the decision to include the "read my lips" sound bite, see Bob Woodward, "The Anatomy of a Decision," *WPNWE*, 12–18 October 1992, pp. 6–9.

An excellent series of interviews with the principals of the 1988 campaign is provided in Michael Gilette, *Snapshots of the 1988 Presidential Campaign: The Bush Campaign* (vol. 1), *The Dukakis Campaign* (vol. 2), and *The Jackson Campaign* (vol. 3) (Austin: Lyndon B. Johnson School of Public Affairs, University of Texas, 1992). There is no fully researched biography of Michael Dukakis. Richard Gaines and Michael Segal, *Dukakis: The Man Who Would Be President* (New York: Avon Books, 1987), is a sycophantic campaign biography. See also William Boot, "Campaign '88: TV Overdoses on the Inside Dope," *Columbia Journalism Review* 2 (January/February 1989): 23–29; Peter Davis and Martin Amis, "The Two-Ring Circus and the White Man's Ball" (on the Republican and Democratic Conventions), *Esquire*, November 1988, pp. 125–136; Gerald M. Pomper, ed., *The Election of 1988: Reports and Interpretations* (Chatham, NJ: Chatham House, 1989); "Quest for the Presidency: The Candidates Debate," *Reader's Digest*, October 1988, pp. 62–73; and Guido H. Stempel and John W. Windhauser, eds., *The Media in the 1984 and 1988 Presidential Campaigns* (Westport, CT: Greenwood Press, 1991). John Gray Geer, *In Defense of Negativity: Attack Ads in Presidential Campaigns* (Chicago: University of Chicago Press, 2006), has a chapter on 1988, which concludes that neither side broke new ground on incivility. See also David Mark, *Going Dirty: The Art of Negative Campaigning* (Lanham, MD: Rowman and Littlefield, 2009).

An excellent analysis of the Reagan legacy to the Bush administration can be found in the 14 May 1988 *NJ*, in an entire issue titled "Reagan's Legacy: The Paradox of Power." See also Walter Dean Burnham, "The Reagan Heritage," in Pomper, ed., *The Election of 1988* (above). Michael Schaller, *Reckoning with Reagan: America and Its President in the 1980s* (New York: Oxford University Press, 1992), though based almost exclusively on secondary sources, nevertheless offers a particularly balanced view of the Reagan legacy. James Pemberton, *Exit with Honor: The Life and Presidency of Ronald Reagan* (Armonk, NY: M. E. Sharpe, 1997), is a largely critical work that combines the first serious usage of the archival material at the Reagan Library with thoughtful, balanced prose.

The vast majority of the available surveys of the Bush presidency still accept the thesis of the English political scientist Richard Rose. In his well-written and significant book *The Postmodern Presidency: George Bush Meets the World* (Chatham, NJ: Chatham House, 1991), Rose advances the belief that Bush was a "guardian president [who] rejects the idea that leadership must be expansive" (p. 308). The surveys of the Bush administration that were written on the heels of the end of that administration—including the first edition of *this* volume (John Robert Greene, *The Presidency of George Bush* [Lawrence: University Press of Kansas, 2000])—adopted Rose's hypothesis. In fact, several of them take his hypothesis beyond the available evidence. Michael Duffy and Dan Goodgame were two White House correspondents for *Time* magazine; their rather long-winded *Marching in Place: The Status Quo Presidency of George Bush* (New York: Simon & Schuster, 1992) is highly critical of its subject and concludes that "Bush was popular, we finally realized, not despite his lip service approach to domestic policy but *because* of it" (p. 12). David Mervin, *George Bush and the Guardianship Presidency* (New York: St. Martin's Press, 1996), the first true scholarly survey of the Bush presidency, uses several oral history interviews as he adopts Rose's hypothesis. Ryan T. Barilleaux and Mark J. Rozell are very critical of their subject in their *Power and Prudence: The Presidency of George H. W. Bush* (College Station: Texas A&M University Press, 2004), but they generally accept Rose's view, as they label Bush an "incrementalist." There is, however, one exception to this trend. Michael Nelson and Barbara A. Perry, eds., *Inside the Presidency of George H. W. Bush* (Ithaca, NY: Cornell University Press, 2014), is an indispensable collection of essays that make heavy use of the Miller Center's George H. W. Bush Oral History Project (above). The breadth of the essays qualifies this book as a survey, and it is the first to attack, as a whole, the "guardian president" moniker popularized by Rose and others.

Surveys offering more limited assistance to the researcher are Ryan J. Barilleaux and Mary E. Stuckey, *Leadership and the Bush Presidency* (Westport, CT: Praeger, 1992); Wesley B. Borucki, *George H. W. Bush: In Defense of Principle* (New York: Nova Science, 2011); Colin Campbell and Bert Rockman, eds., *The Bush Presidency: First Appraisals* (Chatham, NJ: Chatham House, 1991); Dilys Hill and Phil Williams, eds., *The Bush Presidency: Triumphs and Adversities* (New York: St. Martin's Press, 1994); Eric E. Otenyo and Nancy S. Lind, *The First World Presidency: George H. W. Bush, 1989–1993* (Youngstown, NY: Teneo Press, 2009); and Charles Tiefer, *The Semi-sovereign Presidency: The Bush Administration's Strategy for Governing without Congress* (Boulder, CO: Westview Press, 1994).

Surveys of the American presidency are led by the outstanding Lewis L. Gould, *The Modern American Presidency*, 2nd ed., revised and updated (Lawrence:

University Press of Kansas, 2009). Of the several useful chapters on Bush in recent studies on the modern presidency, one should consult Fred Greenstein, *The Presidential Difference: Leadership Style from FDR to George W. Bush* (New York: Free Press, 2000); Paul Brace and Barbara Hinckley, *Follow the Leader: Opinion Polls and the Modern Presidents* (New York: Basic Books, 1992); Charles O. Jones, *Separate but Equal Branches: Congress and the Presidency* (Chatham, NJ: Chatham House, 1995); Robert Shogan, *The Riddle of Power: Presidential Leadership from Truman to Bush* (New York: Dutton, 1991); Stephen Skowronek, *The Politics Presidents Make: Leadership from John Adams to George Bush* (Cambridge, MA: Belknap Press of Harvard University Press, 1993), and Stephen Skowronek, *Presidential Leadership in Political Time: Reprise and Reappraisal* (Lawrence: University Press of Kansas, 2011).

The political background of Bush's vice president is well explored in Richard F. Fenno Jr., *The Making of a Senator: Dan Quayle* (Washington, DC: Congressional Quarterly Books, 1989). Best on the choice of Quayle as Bush's running mate—as well as offering one of the only detailed analyses of Quayle's contributions as vice president—is Bob Woodward and David S. Broder's *The Man Who Would Be President: Dan Quayle* (New York: Simon & Schuster, 1992). The penultimate conclusion of this brief book, taken from the author's reporting for the *WP*, shocked many Washington insiders: "It is clear that—all jokes aside—Dan Quayle has proved himself to be a skillful player of the political game, with a competitive drive that has been underestimated repeatedly by his rivals" (p. 18). Quayle's first autobiography, *Standing Firm* (New York: Harper, 1994) is comparatively well written but serves primarily as a defense of its author from a myriad of political and press-related slights. His second, *Worth Fighting For* (Nashville, TN: Word Publishing, 1999), can be safely dismissed as a campaign mantra, written in advance of his aborted 2000 presidential run. See also "Running Mate" (above) for an interesting interview with Quayle and his wife, Marilyn; and Dan Quayle, "Standing Firm: Personal Reflections on Being Vice President," in Walch, ed., *At the President's Side* (above) for a not-altogether unbiased view of events. One of the best discussions of Quayle in the Bush White House is found in the memoir of Bush's principal adviser for space exploration, Mark Albrecht, *Falling Back to Earth: A First Hand Account of the Great Space Race and the End of the Cold War* (Washington, DC: New Media Books, 2011).

On Bush and the Republican Party, Geoffrey M. Kabaservice, *Rule and Ruin: The Downfall of Moderation and the Destruction of the Republican Party, from Eisenhower to the Tea Party* (New York: Oxford University Press, 2012), is both provocative and well researched. Also useful is Daniel Galvin, *Presidential Party Building: Dwight D. Eisenhower to George W. Bush* (Princeton, NJ: Princeton University Press, 2009).

Two excellent books analyze the sociocultural scene during the Bush years. William Greider's *Who Will Tell the People? The Betrayal of American Democracy* (New York: Simon & Schuster, 1992) is both superb and caustic in its criticism of the "politics as usual" mentality; his placing the blame squarely on the American people made it one of the most talked-about books of the election year. The second is Kevin Phillips, *The Politics of Rich and Poor: Wealth and the American Electorate in the Reagan Aftermath* (New York: Random House, 1990), which makes a clear case that the Reagan years despoiled the American economy. Nancy Gibbs and Michael Duffy, *The Preacher and the Presidents: Billy Graham in the White House* (New York: Center Street, 2007), offers an excellent primer on the impact of the evangelical movement on Bush's White House.

Bradley H. Patterson, *To Serve the President: Continuity and Innovation in the White House Staff* (Washington, DC: Brookings Institution Press, 2008), despite its authorship by the preeminent authority on the White House staff, is disappointing on Bush. Shirley Anne Warshaw is, at present, the leading student of White House–cabinet relations. Her *Powersharing: White House–Cabinet Relations in the Modern Presidency* (Albany: State University of New York Press, 1996) surveys the effect of the cabinet upon policy from Nixon to Clinton. Regarding Bush, Warshaw argues that one of the reasons for what she believes to be his failed domestic policy was that the cabinet became "coopted and oriented toward departmental rather than presidential objectives," due to a lack of White House control (p. 197). An inside view that challenges this thesis is Dick Thornburgh, *Where the Evidence Leads: An Autobiography* (Pittsburgh: University of Pittsburgh Press, 2010). Kenneth T. Walsh, *Family of Freedom: Presidents and African Americans in the White House* (Boulder, CO: Paradigm, 2011), is marred by the author's proclivity to take the word of his interviewees at face value. Warshaw's *The Domestic Presidency: Policy Making in the White House* (Boston: Allyn & Bacon, 1997), a study of the White House Office(s) of Domestic Policy since 1968, presents the Bush administration as having no coherent policy agenda.

On Bush and Congress, Charles M. Cameron, *Veto Bargaining: Presidents and the Politics of Power* (Cambridge: Cambridge University Press, 2000), offers a strong analytical survey. Also quite useful is the work of Richard S. Conley: "A Revisionist View of George Bush and Congress, 1989: Congressional Support, 'Veto Strength,' and Legislative Strategy," *White House Studies* 2 (2002): 359–374, and "George Bush and the 102nd Congress: The Impact of Public and Private Veto Threats on Policy Outcomes," *Presidential Studies Quarterly* 33 (2003): 730–750. See also John Burke, *The Institutional Presidency* (Baltimore: Johns Hopkins University Press, 1992); Kenneth E. Collier, *Between the Branches: The White House Office of Legislative Affairs* (Pittsburgh: University of Pittsburgh Press, 1997); John Hart, *The Presidential Branch: The Executive Office of the President from Washington to Clinton* (Chatham, NJ: Chatham House, 1995); Judith E. Michaels, *The President's Call: Executive Leadership from FDR to George Bush* (Pittsburgh: University of Pittsburgh Press, 1997); and Judith E. Michaels, "A View from the Top: Reflections of the Bush Presidential Appointees," *Public Administration Review* 55 (1995): 273–283.

Although I take issue with the hypothesis stated in its subtitle, James P. Pfiffner's *The Bush Transition: A Friendly Takeover* (Richmond, VA: Institute of Public Policy, George Mason University, 1995) is an important work. Martha Joynt Kumar and Terry Sullivan, eds., *The White House World: Transitions, Organization, and Office Operations* (College Station: Texas A&M University Press, 2003), makes wide use of the White House Interview program but offers little new information on the transition. No fully researched biography of John Tower yet exists, nor is there a balanced secondary study of his catastrophic appointment process. We are left only with Tower's *Consequences: A Personal and Political Memoir* (Boston: Little, Brown, 1991), an angry and ultimately completely unconvincing book, which blames Sam Nunn for personally scuttling the nomination to advance his own presidential ambitions, hints at gossip about the private life of a reporter who covered Tower's bid for cabinet confirmation, and attempts an explanation for all the charges against him (his explanation for the charges of drunkenness is particularly unconvincing). *Consideration of the Honorable John G. Tower to Be Secretary of Defense: Report Together with Minority, Supplemental, and Additional Views* (Washington, DC: Government Printing Office, 1989) is the committee report presented to the Senate. For the inevitable fallout from the Tower defeat, see John M. Barry, *The Ambition and the Power: The Fall of Jim Wright—A True Story of Washington* (New York: Viking, 1989).

Each of the memoirs written by Bush's domestic policy aides is defensive in tone and offers no balanced treatment of policy development. See, for example, Charles Kolb, *White House Daze: The Unmaking of Domestic Policy in the Bush Years* (New York: Free Press, 1993); James P. Pinkerton, *What Comes Next: The End of Big Government—and the New Paradigm Ahead* (New York: Hyperion, 1995); and John Podhoretz, *Hell of a Ride: Backstage at the White House Follies, 1989–1993* (New York: Simon & Schuster, 1993).

But there are several interesting and often strong specific studies of domestic decision making under Bush.

THE AMERICANS WITH DISABILITIES ACT (ADA)

The best short survey of the genesis of the ADA is Susan Gluck Mezey, *Disabling Interpretations: The Americans with Disabilities Act in Federal Court* (Pittsburgh: University of Pittsburgh Press, 2005). While marred by problems of editing, Fred Pelka, ed., *What We Have Done: An Oral History of the Disability Rights Movement* (Amherst: University of Massachusetts Press, 2012), fills in, with testimony, Gluck Mezey's excellent narrative. Two government publications, Rodman D. Griffin, "The Disabilities Act: Protecting the Rights of the Disabled Will Have Far-Reaching Effects," *CQ Researcher* 1, no. 32 (1991), and Major R. Owens, *Americans with Disabilities Act: Initial Accessibility Good but Important Barriers Remain*

(Washington, DC: U.S. General Accounting Office, 1993), are indispensable to a study of the ADA. Less helpful, and containing errors, is Ruth Colker, *The Disability Pendulum: The First Decade of the Americans with Disabilities Act* (New York: New York University Press, 2007). See also Susan Dudley Gold, *Americans with Disabilities Act* (Salt Lake City, UT: Benchmark Books, 2010).

CIVIL RIGHTS

Kenneth O'Reilly, in his *Nixon's Piano: Presidents and Racial Politics from Washington to Clinton* (New York: Free Press, 1995), is quite critical of Bush's civil rights policies; in his chapter on Bush, "The Quota Kings," he concludes that Bush appealed to white nationalism in an effort to protect his electoral base. More balanced, although also critical of its subject, is John Berlau's "The Quota Paradox," *Policy Review*, no. 68 (Spring 1994): 7, which analyzes Bush's high approval ratings among African Americans despite his opposition to racial quotas and his initial refusal to sign the civil rights bill of 1991. See also Stephen Schull, *A Kinder, Gentler Racism? The Reagan-Bush Civil Rights Legacy* (New York: M. E. Sharpe, 1993).

CLEAN AIR ACT AMENDMENTS

Richard E. Cohen's well-written *Washington at Work: Back Rooms and Clean Air* (New York: Macmillan, 1992) takes the reader through the complexities of crafting and adopting the Clean Air Act Amendments of 1990, concluding that the lion's share of the credit for the bill goes not to Bush but to Senate majority leader George Mitchell. Less helpful are Johnathan M. Davidson and Joseph M. Norbeck, *An Interactive History of the Clean Air Act: Scientific and Policy Perspectives* (Waltham, MA: Elsevier, 2012); and Byron W. Daynes and Glen Sussman, *White House Politics and the Environment: Franklin Roosevelt to George W. Bush* (College Station: Texas A&M University Press, 2010)—which errantly names John Sununu as Bush's secretary of the interior (p. 156).

DRUG POLICY

For studies of Bush's drug policies, see Charles M. Fuss Jr., *Sea of Grass: The Maritime Drug War, 1970–1990* (Annapolis, MD: Naval Institute Press, 1996); Al Giordano, "The War on Drugs: Who Drafted the Press?" *Washington Journalism Review* 12 (January–February 1990): 20–24; and Howard Kohn, "Cowboy in the Capital: Drug Czar Bill Bennett," *Rolling Stone*, 2 November 1989, pp. 41–43.

EDUCATION

One must begin Bush's education policy by reading *A Nation at Risk: The Imperative for Education* (Washington, DC: Government Printing Office, 1983). Patrick J. McGuinn's *No Child Left Behind and the Transformation of Federal Education Policy, 1965–2005* (Lawrence: University Press of Kansas, 2006) is a masterful treatment of its subject. See also Susan Chira, "Lamar Alexander's Self-Help Course," *New York Times Magazine*, 23 November 1991, pp. 52+; and Edith Rasell and Lawrence Mishel, "The Truth about Education Spending," *Roll Call*, 21 May 1990, p. 23.

FLAG DESECRATION

The work of Robert Justin Goldstein is critical to an understanding of the flag-burning controversy. See his *Saving "Old Glory": The History of the American Flag Desecration Controversy* (Boulder, CO: Westview Press, 1995); *Burning the Flag: The Great 1989–1990 American Flag Desecration Controversy* (Kent, OH: Kent State University Press, 1996); and particularly his now-standard treatment, *Flag Burning and Free Speech: The Case of* Texas v. Johnson (Lawrence: University Press of Kansas, 2000).

HURRICANE ANDREW

Eugene F. Provenzo Jr. and Asterie Baker, *In the Eye of Hurricane Andrew* (Gainesville: University Press of Florida, 2002), is based largely on oral history interviews; it includes a balanced view of the failures of FEMA, as well as graphic descriptions of the damage wrought by the storm. It should be joined with David K. Twigg, *The Politics of Disaster: Tracking the Impact of Hurricane Andrew* (Gainesville: University Press of Florida, 2012), which offers a strong section on the storm's impact on the 1992 presidential election.

L.A. RIOTS

Gregory Alan-Williams, *A Gathering of Heroes: Reflections of Rage and Responsibility—A Memoir of the Los Angeles Riots* (Chicago: Academy Chicago Publishers, 1994), is brutally direct, reading as a cathartic venture for the author. Rodney King, *The Riot Within: My Journey from Rebellion to Redemption* (New York: HarperCollins, 2012), is less helpful.

Despite their political importance to the administration, very little of analytical substance has been written on Bush's economic policies. The student is left with four tremendously self-serving memoirs: L. William Seidman, *Full Faith and Credit: The Great S&L Debacle and Other Washington Sagas* (New York: Times Books, 1993), blames his political demise on John Sununu; Richard Darman, *Who's in Control? Polar Politics and the Sensible Center* (New York: Simon & Schuster, 1996), blames the budget crisis of 1990 on Newt Gingrich; Alan Greenspan, *The Age of Turbulence: Adventures in a New World* (New York: Penguin, 2007), attempts to explain why Bush blamed Greenspan's economic policies in part for his 1992 election loss; and Robert A. Mosbacher Sr., *Going to Windward: A Mosbacher Family Memoir* (College Station: Texas A&M University Press), which is more useful for Mosbacher's service as Bush's chief fund-raiser than it is for his service as secretary of commerce.

David Lawrence Mason, *From Buildings and Loans to Bailouts: A History of the American Savings and Loan Industry, 1831–1995* (Cambridge: Cambridge University Press, 2004), offers a strong survey of Bush's response to the S&L crisis. See also James R. Barth, S. Trimbarth, and Glenn Yago, *The Savings and Loan Crisis: Lessons from a Regulatory Failure* (Norwell, MA: Kluwer Academic Publishers, 2004); Martin Mayer, *The Greatest-Ever Bank Robbery: The Collapse of the Savings and Loan Industry* (New York: Scribner, 1990); Steven Pressman, "Behind the S&L Crisis," *Editorial Research Reports*, 4 November 1988, p. 550; and Catherine Yang, "Bush's S&L Plan: Full of Good Intentions—and Holes," *Business Week*, February 1989, p. 32.

The budget fight of 1991 has yet to find its historian. Richard E. Cohen, *Rostenkowski: The Pursuit of Power and the End of the Old Politics* (Chicago: Ivan R. Dee, 1999), offers the best analysis. Bits are found in David Wessell, *Red Ink: Inside the High-Stakes Politics of the Federal Budget* (New York: Crown, 2012). Less helpful is Richard M. Pious, "The Limits of Rational Choice: Bush and Clinton Budget Summitry," *Presidential Studies Quarterly* 29 (1999): 617–637. For other facets of domestic and economic policy, see D. Alan Bromley, *The President's Scientists: Reminiscences of a White House Science Advisor* (New Haven, CT: Yale University Press, 2004); Philip J. Funigiello, *Chronic Politics: Health Care Security from FDR to George Bush* (Lawrence: University Press of Kansas, 2005); Robert Goodwin and Thomas Kinkade, *Points of Light: A Celebration of the American Spirit of Giving* (New York: Center Street, 2006); and Robert J. Spitzer, *The Politics of Gun Control*, 5th ed. (Boulder, CO: Paradigm, 2012).

Jan Crawford Greenburg, *Supreme Conflict: The Inside Story of the Struggle for Control of the United States Supreme Court* (New York: Penguin, 2007), offers a full chapter of "inside baseball" on the choice of David Souter. Tinsley E. Yarbrough, *David Hackett Souter: Traditional Republican on the Rehnquist Court* (New York: Oxford University Press, 2005), includes less on Souter's choice than does Crawford Greenburg but offers much more on the confirmation process.

Each of the major studies on the nomination of Clarence Thomas to the Supreme Court has been openly challenged as to both balance and accuracy. The book that makes the most obvious attempt at objectivity (despite the author's ultimate conclusion that Thomas was guilty of the charges levied against him) was written by *Wall Street Journal* reporters Jane Mayer and Jill Abramson, *Strange Justice: The Selling of Clarence Thomas* (Boston: Houghton Mifflin, 1994). Nevertheless, because this is a work of journo-history, one must be wary of their sources. More skewed in its analysis is Timothy M. Phelps and Helen Winternitz, *Capitol Games: The Inside Story of Clarence Thomas, Anita Hill, and a Supreme Court Nomination* (New York: Harper Perennial, 1992). One must obviously be cautious when using both Clarence Thomas, *My Grandfather's Son: A Memoir* (New York: Harper, 2007), and Anita Hill's *Speaking Truth to Power* (New York: Doubleday, 1997), although they are both necessary reads on the subject, if for no other reason than to help reconstruct the maze of depositions and testimony in a logical manner. Although Jan Crawford Greenburg, *Supreme Conflict* (above), covers the period of Thomas's choice and confirmation, the book offers less than two pages on it. Ultimately, then, there has been no satisfying statement of "who lied" in their testimonies. Historians must at this point judge for themselves by reading Anita Miller, ed., *The Complete Transcripts of the Clarence Thomas/Anita Hill Hearings* (Chicago: Academy Chicago Publishers, 1994), which also includes samples of the submitted evidence.

Each of the major players in the formation of the Bush administration's foreign and national security policies has contributed a memoir to the literature. George Bush and Brent Scowcroft, *A World Transformed*, is discussed above. James A. Baker III, *The Politics of Diplomacy: Revolution, War, and Peace* (New York: Putnam, 1995), is an encyclopedic tome, seemingly including every detail on Baker's tenure at the State Department. Baker's second volume of memoirs, *"Work Hard, Study . . . and Keep Out of Politics!": Adventures and Lessons from an Unexpected Public Life* (New York: Putnam, 2006), is the complete antithesis of his first memoir—written with wit and style, this volume shows Baker to be a good storyteller. Richard Cheney, *In My Time: A Personal and Political Memoir* (New York: Threshold Editions, 2011), is an unabashed attempt to make its author look both correct and prescient on all matters, taking unveiled shots at Baker, Scowcroft, and Schwarzkopf in the process. Colin Powell, *My American Journey* (New York: Random House, 1995), serves largely to document Powell's opposition to the haste with which the administration went to war in 1991. See also Zbigniew Brzezinski and Brent Scowcroft, *America and the World: Conversations on the Future of American Foreign Policy* (New York: Basic Books, 2008); Richard A. Clarke, *Against All Enemies: Inside America's War on Terror* (New York: Free Press, 2004); Robert M. Gates, *From the Shadows: The Ultimate Insider's Story of Five Presidents and How They Won the Cold War* (New York: Simon & Schuster, 1996); Richard N. Haass, *War of Necessity, War of Choice: A Memoir of Two Iraq Wars* (New York:

Simon & Schuster, 2009); Roman Popadiuk, *The Leadership of George Bush: An Insider's View of the Forty-First President* (College Station: Texas A&M University Press, 2009); Condoleezza Rice, *No Higher Honor: A Memoir of My Years in Washington* (New York: Broadway Paperbacks, 2011); George Tenet, *At the Center of the Storm: My Years at the CIA* (New York: HarperCollins, 2007); and Philip Zelikow and Condoleezza Rice, *Germany United and Europe Transformed: A Study in Statecraft* (Cambridge, MA: Harvard University Press, 1997).

With a strong sense of analysis as well as a strong use of primary source material, Christopher Maynard, *Out of the Shadows: George H. W. Bush and the End of the Cold War* (College Station: Texas A&M University Press, 2008), is the established starting point for any study of Bush's foreign policy. Maynard has largely supplanted Steven Hurst, *The Foreign Policy of the Bush Administration* (London: Cassell, 2000), a worthy survey but based almost exclusively on secondary sources. One should also consult Jeffrey A. Engel's excellent essay "The Making of a Global President," found in his *The China Diary of George H. W. Bush* (above). Useful, albeit brief on Bush, is George C. Herring, *From Colony to Superpower: U.S. Foreign Relations since 1776* (New York: Oxford University Press, 2008). For a criticism of both Bush and his foreign policy (at least until the Gulf War), see Margaret Thatcher, *The Downing Street Years* (New York: HarperCollins, 1993).

John P. Burke's chapter on Brent Scowcroft in his *Honest Broker? The National Security Advisor and Presidential Decision Making* (College Station: Texas A&M University Press, 2009) is a good summary on the foreign policy/national security structure in the Bush White House. Ivo H. Daalder and I. M. Destler, *In the Shadow of the Oval Office: Profiles of the National Security Advisers and the Presidents They Served—From JFK to George W. Bush* (New York: Simon & Schuster, 2009), is also of value. David F. Schmitz, *Brent Scowcroft: Internationalism and Post–Vietnam War Foreign Policy* (Lanham, MD: Rowman and Littlefield, 2011), is a disappointment that reveals very little about its subject.

Jean Garrison, *Making China Policy: From Nixon to George W. Bush* (Boulder, CO: Lynne Rienner, 2005), offers a chapter on Bush that is a particularly useful starting point. On the post-Tiananmen struggle with Congress over China policy, see David Skidmore and William Gates, "After Tiananmen: The Struggle over U.S. Policy toward China in the Bush Administration," *Presidential Studies Quarterly* 27 (1997): 514–539.

Bob Woodward, *The Commanders* (New York: Simon & Schuster, 1991), studies military decision making in the Bush administration. It is also the best available study of the decision making associated with both Operation Desert Shield and the Panamanian operation (Operation Just Cause). Additional works on the Panamanian episode are John Dinges, *Our Man in Panama: How General Noriega Used the U.S.—and Made Millions in Drugs and Arms* (New York: Random House, 1990); Eytan Gilboa, "The Panama Invasion Revisited: Lessons for the Use of Force in the Post–Cold War Era," *Political Science Quarterly* (1995–1996): 539–562; Seymour Hersh, "Our Man in Panama: The Creation of a Thug," *Life*,

March 1990, pp. 81–85+; and Frederick Kempe, *Divorcing the Dictator: America's Bungled Affair with Noriega* (New York: Putnam, 1990).

Michael Beschloss and Strobe Talbott, *At the Highest Levels: The Inside Story of the End of the Cold War* (Boston: Little, Brown, 1993), continues to be an excellent analysis of Soviet-American relations during the Bush presidency. Their Bush is a cautious Bush, moving slowly toward an inevitable denouement with Gorbachev. John Lewis Gaddis, *The Cold War: A New History* (New York: Penguin, 2005), portrays both Bush and Gorbachev as having little control over events. Vladislav M. Zubok, *A Failed Empire: The Soviet Union in the Cold War from Stalin to Gorbachev* (Chapel Hill: University of North Carolina Press, 2007), puts the blame for the fall of the USSR squarely on Gorbachev's shoulders. Serhii Plokhy, *The Last Empire: The Final Days of the Soviet Union* (New York: Basic Books, 2014), is a fast-reading survey that expertly traces the events of late 1991. Also useful are Raymond L. Garthoff, *The Great Transition: American-Soviet Relations and the End of the Cold War* (Washington, DC: Brookings Institution, 1994); and Jack F. Matlock, *Autopsy of an Empire: The American Ambassador's Account of the Collapse of the Soviet Union* (New York: Random House, 1995). Valuable on Gorbachev is Archie Brown, *The Gorbachev Factor* (New York: Oxford University Press, 1997); Dusko Doder and Louise Branson, *Gorbachev: Heretic in the Kremlin* (New York: Viking, 1990); Mikhail Gorbachev, *Memoirs* (New York: Doubleday, 1996); and Mikhail Gorbachev, *Gorbachev: On My Country and the World* (New York: Columbia University Press, 2000). Timothy J. Colton, *Yeltsin: A Life* (New York: Basic Books, 2008), is detailed and engagingly written; Leon Aron, *Yeltsin: A Revolutionary Life* (New York: St. Martin's Press, 2000), and Herbert J. Ellison, *Boris Yelstin and Russia's Democratic Transformation* (Seattle: University of Washington Press, 2006), are less so.

Jeffrey A. Engel, *The Fall of the Berlin Wall: The Revolutionary Legacy of 1989* (New York: Oxford University Press, 2009), is a collection of essays that are quite illuminating on its subject, particularly the author's introduction and Melvyn P. Leffler's "Dreams of Freedom, Temptations of Power," which offers a useful survey of the events leading up to the reunification of Germany. Elizabeth Pond, *Beyond the Wall: Germany's Road to Unification* (Washington, DC: Brookings Institution, 1993), is the standard work on the subject.

Not surprisingly, the richest part of the Bush literature deals with the Persian Gulf War. The student should begin with Richard W. Stewart, *War in the Persian Gulf: Operations Desert Shield and Desert Storm, August 1990–March 1991* (Washington, DC: U.S. Army Center of Military History, U.S. Government Printing Office, 2010). A seventy-page pamphlet, Stewart's work is nevertheless a strong survey of the military story of the war. Lawrence Freedman and Efraim Karsh, *The Gulf Conflict, 1990–1991: Diplomacy and War in the New World Order* (Princeton, NJ: Princeton University Press, 1993), is a masterful study of the international origins of the war. Woodward, *The Commanders* (above) offers a sage "insider's" treatment of the White House national security decision-making process. For the military decision making during Desert Storm, first consult Rick Atkinson, *Crusade: The Untold Story of the Persian Gulf War* (Boston: Houghton Mifflin, 1993). The buildup to war and Desert Shield receive little attention here, but his is an accessible survey that draws many interesting historical parallels in a first-rate analysis. Atkinson should be joined with Thomas E. Ricks, *The Generals: American Military Command from World War II to Today* (New York: Penguin, 2012). Ricks offers chapters that compare and contrast different styles of military leadership (Powell vs. Schwarzkopf; Schwarzkopf vs. Frederick Franks), and in these chapters reside a host of new information, as well as an incisive assessment of the Gulf War as the anti-Vietnam. Michael F. Cairo, *The Gulf: The Bush Presidencies and the Middle East* (Lexington: University Press of Kentucky, 2012), provides a strong survey introduction to the Persian Gulf War (as well as an excellent survey of the steps that led to the Middle East peace conference in Madrid), as it offers a comparison to the policies of Bush the younger in Iraq. A much less judicious comparison is Alex Roberto Hybel and Justin Matthew Kaufman, *The Bush Administrations and Saddam Hussein: Deciding on Conflict* (New York: Palgrave Macmillan, 2006).

Bush and Scowcroft, *A World Transformed* (above), offers an interesting view of how Scowcroft won the battle for Bush's mind, helping to position the administration toward the offensive option that would become Desert Storm. Powell, *My American Journey* (above), offers the other side of the policy debate, as Powell admits that he argued in favor of giving the economic sanctions more time to work (a revelation first released in Woodward, *The Commanders*). General Norman H. Schwarzkopf, *The Autobiography: It Doesn't Take a Hero* (New York: Bantam Books, 1992), is hagiographic and self-effacing.

Mark Grossman, ed., *Encyclopedia of the Persian Gulf War* (Santa Barbara, CA: ABC-Clio, 1995), is particularly useful, not only for its entries but also for its 144-page appendix of documents and its 162-page chronology. Micha L. Sifry and Christopher Cerf, eds., *The Gulf War Reader: History, Documents, and Opinions* (New York: Times Books, 1991), is a particularly useful collection of primary sources. Other useful reference pieces on the war include Colonel Arthur H. Blair, *At War in the Gulf: A Chronology* (College Station: Texas A&M University Press, 1992); and *The Gulf Crisis: A Chronology, July 1990–July 1991* (London: U.S. Information Service, U.S. Embassy, 1991).

"The Gulf War" (first broadcast on the PBS series *Frontline* on 9 and 10 January 1996) makes for fascinating viewing. With the notable exception of Bush, each of the major American decision makers and generals is interviewed for the program. It also features comments from Margaret Thatcher and Tariq Aziz, as well as scholarly appraisals. The program's chronology is true to events, and it is quite gripping in its narration (complete transcripts of the interviews are also available online at http://www.wgbh.org).

Theodore Draper's commentaries for the *New York Review of Books* ("The Gulf War Reconsidered," 16 January 1992, pp. 46–53, and "The True History of the Gulf War," 30 January 1992, pp. 38–45) are critical essays that offer an interesting overall view of the conflict. Alan Friedman, *Spider's Web: The Secret History of How the White House Illegally Armed Iraq* (New York: Bantam Books, 1994), explores the relationship between the United States and Iraq prior to the 1990–1991 crisis. For a strong look at the military strategies, see Michael R. Gordon and General Bernard E. Trainor, *The General's War: The Inside Story of the Conflict in the Gulf* (Boston: Little, Brown, 1995). Malcolm Browne, "The Military vs. the Press," *New York Times Magazine*, 3 March 1991, pp. 27–30+, is the best view of its subject. See also W. Lance Bennett and David L. Paletz, eds., *Taken by Storm: The Media, Public Opinion, and U.S. Foreign Policy in the Gulf War* (Chicago: University of Chicago Press, 1994); Andrew Sullivan, "The Big Schmooze," *Esquire*, October 1990, pp. 105–106; and Stanley Cloud, "Volleys on the Information Front," *Time*, 2 February 1991, pp. 44–45. For insights into the opposition to the war in the United States, see Pat Buchanan, "How the Gulf Crisis Is Rupturing the Right," in Sifry and Cerf, eds., *Gulf War Reader* (above); and Ted Galen Carpenter, ed., *America Entangled: The Persian Gulf War and Its Consequences* (San Francisco: Cato Institute Books, 1991). On the question of Bush's authority to commit troops within the purview of the War Powers Act, Michael Glennon, "The Gulf War and the Constitution," *Foreign Affairs* 70 (Spring 1991): 84–101, offers a full analysis; see also Douglas L. Kriner, *After the Rubicon: Congress, Presidents, and the Politics of Waging War* (Chicago: University of Chicago Press, 2010). The question of international law is explored in two articles by Christopher Greenwood, "Iraq's Invasion of Kuwait: Some Legal Issues," *World Today*, March 1991, pp. 39–43, and "New World Order or Old? The Invasion of Kuwait and the Rule of Law," *Modern Law Review* 55 (1992): 153–178. Human Rights Watch, *Needless Deaths in the Gulf War: Civilian Casualties during the Air Campaign and Violations of the Laws of War* (New York: Human Rights Watch, 1991), is the most thorough study on the war's fatalities.

The post–Gulf War downsizing of the military is best addressed in Defense Base Closure and Realignment Commission, *Report to the President, 1991* (Washington, DC, 1991), and David S. Sorenson, *Shutting Down the Cold War: The Politics of Military Base Closure* (New York: St. Martin's Press, 1998). Dina G. Levy et al., *Base Realignment and Closure (BRAC) and Organizational Restructuring in the Department of Defense* (Santa Monica, CA: RAND, National Defense Research Institute, 2004), does not adequately address the issue.

A truly balanced study of the often acerbic relationship between Bush and the press has yet to be written. The student must consult sections in virtually all the secondary sources on the administration—the richest information is found in the literature on the press and the Persian Gulf War (above)—and the newsmagazines and newspapers of the period. Mark J. Rozell, *The Press and the Bush Presidency* (Westport, CT: Praeger, 1996), suffers by completely ignoring the broadcast media; however, the author includes a rather interesting chapter based on seven interviews with Bush's press advisers. Marlin Fitzwater, *Call the*

Briefing! Bush and Reagan, Sam and Helen: A Decade with Presidents and the Press (New York: Times Books, 1995), offers wonderful anecdotes and insight. The eminently quotable Daniel Schorr, *Come to Think of It: Notes on the Turn of the Millennium* (New York: Viking, 2007), and equally quotable Leslie Stahl, *Reporting Live* (New York: Simon & Schuster, 1999), offer us the views of two reporters who were largely critical of Bush. Less helpful is Woody Klein, *All the President's Spokesmen: Spinning the News—White House Press Secretaries from Franklin D. Roosevelt to George W. Bush* (Westport, CT: Praeger, 2008).

The fullest and most thoughtful book available on Bush's public presidency is Lori Cox Han, *A Presidency Upstaged: The Public Leadership of George H. W. Bush* (College Station: Texas A&M University Press, 2011). The chapter on Bush in Robert Schlesinger, *White House Ghosts: Presidents and Their Speechwriters* (New York: Simon & Schuster, 2008), is quite useful, particularly for the telling of the tale of Bush's speech on his drug policy. See also Heidi Erica Hamilton, "A Call to Arms: A Rhetorical Analysis of Two Speeches by President George Bush" (master's thesis, University of North Carolina, 1993), and Michael J. Maguire, "The Ritual of Rebirth: Images of Savagery in George Bush's Persian Gulf Rhetoric" (master's thesis, Mankato State University, 1992). For a comic look at Bush's penchant for the malapropism, see *New Republic, Bushisms: President George Herbert Walker Bush, in His Own Words* (New York: Workman, 1992). My personal favorite: a Bush quip at the 1991 Country Music Awards ceremony in Nashville, when he referred to the Nitty Gritty Dirt Band as the "Nitty Ditty Nitty Gritty Great Bird" (p. 24).

Not surprisingly, Barbara Bush's *A Memoir* (New York: St. Martin's Press, 1994) is a defense of her husband's actions and policies. Mrs. Bush's fleshing out of the scenes of their life together is singular in its contribution to the literature—particularly interesting are her treatment of the death of their daughter from leukemia, the diagnosis of their son with dyslexia, and the pain of the campaign of 1992. An engaging writing style also separates this book from others of the species; like her husband, the author has a keen eye for the telling anecdote. This style is not as evident in *Reflections: Life after the White House* (New York: Scribner, 2003), which offers very little in the way of "reflections" and is rather a prose rewording of her diaries that seems to include detail on every function that Mrs. Bush went to and every dinner she attended. Mrs. Bush's other two books, "coauthored" with her dogs, *C. Fred's Story* (Garden City, NY: Doubleday, 1984) and *Millie's Book: As Dictated to Barbara Bush* (New York: Morrow, 1990), are delightful reading, occasionally offering an interesting insight into life in the White House, as well as into the personalities of the "authors'" owners. The royalties from these two books raised a sizable sum for literacy groups. Myra R. Gutin, *Barbara Bush: Presidential Matriarch* (Lawrence: University Press of Kansas, 2008) is the only full scholarly biography of the First Lady; Gutin's Barbara Bush is a fully engaged Barbara Bush, whom Gutin finds to ultimately be more successful than her husband. All other biographies of Mrs. Bush suffer by comparison to

Gutin's. Donnie Ratcliffe, *Simply Barbara Bush: A Portrait of America's Candid First Lady* (New York: Warner Books, 1989), is a hastily written work, done during the 1988 campaign. Pamela Kilian, *Barbara Bush: A Biography* (New York: St. Martin's Press, 1992), is the same, only written during the 1992 campaign (although Kilian does include five pages of Mrs. Bush's favorite recipes). For a less superficial study of Mrs. Bush's role in the 1988 campaign, see Ann Grimes, *Running Mates: The Making of a First Lady* (New York: Morrow, 1990). In *Mr. and Mrs. President: From the Trumans to the Clintons* (Lawrence: University Press of Kansas, 2000), Gil Troy argues unconvincingly that the Bushes had a "co-presidency" (p. 313), but in his *Hilary Rodham Clinton: Polarizing First Lady* (Lawrence: University Press of Kansas, 2006), Troy treats Mrs. Bush in an unflattering comparison to his subject, seeing her both as an apolitical, low-profile traditionalist and as somewhat of a phony (calling her books to raise money for literacy a "stunt"; p. 64).

The best analytical treatment of the presidential election of 1992 is Bennett, *The Governing Crisis* (above). His thesis of the "constant campaign," discussed in chapter 11 of this book, is an important premise that sheds new light on modern presidential campaigning. Jack Germond and Jules Witcover's *Mad as Hell: Revolt at the Ballot Box, 1992* (New York: Warner Books, 1993), offers more coverage on the general election campaign than did their *Whose Broad Stripes and Bright Stars?* (above). Also, their 1992 entry does a better analytical job; their dissection of voter anger is particularly useful. Gil Troy, "Stumping in the Bookstores: A Literary History of the 1992 Presidential Campaign," *Presidential Studies Quarterly* 25 (1995): 697–710, is a useful bibliographical essay, although it tends to overemphasize books that critique the political system of the time instead of reviewing the available survey treatments of the campaign.

The three best biographies of Bush's main opponents are David Bennett, *Bill Clinton: Building a Bridge to a New Millennium* (New York: Routledge, 2014); Gerald Posner, *Citizen Perot: His Life and Times* (New York: Random House, 1996); and Timothy Stanley, *The Crusader: The Life and Tumultuous Times of Pat Buchanan* (New York: Dunne Books, 2012). On the Clinton campaign, Joe Klein, *The Natural: The Misunderstood Presidency of Bill Clinton* (New York: Broadway Books, 2002), is well written and evenhanded. Kenneth D. Nordin, "The Television Candidate: H. Ross Perot's 1992 and 1996 Presidential Races," in Ted G. Jelen, ed., *Ross for Boss: The Perot Phenomenon and Beyond* (Albany: State University of New York Press, 2001), is a worthy survey of the Perot campaign. Most of the alumni of the Bush administration have discussed their role in the campaign in their memoirs, mentioned elsewhere in this essay. Other memoirs, each of them presenting the election in a manner that is completely biased toward their candidate, are Sidney Blumenthal, *The Clinton Wars* (New York: Farrar, Straus and Giroux, 2003); Bill Clinton, *My Life* (New York: Knopf, 2004); Mary Matalin and James Carville, *All's Fair: Love, War, and Running for President* (New York: Random House, 1994); and Ed Rollins, *Bare Knuckles and Back Rooms: My Life in American Politics* (New York: Broadway Books, 1996).

The 1992 presidential primary process is critically analyzed in Robert D. Loevy, *The Flawed Path to the Presidency, 1992: Unfairness and Inequality in the Presidential Selection Process* (Albany: State University of New York Press, 1995). The impact of the new media on the campaign is best seen in Larry King, *On the Line: The New Road to the White House* (New York: Harcourt Brace, 1993). See also *1-800-President: The Report of the Twentieth Century Fund Task Force on Television and the Campaign of 1992* (New York: Twentieth Century Fund Press, 1993), and Tom Rosensteil, *Strange Bedfellows: How Television and the Presidential Candidates Changed American Politics, 1992* (New York: Hyperion Press, 1992). On campaign rhetoric, see Robert E. Denton, ed., *The 1992 Presidential Campaign: A Communication Perspective* (Westport, CT: Praeger, 1994). On the "Dump Quayle" movement, see James A. Baker III, *"Work Hard, Study . . . and Keep Out of Politics"* (above), and Thomas M. DeFrank, *Write It When I'm Gone: Remarkable Off-the-Record Conversations with Gerald R. Ford* (New York: Putnam, 2007). On the role of the conservatives in the election, see Steven J. Allen and Richard A. Viguerie, *Lip Service: George Bush's 30-Year Battle with Conservatives* (Chautilly, VA: CP Books, 1992); Donald T. Critchlow, *The Conservative Ascendancy: How the Republican Right Rose to Power in Modern America*, 2nd ed. (Lawrence: University Press of Kansas, 2011); and John Karaagac, *The Fate of the Father: The Bush Policy Paradox* (Tucson, AZ: Fenestra Books, 2004). Of the many available postmortems, the most thought-provoking are Seymour Martin Lipset, "The Significance of the 1992 Election," *Political Science and Politics* 26 (1993): 7–16, and Grover G. Norquist, "The Unmaking of the President: Why Bush Lost," *Policy Review*, Winter 1993, 10–17. For conspiracy buffs, Anne DuBose Joslin, *Ambushed: Why George Herbert Walker Bush Really Lost in 1992* (Boston: Henley and Luce, 2003), argues that Bush lost because "Jim Baker and his former Reaganite cronies did not want Bush reelected" (p. 496).

Bush's lame-duck period was particularly active. On the pardons of Caspar Weinberger and others, see Benjamin Wittes, *Starr: A Reassessment* (New Haven, CT: Yale University Press, 2002), and Bob Woodward, *Shadow* (above). James Dobbins, Michele A. Poole, Austin Long, and Benjamin Runkle, *After the War: Nation-Building from FDR to George W. Bush* (Santa Monica, CA: RAND National Security Research Division, 2008), offers an excellent short history of the American intervention in Somalia. Walter Clarke and Jeffrey Herbst, eds., *Learning from Somalia: The Lessons of Armed Humanitarian Intervention* (Boulder, CO: Westview Press, 1997), is also particularly useful. See also John G. Summer, *Hope Restored? Humanitarian Aid in Somalia, 1990–1994* (Washington, DC: Refugee Policy Group, Center for Policy Analysis and Research on Refugee Issues, 1994).

Several studies on the post-presidency highlight Bush's activities since 1993. The best written and most broadly researched is Nancy Gibbs and Michael Duffy, *The Presidents Club: Inside the World's Most Exclusive Fraternity* (New York: Simon & Schuster, 2012). Also useful is Leonard Benardo and Jennifer Weiss, *Citizen-in-Chief: The Second Lives of the American Presidents* (New York: Morrow,

2009); Burton I. Kaufman, *The Post-presidency from Washington to Clinton* (Lawrence: University Press of Kansas, 2012); and Mark K. Updegrove, *Second Acts: Presidential Lives and Legacies after the White House* (Guilford, CT: Lyons Press, 2006). While hyperbolic and conspiratorial, Dan Brody, *The Iron Triangle: Inside the Secret World of the Carlyle Group* (Hoboken, NJ: Wiley, 2003), is a usable history of the company that employed Bush in the post-presidency. Taylor Branch, *The Clinton Tapes: Wrestling History with the President* (New York: Simon & Schuster, 2009), is particularly helpful in tracing the development of the Bush-Clinton friendship; Bill Clinton, *My Life* (above) is less forthcoming about the relationship.

Several entries in the growing literature dealing with the life and presidency of George W. Bush serve to illuminate certain areas of the life and presidency of his father. George W. Bush, *A Charge to Keep: My Journey to the White House* (New York: Morrow, 1991), goes well beyond the expected "I-love-my-dad" vignettes; the author offers several sharp criticisms—some more overt than others—of his father and his presidency. The second volume of memoirs, *Decision Points* (New York: Crown, 2010), offers much less on his father. First Lady Laura Bush, in *Spoken from the Heart* (New York: Scribner, 2010), is also surprisingly critical of both her father-in-law and mother-in-law. While the reader should consult earlier entries in this essay for material dealing with parallels between the administrations of the two Bushes (particularly the newer literature on the Gulf War, and the literature on Hurricane Andrew, which makes the obvious parallels to Hurricane Katrina), the best analysis of the relationship between father and son is Bill Minutaglio, *First Son: George W. Bush and the Bush Family Dynasty*, rev. ed. (New York: Times Books, 2001). Other books on the second Bush and his presidency that were helpful in understanding the policies and personality of the first Bush are Peter Baker, *Days of Fire: Bush and Cheney in the White House* (New York: Doubleday, 2013); Sidney Blumenthal, *How Bush Rules: Chronicles of a Radical Regime* (Princeton, NJ: Princeton University Press, 2006); Lou Cannon and Carl M. Cannon, *Reagan's Disciple: George W. Bush's Troubled Quest for a Presidential Legacy* (New York: Public Affairs, 2008); Robert Draper, *Dead Certain: The Presidency of George W. Bush* (New York: Free Press, 2007); Barton Gellman, *Angler: The Cheney Vice Presidency* (New York: Penguin, 2008); Robert G. Kaufman, *In Defense of the Bush Doctrine* (Lexington: University Press of Kentucky, 2007); Elizabeth Mitchell, *W: Revenge of the Bush Dynasty* (New York: Berkley Books, 2003); James Risen, *State of War: The Secret History of the CIA and the Bush Administration* (New York: Free Press, 2006); and Shirley Anne Warshaw, *The Co-presidency of Bush and Cheney* (Stanford, CA: Stanford University Press, 2009). Less helpful, but also mentioning father and son, were Terry H. Anderson, *Bush's Wars* (New York: Oxford University Press, 2011); Russ Baker, *Family of Secrets: The Bush Dynasty, America's Invisible Government, and the Hidden History of the Last Fifty Years* (New York: Bloomsbury Press, 2009); and Kitty Kelley, *The Family: The Real Story of the Bush Dynasty* (New York: Doubleday, 2004).

Defying an easy categorization is Donald Rumsfeld's wide-ranging autobiography, *Known and Unknown: A Memoir* (New York: Sentinel, 2012), which serves to document the author's antipathy toward the elder Bush. Of particular note are Bob Woodward's four volumes on George W. Bush's wartime decision making, each of which offers useful information on the father: *Bush at War* (New York: Simon & Schuster, 2002); *Plan of Attack* (New York: Simon & Schuster, 2004); *State of Denial: Bush at War, Part III* (New York: Simon & Schuster, 2006); and *The War Within: A Secret White House History, 2006–2008* (New York: Simon & Schuster, 2008).

A particularly fertile area of study—indeed, one that is calling for a full treatment—lies in the area of comparative history, looking at the entirety of the two Bush presidencies side by side. Anthony J. Eksterowicz and Glenn P. Hastedt have attempted this in *The Presidencies of George Herbert Walker Bush and George Walker Bush: Like Father Like Son?* (New York: Nova Science, 2008), but theirs is a collection of articles, and their effort is marred by a self-published format that contains more than the usual number of mistakes and typos. Hybel and Kaufman, *The Bush Administration and Saddam Hussein*, and Cairo, *The Gulf: The Bush Presidencies and the Middle East* (above) each offers such a joint treatment, but their studies are limited to foreign and national security policy. Scholars interested in pursuing such a comparison can begin with the memoirs of those who served in both presidencies (e.g., Cheney, Haass, Rice, Tenet).

INDEX

ABC News, 47, 50, 197
Abortion policy, 13, 22–23, 33, 60,
    76–78, 197, 226, 258
Abrams, Elliot, 242, 316n33
ADA. *See* Americans with Disabilities
    Act
Affirmative action, and education
    reform, 84, 86
African Americans, 304n14; and
    appointment of Powell to JCS,
    129; and Bush, 60, 78–79; and civil
    rights act (1990), 79; and civil rights
    act (1991), 80; and election of 1964,
    12; and election of 1988, 45–46;
    and election of 1992, 218; and
    nomination of Clarence Thomas,
    195–196
Agnew, Spiro T., 14, 15
Aidid, General Mohammed, 240
AIDS, 91
Ailes, Roger, 34, 35, 36, 40, 43, 194,
    230, 233
Air Force One, 187, 215, 224, 253

Alexander, Lamar, 85, 86
Al Firdos bunker, 169–170
*All the Best, George Bush: My Life in
    Letters and Other Writings* (Bush),
    42, 245
Almanac of American Politics (Barone &
    McCutcheon), 42
Al-Sabah, Salem, 171
"America 2000," 85–86
American Achievement Tests, 85
American Civil Liberties Union
    (ACLU), 44
American Heart Fund, 19
American Red Cross, 228
Americans for Tax Reform, 35
Americans with Disabilities Act
    (ADA), 25, 90–92, 181, 216, 233, 255
Amnesty International, 156
Anderson, John, 21
Anderson Center, M. D., 243
"Andover," 3, 19. *See also* Phillips
    Academy
Andrews Air Force Base, 237

Andropov, Yuri, 23
Anti-Drug Abuse Act (1988), 86
Appalachian Regional Commission, 186
Apple, R. W. ("Johnny"), 133
Aquino, Corazon, 131–132
Arab League, 141, 149
Arens, Moshe, 168
Armenia, 135
Armey, Dick, 250
Arnett, Peter, 169, 298n24
Asbestos, 92
Ashley, Lud, 15
Ashley Hall, 3
Aspen Institute, 144
Assad, Hafez el, 176–177
Atkinson, Rick, 142, 165, 168, 170, 172
Atlanta Constitution, 61
Atwater, Harvey LeRoy ("Lee"), 31–33, 34, 35, 36, 39, 40, 45, 47, 55, 61, 70, 74, 230, 233; and civil rights act (1990), 80; death of, 193–194; and election of 1988, 183; and George W. Bush, 33; and transition to Bush administration, 54
Australia, and Persian Gulf War, 294n34
Azerbaijan, 135
Aziz, Tariq, 151, 159–160

Ba'ath Party (Iraq), 139
Baghdad, 164, 166, 169, 174
Baker, Howard, 21, 30, 234
Baker, James A., III, 17, 19, 54, 57 (photo), 58, 60, 81, 109, 117, 123, 125 (photo), 187, 224, 253, 267n112, 315n23; and American invasion of Panama, 132, 133; appointment as secretary of state, 53, 56; and Bush, 53, 179; and Carlyle Group, 244; and charges of conflict of interest, 65; on Cheney, 129; as chief of staff to Reagan, 23; and choice of Cheney

as Secretary of Defense, 68; and "Dump Quayle" movement (1992), 223–224; and election of 1962, 10–11; and election of 1980, 21; and election of 1988, 271n57; and election of 1988, 42, 44, 46, 272n72; and election of 1992, 231, 312n86, 312n87, 315n23; and election of 2000, 249; on Gates, 285n20; and Kurds, 176; and Madrid Conference, 176–178; and North American Free Trade Agreement, 222; and Panama, 127, 130–131; and "Passportgate," 312n91; and the *pauza*, 111, 112; on Perot, 213; and Persian Gulf War, 142, 146, 149, 150, 151, 152, 152 (photo), 153, 154, 156, 157, 158, 159–160, 161, 174, 295n68, 297n103; and reunification of Germany, 133, 137; and Tiananmen Square massacre, 116; and transition to Bush administration, 54, 274n20; on Weinberger re-indictment, 235–236; on withdrawal of U.S. and Soviet troops in Europe, 114; on Yeltsin, 121
Baker and Botts (law firm), 10
Baker v. Carr (1963), 12
Banca Nazionale del Lavoro, 313n105
Barbara Bush Foundation for Family Literacy, 190
Barilleaux, Ryan J., 256
Barnes, Fred, 172
Barr, William, 241, 312n91, 313n105
Barry, Marion, 89
Basra, 164
Bates, David, 193
Bates College, 38
Bauer, Gary, 84
Bayh, Birch, 40
Baylor University School of Medicine, 19
Becker, Jean, 245

Beijing, 115, 117
Bell, Terrel, 83
Bennett, W. Lance, 50–51, 219
Bennett, William, 194; and drug
    policy, 86, 87, 89; and education
    reform, 83, 86
Benton, William, 9
Bentsen, Lloyd, 14–15, 67, 272n88
Bergen, Candice, 223
Berlau, John, 78–79
Berlin Wall, opening of, 122–126,
    207, 226, 255, 257. *See also* East
    Germany: fall of communism in
Beschloss, Michael, 107, 110
Bethesda Naval Hospital, 195
Biden, Joseph, 38, 82
Black, Charles, 230
Blue Spoon, Operation, 132–133. *See
    also* Panama: American invasion of
Boehlert, Sherwood, 94
Boehner, John, 211
Bolivia, 89
Bond, Rich, 194, 225
Boot, William, 50
Boren, David, 252
Bork, Robert, 80–81
Boskin, Michael, 96
Bosnia, 315n21
Boston Globe, 81
Boston Herald, 97
Boutros-Ghali, Boutros, 241
Boyd, Gerald, 50
BRAC, 208–209. *See also* Defense
    Base Closure and Realignment
    Commission
Bradley, Bill, 203, 217
Bradley, Tom, 221
Brady, John, 32, 47
Brady, Nicholas, 32–33, 44, 56, 57
    (photo), 61–62, 207, 253; and 1990
    budget fight, 101 (photo); and
    Persian Gulf War, 150; and savings
    and loan crisis, 98, 99

Branch, Taylor, 317n72
Brando, Marlon, 8
Branstad, Terry, 85 (photo)
Breen, John, 268n123
Brennan, William, 74, 80, 81, 195
Brezhnev Doctrine, 22, 119
Bridge of the Americas (Panama), 130
Brigham Young University, 46
Briscoe, Frank, 13
British Aerospace, 65
British Red Cross, 239
Brock, William, 266n91
Broder, David, 25, 37–38, 40, 41
Brokaw, Tom, 36
Brook, Douglas, 295n56
Brown, Jerry, 218
Brown, Murphy, 223
Brown Brothers Harriman, 1, 8
Buchanan, Patrick J. ("Pat"), 158,
    210, 216–217, 220, 221, 222–223,
    225–226, 233
Buckley, Christopher, 185
Buckley, James, 266n91
budget cuts, defense, 129–130
budget fight (1990), 100–106, 200, 208,
    210, 258
Bulgaria, 123
Bundestag (German Parliament), 125
Burke, John P., 60
Bush, Barbara Pierce, 3, 36, 143, 188–
    191, 189 (photo), 229, 236, 237, 238,
    242, 243–244, 247 (photo), 248, 253,
    254, 302n46, 302n48, 303–304n10,
    316n41
Bush, Dorothy Walker, 1, 2, 181
Bush, George H. W. (Herbert Walker)
    and abortion issue, 13, 22–23, 33,
    76–78, 258
    as activist president, 255–259
    and African Americans, 78–79,
    95–196, 129, 304n14
    and Americans with Disabilities
    Act, 90–92, 181, 255

Bush, George H. W., *continued*
analysis of presidency of, 254–259
and attacks of 11 September 2001,
250–251
and Atwater, 32
and Baker, 10–11, 53
and base closures, 208–209
and Berlin Wall, 123–126, 255, 257
on Buchanan, 216
and cabinet, 53, 56–58
as campaigner, 29–30, 32, 44–51,
108, 181
and Carlyle Group, 244
as chair of Harris County (Texas)
Republican Party, 11, 22
as chair of Republican National
Committee, 265–266n85
and "Chicken Kiev" speech, 257
childhood of, 1–3
China diary of, 17
chosen as Reagan's vice
presidential running mate
(1980), 22–23
and civil rights act (1964), 264n56,
264n61
and civil rights act (1968), 13–14, 79
and civil rights act (1990), 79–80,
258
and civil rights act (1991), 80, 258
and Clean Air Act Amendments of
1990, 92–94, 255
and Clinton (during post-
presidency), 84, 85, 242–243,
252–254
on Clinton, 254
and coalition against Iraq (1990–
1991), 109, 185, 203
competitive nature of, 179–180
and Congress, 64, 66–67, 72–73,
184
and conservation, 92–94
and conservatives, 11, 13–14, 21–22,
24–25, 190, 221, 233–234

and coup attempt against Corazon
Aquino, 132
as crisis manager, 185–186
and criticism of Reagan legacy, 64,
184
and cuts in defense spending,
208–209
and Dana Carvey, 238
and Dan Rather interview (January
1988), 34–35
as decision maker, 40, 151–152
and decision to raise taxes (1990),
95–97, 100–106, 194, 232, 233,
255
and decision to run for reelection
(1992), 193, 303n3
and Deng Xiaoping, 114
diplomatic philosophy of (realist),
127, 285n10
as director of central intelligence,
18–19, 108, 110, 147
at Dresser Industries, 6–7
and drug policy, 86–90, 258
and drug summit (Colombia,
February 1990), 187
and "Dump Quayle" movement
(1992), 223–224
and economic regulation, 24
and economy, 206–207, 215, 249
and education reform, 83–86, 258
and election of 1962, 10–11
and election of 1964, 11–12, 181,
264n61
and election of 1966, 12–13, 264n65
and election of 1968, 13
and election of 1970, 14–15
and election of 1980, 20–23, 31
and election of 1988, 27, 29–51, 183,
216
and election of 1992, 103, 184, 215–
236, 237, 248–249, 303n3
and election of 2000, 248–249
as elitist, 33, 41

as envoy to People's Republic of China, 17–18, 108, 110, 114
and ethics in his administration, 64–65, 69–70, 210
and fall of communism in Eastern Europe, 119–126, 257, 289n95
and fall of USSR, 202–206, 257
and Family Leave Act, 222
and family of, 8–9, 190
and flag desecration issue, 74–76, 258
on gays in his administration, 222
and George Bush Presidential Library and Museum, 74, 245–246, 247 (photo), 255, 258, 263n45, 289n108
on Gingrich, 283n28, 284n41
and Giroldi coup attempt (Panama), 130, 187
and Gorbachev, 107, 110, 112, 121–122, 137, 146, 203–206, 289n95
and Graves' disease, 194–195, 200, 229–230, 303–304n10
on Hirohito, 276n61
and Hungary, 119–120
and Hurricane Andrew, 227–228, 254
and Hurricane Katrina, 254
and image-makers, 183
and inauguration of George W. Bush, 250
and invasion of Iraq (2003), 251–252
and Iran-Contra scandal, 25–26, 234–236, 242
and "Iraqgate," 234–236, 313n105
and Israel, 167–168, 222
on Jaruzelski, 120
and King Hussein (Jordan), 177–178
and Lithuania, 135–136
and Los Angeles Riots (1992), 221–222

and Madrid conference, 176–178, 257
managerial style of, 54–55, 56
marriage of, 5
memoirs of, 245
and Middle East, 222
and minimum wage, 73
and Mosbacher, 10–11
and National Security Council, 59–60
and 1990 budget deal, 258
on Nixon, 16
and nomination of Clarence Thomas to Supreme Court, 80, 195–200, 304n26
and nomination of David Souter to Supreme Court, 80–83, 195, 196–197
and Noriega, 26–27, 127, 128, 289n108
and North American Free Trade Agreement, 222–223, 234
and Panama, 130, 132–133, 173, 187
parachute jumps of, 244–245
and pardon of Weinberger and others, 241–242
and "Passportgate," 312–313n91
and patriotism, 44
and *Patterson v. McLean Credit Union*, 79
and *pauza* with the Soviet Union, 110–114, 118, 204
and People's Republic of China, 17–18, 108, 110, 114, 116–118, 286n34
and Perot, 213, 216, 234
personality of, 181–184
philosophy of diplomacy, 108–109, 113, 117
philosophy of the presidency, 184–186
photo of, 4, 24, 48, 57, 85, 88, 101, 125, 126, 135, 152, 171, 180, 232, 247

INDEX

Bush, George H. W., *continued*
and Points of Light movement,
190–192, 303n58
and Poland, 119–120
and political ambitions of his sons,
246–250
and polls, 158, 172, 189, 193
post-presidency of, 243–255
and Powell, 129
and presidency of George W. Bush,
244, 250–252
and presidential war making
power, 160–161
and press, 55, 170–171, 186–188,
229, 255, 297n103, 298n24
promise not to lower taxes, 43–44,
91, 95, 158, 190, 191, 226
as public speaker, 181
and Quayle, 40–43, 186
reaction to 1992 defeat, 237
and Reagan, 23–27, 29, 184
on Reagan's foreign policy, 110
and recession of 1991–1992, 207
and removal of Reagan appointees,
56, 233, 274n20
as Republican National Committee
chair, 16
and Republican National
Convention (1988), 39, 40, 43–44,
190, 191, 226
and Republican National
Convention (1992), 225–226
and reunification of Germany,
124–126, 133–137, 150, 203,
257
and rumors of marital infidelity, 33,
229
on Saddam Hussein, 174
and Savings and Loan Crisis, 255,
259
and Scowcroft, 145, 252
and Somalia, 239–241
as sportsman, 92

and Strategic Arms Reduction
Treaty (START I), 204, 238–239
and Strategic Arms Reduction
Treaty (START II), 239
and summit with Gorbachev
(Malta, December 1989), 110–111,
121–122, 126, 131, 133, 136
and summit with Gorbachev
(Washington, June 1990), 136,
180
and summit with Gorbachev
(Helsinki, September 1990), 151,
176
and summit with Gorbachev
(Moscow, July 1991), 204
and Sununu, 201–202
as Texas oilman, 7–9, 10
as Texas "transplant," 180–181
and *Texas v. Johnson*, 75
and Thatcher, 144, 145
and Tiananmen Square crisis,
116–118
and Tower nomination, 62, 66–67,
68, 93–94
and transition to Clinton
administration, 237–243
and Tsunami relief (2004), 253–254
and Ukraine, 204
as United Nations ambassador, 15,
17, 57, 190
and veto strategy, 72–73, 79–80, 94,
118, 184, 258
as vice president, 23–27, 53, 54,
90, 107, 110, 127, 183, 186, 235,
273n88
as vice presidential prospect (1968),
14, 265n74
as vice presidential prospect (1974),
266n91
as vice presidential prospect (1975),
16–17
as vice presidential prospect (1976),
19

352

and "vision thing," 72, 277n4
visit to Vietnam Memorial, 238
on Walesa, 120
and *Wards Cove Packing Co. v.
   Atonio,* 79
wealth of, 243–244
and *Webster v. Reproductive Health
   Services of Missouri,* 77–78
and Weinberger re-indictment,
   235–236
and "wimp factor," 34, 49, 131, 187
and World War II, 3–6, 263n26
and Yale University, 6, 263n29
and Yeltsin, 121, 203–206
Bush, George H. W., and Persian Gulf
   War
and aid to Iraq (1989–1990), 140,
   141, 234–235
and decision not to invade Iraq,
   143–144
and decision to end conflict,
   172–175
and decision to expel Iraq from
   Kuwait, 152–154
and Egypt, 294n34
and formation of coalition against
   Iraq, 144–151
and Gorbachev, 146, 203
and hostages in Iraq, 155–156,
   159
and invasion of Kuwait by Iraq,
   103, 257
and Israel, 149, 167–168
and *Khaneqan* incident, 151
letter to his children, 163
letter to Saddam Hussein, 159–160
and National Security Council,
   143–144
and 1990 budget fight, 103–104
and peace initiatives, 159–160
and presidential war making
   power, 160–161
and press, 170–171, 298n24

and Prince Bandar bin Sultan, 145
on Saddam Hussein, 141, 156,
   159–160
and Scowcroft, 145
speech, 8 August 1990, announcing
   Operation Desert Shield, 148
speech, 20 August 1990 (Baltimore,
   Veterans of Foreign Wars
   convention), 155–156
speech, 10 September 1990 (Joint
   Session of Congress, on Kuwait
   Crisis), 103–104, 154
speech 16 January 1991 (Oval
   Office, announcing Allied
   military action in Persian Gulf),
   164
speech, 29 January 1991
   (Washington, State of the Union
   Address), 156, 190
speech, 6 March 1991 (Washington,
   Joint Session of Congress),
   proclaiming end of Persian Gulf
   War, 170
summit with Gorbachev (Helsinki,
   September 1990), 151, 176
televised interview, 2 January 1991
   (with David Frost), 156
and Thatcher, 145
and "This Will Not Stand"
   comment (August 5), 147–148
and United Nations, 144–145, 257
war aims of, 161–162
Bush, George H. W., speeches,
   statements, and television
   appearances
17 April 1968 (Houston, on Fair
   Housing Act of 1968), 14, 79
12 October 1987 (Houston,
   announcement of presidential
   candidacy), 27, 61
25 January 1988 (Television
   interview with Dan Rather),
   34–35, 186

Bush, George H. W., speeches, statements, and television appearances, *continued*
29 May 1988 (Boston, Harvard University), 254–255
18 August 1988 (New Orleans, acceptance speech at Republican Convention), 43–44, 91, 190, 191, 226
13 October 1988 (Los Angeles, Second Presidential Debate), 47–49
8 November 1988 (Houston, victory speech), 54
20 January 1989 (Washington, Inaugural Address), 63–64, 86, 91, 190
9 February 1989 (Washington, Joint Session of Congress), 83–84
6 March 1989 (Washington, Veterans of Foreign Wars convention), 89
12 May 1989 (Texas A&M University, on foreign policy), 113
14 May 1989 (Mississippi State University), 128
12 July 1989 (Budapest, Karl Marx University), 120
5 September 1989 (Washington, DC, Oval Office, on drug policy), 86–87
5 August 1990 (White House, "This Will Not Stand" comment), 147–148
8 August 1990 (Oval Office, announcing Operation Desert Shield), 148
20 August 1990 (Baltimore, Veterans of Foreign Wars convention), 155–156
10 September 1990 (Washington, Joint Session of Congress, on Kuwait), 103–104, 154

2 January 1991 (televised interview with David Frost), 156
16 January 1991 (Oval Office, announcing Allied military action in Persian Gulf), 164
29 January 1991 (Washington, State of the Union Address), 156, 190
1 August 1991 (Kiev, Ukraine, the "Chicken Kiev" speech), 204, 206
10 May 1991 (Princeton University), 184–185
20 August 1992 (Houston, Acceptance speech to Republican National Convention), 226
Bush, George, Presidential Library and Museum, 74, 188, 245–246, 255, 258, 263n45, 289n108
Bush, George W., 8, 19, 33, 34, 36, 54, 173, 181, 190, 193, 202, 247–250, 270n23, 303n3, 314n10, 318n90; and attacks of 11 September 2001, 250–251; and "Dump Quayle" movement (1992), 224, 310n49; and election of 1992, 215, 231; and election of 2000, 248–249; and firing of Sununu, 201–202, 305n34; and Hurricane Katrina, 228, 254; inauguration as president, 250; on nomination of Thomas, 304n26; and political philosophy of his father, 250; and retaliation against Afghanistan and Iraq, 251–252; and Scowcroft op. ed. in *Wall Street Journal*, 252; on Souter, 82; and transition "scrub team," 54; and tsunami relief (2004), 253–254
Bush, John Ellis ("Jeb"), 8, 190, 228, 247, 248, 249, 250
Bush, Laura, 202
Bush, Marvin, 9
Bush, Mildred Kerr ("Millie," dog), 190, 229, 231, 303–304n10

Bush, Neil, 9, 90, 190, 191, 254, 303n3;
and savings and loan crisis, 99–100
Bush, Noelle, 229
Bush, Pauline Robinson ("Robin"),
8–9
Bush, Prescott, 1, 2, 7, 8, 9, 10
Bush, Prescott, Jr., 3
Bush, Robin, 27, 90, 263n45
Bush-Clinton Katrina Fund, 254
Bush-Clinton Tsunami Relief Fund,
254
Bushnell, John, 133
Bush-Overbey Oil Development
Company, 8
Bush v. Gore (2000), 249
Byrd, Robert, 93

C. Fred's Story (Barbara Bush), 302n46
Cabinet (Bush), composition of,
53, 56–58. *See also* Tower, John:
nomination as secretary of defense
Cable News Network (CNN), 47, 117,
129, 164, 169, 170, 171, 173, 188,
210, 220, 229, 271n39, 298n24
Cable Television Protection and
Competition Act (1992), 277n8
Cairo, Michael, 285n10
California, 139
*Call to Economic Arms: Forging a New
American Mandate, A* (Tsongas), 218
Campbell, Carroll, 31, 224
Camp David, 74, 147, 159, 182, 195,
216, 232, 251
Canada, 222
Canal Zone, 128. *See also* Panama
capital gains tax, 100
Card, Andrew, 35, 39, 45, 272n72;
and firing of Sununu, 202;
head of transition to Clinton
administration, 237; and Hurricane
Andrew, 228; on Skinner, 202; on
Sununu, 55, 202
Carlucci, Frank, 208, 244

Carlyle Group, 244
Carson, Johnny, 42–43
Carter, Jimmy, 19, 23, 92, 95, 127, 131,
145, 155, 157–158, 227, 234, 247
(photo), 253, 289n105, 291n145
Carter, Rosalyn, 247 (photo)
Carter Center, 127
Carvey, Dana, 183, 238
Carville, James, 206–207, 211
Casey, William, 169
Castro, Fidel, 128
Cato Institute, 158
Cavasos, Lauro, 56, 57 (photo), 83, 85,
85 (photo)
CBS News, 22, 59, 124, 219
Ceauşescu, Nicolae, 123, 140, 174, 206
CENTCOM. *See* Central Command;
Persian Gulf War
Central Command (CENTCOM), 142,
143, 169, 170
Central Intelligence Agency (CIA),
26, 61, 108, 129, 147, 169, 242, 251,
287n64, 292n1; and assassination
attempt against Bush, 253; Bush
as director of, 18–19; Chapman
Amendment (to ADA bill), 91; and
Panama, 127; and Persian Gulf
War, 168
Chappaquiddick Bridge, 199
Chase Bank, 19
check overdraft scandal (Congress),
210, 307n95
Cheney, Richard B. ("Dick"), 69, 206,
224, 310n49; and base closures,
208–209; and choice of secretary
of defense, 68; and coup attempt
against Corazon Aquino, 131–132;
and cuts in defense spending, 129–
130, 208–209, 307n84; and election
of 2000, 249; and Giroldi coup
attempt, 131; on Gorbachev, 129;
managerial style of, 128–129; and
invasion of Panama, 128, 132;

Cheney, Richard B., *continued*, and the *pauza*, 112; and Persian Gulf War, 142, 145, 147, 148, 149, 151, 152–153, 152 (photo), 155, 160, 161, 167, 173, 294n34, 296n71; popularity after Persian Gulf War, 172; and Powell, 129; and reproach of Welch, 128–129, 290n110; and Tower nomination, 66; as vice president, 174, 251; on withdrawal of U.S. and Soviet troops in Europe, 113–114
Chichi Jima, 5
"Chicken Kiev" Speech (1 August 1991), 204, 206, 257
Chief of Staff. *See* Baker, James A., III; Skinner, Samuel; Sununu, John; Yeutter, Clayton
Chiles, Lawton, 248
China. *See* People's Republic of China
Christie's (Auction House), 201
Chrysler Motor Company, 30, 207
Churchill, Winston, 237
CIA. *See* Central Intelligence Agency.
Cicconi, James, 103
Civil Rights Act (1866), 79
Civil Rights Act (1964), 11, 12, 13, 90, 264n56, 264n61
Civil Rights Act (1968), 13–14, 79
Civil Rights Act (1988), 37
Civil Rights Act (1990), 79–80, 258
Civil Rights Act (1991), 80, 210, 217, 220
Civil War (American), 295n56
Clarke, Richard A., 109, 294n34
Clarridge, Duane, 242, 316n33
Clean Air Act (1970), 92
Clean Air Act Amendments (1990), 92–94, 216, 233, 255
Clinton, Hillary, 219, 247 (photo)
Clinton, William J. ("Bill"), 106, 172, 184, 206, 211, 213, 226, 232 (photo), 233, 241, 243, 247 (photo), 248, 249, 250, 284n41; and African American voters, 218; and assassination attempt against Bush, 252–253; and Bush (during post-presidency), 252–254; character issue, 229, 231, 253; and Education Summit (1989), 84, 85 (photo); and election of 1988, 38, 50; and election of 1992, 218–220, 222, 227, 228, 229, 231, 232, 233; and election of 2000, 317n72; and Hurricane Andrew, 227–228; and Hurricane Katrina, 254; inauguration of, 242–243; and "Iraqgate," 234–236, 313n105; and North American Free Trade Agreement, 223, 234; and "Passportgate," 231, 312n91; and philosophy of the "New Democrat," 219; and the press, 229; and Roger Porter, 312n89; transition from Bush administration, 237–238; and tsunami relief (2004), 253–254; and Weinberger re-indictment, 235–236
Clinton, William Jefferson, Presidential Library, 253
CNN. *See* Cable News Network
Coehlo, Tony, 73, 90, 91
Cohen, David, 256
Cohen, Richard, 92–93, 94
Colby, William, 18
Cold War, 122, 155, 204, 233
Colombia, 89, 187
Color Purple, The (Walker), 189
Colson, Charles, 15
Commandancia Building (Panama), 133
Commanders, The (Woodward), 130
Commission on National and Community Service, 191
Commonwealth of Independent States, 206. *See also* USSR: fall of
Communism: fall of in Eastern

Europe, 118–122, 140; fall of in East Germany, 122–126

Congress, 128, 184; and amendments to Clean Air Act (1990), 92–94; and Americans with Disabilities Act, 90–92; and base closures, 208–209; and budget deficits, 95; and Bush decision to raise taxes, 96, 100–106; and Bush domestic policies, 72–73; and Bush veto strategy, 72–73, 79–80, 258; and Bush's executive office appointments, 60, 62, 64–68; and check overdraft scandal, 210, 307n95; and civil rights act (1990), 79–80; and civil rights act (1991), 80; and education reform, 84; and ethics, 210–211; and minimum wage, 73; and nomination of Clarence Thomas, 195, 197–200; and nomination of David Souter, 81–82; and nomination of John Tower, 62–68; and North American Free Trade Agreement, 222–223; and pay-raise (November 1990), 210–211; and Persian Gulf War, 150, 158, 160–161; and Savings and Loan crisis, 97; and Tiananmen Square massacre, 117–118

Congressional Leadership Committee, 20

Congressional Quarterly, 42

Connally, John, 10, 11, 21, 32, 226n91, 265n79

Connor, Sandra Day, 77

Conservation Fund, 92

Conservatives, 24–25, 40, 41, 65, 72, 190; and abortion issue, 76, 77; and the ADA, 91; and Bennett, 86; and Buchanan candidacy, 209–210, 221; and "Chicken Kiev" speech, 204; and China policy, 114; and Darman, 58; and decision to raise taxes, 105; and drug policy, 86; and education

reform, 84, 86; and election of 1988, 36, 49, 234; and election of 1990, 106; and election of 1992, 216, 221, 228, 233–234, 250; and fall of USSR, 206; and Lithuania, 203; and 1990 budget, 80, 161; and nomination of Clarence Thomas, 196, 197, 198; and nomination of David Souter, 80, 82; and nomination of Richard Thornburgh, 56; opposition to Congressman Bush, 13–14; and Persian Gulf War, 158, 161; and Reagan, 56; and Sununu, 54, 200

Consolidated American Life Insurance Company, 14

"Contras" (Nicaragua), 25, 26

Cooley, Denton A., 249

Costa Rica, 102

Cramer, Richard Ben, 33

Crane, Philip, 21

Crawford-Greenburg, Jan, 81, 82

Critchlow, Donald T., 234

Cronkite, Walter, 22

Crosby, Bing, 7

Crossfire (CNN), 210

Crowe, Admiral William, 128

Crusade: The Untold Story of the Persian Gulf War (Atkinson), 165

Cuba, 26, 159

Cuomo, Mario, 37–38, 217–218

Curtis, Lieutenant Adam J., 132

Cutler Ridge Mall, 227

Czechoslovakia, 122, 123

Dade County (Florida), 227, 247

Dallas City Hall, 74

Danforth, John, 40, 198

Dannemeyer, William, 91

Darman, Richard, 43, 57 (photo), 100, 202, 232, 244, 256; and Bush's decision to raise taxes, 96; choice as OMB director, 58; and 1990 budget fight, 101, 101 (photo), 103, 104

David, Charles-Philippe, 294n35
Deaver, Michael, 37
De Borchgrave, Arnaud, 128
Defense Base Closure and
    Realignment Act, 208–209
Defense Base Closure and
    Realignment Commission, 208–209.
    See also BRAC
defense spending, 71; cuts in, 207–
    209, 307n84
DeFrank, Thomas, 224, 266n91
Delta Force, 167
Demarest, David, 183, 231
Democratic Leadership Council,
    218–219
Democratic National Committee
    (DNC), 15
Democratic National Convention
    (1988), 1, 37
Democratic National Convention
    (1992), 224–225
DePauw University, 40
Deputies Committee (NSC), 59–60,
    112, 131, 143
Derwinski, Edward, 57, 57 (photo),
    202
Desert Shield/Desert Storm,
    Operations. *See* Persian Gulf War
Détente, 110, 111, 112
Devroy, Ann, 70, 201
Dewey, Thomas, 9, 47, 265n74
DiGenova, Joseph, 312n91
Dignity Battalions (Panama), 127
Dingell, John, 93
District of Columbia: appropriations
    bill (1990), 78; and drug war, 89
Dodd, Christopher, 67
Dole-Michel Amendment (flag
    protection amendment), 75–76
Dole, Elizabeth, 40, 56, 57 (photo)
Dole, Robert ("Bob"), 15, 21, 30–31,
    35, 36, 37, 40, 45, 67, 75, 101, 101
    (photo), 265–266n85

Domenici, Pete, 40
Domestic Policy Council, 58, 182
Doonesbury (comic strip), 33–34, 45
Dowd, Maureen, 65, 180, 185
Dow Jones Industrial Average, 100
Draper, Robert, 201
Dresser Industries, 6, 7
Drug Enforcement Agency (DEA), 86
drug policy, and Bush, 86–90, 258;
    and Reagan, 86
Duffy, Michael, 256, 265n74, 273n4
Dukakis, Kitty, 47
Dukakis, Michael, 37, 38–39, 40, 44,
    45, 46, 47, 48 (photo), 49, 50, 194,
    233
Duke, David, 80, 211
DuPont, Pierre S. (Pete), 30, 36
Durenburger, David, 70

Eagleburger, Lawrence, 60, 111, 117,
    118, 145, 167, 241, 315n23
East Berlin, 122
East Germany: fall of communism in,
    122–126; reunification with West
    Germany, 124–126, 133–137, 150,
    203, 206, 257
Economic Policy Council, 58
economy: and Bush, 249; and election
    of 1992, 206–207, 215; recession of
    1991–1992, 206–207
Ecuador, 89
Educational Excellence Act (1989),
    84, 86
education policy, and Bush, 83–86,
    258; and Reagan 83
Education Summit (Charlottesville,
    1989), 84
Edwards, Edwin, 211
Egypt, 139, 143, 144, 149, 177
Eisenhower, Dwight D., 1, 9, 65, 113,
    172, 235, 256, 291n145
Eisenhower, Mamie, 188
Election of 1928, 9

Election of 1948, 9, 47
Election of 1950, 9
Election of 1952, 9
Election of 1956, 9
Election of 1960, 10, 61
Election of 1961, 61
Election of 1962, 10–11
Election of 1964, 9, 11–12, 181, 264n61
Election of 1966, 12–13, 264n65
Election of 1968, 13, 265n74
Election of 1970, 14–15, 53
Election of 1972, 16
Election of 1976, 19
Election of 1978, 19, 31–32, 47
Election of 1980, 20–23, 31, 32, 33, 50, 53, 61
Election of 1984, 50
Election of 1988, 53, 57, 75, 76, 91, 110, 183, 216, 233; and African Americans, 45–49; analysis of, 49–50; and Atwater, 31–33, 34, 35, 36, 39, 40, 45, 47; Bush's announcement of candidacy, 27; and Bush's "flexible freeze," 95; and Bush's southern "firewall" strategy, 36–37; and choice of Quayle as Bush's running mate, 40–43, 44, 186, 271n57; and conservatives, 234; and Dan Rather interview (January 1988), 34–35; Democratic candidates for nomination, 37–39, 271n39; and Democratic convention, 1, 37; and education policy, 83; Dukakis campaign, 38–39, 40, 44, 45, 46, 47, 49–50, 194; Iowa caucuses, 35; and Iran-Contra, 34, 35, 37; and negative campaigning, 32–33, 35–36, 44–47, 49–50; New Hampshire primary, 35–36, 54; and pledge of allegiance issue, 44, 46, 74, 272n78; and press, 187; Republican candidates for nomination, 30–31; and Republican National Convention, 39, 40, 43–44, 190, 191, 226; results of, 49, 272–273n88; rumors of Bush marital infidelity, 270n19; Second Presidential Debate (Los Angeles), 47–49; and Willie Horton issue, 45–46, 47–49, 186, 272n72, 272n78; and the "wimp factor," 34, 49
Election of 1990, 75, 76, 79–80, 106
Election of 1991, 211
Election of 1992, 26, 80, 179, 183, 184, 292n11; analysis of results, 228–236; and Buchanan, 210, 220–221; and Bush, 193, 215–236, 237, 303n3; Bush acceptance speech to Republican convention, 226; and Clinton, 218–220, 227; and conservatives, 216, 228, 233–234, 250; and debates, 232; Democratic candidates for nomination in, 217–220; and Democratic Convention, 224–225; and "Dump Quayle" movement, 223–224, 310n49; and economy, 206–207, 215; and George W. Bush, 231; and Hurricane Andrew, 227–228, 232–233; and Iran-Contra, 234–236; and "Iraqgate," 234–236, 313n105; and James Baker, 231; and Los Angeles Riots, 221–222; and New Hampshire primary, 216–217, 249; and North American Free Trade Agreement, 222–223; and "Passportgate," 231, 312–313n91; and Perot, 212–213, 220, 225, 226–227, 234, 308n101; and Persian Gulf War, 172; and polls, 236; and press, 188, 229; and Republican National Committee, 194; and Republican National Convention, 226, 310n53; results of, 228; and Weinberger re-indictment, 235–236
Election of 2000, 248–249, 317n72

Electoral College system, 272–273n88
Electronic Data Systems (EDS), 212
Ellis Island, 30
Emir of Kuwait, 141, 143
Endara, Guillermo, 127, 133
Engel, Jeffrey A., 17, 109
Environmental Protection Agency
    (EPA), 92, 94
Equal Employment Opportunity
    Commission (EEOC), 90, 195, 197,
    198
Estonia, 120
Ethics: and Bush administration, 64–
    65, 69–70, 201, 210; and Congress,
    210–211
Evangelical Christians, as political
    constituency, 30–31, 36, 37. *See also*
    conservatives
Evans, Rowland, 224
Exorcist, The (Blatty), 199
Exxon Oil Company, 93
Exxon Valdez, 93, 202

Fahd, King (Saudi Arabia), 145, 146,
    147, 148
Fahrenheit 9/11, 244
Falwell, Jerry, 36
Family Leave Act, 222
Family of Freedom (Walsh), 196
Feder, Don, 97
Federal Bureau of Investigation (FBI),
    66, 89, 197
Federal Communications
    Commission (FCC), 64, 91
Federal Deposit Insurance
    Corporation (FDIC), 98, 99, 100
Federal Emergency Management
    Agency (FEMA), 227, 254
Federal Home Loan Bank Board
    (FHLBB), 98
Federalist Society, 90
Federal Republic of Germany. *See*
    West Germany

Federal Reserve Board, 100, 207,
    283n21
Feed and Forage Act (1861), 295n56
Fiers, Alan, 242, 316n33
Financial Institutions Reform,
    Recovery, and Enforcement Act
    (1989), 99
Finback, USS, 5
Fineman, Howard, 33
First International Bank (Houston), 19
Fitzgerald, Jennifer, 229
Fitzwater, Marlin, 53–54, 102, 135,
    164, 186, 201, 229, 230, 233
flag (American): and Dole-Michel
    Amendment, 75–76; and Flag
    Protection Act of 1989, 75–76; and
    Pledge of Allegiance issue (1988),
    44, 46, 74, 272n7; and *Texas v.
    Johnson*, 74–75; and *U.S. v. Eichman*,
    75
Flag Protection Act of 1989, 75–76, 258
"Flexible Freeze," 95, 97
Florida, 227, 247
Foley, Thomas, 69, 75, 258; and 1990
    budget fight, 100–101, 101 (photo),
    103, 104
Ford, Betty, 188, 247 (photo)
Ford, Gerald R., 16–17, 18, 19, 20,
    22, 30, 53, 58, 59, 68, 73, 95, 108,
    109, 230, 234, 237, 247 (photo),
    253, 266n91, 291n145; and "Dump
    Quayle" movement (1992), 224
Ford Motor Company, 207
Fort Amador (Panama), 130
Fort Hood, 246
France, 134, 137, 139, 144, 150; and
    Persian Gulf War, 159
Frank, Barney, 70
Freedman, Sir Lawrence, 150
"Free Trade." *See* North American
    Free Trade Agreement
Freie, John, 257
Frohnmeyer, John, 220

Frost, David, 156, 172
Fuller, Craig, 40, 53, 54, 55, 62, 182
Fund for Limited Government, 20, 267n112

G.I. Bill, 6
Gallup Poll, 225
"Gang of Eight" (Persian Gulf War), 152, 152 (photo), 200
Gantt, Harvey, 80
Gardner, Booth, 85 (photo)
Garn-St. Germain Act (1982), 97
Gates, Robert M., 59–60, 112, 131, 152, 152 (photo), 173, 175, 206, 285n20, 290n133
gays, 225; in Bush administration, 222
General Accounting Office, 95
General Dymanics, 47
General Motors, 207
Generals, The (Ricks), 165
Genscher, Hans-Dietrich, 134
George Bush and the Guardianship Presidency (Rose), 255–256
George Bush School of Government and Public Policy (Texas A&M University), 246
George, Clair, 242, 316n33
Georgia, Republic of, 120. See also USSR
Gephardt, Richard, 38, 124, 217, 223
German Democratic Republic. See East Germany
Germany (referring to post-1990 reunified Germany), 150
Giamatti, A. Bartlett, 44
Gibbs, Nancy, 265n74, 273n4
Gingrich, Newt, 69, 70, 102, 105, 106, 210, 283n28, 284n41
glasnost, 107
Glaspie, April, 143, 293n28
"God Bless the U.S.A." (song, Greenwood), 171

Golan Heights, 177
Golden Knights (U.S. Army Parachute Team), 244
Goldwater, Barry, 9, 11, 12, 37, 264n56
Goldwater-Nichols Act (1986), 129
Gonzalez, Henry, 234, 313n105
Goodgame, Dan, 256
Goodin, Mark, 69–70
Gorbachev, Mikhail, 23, 108, 110, 111, 112, 126 (photo), 127, 129, 180 (photo), 257, 285n20, 287n64; and Bush, 121–122, 203–206; coup against (August 1991), 204–205, 257; and dissent in Soviet republics, 120–122, 134–136, 203–205; and fall of communism in Eastern Europe, 118–124; and fall of communism in East Germany, 122–126; and fall of USSR, 202–206; and Governor's Island meeting, 107, 112; and Helsinki Summit (with Bush, September 1990), 151, 176; and Kissinger, 107–108; and Lithuania, 135–136; and Madrid conference, 176–178; and Malta Summit (with Bush, December 1989), 110–111, 121–122, 126, 131, 133, 136; and Moscow Summit (with Bush, July 1991), 204; and pauza, 112; and Persian Gulf War, 146, 151, 159, 176, 203, 206, 257; popularity of, 112; and Reagan, 59, 63; and reunification of Germany, 124–126, 133–137, 203, 206; and Soviet economy, 118, 134, 146; and START I, 204, 238–239; on Tiananmen Square massacre, 123; visit to People's Republic of China (May 1989), 115–116; and Washington Summit (June 1990), 136, 180; and withdrawal of Soviet troops in Europe, 113

Gorbachev, Raisa, 189
Gore, Al, Jr., 38, 45, 94, 161, 225, 231, 249
Gorgas Army Hospital, 132
Governing Crisis: Media, Money, and Marketing in American Elections, The (Bennett), 50–51, 219
Government Accountability Office, 211
Governor's Island meeting (1988, Reagan, Bush, and Gorbachev), 107, 110, 112
Grady, Robert, 93
Graham, Billy, 265n74
Gramm, Phil, 194
Gramm-Rudman-Hollings Act (1985), 96, 100, 103, 105, 233
Grand Canyon, 92
Grassley, Charles, 161
Graves' disease, 195, 303–304n10
Gravois, John, 297n103
Gray, C. Boyden, 23, 25, 201; on ADA, 91; and amendments to Clean Air Act, 93; and charges of conflict of interest, 64–65; and pardon of Weinberger (and others), 242; and Persian Gulf War, 160; and Souter nomination, 81; and Thomas nomination, 196; and Tower nomination, 66; and transition to Bush administration, 53; as White House counsel, 65
Great Britain, 134, 137, 141, 144, 150, 159
Great Hall of the People (Beijing), 115
"Great Society" (Johnson), 13, 72
Green, Fitzhugh, 2
Greene, Bob, 246
Green Party (West Germany), 183
Greenspan, Alan, 100, 283n17, 283n21
Greenwich Country Club, 3
Greenwich Country Day School, 3
Greenwood, Lee, 171

Greider, William, 211–212
Guam, 5
Gutin, Myra G., 188
Gutman, Roy, 315n21

Haass, Richard N., 103, 140, 144, 294n47
Haig, General Alexander, 23, 24, 30, 34
Haiti, 253
Halabja (Iraq), 140
Haldeman, H. R., 14, 200
Hale, Kate, 227
Hamilton, Kathy, 303n58
Hammer, Floyd, 303n58
"Hammer Rick" (satellite line), 167
Han, Lori Cox, 186
Harkin, Tom, 91, 218
Harlow, Bryce, 266n91
Harris County (Texas) Republican Party, 10–11
Hart, Gary, 38
Hartmann, Robert, 266n91
Harvard Law School, 38
Harvard Medical School, 38
Harvard University, 7, 8, 254
Hatch, Orrin, 198, 199
Hatfield, Mark, 161
Havel, Václav, 123
Heflin, Howell, 67
Heimbach, Daniel, 182
Heinz, John, 21, 31
Helms, Jesse, 80, 91, 117–118, 131
Helsinki Summit (Bush and Gorbachev, September 1990), 151, 176
Herring, George, 292n160
Hersh, Seymour, 26
"Highway of Death" (Iraq), 164, 173
Hill, Anita, 197–200
Hills, Carla, 57–58, 57 (photo)
Hippocratic Oath, 256
Hirohito, 127, 276n61

Hitler, Adolf, 127, 149, 156, 158, 296n86

HIV, 91

Hoffman, David, 54, 70

Hofstra University Conference on Bush Presidency (1997), 196, 256, 274n20

Home Box Office (HBO), 234

Honduras, 191

Honecker, Erich, 122, 127

Hoover, Herbert, 9

Hope, Bob, 7

Horton, Willie, 45–46, 186

Houston Post, 297n103

Houston, University of, 245–246

Houstonian Hotel, 236

Hoyer, Steny, 91

Hubbard, Al, 248

Human Rights Watch, 170

Hungary, 119–120, 121, 122

Hunt, Al, 33

Huntington Herald-Press, 40

Hurricane Andrew, 93, 227–228, 232–233, 254

Hurricane Katrina, 254

Hurricane Mitch, 191

Husak, Gustav, 123

Hussein, King (Jordan), 144, 147, 177–178, 253, 293–294n34

Hussein, Saddam, 103, 127, 133, 144, 145, 146, 147, 149, 150, 151, 152, 153, 154, 157, 158, 159, 160, 163, 164, 166, 167, 172, 173, 174, 210, 234, 235, 251, 291n1, 293n28; and assassination attempt on Bush, 253; background of, 139–140; Bush on, 141, 156; and genocide of Kurds and Shiites, 175; and hostages in Iraq, 155–156; and invasion of Iraq, 143; and Israel, 140; preparations for war against Kuwait, 140–141, 142, 143; and reaction to Desert Shield, 149; and Safwan cease fire,

165; and use of chemical weapons, 140, 159–160

Iacocca, Lee, 30

Idealism (philosophy of diplomacy), 108

Ideco. *See* International Derrick and Equipment Company

Inchon, 173

Independence, USS, 144

Indiana University School of Law, 40

International Business Machines (IBM), 212

International Derrick and Equipment Company, 7

Iowa, USS, 181–182

Iran, 25, 174, 212, 299n47; hostage crisis (1979–1980), 155; war with Iraq, 139–140, 141, 159–160

Iran-Contra scandal, 25, 34, 37, 59, 61, 62, 68, 81, 210, 242; and Bush, 25–26, 234–236, 242; and Reagan, 25–27, 59, 235

Iraq, 139, 141, 148, 150; aid from United States, 139–140, 141; invasion of Kuwait, 103, 140, 142, 143, 257; war with Iran, 139–140, 141, 159–160; and weapons of mass destruction, 165. *See also* Persian Gulf War

"Iraqgate," 234–236, 313n105

Isikoff, Michael, 87

Israel, 222; and Madrid conference, 176–177; and Persian Gulf War, 149, 167–168, 176, 210; Saddam Hussein on, 140

Ivins, Molly, 226

Iwo Jima, Battle of, 5

Iwo Jima monument, 75

Jackson, Keith, 86

Jackson, Reverand Jesse, 38, 55, 79, 217, 218

Japan, 114, 127, 144, 150, 229
Jaruzelski, Wojciech, 119, 120
Jaycees, 32
job discrimination, 79–80
Job Training Partnership Act (1982), 41
John Birch Society, 10, 11, 12, 13, 41
John Paul II, Pope, 119
Johnson, General Robert, 168
Johnson, Gregory Lee, 74
Johnson, Lady Bird, 247 (photo)
Johnson, Lyndon B., 10, 12, 14, 181, 291n145, 301n31
Joint Chiefs of Staff (JCS), 79, 128, 129, 142
Jones, Edith, 81–82
Jong, Erica, 76
Jordan, 144; and Madrid conference, 177–178; and Persian Gulf War, 293–294n24
Jordan, Hamilton, 220
Just Cause, Operation, 132–133. *See also* Panama: American invasion of
Juster, Kenneth, 241

Kaifu, Toshiki, 150
Kansas State University, 186
Karl Marx University (Budapest), 120
Karsh, Efraim, 150
Kassenbaum, Nancy, 67–68
Kaufman, Burton I., 7
Keating, Charles, 70
Kelly, Petra, 183
Kemp, Evan J., Jr., 90
Kemp, Jack, 30, 33, 36, 37, 40, 56, 57 (photo), 78, 228
Kemp-Roth Bill (1981), 30
Kennan, George, 137
Kennebunkport (Maine), 180, 195, 229, 244
Kennedy, Anthony, 81
Kennedy, Edward M., 37, 38, 41, 73, 79, 81, 271n39; and ADA, 91; and

nomination of Clarence Thomas, 198, 199; and Persian Gulf War, 161
Kennedy, John F., 10, 11, 128, 133, 195, 291n145, 302n31
Kennedy, Robert F., 128
Kennedy Center for the Performing Arts, 238
Kentucky Fried Chicken, 231
Kenya, 239, 240
Kermit the Frog, 186
Kerrey, Bob, 218
Keys to Power: Managing the Presidency, The (Warshaw), 257
Khanequan (Iraqi freighter), 151
Khmer Rouge, 17
Khrushchev, Nikita, 120
Kiev, 204
Kimmitt, Robert, 42
King, Martin Luther, Jr., 13
King, Rodney, 221
Kippy of Rechov Sumsum, 168
Kissinger, Henry, 14, 18, 107–108
Klein, Joe, 232
Knoche, Hank, 21
Koch, Doro(thy) Bush, 2, 9, 15
Kohl, Helmut, 24, 135 (photo), 183; and Persian Gulf War, 150; and reunification of Germany, 124–126, 133–137, 150
Kopechne, Mary Jo, 199
Korean War, 37, 173, 212
Kremlin, 107, 122
Krenz, Egon, 122, 123
Ku Klux Klan, 80, 211
Kurdistan, 175
Kurds, 140, 174, 175–176, 203
Kuwait, 103, 140, 141–142, 143, 145, 146, 147, 148, 149, 150, 151, 152, 153, 154, 155, 159, 165, 169, 173, 175, 203, 251, 253, 257. *See also* Persian Gulf War
Kuwait City, 143, 164, 166

Laboa, Monsignor Sebastian, 133
Lacey, Frederick B., 313n105
Laden, Osama bin, 244
Laird, Melvin, 266n91
Land and Water Conservation Fund, 92
Larry King Live (CNN), 213, 220, 230
Latvia, 120
Laubach Literacy Action, 190, 302n46
Laxalt, Paul, 31
Leach, Margarette, 272–273n88
Leahy, Patrick, 81
Lebanon, 23, 25
Lee, Dr. Burton, 229
Liedke, Bill, 8, 12, 265n74
Lilley, James, 114, 116
Lincoln Bedroom, 238
Lincoln Memorial (Washington), 238
Lincoln Savings and Loan, 70
Literacy Volunteers of America, 302n46
Lithuania, 120, 135, 136, 203; and "Chicken Kiev" speech, 257; and Gorbachev, 146. *See also* USSR
Lockwood, Stuart, 155
Lofton, John, 76
Lone Star Yankee (Parmet), 181
Los Angeles Riots (1992), 221–222, 223
Los Angeles Times, 21
Lott, Trent, 102
Louisiana Superdome (New Orleans), 43
Lugar, Richard, 41
Lujan, Manuel, 57, 57 (photo)

M1 tank, 47, 155
MacArthur, General Douglas, 142, 173, 174
Madrid Conference on the Middle East (October–November 1991), 151, 176–178, 206, 257; and Gorbachev, 176–178
Malek, Frederic, 179, 230, 244

Mallon, Neil, 6, 7, 265n74
Malta Summit (Bush and Gorbachev, December 1989), 110–111, 121–122, 131, 133, 136
Manchester Union-Leader, 20, 216–217
Mandela, Nelson, 79
Man from Hope, The (Clinton campaign documentary), 224–225
Mansfield, Mike, 19
Maoist Revolutionary Communist Party, 74
Marianas campaign (World War II), 5
Marine One, 237
Marshall, Thurgood, 195
Martinez, Bob, 89–90
Matalin, Mary, 194
Matlock, Jack, 111
Maxim Gorky, 126
Mayaguez, USS, 17
Mayo Clinic, 243
McCain, John, 250
McCall's Publishing Company, 3
McCarthy, Joseph, 9, 10
McCarthyism, 69
McClure, Fred, 234
McCullough, David, 101
McCurdy, David, 131
McFarlane, Robert, 25–26, 242, 316n33
McKay, Buddy, 248
McLaughlin Group, The (PBS), 210
McNamara, Robert, 128
Medicaid, 71, 212
Medicare, 71, 105, 212
Medina Ridge, Battle of, 164
Meese, Edwin M., 37
Mervin, David, 181, 255–256
Mexico, 222–223
Mexico City Policy (on abortion), 77
Michel, Robert, 75, 101, 101 (photo), 161
Middle East. *See* Iran; Iraq; Israel; Madrid Conference on the Middle East; Persian Gulf War

Mike Douglas Show, 34
Millie's Book (Barbara Bush), 190
minimum wage, 73
Minutaglio, Bill, 305n34
Mitchell, George, 67, 93–94, 97, 101, 101 (photo)
Mitterrand, François, 129, 159
Miyazawa, Kiichi, 229, 255
Mogadishu, 239, 240, 241
Mondale, Walter, 38
Mongolia, 146
Monument to the People's Heroes (Beijing), 115
Moore, Michael, 244
Morehouse College of Medicine, 57
Morning in America: How Ronald Reagan Invented the 1980s (Troy), 256
Mosbacher, Robert A., 11, 13–14, 15, 19, 20, 22, 39, 44, 56–57, 57 (photo); and election of 1992, 230; and Perot, 308n101; on Weinberger re-indictment, 236
Mosbacher Energy Company, 11
Moynihan, Daniel Patrick, 97
Ms. (magazine), 78
Mubarak, Hosni, 143, 144, 147, 149, 294n34, 296n86
Mulins, Janet, 312n91
Mulroney, Brian, 204–205, 222, 249
Muris, Timothy, 64
Muse, Kurt, 128, 133
Muskie, Edmund, 92
Mussolini, Benito, 127
My Grandfather's Son (Thomas), 199

NAFTA. *See* North American Free Trade Agreement
Naftali, Timothy, 13, 265n74
Nagy, Imre, 119–120
Nation, 157
National Cathedral (Washington), 251

National Center for Community Risk Management and Insurance, 191
National Commission on Excellence in Education, 83
National Council on the Handicapped, 90
National Drug Policy Board, 86
National Endowment for the Arts, 220
National Environmental Protection Act, 208
National Governor's Association, 218
National Guard: and drug policy, 89; and Quayle, 40, 42
National Literacy Act, 190
National Public Radio, 197
National Review, 216
National Rifle Association, 92
National Science Scholars Program, 84
National Security Council, 42, 59–61, 112, 121, 131, 173, 235, 248, 290n133; Deputies Committee, 59–60; and Iran-Contra, 81; and Persian Gulf War, 143, 145, 152, 156; Principals Committee, 59; restructuring under Bush, 59–60; under Reagan, 23
National Security Directives: NSD-1, 59; NSD-26, 157; NSD-54, 161
National Security Political Action Committee, 45
Nation at Risk: The Imperative for Educational Reform, A (1983), 83
NATO. *See* North Atlantic Treaty Alliance
NBC News, 31, 36
Neustadt, Richard, 185
New Federalism, 72
New Frontier, 72
New Republic, 172
Newsday, 197
Newsweek, 33, 34, 315n21

New York Post, 102
New York State, 141
New York Times, 26, 50, 55, 64, 65, 95, 112, 117, 133, 135, 151, 170, 180, 181, 195, 199, 200, 201, 212, 235, 244, 313n105
New York Times Book Review, 211
New York Times/CBS Poll, 110, 291n145
Nicaragua, 25, 26, 68
Nightline (ABC News), 197
Nixon, Richard M., 14, 15, 16, 20, 25, 26, 30, 34, 53, 58, 59, 92, 108, 109, 114, 158, 210, 212, 221, 264n65, 265n79, 291n145, 310n53
Noonan, Peggy, 43–44, 113, 191
Noriega, Manuel, 127, 128, 130–133; aborted coup against (October 1989), 130–131; and American invasion of Panama, 132–133, 173; and Bush, 289n108; capture of, 133; disputed reelection (May 1989), 127; and Perot, 213; and proposed deal with Reagan (1988), 26–27, 127
Norquist, Grover G., 233–234
North, Oliver, 81, 235
North American Free Trade Agreement, 222–223, 234
North Atlantic Treaty Alliance (NATO): 40th anniversary meeting of, 113–114; and reunification of Germany, 124, 134, 135, 136, 137
Northern Illinois Regional Transportation Authority, 57
North Korea, 174
North Vietnam, 212
Novak, Robert, 47, 224
NSC. *See* National Security Council
Nuclear Test Ban Treaty (1963), 12
Nunn, Sam, 62, 66, 69, 158, 160, 217

Oak Ridge Boys, 181
Obama, Barack, 191

O'Brien, Lawrence, 15
Observatory Circle, 190
Office of Management and Budget (OMB), 43, 58, 93, 96
Office of National Service (ONS), 191
Office of Personnel Management, 66
Office of Thrift Supervision (OTS), 98, 100
oil, and Persian Gulf War, 156–157
Oklahoma, University of, 197
OMB. *See* Office of Management and Budget
Omnibus Budget Reconciliation Act of 1990, 105. *See also* budget fight (1990)
Omnibus Water Bill (1992), 92
Opa Locka Airport, 227
"Open Skies" proposal, 113
Operation Instant Thunder (Persian Gulf War), 154–155
Operation Restore Hope, 315n21. *See also* Somalia
Operations Plan 1002-90, 142
Operation Spring Colt, 244
Organization of Petroleum Exporting Countries (OPEC), 141
"Out Now," 157
Overbey, John, 8

Pacific Pumps, 7
Pakistan, 240, 241
Palestine Liberation Organization, 149, 176, 178
Panama: American invasion of, 132–133, 173, 187; capture of Noriega, 133; and disputed reelection of Noriega (May 1989), 127; and Giroldi Coup, 130–131; and proposed deal between Reagan and Noriega (1988), 26–27, 127
Panamanian Defense Force, 130, 132
Parkinson, Paula, 41, 42

Parmet, Herbert S., 41–42, 44, 131, 179, 181, 215, 229

"Passportgate," 231, 312–313n91

Patriot missile, 167, 169, 170

Patterson v. McLean Credit Union, 79

Pauza, 118, 129, 204. *See also* USSR

Paz, Lieutenant Robert, 132

"Peace dividend," 207–208

Pearl Harbor, 3

Pell, Claiborne, 296n86

Pelosi, Nancy, 118

Pennzoil, 8, 12

People's Liberation Army (Chinese military), 115

People's Republic of China, 24; Bush as envoy to, 17–18, 114; and inclusion in United Nations, 15; and massacre at Tiananmen Square, 115–118, 119, 123, 257; Most Favored Nation status, 115, 118, 286n34; and Persian Gulf War, 158, 159, 174

Permian Basin (West Texas), 7

Perot, H. Ross, 19, 70, 172, 184, 232 (photo), 248; background of, 212–213; and Bush, 213, 234; and election of 1992, 216, 220, 225, 226–227, 228, 231, 232, 233, 234, 308n101, 312n86; and Los Angeles riots, 221; and Mosbacher, 308n101; and North American Free Trade Agreement, 222–223

Persian Gulf War, 106, 203, 207, 209, 255
    airwar, 163–164, 166, 167, 168–170
    and Al Firdos bunker, 169–170
    American technology, 168–170
    antiwar protests, 157–158
    and April Glaspie, 293n28
    and Australia, 294n34
    Battle of Medina Ridge, 164
    Battle of 73 Easting, 164
    and budget fight of 1990, 105, 106
    and Bush creation of coalition against Iraq, 109, 185, 203, 206
    and Bush decision to expel Iraq from Kuwait, 152–154
    and Bush formation of coalition against Iraq, 144–151
    and Bush letter to Saddam Hussein, 159–160
    and Bush on Saddam Hussein, 156, 159, 174
    and Bush speech, 20 August 1990 (Baltimore, Veterans of Foreign Wars convention), 155–156
    and Bush speech, 10 September 1990 (Joint Session of Congress, on Kuwait Crisis), 154
    and Bush speech, 16 January 1991 (Oval Office, announcing Allied military action in Persian Gulf), 164
    and Bush speech, 29 January 1991 (Washington, State of the Union Address), 156, 190
    and Bush Speech, 6 March 1991 (Washington, Joint Session of Congress, proclaiming end of war), 170
    and Bush televised interview, 2 January 1991 (with David Frost), 156
    and Bush and "This Will Not Stand" comment (5 August 1991), 147–148
    and Bush war aims, 161–162
    and C. Boyden Gray, 160
    casualties of, 165, 169–170
    cease-fire (terms dictated at Safwan), 165, 175
    and Central Intelligence Agency, 168
    and Cheney, 142, 145, 147, 148, 149, 151, 152–153, 152 (photo), 155, 160, 161, 167, 173, 294n34, 296n71

and civilian deaths, 169–170
and Colin Powell, 142, 145, 147,
148, 151, 152–153, 152 (photo),
153–154, 164, 171, 172–173, 251,
294n47, 299n47
and Congress, 150, 158, 160–161
and conservatives, 158, 161
and decision to end conflict,
172–175
and Delta Force infiltration, 167
and Eagleburger, 145, 167
and Edward Kennedy, 161
and Egypt, 294n34
and election of 1992, 172
and France, 159
and "friendly fire" casualties, 169
and the "Gang of Eight," 152, 152
(photo), 200
and Gates, 152, 152 (photo), 173
and George Mitchell, 160–161
and Gorbachev, 146, 151, 159, 176,
203, 257
Great Britain, 159
ground attack, 164–167, 173, 174
and Haass, 294n47
and Helsinki Summit (Bush and
Gorbachev, September 1990),
151, 176
and hostages in Iraq, 155–156, 159
inevitability of outcome, 166
and invasion of Iraq (2002), 143
and Israel, 149, 167–168, 176, 210
and issue of oil, 156–157
and James Baker, 142, 146, 149, 150,
151, 152, 152 (photo), 153, 154,
156, 157, 158, 159–160, 161, 174,
295n68, 297n103
and Jimmy Carter, 157–158
and Jordan, 293–294n34
and *Khaneqan* incident, 161
and King Hussein, 293–294n34
and Michel, 161
and Mitterrand, 159

and Mubarak, 294n34, 296n86
and National Security Council,
143–144, 145, 152, 156
and National Security Directive
(NSD-54), 161
and 1990 budget fight, 103–104
and Nunn, 160 and Operation
Instant Thunder, 154–155
and Pat Buchanan, 158
and peace initiatives, 159–160
and People's Republic of China,
158, 159, 174
and post war patriotic fervor, 258
and press, 170–171, 187, 297n103,
298n24
and Prince Bandar bin Sultan,
145–146
and Quayle, 152, 152 (photo)
and Saudi Arabia, 143
and Schwarzkopf, 142–143, 145–
146
and Scowcroft, 143–144, 145, 147,
151–152, 152 (photo), 154, 165,
172, 173, 174, 175
and Shevardnadze, 143, 146
and Sununu, 152, 152 (photo), 167,
200
and Thatcher, 145, 151, 155, 159
and U.S. financing of the war, 150,
295n56
and United Nations, 144–145, 146,
148, 151, 157, 158–159, 161, 163,
165, 172, 175, 241, 257
and USSR, 146–147, 148, 151, 159,
176, 257
and Wolfowitz, 167
Peru, 89
Petersmeyer, C. Gregg, 191
Philippines, 5, 131–132
Phillips, Kevin, 221
Phillips Academy ("Andover"), 3, 19
Pierce, Franklin, 3
Pincus, Walter, 270n19

Pinkerton, James, 45
Plan of Attack (Woodward), 252
Playboy, 41
Pledge of Allegiance issue (1988), 44, 46, 74, 272n78. See also flag (American)
PLO. See Palestine Liberation Organization
Plokhy, Serhii, 204, 205
Poindexter, Admiral John, 25–26, 235
Points of Light Foundation, 190–192, 243, 248, 303n58
Poland, 119–120, 121, 122
Policy Coordinating Group, 202
Policy Review, 233
Polls: popularity, 158, 172, 189, 193, 225, 236; "push polling," 31
Porter, Roger, 93, 103, 312n89
Portman, Rob, 81
Postmodern Presidency: George Bush Meets the World, The (Rose), 255
Powell, General Colin, 79, 196, 224, 252; and American invasion of Panama, 132–133; on Cheney, 68; choice as head of JCS, 129; and coup attempt against Corazon Aquino, 132; and defense budget cuts, 129–130; and election of 1992, 218; on genocide of Kurds, 175; and Giroldi Coup (Panama), 130–131; and Persian Gulf War, 142, 145, 147, 148, 151, 152–153, 152 (photo), 153–154, 164, 171, 172–173, 251, 294n47, 299n47; popularity after Persian Gulf War, 172
Power and Prudence: The Presidency of George H. W. Bush (Barilleaux and Rozell), 256
PRC. See People's Republic of China
Presidency: activist theory of, 255–257; guardian theory of, 255
President Ford Committee (1975–1976), 11

Presidential Libraries Act (1986), 246
Presidential Power (Neustadt), 185
Presidential Records Act (1978), 246
President's Foreign Intelligence Advisory Board (PFIAB), 276n66
President's Special Review Board on Iran-Contra ("The Tower Commission"), 61, 62
press: and Bush, 55, 170–171, 186–188, 229, 255, 298n24; and election of 1992, 229; and Panamanian invasion, 187; and Perot campaign, 220; and Persian Gulf War, 187, 297n103; and Reagan, 188
Prince William Sound (Alaska), 93
Principals Committee (NSC), 59
Public Broadcasting System, 210
Puerto Rico, 181
Pusan Perimeter, 173
"push polling," 31
Putin, Vladimir, 314n10

Qasr Prison (Iran), 212
Quayle, J. Danforth ("Dan"), 32, 57 (photo), 61, 66, 182, 191, 217, 248; chosen as Bush's vice presidential running mate (1988), 40–43, 44, 186, 271n57; and coup attempt against Corazon Aquino, 132; and "Dump Quayle movement" (1992), 223–224, 310n49; and election of 2000, 249; and Murphy Brown remark, 223; and opposition to gay rights, 222; and Persian Gulf War, 152, 152 (photo)
Quayle, Marilyn, 40, 226
"quotas." See Civil Rights Act (1990)

Rabin, Yitzhak, 229, 253
Rather, Dan, 34–35, 186
Reader's Digest, 49
"Reading is Fundamental," 190

Reagan, Nancy, 22, 37, 64, 247
(photo)
Reagan, Ronald W., 24 (photo), 30,
31, 33, 34, 35, 37, 39, 40, 42, 43, 44,
45, 49, 53, 58, 59, 60, 63, 64, 65, 112,
129, 169, 179, 186, 191, 219, 233,
250, 251, 291n145; and abortion
issue, 76–77; and aid to Iraq,
139–140; assassination attempt
on (1981), 23; and base closures,
208, 209; and Bork appointment,
80–81; and budget deficits, 71, 95,
96; and Bush, 23–27, 29, 184; and
clean air act, 92–93; and Cold War,
233; and conservatives, 31, 56; as
crisis manager, 185; and defense
spending, 71; and deregulation
of Savings and Loans, 97; and
disability rights, 90; and drug
policy, 86, 87; and economy, 210;
and education policy, 83, 84; and
election of 1980, 20–23, 32, 50;
and election of 1984, 50, 216; and
election of 1988, 40; and fall of
communism in Eastern Europe,
118, 258; Farewell Address
(11 January 1989), 62–63; and
Gorbachev, 59, 107, 111; as "great
communicator," 72; as idealist
in foreign policy, 108, 109, 110,
111; and Iran-Contra, 210, 235,
242; and press, 55, 187, 188; and
"Reaganomics," 233; and Souter,
81; suggested as Ford's vice
president (1974), 266n91; and tax
increase, 104
Realism (philosophy of diplomacy),
108–109, 117
recession, 100, 249. *See also* economy
Rehabilitation Act of 1973, 90
Rehnquist, William, 77
Reilly, William, 92, 93
Reno, Janet, 313n105

Republican Guard (Iraq), 142, 154,
164, 166
Republican National Committee
(RNC), 39, 69, 106, 194, 202, 225;
Bush as chair of, 16, 18; and 1992
election, 194
Republican National Convention
(1984), 74
Republican National Convention
(1988), 39, 40, 43–44, 190, 226
Republican National Convention
(1992), 225–226, 310n53
Republican Senate Campaign
Committee, 61
Reserve Officers Training Corps
(ROTC), 219
Resolution Trust Corporation (RTC),
98, 99, 283n17
Revere, Paul, 3
"Revolving Door" (Willie Horton Ad,
1988), 45–46
Ribicoff, Abraham, 9
Rice, Condoleezza, 121, 248, 252,
318n98
Rice University, 245
Richards, Ann, 1, 248
Richardson, Elliot, 266n91
Ricks, Thomas, 165
Risen, James, 251
Riyadh, 148
Robertson, Pat, 30–31, 35, 36, 37, 41
Rockefeller, Nelson A., 16–17, 266n91
Roe v. Wade, 76, 77, 78, 82, 195
Rogers, Fred ("Mr. Rogers"), 238
Rogich, Sig, 35, 36, 39, 47, 93
Rollins, Edward, 22, 32, 106, 182, 220,
225, 227
Romania, 123, 140, 206
Roosevelt, Eleanor, 188
Roosevelt, Franklin D., 184, 280n67
Roosevelt, Theodore, 92, 280n67
Rose, Richard, 255
Rosenberg, William, 93

Rosenthal, A. M., 117
Rostenkowski, Dan, 97, 100–101, 105, 258
Rove, Karl, 267n112
Rozell, Mark J., 256
Rudman, Warren, 81, 96, 279–280n55
Rumaylah Oil Field, 141
Rumsfeld, Donald, 18, 30, 68, 251, 266n91
Russia, 120–121, 205–206. *See also* USSR
Ryan, Richard, 270n19

S&Ls. *See* Savings and Loan crisis
Safire, William, 201, 204
Safwan (Iraq), 165, 175
Saipan, 5
Sakharov, Andrei, 117
Salinas de Gortari, Carlos, 222
Salinger, Pierre, 302n31
San Jacinto, USS, 5, 164
Saturday Night Live, 238
Saudi Arabia, 143, 145, 147, 148, 150, 153, 155, 174, 177. *See also* Persian Gulf War
Savings and Loan crisis, 70, 97–100, 255, 258–259, 283n17
Schlesinger, Arthur M., Jr., 14
Schlesinger, Robert, 86
Schorr, Daniel, 176
Schroeder, Patricia, 38
Schwarzkopf, General Norman, 164, 168; on decision to end Persian Gulf War, 172–173; and hunt for Scud missiles, 167; meets with King Fahd, 147, 148; and Operation Instant Thunder, 154–155; personality of, 142; plans to deter Iraqi aggression, 142–143, 145–146; plan to counter Iraqi invasion of Kuwait, 147, 148; popularity after war, 171–172; and Safwan cease-fire, 165, 175

Scowcroft, General Brent, 19, 109, 110, 125 (photo), 206, 250, 294n35; and American invasion of Panama, 132–133; on Bush's philosophy of diplomacy, 109, 285n10; and choice of Cheney as secretary of defense, 68; choice as national security advisor, 58–59; as critic of Reagan's foreign policy, 112; and election of 1992, 231; on fall of communism in eastern Europe, 120; and Giroldi coup attempt, 131; on Iran-Iraq War, 140; and op. ed. in *Wall Street Journal* (15 August 2002), 252; on "Open Skies" proposal, 113; and the *pauza*, 111–112; and Persian Gulf War, 143–144, 145, 147, 151–152, 152 (photo), 154, 165, 172, 173, 174, 175; and Somalia, 240–241; style as national security advisor, 60; and Tiananmen Square massacre, 116–118; on Ukraine, 204; on withdrawal of U.S and Soviet troops in Europe, 113; and *A World Transformed*, 245; and Yeltsin, 121
Scranton, William, 266n91
Scud missile, 140, 167, 169, 170, 176
Seidman, L. William, 98, 99
Sessions, William, 66
700 Club, The, 31
73 Easting, Battle of, 164
Shadow: Five Presidents and the Legacy of Watergate (Woodward), 245, 312n91
Shah of Iran, 139, 149, 167, 168, 176, 177, 178
Shaw, Bernard, 47–49
Shevardnadze, Eduard, 203; and fall of communism in eastern Europe, 123; and Persian Gulf War, 143, 146, 151; and reunification of Germany, 134
Shiites, 174, 175–176, 203

Shivers, Allan, 9
Shultz, George, 24, 25, 26, 27, 111, 266n91
Sidey, Hugh, 181, 186, 216, 249, 251
Silberman, Lawrence, 81
Silverado Savings and Loan, 99–100, 303n3
Simmons Hardware Company, 1
Simon, Paul, 38, 190
Simpson, Alan, 40, 197, 254
60 Minutes, 219, 226
Skinner, Samuel, 57, 57 (photo); and chief of staff, 202; and Exxon Valdez, 93; and Los Angeles riots, 221
Skowronek, Stephen, 109
Skull and Bones Club (Yale University), 6
Sloan-Kettering Hospital, 8
Snowe, Olympia, 117
Social Security, 71, 100
Socrates, 255
Solarz, Stephen, 117
Solidarity, 119, 120
Somalia, 239–241, 315n21
Souter, David, 80–83, 195, 196–197, 249, 279–280n55
South Korea, 150, 174
South Penn Oil Company, 8
Southwestern University, 61
Special Prosecutor Act, 312n91
Specter, Arlen, 198, 199
St. Louis Post Dispatch, 210
staff, White House (Bush), composition of, 58–60
Stahl, Lesley, 59, 124, 125 (photo), 288n93
Starek, Roscoe B., III, 274n20
Starr, Kenneth, 75, 81
"Star Wars." See Strategic Defense Initiative
Statue of Liberty, 30
"Stealth Bomber," 133, 164
Stennis, John, 19

Stevens, John Paul, 74–75
Stimson, Henry, 3
Stockdale, Admiral James, 220
stock market, 100, 201
Stolberg, Sheryl Gay, 199
Stone, Roger, 35
Strategic Arms Reduction Treaty (START I), 204, 238–239
Strategic Arms Reduction Treaty (START II), 238–239
Strategic Defense Initiative ("Star Wars"), 65
Sullivan, Louis, 57, 57 (photo), 60, 77, 79, 196, 228
Sultan, Prince Bandar bin, 141, 145–146, 248
Summit Communication Group, 65
Sununu, John, 58, 125 (photo), 182, 186, 253, 256, 259; and "Air Sununu" scandals, 200–201; and Americans with Disabilities Act, 91; as chief of staff, 200; and choice of Cheney as Secretary of Defense, 68; choice as chief of staff, 54–55; and election of 1988, 35, 54, 183; on election of 1992, 230; firing of, 200–201, 217, 305n34; and 1990 budget fight, 101, 101 (photo), 102, 105; and nomination of Clarence Thomas, 197; and NSC, 59; and Persian Gulf War, 152, 152 (photo), 167, 200; and Savings and Loan crisis, 98; and Souter nomination, 81–82; and the pauza, 112
Supreme Court: and Baker v. Carr, 12; and Bush v. Gore, 249; and election of 2000, 249; and nomination of Clarence Thomas, 80, 195–200, 304n14, 304n26; and nomination of David Souter, 80–83, 195, 196–197, 279–280n55; and Patterson v. McLean Credit Union, 79; and Roe v. Wade, 76, 77, 78, 82, 195;

Supreme Court, *continued*, and *Texas v. Johnson*, 44, 74–75; and *U.S. v. Eichman*, 75; and *Wards Cove Packing Company v. Atonio*, 79; and *Webster v. Reproductive Health Services of Missouri*, 77–78
Swarthmore College, 38
Syracuse University, 38
Syria, 149, 174, 176–177

Taiwan, 15, 24, 114
Talbott, Strobe, 107, 110
Tamposi, Elizabeth M., 312n91
Task Force on Regulatory Relief (Reagan administration), 24, 90
Tate, Sheila, 53, 186
Taxes, Bush decision to raise (1990), 95–97, 100–106, 194, 232, 233, 255; Bush promise not to lower, 43–44, 91, 95, 158; capital gains, 96
Tbilisi, 120
Teeter, 53, 54, 62, 213, 224, 230–231
Tenet, George, 251
Tet Offensive (Vietnam), 149
Texarkana Junior College, 212
Texas, politics of, 9–15
Texas, University of, 7
Texas A&M University, 246
Texas Congressional Boosters, 11
Texas Heart Institute, 249
Texas Law School, University of, 10, 81
Texas Rangers (major league baseball club), 248
Texas Select Committee on Public Education, 213
Texas v. Johnson (1989), 44, 74–75
Texas War on Drugs Committee, 212
Thatcher, Margaret, 24, 112, 114; and Persian Gulf War, 144, 145, 151, 155, 159; and reunification of Germany, 125

Thomas, Clarence, 80, 81, 90, 195–200, 196 (photo), 249, 304n14, 304n26
Thomas, Helen, 187
Thompson, James, 30, 57
Thornburgh, Richard, 56, 57 (photo), 58; and drug policy, 89; and election of 1991, 211; and Souter nomination, 81
Thrifts. *See* Savings and Loan crisis
Thurman, General Max, 130, 131, 132, 290n122
Thurmond, Strom, 31, 32
Tiananmen Square (China), massacre at, 115–118, 119, 123, 126, 257
Tidelands Oil controversy (1952), 9
Tillotson, Mary, 229
Time, 36, 249
Tomahawk missiles, 164, 253
Toner, Robin, 95
Tower, John, 49, 57 (photo), 68, 69, 93–94, 182, 198; background of, 61; choice as secretary of defense, 56; death of, 276n66; election to Senate (1961), 10, 11; and Iran-Contra investigation, 59, 61, 62; nomination as secretary of defense, 61–68, 93–94, 128, 210
TOW missiles, 25, 26
Townhouse Operation, 15, 16
Trade Representative, Office of the United States, 56, 57
Transition: from Reagan to Bush administration (1988–1989), 53–70, 273n4; from Bush to Clinton administration (1992–1993), 237–243
Treleaven, Harry, 12, 264n65
Trinity University, 19
Troy, Gil, 188, 190, 256, 302n48
Trudeau, Garry, 33–34, 45
Truman, Harry, 47, 174
Tsongas, Paul, 218
Turkey, 174
Turner, John, 92

Tutweiler, Margaret, 54
"Two-Plus-Four Talks," 134–137. *See also* West Germany: reunification with East Germany

U.S. Armed Forces Joint Information Bureau, 170
U.S. Constitution: and due process clause, 77; First Amendment issues, 74–75; and proposed flag protection amendment, 75–76, 77–78; Twenty-Fifth Amendment, 16
U.S. Defense Intelligence Agency (DIA), 142
U.S. Golf Association, 2
U.S. Government Accounting Office, 17
U.S. House of Representatives, 284n41; Banking Committee, 100; Credit Union of, 210–211; Republican Research Committee Task Force on Earth Resources and Population, 13; Ways and Means Committee, 96–97
U.S. Military Academy ("West Point"), 59
U.S. Naval Academy (Annapolis), 212
U.S. News and World Report, 34, 93
U.S. Open Tennis Tournament, 35
U.S. Secret Service, 251
U.S. Senate, 14–15; Appropriations Committee, 86; Armed Services Committee, 19, 62, 65–67, 158; Judiciary Committee, 81, 83; Labor and Human Resources Committee, 73; and nomination of Clarence Thomas, 197–199; and nomination of David Souter, 81–82
U.S. v. Eichman, 75
Ukraine, 204
Unemployment Insurance Reform Act, 207
United Arab Emirates (UAE), 150

United Nations, 12, 108, 176; Bush as ambassador to, 15, 17, 57, 190; and Madrid conference, 176; and Persian Gulf War, 144–145, 146, 148, 151, 157, 158–159, 161, 163, 165, 172, 175, 241, 257; Security Council, 145; and Somalia, 239–241
United Nations Fund for Population Activities, 77
United Press International (UPI), 187
United Steelworkers Union, 7
University of California, Los Angeles, 47
UNOSOM (United Nations Operation in Somalia), 240
Untermeyer, Chase, 16, 54, 81
USSR, 59, 63, 108, 109, 113, 215; and "Chicken Kiev" speech, 257; and cooling off period (*pauza*), 110–114, 118, 204; coup attempt against Gorbachev (August 1991), 204–205; and dissent in Republics of, 120–122, 134–136, 203–205; fall of, 202–206, 207, 257; and fall of Communism in Eastern Europe, 118–126; Gorbachev and Bush summit (Washington, June 1990), 136, 180; Gorbachev and Bush summit (Moscow, July 1991), 204; Governor's Island Meeting (1988—Reagan, Bush, and Gorbachev), 107, 110, 112; Helsinki Summit (Bush and Gorbachev, September 1990) 151, 176; and Hungary, 119–120; and Lithuania, 146; and Madrid conference, 176–178; Malta Summit (Bush and Gorbachev, December 1989), 110–111, 121–122, 126; and Persian Gulf War, 146–147, 148, 151, 159, 176, 257; and Poland, 119–120; and reunification of Germany, 124–126, 133–137, 146, 203; and Yeltsin, 121

Vega, Major Moises Giroldi, 130–131
"Velvet Revolution," 123. *See also*
    communism: fall of in eastern
    Europe
Veteran's Affairs, Department of, 57,
    202
Veterans of Foreign Wars, 155–156
veto strategy (of Bush), 72–73, 79–80,
    94, 184, 258
Vietnam Memorial (Washington, DC),
    212–213
"Vietnam Syndrome," 129–130
Vietnam War, 12, 13, 129–130, 142,
    149, 155, 157, 166, 170, 174, 175,
    208, 212, 220, 255
Vietnam War Memorial (Washington,
    DC), 238
Vilnius (Lithuania), 203
"Vision Thing," 72, 277n4
Vnukovo II Airport (USSR), 146
Volkskammer (East German House of
    Representatives), 136

Wałęsa, Lech, 119, 120
Walker, Alice, 189
Walker, Herbert, 6
Walker's Cup (Tennis), 2
Wall Street Journal, 205, 252
Walsh, Kenneth T., 195–196
Walsh, Lawrence, 235–236, 241–242
Warba, 141
Wards Cove Packing Co. v. Atonio, 79
Warner, Margaret, 34
War Powers Act, 160
Warsaw Pact, 114, 119, 134, 136
Warshaw, Shirley Anne, 257
Washington, George, 63
Washington Post, 25, 37, 40, 54, 70,
    73, 87, 102, 140, 149, 201, 202, 211,
    270n19, 313n105
Washington Times, 76, 81, 128
Watergate Crisis, 15–16, 17, 92, 211,
    231

Watkins, Admiral James, 57 (photo),
    58
Wayne, John, 238
Wayne, Steven, 49
Weapons of Mass Destruction, 165
Webster, William, 62, 130, 143, 169,
    292n1, 298n24
*Webster v. Reproductive Health Services
    of Missouri*, 77–78
Weicker, Lowell, 90, 91
Weinberger, Caspar, 25, 26, 235,
    241–242
Welch, Larry, 128–129, 290n110
Wellesley College, 189
West Bank, 149
West Berlin, 122–123
West Germany, 123, 144, 183;
    reunification with East Germany,
    124–126, 133–137, 146, 150, 203,
    206, 257
Weyrich, Paul, 65
White, Byron, 195
White House: Office of
    Communications, 167; Office of
    Political Affairs, 32
White House Council of Economic
    Advisers, 96
White House Ghosts (Schlesinger), 86
White House Press Corps, 179, 187,
    201, 297n103
*Who Will Tell the People? The Betrayal
    of American Democracy* (Greider),
    211–212
Wilder, Douglas, 218
Will, George, 34, 50, 131, 226
Willey, Malcolm, 64
Williams, Edward Bennett, 18
Wilson, Donald M., 246
Wilson, Pete, 80
Wilson, Woodrow, 108, 109, 164
"Wimp Factor," 49, 131
Winston, Chriss, 86
Witness to Genocide (Gutman), 315n21

Woerner, General Fred, 290n122
Wofford, Harris, 211
Wohlfart-Kugelberg-Welander
    syndrome, 90
Wolfowitz, Paul, 167
Woodward, Bob, 40, 41, 130, 131, 132,
    147, 154, 245, 251–252, 270n19,
    279–280n55, 312n91, 318n90
Woolsey, R. James, 253
*Work Hard, Study . . . and Keep Out of
    Politics!* (Baker), 46
World Bank, 116
World Food Programme, 239
World Trade Center, 250
World Transformed, A (Bush and
    Scowcroft), 245
World War I, 1
World War II, 6, 30, 61, 63, 109, 127,
    134, 150, 168, 181
Wright, James, 69

Xiaoping, Deng, 23, 24, 114, 115, 116–
    117, 118, 127
Xu, Han, 116

Yale University, 1, 2, 3, 6, 7, 19, 254
Yalu River, 174
Yaobang, Hu, 115
Yarborough, Ralph, 10, 11, 12, 14
Yeltsin, Boris: and Bush, 203–206;
    and fall of USSR, 203–206; and
    Gorbachev, 121, 203–206; and
    Strategic Arms Reduction Treaty
    (START II), 238–239
Yemen, 145, 151, 159
Yenayev, Genady, 205
Yeutter, Clayton, 56, 57 (photo), 194,
    202, 225, 231
Yom Kippur War (1973), 167
Young Americans for Freedom (YAF),
    13
Yugoslavia, 123, 204, 240

Zapata Offshore, 8, 11, 12
Zapata Petroleum Company, 8
Zedong, Mao, 115
Zhi, Fang Li, 114–115
Zubok, Vladislav M., 123